SPORT IN CANADIAN SOCIETY

SPORT IN CANADIAN SOCIETY

Ann **H**all
Trevor **S**lack
Garry **S**mith
David **W**hitson

M&S

Reprinted 1992

Canadian Cataloguing in Publication Data

Main entry under title:

Sport in Canadian Society

Includes bibliography references and index.
ISBN 0-7710-3783-X

1. Sports - Social aspects - Canada.
I. Hall, Ann.

GV585.S677 1991 306.4'83'0971 C91-093367-7

McClelland & Stewart Inc.
The Canadian Publishers
481 University Avenue
Toronto, Ontario
M5G 2E9

Printed and bound in the United States of America

Text Design: James Loates

Typesetting: Jennifer Loates
                Loates Desktop Publishing

TABLE OF CONTENTS

To Peter McIntosh, whose little book *Sport in Society* inspired us all very early in our careers; and to Donald Macintosh, whose continuing support and encouragement we very much appreciate.

Acknowledgements

This book could not have been written without the many students, both undergraduate and graduate, who have passed through our courses at the University of Alberta. They have consistently provided the feedback, often critical yet always insightful, that helped us develop the material and ideas in this book.

We are also grateful to the Secretary of State, through its Canadian Studies Program, and to the University of Alberta, through its Support for the Advancement of Scholarship Fund, for financial assistance in preparing the manuscript.

Thanks must also go to Betty Millman, who assisted us in tracking down elusive references through the computerized data base (SIRLS) at the University of Waterloo, and to Brian Gavriloff, one of our former students, who helped us assemble the photographs.

Our appreciation also extends to two of our colleagues, Nancy Theberge and Peter Donnelly, who as the publisher's reviewers provided us with many thoughtful and constructive suggestions that helped us improve the text. We have also been been very fortunate in having as our editor Michael Harrison. He was never anything but patient, supportive, and encouraging, particularly when we needed it most.

Finally, we are especially indebted to Jane Haslett for her editorial and proofreading contributions.

PREFACE

This book originated out of our frustration at the lack of a textbook suitable for Canadian undergraduate students in physical education or sociology taking their first course in the sociology of sport. It has, therefore, a twofold purpose: to provide students with an introduction to the sociology of sport, and to challenge them to think critically about sport in Canadian society. It is a deliberately Canadian book in the sense that all our examples are Canadian, and wherever possible we have relied on scholarship and research by our colleagues across this country. Where that scholarship is lacking, or the research simply has not been done, we have utilized studies often originating in the United States, but in other countries as well, always being careful to point out the possible differences within a Canadian context.

We cover the topics that have become standard fare in most introductory courses in this area: what is sociology and how it relates to the study of sport; sport in Canadian culture; the emergence of modern sport in Canadian society; politics and the state; business and capital; media and ideology; social inequality and conflict; youth and education; issues and controversies (violence, drugs, and gambling); and finally, continuity and change. What is different about our approach, however, is that, first, it draws on our belief that sociology is an historical and critical science, and that it is important to bring a "sociological imagination" to the study of sport. Second, throughout the text we have made a conscious effort to demonstrate the significance of sport to one of the central problems of sociology: the explanation of structures of gender, class, racial, and ethnic inequality.

Most students, we believe, will find this a challenging book. Although the level of discussion does not presume prior courses in sociology or a prior knowledge about sport, we do invite students to see what is probably a familiar phenomenon, sport, in a different light. Our intent is always to challenge existing assumptions about sport and its place in Canadian society. We have also tried to keep the sociological jargon to a minimum, but at the same time we have made use of appropriate sociological terms and concepts. They are all fully explained in the text, and a comprehensive index assists readers in locating definitions and examples throughout the book. Finally, students are encouraged to extend their knowledge through the many references cited as well as through the supplementary reading suggestions provided at the end of each chapter.

Chapter 1

SPORT AND THE SOCIOLOGICAL IMAGINATION

Sport today is a pervasive phenomenon in Canadian society. Most Canadians, even if they are not active participants, are touched in some way by sport. From our childhood days on the playground to the televised sports events that bring the big names into our living rooms, sport is such a significant aspect of our culture that we sometimes take it for granted. It is inextricably linked to the major social institutions that regulate Canadian society – government and politics, the economy and big business, the mass media and the educational system to name just a few. Its opportunities and weaknesses are those of the society in which we live.

We study sport from a sociological perspective for a variety of reasons. The most common of these is to enhance our understanding of aspects of sport itself, ranging from patterns of participation or ownership, for example, to increases in performance standards or levels of violence (either on the ice or in the stands). Sociology suggests to us that both patterns and standards as well as changes in sport can only be fully understood in relation to developments in other social institutions – economic institutions, educational institutions, the family, the mass media. These in turn point to broader structures of inequality between men and women, rich and poor that affect all social institutions. Here we are using concepts and theories that emphasize social as opposed to individual causes and that point toward structural solutions to problems identified in sport. The need to understand and solve problems within sport was primarily why the sociology of sport began more than twenty years ago, as a sub-field of physical education (Sage, 1987). Today it is increasingly important that those whose work involves sport, whether as teachers or coaches, administrators or entrepreneurs, have a clear understanding of sport as a social phenomenon.

Beyond this, however, some sociologists have become increasingly interested in the effects of sport, as an ever-present aspect of popular culture, on other social institutions and structures. At the institutional level, this is simply to say that the relationship between sport and other institutions is two-way and that sport is structured in different ways by economic and political interests or by the realities of family life. Sport has itself become an important part of the Canadian economy, and the lives of many Canadian families are today structured (and restructured) around the time and financial demands of members' involvements with sport.

At the broader structural level, the structures of organized sport (amateur as well as professional) and the attention our culture gives to sport both reflect and reinforce patterns of class, race, ethnic, and gender inequality. In the case of class, race, and ethnicity, it is a matter of debate whether sport provides significant opportunities for social mobility to individuals from poor families and minority ethnic or racial groups, or whether the highly publicized success of a few individuals creates illusions of mobility and meritocracy in a society where money still counts. In the case of gender relations, the amount of public attention and money that is lavished on male professional team sports and the continued association of prowess in these sports with masculinity have the effect of trivializing not just women's sport but fe-

maleness and female activities. When masculinity is so publicly celebrated, the corollary is a devaluation of anything feminine. In addressing questions like these, the sociology of sport is going beyond a concern with phenomena within sport. It is seeking to demonstrate the significance of sport to some of the central problems of sociology: the explanation of structures of class, gender, and racial inequality, as well as the processes through which social change is achieved and circumscribed.

It is also important that Canadian students understand sport within the context of *Canadian* society as opposed to North American society in general. Certainly there are similarities between organized sport in the United States and Canada, but there are also major differences. For instance, the role of the federal government in developing the Canadian amateur sport bureaucracy is considerably different from the American system, where private enterprise plays a more significant role. The attempts by women in Canada to achieve sex equality in sport have been very different from the struggles of our American counterparts, where specific legislation, like Title IX, is in place. No such legislation exists in Canada. The role of sport within the Canadian university and college system is very different from the big business approach of American college sport; it produces different problems from those that American texts necessarily address. Likewise, the analysis of race and sport requires a somewhat different accent than the focus on blacks, which is a necessary feature of American sport sociology. To say this is not to say that Canadian blacks do not encounter racism; they do. However, the size of the American black community, the history of race relations in America, and the presence of black stars in all the major American sports together create a context that is different from the Canadian one. Conversely, our own history requires a fuller recognition of native and Francophone issues. In sum, organized sport is different in Canada because Canadian society is unique.

Defining Sport

First, it will be necessary to say something about how we will define sport. Some of the earliest work that addressed the social significance of sport was concerned with drawing distinctions between play, games, and sport, and with the classification of particular activities as sports or as something else. In one sense, this is an important task, for if one is going on to make claims about the "functions" of sport in transmitting social norms and values, or to criticize the effects of the introduction of "southern" sport into native communities in the Canadian North, it is necessary to distinguish between basketball and hiking, and between cross-country ski-racing and travel on skis.

At the same time, however, it is important to recognize that any classification scheme is to some extent arbitrary. Most people would likely agree that the major team games are "sports," and so, too, are tennis (and other racquet games), boxing and other combat sports, and the internationally recognized "racing" sports (including swimming, running, skiing, cycling, and sailing). But even within these categories there is room for dispute. Are the latter activities, for example, sports only when one is training for or competing in formally organized races? What makes boxing a sport, and when is wrestling a sport, and what about the "martial arts"? When we go beyond these familiar categories to consider activities like gymnastics and rhythmic gymnastics, diving and synchronized swimming, biathlon and rock climbing, the difficulties of classification are magnified.

Most definitions begin by positing the presence of complex physical skills and the presence of competition using these skills as necessary conditions for sport. This would allow us to eliminate chess on the first grounds and to raise questions at least about aesthetic sports (e.g., ice dance and rhythmic gymnastics) and wilderness sports (e.g., climbing, hiking, canoeing) on the second. Yet there are some who would argue that dancers and gymnasts are among the greatest athletes, that climbing is highly competitive, and that wilderness activities are among the most Canadian of sports.

Also common to many definitions is the existence of formal organization on a national and preferably international level. This usually means that the rules of the activity are standardized so that international competition can take place. However, in the case of football, we can identify *six* different codes of rules, each of which is simply considered to be "football" by its proponents and fans: Canadian football and American football, which Europeans call "gridiron football"; soccer, which Europeans call simply "football"; rugby union and rugby league, which are quite different in Britain, France, and Australia but are often lumped together as "rugby" elsewhere; and Australian rules football, which is a distinctive blend of all of the above! In each instance, authority to organize competitions and enforce rules is vested in official bodies recognized by the participants.

Formal organization also means that the learning of game skills becomes the object of teaching and systematic preparation, and that organizations evolve (clubs, schools, national and provincial sport organizations) whose purposes are to prepare competitors. What we are talking about, in short, is the *institutionalization* of sport and the *rationalization* of both sports

Ann Hall photo

Ski touring in the Canadian Rockies.

training and the sports organizations that sponsor training, and under whose auspices competition occurs. It is common for sport sociologists to restrict their use of the term "sport" to institutionalized, formally organized sport. Not only is hockey in its institutionalized form(s) more visible than children playing shinny on ponds or corner rinks, but these formal institutions have the widest social effects and are, therefore, of the greatest sociological interest. Institutionalization is also often a prerequisite for getting more resources and thereby growing, as opposed to remaining an interest of only a

few. Sport Canada's "Sport Recognition System," for example, recognizes as sports only those activities in which Canadian national organizations participate in recognized international competitions and run development programs aimed at producing competitive excellence. Luge is recognized as a sport because it is an Olympic sport, while white-water canoeing and triathlon are not eligible for Sport Canada funding, despite the fact that each enjoys a higher participation base in this country.

What these and other examples illustrate

is that the institutionalization of particular activities as sports has depended less on the characteristics of the activity itself (i.e., on the complexity and variety of the physical skills required, or the precise nature of the competition) than on the political and economic resources that could be mobilized by its practitioners and sponsors. Thus hockey has prospered in Canada and increasingly in Europe, while lacrosse and jai alai, both highly competitive tests of physical skills, remain marginal activities. Therefore disputes about the supposed essence of sport, or about the defining characteristics that allow particular activities to be classified as sports, are less important than studying the social relations and distributions of political and economic resources that have meant that some games and physical pursuits have become institutionalized features of Canadian life while others have not.

For our purposes, sporting activities characteristically involve the pursuit "of a non-utilitarian objective through the engagement of bodily capacities and/or skills" (Young, 1979: 45). This definition can encompass the wilderness sports that are a growing part of Canadian life, as well as informal (though often quite serious) participation in many more conventional sports. Our analysis will begin with the physical tests and contests that have become institutionalized in Canadian society, but it will extend beyond these where appropriate and will attend in particular to the impact of institutionalized sport on Canadians' participation in these sports as well others. What is the impact of "official" hockey, for example, on Canadian men's and women's participation in hockey? Is there a relationship, either direct or inverse, between the norms and values celebrated in the major team games and Canadians' interest in other forms of physical activity? It is our view that this wider definition of sport will make it easier to recognize the social structures within which the physical activities of dominant groups (e.g., men, whites, Anglophones) have acquired cultural significance, while those of subordinate groups (e.g., women, natives, Francophones) have not.

Understanding Sociology

It is our view that sociology is best understood not so much as a body of knowledge but rather as a way of thinking, and especially of asking questions about aspects of social life. Certainly we will be discussing some of the research findings that today constitute sport sociology as a body of knowledge. However, much of the best sociological research gives us new perspectives on hitherto taken-for-granted aspects of social life (Worsley, 1987). In doing so, it may raise questions about why we have taken them for granted for so long. It is precisely because of this questioning habit of mind that sociology is sometimes accused of having a tendency toward destructive criticism of social institutions rather than an interest in making them work. For instance, when sport sociologists have suggested that violence in sport is a product of the normal practices of sports programs, rather than of aberrant individuals, they have been assailed as destructive (Coakley, 1990). Such findings, as Coakley suggests, point to a need for structural changes that would affect everyone. These changes would likely be most threatening to those who are influential within current sporting structures and those who take them for granted. However, it is precisely the sociologist's willingness to ask new and different questions about old ways of doing things that has pointed the way toward innovative solutions.

On the other hand, radical critics of society have often accused sociology of providing apparent justifications for the shape of existing social structures (e.g., stratification theory) and of integrating their own research with the goals of existing social institutions (Worsley, 1987). It is worth pointing out that much of the early sociology of sport, especially that from the discipline of physical education, was concerned with demonstrating the social value of sport and with making sporting institutions run more effectively.

The point is that thinking sociologically does not in itself either tie one to existing institutions or make one a social critic. In-deed, what American sociologist C. Wright Mills (1959) termed the "sociological imagination" is best understood as the habit of looking for the connections between history and biography.

Sociology and History

> Those who have wanted to model sociology upon natural science, hoping to discover universal laws of social conduct, have tended to sever sociology from history. (Giddens, 1982: 165)

The first component of a sociological imagination, Mills and subsequently Giddens (1982) have insisted, is an appreciation of just how different life was before the days of industrial capitalism, the welfare state, rapid mass communications, and other aspects of the modern condition. We know the facts: that production was once for local markets, that many state benefits and safeguards we now take for granted (e.g., unemployment insurance) were once only political slogans, and that travel and even the mails required far more time than they do now. We have only to reflect on how much the structure of organized sport that we take for granted today – with regional leagues and interregional playoffs at age-group as well as pro-

fessional levels – depends on cheap and rapid transport to begin to imagine how different most sports would have been. The very notion of a world record embodies horizons that did not make sense in an era when news of performances in Australia and Europe took months to reach North America. The fame and importance of figures as various as Ben Johnson, Wayne Gretzky, and Elizabeth Manley depend on access to international audiences. What did people do for entertainment before they could follow the performances of stars? The general point is that the past two hundred years (a relatively short period on an historical time scale) have seen changes so profound and far-reaching in their consequences for people's daily lives that it requires a real effort of imagination to grasp just how different life would have been.

It is a further challenge to break with the assumption that our modern way of life constitutes "progress" and that other societies that have not achieved (and in some cases not aspired to) our levels of material productivity are "backward." Giddens (1982) points out the *ethnocentrism* of this common attitude. He suggests that a proper sociological imagination would help us to consider the institutions of another society in terms of its *own* goals and values, and to recognize that the value we place on material productivity has not always been given the same emphasis in other cultures. It could ultimately help us to appreciate cultural diversity in a less judgemental way and even to learn from other cultures. It might lead us to appreciate the wisdom of the travel writer who once suggested that there are no foreign countries, only foreigners. Canadians who travel to Japan to learn the martial arts understand this, as do Europeans who come to play in the National Hockey League.

We can see very clearly what this imagination might bring to the study of sport if we consider the extent to which the value our culture places on productivity has permeated modern sport. Alan Ingham and John Loy (1974) have described as *ludic structuration* the process by which once playful activities have been transformed into increasingly formal institutions where an unrelenting emphasis on "higher, faster, stronger" has meant that most people's experience of organized sport is more akin to work than to play. This should not surprise us, if we accept the philosopher Herbert Marcuse's (1964) contention that productivity is the quintessential value of Western culture, the ultimate standard that suffuses all our institutions and most of our personal relations. This quest for productivity has given us the four-minute mile and in turn made it a good personal best but no longer a newsworthy feat. The quest for productivity underlies the acclaim we give to record breakers in every area of sport. Yet it may bring with it costs for the performer. Canadian sport psychologists Orlick and Botterill (1975) have offered one kind of evidence of such costs in studies that show many boys and girls drop out of organized sport precisely because the pressures on them to "produce the goods" are more than they are ready to handle at an early age.

Terry Orlick (1977) has also studied the games of Canadian native peoples and has sought to make physical educators aware of the more co-operative games characteristic of cultures organized around very different values. These communities can transform our own games: Orlick describes how in some Dene and Inuit communities, baseball is played so that a batter stays at bat until (s)he gets a hit, and an "inning" continues until everyone on a side has had a hit. Such practices may seem bizarre to Euro-Canadians if we take for granted our own competitive and results-oriented structures.

The sociological imagination, however, would help us to consider such differences non-judgementally and to reflect on the markedly different experiences that such games would offer to the participants and the very different lessons they would teach.

In this way the study of sociology can help us to think freshly about our own society, to formulate questions about things we have always taken for granted, and to imagine alternative futures. Giddens (1982: 15) proposes that:

> It is often precisely by showing that what may appear to those involved as inevitable, as unchallengeable – as resembling a law of nature – is, in fact, an historical product, that sociological analysis can play an emancipatory role in human society.

Perhaps we need to appreciate that the sets of social practices and relations we know as high-performance sport today are not simply in the "nature" of sport but rather are associated with historically specific social relations. Only then are we likely to respond to these practices in an active and if necessary critical manner. The Thérien Committee's recommendation that minor hockey in Quebec de-emphasize body contact is one contemporary example of a willingness to rethink taken-for-granted structures. Court rulings that have permitted girls to play on previously all-boy teams are another. Giddens proposes that sociology can play a constructive role if it can help us to think beyond the realities we have grown up with and to work toward ones that are happier, fairer, and more satisfying. This is important because, "As human beings, we do not just live in history; our understanding of history is an integral part of what that history is, and what it may become" (Giddens, 1982: 15).

Sociology and Science

The history of sociology is itself a history of tension between sociology, conceived as an historical and critical inquiry, and a conception of sociology modelled much more closely on the natural sciences. Indeed, there was a time, spanning the middle part of this century, when sociologists who posed fundamental questions about the way society was evolving, or whose work manifested historical and critical imagination, were in the minority. For several decades, the mainstream of sociological work moved away from the classical questions of the discipline, such as order and conflict, stability and change, and the relationship of individuals to structural processes. There were important exceptions like Mills, but most sociologists of that era saw their task as the development and refinement of techniques – of experimental design, operational definitions, and statistical analyses – that would enable the social sciences to develop along the lines of the natural sciences. They sought to demonstrate concrete relationships between discrete variables and conceived of a gradual accumulation of sociological knowledge, as more and more such relationships could be "proven." Heavily influenced by the natural science model of reality, sociologists sought to disassemble the social world, isolating variables and breaking down problems into their smallest possible components.

This kind of sociology did not (indeed, could not) ignore the "big questions" of structure and power completely. It did address concepts like class, but many studies in which class was a variable were simply not designed to consider whether power is produced and reproduced by the *structured* ways in which men and women in different classes learn to relate to one another. The scope of discrete empirical studies seldom included such discussions. Scientific sociology systematically excluded any treatment of experience (which is, of course, difficult to quantify and measure in any reliable way), let alone the possibility that there are widely shared experiences (e.g., of growing up female or as a native in our society) that are themselves structured, and in ways that have profound effects, by the patriarchal and paternalistic social relations of our society.

The achievement of this approach to sociology was a great deal of factual information. It did demonstrate statistical relationships, and this evidence sometimes challenged the accuracy of cherished social myths (that education is a powerful tool in overcoming class inequalities, for example, or that wage discrimination against women has been substantially overcome). Statistical correlations do not in themselves constitute explanations, however, and in the absence of sufficient critical analysis, these were seldom forthcoming. This approach to sociology also avoided evaluative language, because "value-free" sociology described the way things were, rather than criticizing or speculating about possible alternative arrangements. Most important of all, it did not convey any sense that societies change over time and that this happens in part as a result of the discoveries and the struggles of many different men and women, both famous and anonymous. Sociology as a natural science was, in other words, ahistorical.

The difficulty was that methodological considerations, especially the natural science model of what constituted the "scientific method," too often determined how social phenomena were conceived and addressed. However, Michael Polanyi (1958) has noted that even in the physical sciences there is not *one* scientific method, but rather science requires researchers to tailor their methods to the nature of the phenomenon under investigation. What ultimately distinguishes the scientist from the lay person is not the use of a particular method but the habit of submitting the full details of one's work – a systematic review of evidence-gathering procedures and arguments, together with a reasoned defence of one's choice of that particular approach – for evaluation by others engaged in the study of the same problems. Validity, Polanyi suggests, is not something achieved simply by the use of a particular model of investigation. Rather, it is something that is recognized by, and indeed is often debated within, communities of people who are dedicated to the systematic study of a particular field, people whose familiarity with that field allows them to assess collectively the merit of procedures as well as analysis.

We have drawn attention to Polanyi's discussion of what science is because it emphasizes that if we understand people to differ in important ways from physical objects and from animals, a truly scientific approach demands not that we import techniques from physics or from the study of animal behaviour but rather that we develop techniques appropriate to what is unique about *people*. Here we must note that "scientific" sociology seeks to find, in the patterns of social behaviour it discovers and documents, natural laws of the same order as the laws that govern the behaviour of animals and indeed all matter. Yet as Giddens (1982: 14-15) points out:

> Atoms cannot get to know what scientists say about them, or change their behaviour in the light of that knowledge. Human beings can do so. Thus the relation between sociology and its 'subject matter' is necessarily different from that involved in the natural sciences.

It is different because the reality being studied –

human behaviour – can be changed by the very process of studying it and describing it, if that process leads in some way to increased self-awareness among the people being studied.

BRINGING A SOCIOLOGICAL IMAGINATION TO THE STUDY OF SPORT

Early work in the sociology of sport tended to confine itself to the natural science model. Although there were some exceptions, most of the first generation of sport sociologists were working within departments of physical education, where the dominant mode of research was the natural science one and where the emphasis was on understanding and solving problems *within* sport. Some of this work focused on topics like group cohesion and team effectiveness, motivations for sport involvement, and the effects of role models on patterns of physical activity. These studies typically addressed themselves to coaches and physical educators and made little attempt to connect the research to the general questions of social process that are of interest to sociologists. They did little, therefore, to demonstrate the importance of sport as a field for the study of sociological issues. Indeed, it is fair to say that they drew more on social-psychological concepts than on sociology.

Another body of work was more clearly sociological, in that it sought to demonstrate that interest and participation in various sports were related to the standard sociological variables: gender, social class, race, age, education levels, geographical location, and so forth. It also used standard sociological survey procedures. Unfortunately, the fruits of this research were unremarkable. We learned that more girls than boys dropped out of sport in their teenage years, that middle-class people played more squash and golf than their working-class counterparts, and that older people preferred less physically active forms of recreation (see Chapter 7). What such studies were not designed to address, however, was the wider sociological significance of these fairly obvious facts. Were patterns of male and female participation, for example, products of social structures that favoured and empowered males in a whole host of ways? What is it about the Canadian class structure that perpetuates unequal access to participation? Why have older adults had difficulty gaining suitable access to many sporting facilities? These questions and others would connect the study of sport to the study of change and resistance in relations between dominant and subordinate groups in society. When these questions are asked, and when research uncovers interesting lines of analysis and further investigation, we show that studying sport sociologically is not just of interest to a few fans but something that is important to the understanding of Canadian society.

Today, sociologists in Canada and elsewhere are asking these kinds of questions. They are working not only in departments of physical education and sports studies but in departments of communications and sociology. Together they are demonstrating that sport, as a formative experience in childhood in developed societies, and as a pervasive presence in popular culture, may have significant effects in the development of male and female identities, as well as communal and national identifications. Sport is also, as a major aspect of the entertainment industry and as an object of public policy, an aspect of Canadian life that has increasing economic and political significance. Thus scholars are producing work that addresses the place of sport in the modernization of Canadian

class structures and in the evolution of the Canadian welfare state. Other work, for example, demonstrates the importance of moving on from the study of "women and sport," once a chapter in many sport sociology texts, to an approach that addresses the effects of sport in the overall social structure that is "gender relations" (see Chapter 7). In these cases (and others) sport sociologists are demonstrating an interest not just in sport, but also in the broader significance of sport in processes of socio-historical reproduction and transformation. Work like this helps to demonstrate what bringing a sociological imagination to the study of sport can offer. It is worth making some further and more specific comments on just what the sociological imagination involves.

First, it involves *understanding the institutions we know today as sport in relation to their own history.* We reiterate here the importance of an historical perspective in sociology. It cannot be stressed often enough that a sociology which does not recognize the reality of socio-historical change, and which portrays present realities as if they were "natural," is misleading. We have a tendency, especially when we are too young to have experienced significant changes in our own lives, to take for granted what we know today. Sport is the Olympic Games, the Stanley Cup, the Masters, and the Super Bowl. We hear older men talk of past glories (and it is overwhelmingly more likely to be our grandfathers and uncles, rather than their female counterparts, who we hear reminiscing about yesteryear's heroes), of eras when games were harder and players more heroic. But when we see the sepia photos of men in funny uniforms, men who look very ordinary by today's standards of athletic physique, and when we know that Roger Bannister's four-minute mile, an achievement that stirred the athletic world in 1954, would not now make the Olympic qualifying time let alone the Olympic final, we tend to take for granted that what we know today is all that really matters.

It is a matter of historical fact, however, that less than forty years ago people did not spend their Saturdays watching *Wide World of Sports* on television with its wind-surfing from Squamish, ice skating from England, and golf from Florida. They played, or they watched their friends and neighbours play. Sport has taken many different forms, in different times and different cultures. It has ranged from cock-fighting to figure skating and from agricultural labourers tossing a length of wooden pole to the pharmacologically bolstered weight-athletes of the modern Olympics. Even leisure was not the discrete part of life, or the industry, we know today. For most people their work and their way of life were not easily separable, and if "leisure" had any distinct meaning it referred simply to the traditional pastimes and practices (singing and storytelling, as well as physical contests) in which people engaged in order to inject pleasure into the rhythms of daily and seasonal life.

We may be proud of having advanced from these amateurish self-entertainments. Certainly performance standards have increased, and the settings and organization manifest a lot more slickness and a great deal more investment. Conversely, we may feel that modernization has its costs, that the games of a less organized era offered experiences that are hard to find in an era of rigid training plans and steroids, of agents and endorsements. Yet the point of sociological study is neither to applaud progress nor to become nostalgic for an idealized past. It is to build on the appreciation that things have been different and could be again, and to clarify the dynamics of how change has been (and is) accomplished. These are issues we shall address in greater depth in Chapter 3.

Second, a sociological imagination involves *understanding the significance of these changes for the lives of ordinary men and women.* At first glance, the dramatic increases in performance standards in sport, illustrated by how far we have surpassed the four-minute mile in thirty-seven years, constitute real "progress." Not only have world standards improved, but in many nations, including Canada, public funding for sports facilities and programs has meant that opportunities to excel are more widely distributed in the population than was the case in the days depicted in the film *Chariots of Fire.* A four-minute mile remains a substantial achievement, indicative of courage and determination as well as real athletic ability. Nonetheless, more knowledge about training, better facilities, more financial support for athletes, and a culture that applauds various forms of athletic excellence together mean that yesterday's standards no longer attract much attention. Our point here is that our achievements are not so clearly our own as we typically like to think. What we do as individuals is very much a function of the kinds of opportunities open to us in our particular time and place.

The point is reinforced by a consideration of the phenomenon of sport spectatorship. Ken Dryden's (1983) account of the sheer entertainment value of good hockey serves to remind us that the expansion of professional hockey into new cities like Edmonton, Calgary, and Quebec can be seen as constituting a significant addition to the cultural life of these communities. It is just like being able to see world-class theatre or hear the very best in music. Although the fact that entertainment of this skill level and quality is brought right into our homes via television may no longer seem remarkable, it makes a big difference to the lives of sports fans. It has also made the annual rhythms of professional sport a pervasive part of Canadian popular culture.

At the same time, the very availability of high-quality entertainment (and sport is clearly only a part of this picture) may mean that we do not learn how to entertain ourselves. Entertaining ourselves (and others) usually involves the development of personal skills: in sports, in music, in crafts or hobbies of various kinds, even in conversation; and these are skills that may be less widely developed than in a pre-television age. Again, the point is not to pass judgement but to understand the connections between history and biography. We need to understand that the kinds of people we are, the kinds of experiences we have been exposed to, and the kinds of skills and knowledge we take with us into successive experiences are all products of the opportunities Canadian society offers to women and men like ourselves.

Third, a sociological imagination involves *thinking about the relationships between individuals and social structures in processes of social change.* To suggest that we are formed as individuals, in experiences that we share with others like ourselves, reminds us that there have been great differences over the years in the formative experiences readily available to rich and poor, women and men, Anglophone and Francophone, native and non-native, in Canadian society.

It is clear from historical accounts that the social structures of successive periods in Canada have facilitated cultural accomplishment among privileged population groups, while they have systematically denied to many people the opportunities in which talents could be recognized, let alone developed. Class-conscious social institutions, as we shall see in Chapter 3, meant that many avenues for cultural development were available to members of the Canadian elite at a time when labouring or farming families had to preoccupy themselves with survival. Equally clearly, the structure of

relations between men and women was such that women of all classes were constrained in a variety of ways that men were not. Certainly the reduction of the working week meant that both men and women had more free time, but for women this often meant the servicing of other family members' leisure at the expense of opportunities to develop new and satisfying skills for themselves. Finally, relations between French and English, and between natives and non-natives, relations that became structured through our particular history, continue to limit opportunities for both Francophones and natives in mainstream Canadian sport.

What is perhaps even less obvious is that to whatever extent class, gender, race, and ethnic relations are less restrictive in their effects today, these changes are the result of collective historical efforts on the part of men and women. Working-class struggle did not just seek to increase wages and reduce hours of work; it sought these things so that ordinary people could enjoy a fuller life. Indeed, efforts to widen access to schooling, to operate public recreational facilities at prices most people can afford, and to include child-care facilities in them are all part of a broader project of creating a social structure that enables more people to pursue fuller lives. The historical project of the women's movement, from the suffragettes who fought for the vote to those women who have come together to fight different battles today, has been to oppose and break down what have been revealed as a succession of barriers to women's full participation in society. Similarly, the struggles of Francophones, as well as other ethnic groups, have been to develop and maintain their own unique sporting cultures but at the same time to win unprejudiced access to professional and national teams. Finally, aboriginal peoples who have recorded significant achievements as runners, for example, and as lacrosse and hockey players, continue to struggle to break down stereotypes and to rediscover their sporting culture.

Two additional points are worth noting here. First, historical change seldom occurs without protracted struggles in which the gains of some groups typically require some adjustment on the part of others. Second, it is through the actions of people that structures change. This includes the actions of famous individuals like tennis player Billie Jean King or boxer Muhammad Ali, who placed themselves in the forefront of challenges to particular kinds of barriers and became symbols after whom things were not the same again. It also includes the less dramatic but nonetheless cumulative actions of all those anonymous individuals who ultimately make normal what was once revolutionary. Very often we feel we have no impact on the structures of our society. However, despite the temptation to conceive of "the system" as having a logic and a momentum of its own, social institutions are composed of what people do. Thus children's experience of sport will be constituted by the teammates, coaches, opponents, and spectators they encounter there. The motives they will internalize, as well as the experiences they come to appreciate and enjoy, will come from the cumulative actions of those who initiate them into sport. Orlick and Botterill (1975: 46) capture this all too clearly in an interview with a ten-year-old ice hockey player.

Q. What do you like best about playing hockey?

A. Hitting . . . knocking the guy down . . . I just like hitting.

Q. What does your coach do when you make a good hit?

A. He gets really excited . . . like in practice when you make a good check . . . he yells 'yeah' and slaps his stick on the ice.

Social structures, in other words, are not natural; they are historical creations. They are not immutable, but rather manifest the collective practices of the men and women who make them up. It is also important to remember that the very people who change social structures are themselves products of those structures. Indeed, it is only by realizing the extent to which we are ourselves shaped by existing social institutions that we can begin to appreciate the complexity of social change.

This reciprocal and ongoing relationship between societies and individuals is at the heart of what sociologists debate as the relationship between *structures* and *agents*. On one side of this debate are those who emphasize the powerful effects of social structures: economic structures, political structures, structures of gender or ethnic relations. On the other side are those who emphasize that people individually, and especially collectively, have changed societies. The common ground in the debate is that there is a complex relationship between social structures and the individuals who constitute (and continually reconstitute) them. Understanding this relationship more clearly is the ultimate task of the sociological imagination.

SUMMARY

The approach we have taken in this book reflects our conviction that sociology is an historical science. In our view, a properly sociological analysis of sport cannot help but undermine any preconceptions that contemporary forms of leisure are in any sense "natural," by making it clear that the dominance they enjoy today was achieved (and, crucially, is maintained) by conscious human action. It will show that these cultural transformations cannot be divorced from economic and political developments; on the contrary, they are intimately bound up with them.

What is required in the sociology of sport is an understanding that the observable institutionalization of various games into "sports" manifests a process characteristic of any modern society. But we need to ask what interests and coalitions of interests gave specific shape to the development of modern sport. We need to ask how the development of sport has affected the lives of men and women in different parts of Canada. We need finally to ask how contemporary sport in Canada is both influenced by and an influence on developments in other Canadian institutions.

Sociology as an historical and critical science starts from the assumption that society is an evolving human construction. Thus the particular social patterns and institutional structures we can observe just now are understood neither as natural nor as necessarily ideal, but rather as reflecting currently dominant understandings as to how societies function best. Sociology therefore has to examine the origins of these understandings, as well as the processes by which they have become and are able to remain dominant. This is the task of the next chapter.

SUPPLEMENTARY READING

The approach to sociology we have taken in this book clearly owes much to the sociology of Anthony Giddens. A great deal of Giddens's work is directed at professional sociologists and is difficult for the beginning student; however, his *Sociology: A Brief but Critical Introduction* is the best introduction to sociology as the habit of thinking critically and historically about social institutions. It is lively and readable, without oversimplifying the issues. Chapter One could be read as a companion to this chapter. Another text that can be recommended as an introduction to thinking sociologically is Peter L. Berger's *Invitation to Sociology: A Humanistic Perspective*. This book is somewhat older than Giddens's, and it does not fully register the debates about gender that are in the forefront of sociology today. However, it is extremely well written and makes the connections between sociology, history, and biography that we have emphasized here.

In the sociology of sport, we shall have occasion to introduce many works over the course of this book. As a companion to this chapter, however, John Goldlust's discussion of sport as a sociological problem in *Playing For*

Keeps (Chapter One) is very good. Also, Susan Birrell's (1988) article, "Discourses on the Gender/Sport Relationship: From Women in Sport to Gender Relations," and her "Racial Relations Theories and Sport: Suggestions for a More Critical Analysis" (1989) are excellent analyses of how and why sport sociology is changing, although they will be challenging for students new to these issues.

Finally, Ken Dryden's *The Game* tells a story that will be familiar to most Canadian students interested in sport. Intended as a popular book rather than as sociology, it is nonetheless valuable because it makes connections between changes in Canadian hockey and changes in Canadian society.

Chapter 2
SPORT AND CULTURE

When Canada hosted the 1976 Olympics in Montreal, the Games themselves were accompanied by a variety of other cultural activities. A series of artists' posters was commissioned, musical and dramatic events were staged, a play about the lives of athletes was performed in the Games Village itself. At one level, this demonstrated the Montreal organizers' commitment to breathe new life into the classical idea of the Games as a cultural event, with sport in the forefront of a celebration of different forms of human accomplishment. However, that this tradition had been allowed to lapse and that many people (including many athletes) did not see much connection between sport and "culture" illustrate that sport is not always considered a cultural form, and indeed that some people see sport and culture as antithetical.

SPORT AS CULTURE?

In this section we want to review some historical understandings of culture as well as some academic approaches to the study of culture. We will begin by identifying some ideas about culture that have tended to exclude sport and conclude by arguing for a broader definition that recognizes sport as an important purveyor of cultural meanings and values.

Culture as the "High Arts"

Common to most definitions of culture that would exclude sport is an association (indeed,

Brian Gavriloff, Edmonton Journal.

Wilderness sports – new technologies, new problems.

sometimes an equation) between culture and refinement. This is present in oppositions between culture and nature. It is also present in familiar contrasts between the cultural arts and the practical crafts, and between the "fine" arts, which demonstrate mental and aesthetic achievement, and those more "basic" skills like sports that are associated with the body. It is finally present in the equation of "culture" with the activities of those classes and societies that have been able to portray themselves as models of refinement. Often these different ideas – the idea of culture as refinement and the appropriation of the adjective "cultured" to honour the activities of particular groups or societies – are intimately connected. In what follows, we untangle these ideas.

The opposition between culture and nature tends to equate culture with the habits and artifacts of a "civilized" society. In this version, London and Paris, and in Canada, Montreal and Toronto, were considered centres of refinement and civilization. People who lived on the frontiers were considered cultured only to the extent that they knew what was going on in the centres of cultural activity. Cultural activity referred especially to art forms and intellectual pastimes whose practice became more possible the more removed one's way of life was from subsistence and survival. For a community to support drama and music presumed some level of free time and disposable income, and it was not unheard of for frontier cities to build theatres and opera houses in boom periods and to consider that such facilities made them outposts of civilization in a raw land.

This idea of culture as refinement slides very easily into equating it with "non-productive" activity. This, of course, is made explicit in Veblen's (1934) classic account of the life of the "leisure class," in which the cultivation of skill and knowledge in a range of non-productive pursuits, from music and painting to polo, was considered part of a cultured lifestyle and a public marker of "class."

In addition, the opposition between culture and nature also connects readily with the dichotomy between mind and body that has been deeply etched into Western consciousness. Not only are mind and body separate, but in this view, straining and sweating and running about are throwbacks to our animal nature, while philosophy, mathematics, etc. represent our collective progress away from a state of nature. The idea that "humanity" is represented by the activities of the mind was articulated long ago by the French philosopher Descartes in the saying "I think, therefore, I am." It has gone through many modern variants, including the Freudian thesis that "civilization" requires the discipline and constraint of our natural (i.e., physical and emotional) impulses. It is also present in the prejudices held by some whites, in which blacks are conceded to be good athletes but are stereotyped as lacking the mental qualities to be managers or even to play the "thinking" positions.

These ideas come together in a conception of culture as *the context in which intellectual growth is fostered*. This translates, in turn, into the widely held idea that culture refers to a specific set of activities and skills: the "high arts." People who had the appropriate performance skills in the classical art forms or who knew how to "appreciate" good performances were considered cultured, while others were not. To become cultured, in this sense, was to become familiar with "the best" that had been written, composed, and painted. It was to absorb this heritage of Shakespearean drama, Bach and Beethoven, classical Dutch and French painting, and opera and to make it one's own. Culture, according to this view, would have little or nothing to do with sport.

The Power to Define: Whose Activities "Count"?

The several dimensions of snobbery and privilege embedded in this definition are worth noting. There is an obvious class bias in equating "culture" with the leisure pursuits of the wealthier and more educated classes of society. What is perhaps less obvious is the devaluation of a variety of working-class skills, often very intricate skills, that are demonstrated in the making of many practical yet beautiful things. Cabinetmaking, wrought-iron work, and in Canada the making of canoes and other fine wooden boats, for example, were all recognized as skilled trades or *crafts*. However, the knowledge and craft of the violin maker have always had much less social status than those of the violinist or the composer, and the distinction between art and craft, which builds on the distinction between leisure and work, puts a much lower cultural value on artistry displayed in the making of practical things. As well, the crafts developed by women around the world to bring beauty and comfort to the home – quilting, crochet, and embroidery, as well as the culinary arts – have seldom been accorded the status of art forms.

A similar devaluation of practical artistry is often present in the special categories of "folk art" or "ethnic art." Here, such items as ceremonial clothing (e.g., moccasins, wedding shirts and dresses), carved utensils and furniture, and fine Persian rugs are recognized as highly artistic but not quite "art." The ethnocentrism of such categories is taken a step further when even strictly decorative objects or religious artwork, for example bark paintings or carved masks, are not typically accorded the same status as Western painting and sculpture (which themselves have often been religious in their themes and imagery). Yet Europeans saw themselves as bringing culture to the native peoples of the Americas and Africa, as if their own cultural forms were inferior or non-existent.

Mass or Popular Culture

The equation of culture with the intellectual and the aesthetic set up an opposition, actively articulated in some circles, between culture and entertainment, and between "culture" and mass or popular culture. Mass culture originated as a derogatory label for what were often described as the "mindless" entertainment forms that had developed with the growth of a mass market for leisure experiences. These included romance novels and hit parade music, as well as Hollywood films and professional sport. Popular culture had more positive connotations, referring to the self-produced "folk" entertainments of particular regions: for example, local and regional music (e.g., country, blues), as well as local and regional sports. Today, however, this distinction becomes blurred when "sport, born of truly popular games, i.e. games produced by the people, returns to the people, like 'folk music', in the form of spectacles produced for the people" (Bourdieu, 1978: 828). Popular culture now generally refers to all those spectator entertainments, including sport, whose appeal is primarily an emotional or sensual one and whose "fans" are seeking excitement or entertainment rather than intellectual development in their leisure time.

This is not to say that popular cultural forms are without intellectual interest. Baseball and cricket are examples of sports that have become the subjects of large and often imaginative literatures, and the late Baseball Commissioner, A. Bart Giammati, is often cited as an example of a "Renaissance Man" whose strength was his deep love of sport *and* ideas. Nonetheless, intellectuals who are interested in "low brow" cultural forms often find themselves having to defend these interests. Therefore, one of the recurring questions in the study of culture is precisely how the "high arts" are able to maintain their privileged status when popular culture speaks to more people and popular culture more clearly expresses the character of a society.

Culture as a "Way of Life"

Independent of this whole debate, however, is another tradition in the analysis of culture, derived from anthropology, in which culture refers to a whole way of life. In this tradition, questions of the power to define what counts as culture are postponed, because culture is not treated as a specific set of "cultural" activities, with other activities therefore non-cultural. Instead, "a culture" includes all those activities and ideas that go to make up a way of life: economic activities as well as leisure pastimes, decision-making structures, patterns of male-female relationships, and other behavioural norms and values.

This conception of culture as a whole way of life was what anthropologists meant when they spoke of the cultures of the Aztecs or Mayans in Mexico, the Nuer in Africa, the Haida or Kwakiutl in what is today British Columbia. On a smaller scale, it is also what social historians mean when they talk about the cultures of prairie cities or of a working-class city like Hamilton (Palmer, 1979). It is finally what sociologists mean when they talk about "subcultures" within contemporary society: about youth subcultures, ethnic subcultures, or even sporting subcultures. Gary Alan Fine (1987), for example, offers us a detailed account of the subculture of Little League baseball. This all-inclusive conception of culture is captured by an Australian cultural analyst:

Culture is what we are all about. It is a crystallization of what we feel, what we want, what we fear, what we live for. We shape it, it shapes us, it both reflects and determines our being, it is the way we try to understand and give meaning to our lives. Our culture is us. (McGregor, 1983: 99)

Culture, from this view, includes what might be called formalized practices or *cultural forms* (including hockey and golf as well as sculpture and poetry), each of which has its own formal characteristics, its own history, and has produced its own examples of human achievement. But it also includes other kinds of social practice, including skateboarding, weekends at the cottage, hunting and snowmobiling, as well as practices of neighbourliness or community service, including the volunteer activity that makes minor sport possible. All these *cultural practices*, both the formal and the informal, contribute to making us who we are as Canadians.

The "whole way of life" definition of culture has many attractions in our view. It helps to legitimize the recognition and study of sport, both formal and informal, as an important aspect of Canadian culture. The "high art" definition, in contrast, made it difficult to take sport seriously. However, there is an irony here that should not go unnoticed. Central to the "whole way of life" definition is that culture includes the social practices of ordinary people, rather than starting from notions of "excellence" that focus attention on the achievements of a creative minority. Yet much sport sociology has focused precisely on the most visible and achievement-oriented forms of sport – professional sport and high-performance amateur sport – at the expense of the many other kinds of sporting practice that are important aspects of contemporary culture.

Professional sports and events like the Olympics, which celebrate the meanings and values associated with "excellence," are indeed features of life in contemporary developed societies that an observer from another world might find worthy of analysis. Yet if we confine our attention to high-performance sport (whether professional sport, the Olympic sports, or highly competitive college and youth sport), we overlook the significance in contemporary life of many kinds of athletic participation that carry on unheralded and outside any official framework. We also reproduce, however unwittingly, the "high art" notion that the activities of elites are most worthy of our attention.

There is one further problem with the "whole way of life" definition, despite its attractions. When "culture" comes to refer to everything, it loses some of its usefulness as a conceptual tool for the analysis of social processes. If everything in a way of life is seen as "culture," it becomes difficult to distinguish relationships between different aspects of culture, or between *cultural* practices and other practices that are *not* cultural. In particular, there is no framework for clarifying relationships between changes in cultural traditions and practices, and changes in the structural relations of Canadian society: specifically, gender relations, class relations, and ethnic relations.

Culture and Sport: A Sociological Perspective

These kinds of questions make culture sociologically interesting because they have placed the analysis of culture increasingly in the forefront of efforts to understand social change. Sociologists have tried to be more specific about culture than the "whole way of life" approach, without tying themselves either to the specific activities of the "high art" definition or to the elitist ideologies that underlie it. Most sociologists now use culture to refer to the practices of everyday life through which meanings are daily expressed, as well as the symbolic forms through which meanings are publicly rehearsed or challenged. There are important differences, of course, between schools of sociology that use the consensual language of "socialization" to emphasize the teaching of "core" meanings and values and those that use such terms as "dominant" to emphasize that cultural institutions can be the focus of conflicts between social groups. There is agreement, though, that the creation and diffusion of meaning comprise an important factor in patterns of cohesion and conflict in societies, and that the activities through which meanings and values are popularized are therefore important.

We define culture, then, as the *symbolic forms and the everyday practices through which people express and experience meaning.* This will allow us to focus on formalized practices, including sports and art forms, that develop their own rules and disciplines and recognized standards of excellence. It also allows us to focus on the significance of the many less formalized cultural practices that for many Canadians constitute the rhythms of daily and seasonal life. Our approach to sport explicitly recognizes both the formal and the informal, the excellent and the participatory. We are interested, of course, in the place of highly visible forms of sport in Canadian culture, such as the NHL, the CFL, the Expos and Blue Jays, as well as Canadian standard-bearers in the Olympics or in World Cup skiing. However, we are also interested in the many less visible kinds of sporting practice that are for many Canadians their most significant (and sometimes their only) involvement in sport. We include here recreational involvement in the major games: the "beer leagues" and pickup games in local rinks and parks. We could cite as an example the place of the local baseball team, the Field Mice, in life in tiny Field, B.C. (and we think the symbolism of the name is important). We also include the thriving participation in a variety of other games – soccer, curling, bowling – that are a vital part of life for many Canadians but seldom get much media attention. Finally, we include the burgeoning participation in aerobic and "wilderness" sports, including running and cycling and swimming, cross-country and downhill skiing, hiking and camping, fishing and hunting. All of these are significant parts of Canadian sporting culture.

Our intention is not simply to insist on the cultural significance, in Canada, of sports other than major spectator sports, though we *do* want to do that. What also needs to be raised, as a question to be kept in mind in the discussion that follows, is how and why some sports get more recognition and attention – and a lot more public money and/or commercial sponsorship – than others. The standard answers have been tradition and popularity, but it can be suggested that fishing, for example, is both more traditional and more popular in Canada than either football or baseball. It is necessary to factor in, then, the structures of class, gender, and ethnicity, as well as the straightforward commercial interests, which have meant that some popular sporting practices have benefited from active promotion while others have remained relatively obscure outside their own circles of participants (for example, candlepin bowling in the blue-collar towns of New Brunswick and Nova Scotia). It is also important to recognize that popular practices have become one site of struggle between different meaning and value systems. (It

is not the only such site.) However, if McGregor's suggestion that "Culture is what we are all about" has any merit, it follows that the meanings and values that come to prevail in Canadian sport will say something about who we are, and who we are becoming, as a people.

Sport and Popular Culture

In this section we discuss why sport is such a visible aspect of popular culture, not just in Canada but in many other developed countries as well. Australians, for example, have been described as "sports mad" (Stoddart, 1986). Sport has been described as a metaphor for contemporary American life and important to the understanding of American society (Eitzen and Sage, 1989). Cycling's Tour de France is a major cultural event each summer, not only in France itself but in Belgium and other adjacent countries (Nicholson, 1978). Soccer, though not a major sport in North America, arouses passions in many European and Latin American nations that are difficult for even sports-conscious North Americans to fully appreciate (Tomlinson and Whannel, 1986; Lever, 1983).

Why does sport occupy the place it does in popular culture? At one level, Wilson (1988: 4-5) is doubtless correct in suggesting that "People want to be entertained in their leisure time, and those who run sports as a business have responded adroitly and zealously to this demand." Our attention is drawn here to the importance of entertainment in much of popular culture, and also to the centrality of money and marketing in what are now the entertainment industries. The music and film industries and commercial television, as well as professional sport, spring to mind. We shall have more to say about the business and promotion of sport as an entertainment form in Chapters 5 and 6.

But, this does not explain everything. To begin with, the success of sport as spectator entertainment does not in itself explain the varied participation in recreational sport. Industries are involved here, too, of course. However, our point, with respect to watching and playing sport alike, is that promotion alone is not enough. Sports would not enjoy the popularity they do around the world if they did not speak to widely felt needs and desires in contemporary societies. Three themes have been articulated in most discussions about the attraction of sport: excitement, physicality, and community.

Excitement

The essence of this first dimension is captured in Elias and Dunning's (1986) proposal that widespread involvement in sport, whether as a spectator or a player, manifests "the quest for excitement in unexciting societies." The appeal of sport, they suggest, is that it offers opportunities for excitement, emotional expression, and physical trial that are otherwise hard to find in contemporary societies. Physical trial is an issue we shall return to, but to appreciate Elias and Dunning's analysis of excitement it is necessary to recall our discussion of the rationalization of life in modern societies (see Chapter 1).

Rationalization is not just a method for the organization of more efficient production or administration. It is also the normative value placed today on planning and calculation, predictability and control, a norm that has encouraged us to divide our time and indeed our lives into managed and purposeful segments. The corollary of our carefully planned achievements is the progressive elimination of opportunities for the impractical, the spontaneous, the emotional, and the surprising in most aspects of our lives. Rationalization has certainly penetrated sport, and the result is precisely as Dryden (1983: 134) suggested, that "once a game has been organized, unorganized games seem a waste of time." Indeed, Guttmann (1978) credits the force of this rationalizing world view with the transformation of spontaneous and playful pastimes into highly organized and performance-oriented sports.

Nonetheless, the potential for excitement and spontaneity in sport constitutes one of the major sources of its appeal. For all but the most partisan fans, the suspense that attends seeing a genuine contest sustains the entertainment value. Whether we are talking about team games, racquet games, or races, if we realize the outcome is not in doubt our interest is sharply diminished. This is why professional leagues must try to sustain some level of parity; it is also why we are offended and even outraged if we believe that players are not trying. Suspense is not the only source of pleasure in sports; some fans would rather that their favourites win by a large margin than see a close game. For most of us, however, a belief that there is something open about the outcome and that the contestants are trying their hardest is fundamental to arousing our interest and involvement. This belief is also absolutely fundamental to the widespread gambling among sports followers, and it is why the penalties against gambling on the part of the contestants are so severe (recently the case of Pete Rose, as well as the famous Black Sox scandal involving Shoeless Joe Jackson).

For the participant, the opportunity for complete emotional commitment can make sport a "special" kind of experience. For the soccer player or runner or rock climber, the result may not be as important as total involvement in the activity itself (though for some it clearly is). Again, the background is the rationalized world, in which we spend most of our time engaged in tasks that involve only some small part of our mental and physical capacities, and even less of our desire. Time passes slowly, our commitment of ourselves is partial at best, part of us is elsewhere. In contrast, sports offer opportunities for commitments that are voluntary in a way that school and work seldom are, and they are "total" in the sense that they combine physical, mental, and emotional challenges as few other activities can.

The literature on climbing and other "adventure" sports offers some of the best descriptions of how completely engrossing athletic activities can be: engaging our emotions and our minds as well as requiring total physical commitment (see Mitchell, 1983). What Csikszentmihalyi (1975, 1990) has characterized as "flow," as the experience of total commitment to and absorption in the challenge, has been well represented in books about many different sports. The literature, for instance, on "inner" tennis and skiing, and more generally about the mental and emotional sides of "peak performance," has given expression to what many top athletes have long known about these experiences. It has always been a part of popular knowledge of sport that a player or team of moderate talents can overcome superior opponents through emotional commitment and readiness. Whether we call it willpower, "wanting it badly enough," being "psyched up," or

Competitive kayaking.

Brian Gavriloff, Edmonton Journal.

"rising to the occasion," this emotional factor is why the best teams do not always win, and it is a major part of what makes sport exciting for players and fans alike. Indeed, fans' understanding of this makes rooting for the underdog meaningful and allows us to share vicariously in the "thrill of victory and the agony of defeat."

Physicality

Alongside the excitement generated by sporting contests and challenges, another important aspect of sport's popular appeal is a widespread appreciation of the physical skills displayed. Leonard Koppett (1981) has suggested that sport is widely appreciated precisely because the accomplishments of the elite athlete are comprehensible to any adult or child who has tried to perform the same feats. The individual thus understands just how difficult they are. The mastery of the body and some of the general skills of physical play – balance and dexterity, strength, speed, co-ordination – are part of growing up for most children, and they remain part of the remembered experience of most adults. "This is not the same with opera, abstract art, or a Fellini movie" (Smith 1988:56). In these and other cases, the absence of any direct experience means that we have to learn to appreciate the achievements of those who become the masters. Opportunities for personal experience of these more refined cultural skills, especially some of the more esoteric and expensive ones, are not widely distributed in most societies. Therefore, appreciation of them is likely to be less widely distributed than is the appreciation of physical prowess. Sport is popular in part because it showcases forms of human accomplishment that most of us can appreciate precisely because we have first-hand experience of how difficult they are. Indeed, the importance of familiarity to appreciation is under-

lined by the indifferent response of some American audiences to hockey and by the inability of many Canadians to see what others enjoy in games like soccer and cricket.

An important qualification points to the relationship of sport, as a popular cultural form, to ideologies of masculinity and femininity in contemporary Western societies. Australian sociologist R.W. Connell (1983) has suggested that intellectuals often fail to register just how important sport is in the culture of boys. Sport is quite simply *the* socially legitimated way, now that fighting is actively discouraged in most sectors of society, in which boys can acquire and demonstrate the physical prowess our culture still associates with masculinity. Boys are actively, and in many cases ardently, encouraged by schools and parents to practise these skills. Thus most adult males not only appreciate the physical skills of the professionals; they also relate to the emotional struggles described above: the triumph over tension, the difficulties of coming through in the clutch or of coming back after the loss of a close game or close point. Finally, they can enter into the tactical decisions and judgements, so that the "armchair quarterback" is a familiar figure wherever men gather to watch sport.

The continuing barriers to girls' participation in the team games that remain the most popular spectator sports among Canadian men (see Chapter 7) mean that many women are not in the same position to appreciate the skills of these games or to relate in any active way to the competitors. The same women may have a first-hand appreciation of tennis, skating, or any of the other sports that girls now routinely play. What is pertinent here is that the most actively promoted sports in the mainstream Canadian media – baseball, football, and especially hockey – remain very much male cultural forms. Moreover, the attention given to them and the

To the winner go the spoils.

Brian Gavriloff, Edmonton Journal.

public celebration of the "male" qualities of these sports, according to some observers, help to legitimize a particular version of masculinity (i.e., forceful, confrontational, dominant) in the broader culture. We discuss this further in Chapter 7.

Community

The final aspect of sport's prominence in popular culture that we want to introduce here is its significance in the construction and organization of social identifications and rivalries. At the interpersonal level, sociologists – and athletes themselves – have depicted how the friendships that develop within teams and sporting subcultures, and the sense of belonging and bonding that can develop within such groups, constitute an important aspect of the joy of sports for many participants (see, for example, Donnelly and Young, 1988; Dryden, 1983; Stebbins, 1987). However, there is a fur-

ther and more sociologically significant sense of "community," in which sport helps to construct and reinforce public identifications with nations or cities. This will be the focus of our discussion here. The distinction, following Foley (1990), is between community as a group of individuals pursuing a particular sport together and communities as historical or geographical entities that mobilize a sense of emotional identification among complete strangers.

Political and economic elites have long been aware of the value of symbolic representatives in building popular identification with a larger collectivity, whether a city or a state. Sport has been particularly well suited to the annual rehearsal of civic and national identifications because most citizens "are much more likely to identify with the elite athletes representing their country than they would identify with artists, or even politicians" (Wilson, 1988: 149). Few Canadians who were old enough at the time will forget the intensity with which the nation followed the progress of the first Canada-Soviet hockey series in 1972, or the national celebration that followed Paul Henderson's dramatic goal in the final minutes of the deciding game. We celebrated not only the victory itself, but what we liked to believe it demonstrated about Canadians' flair, skill, desire, and *individualism* in comparison with our Soviet opponents. The result of this powerful public identification with athletic "representatives" is that governments in many nations have been anxious to identify themselves with international sporting successes and thus have sought to create them. There is no question that the Canadian government's increasing support for our Olympic athletes has been very much a part of the "nation-building" strategies of successive federal governments from the 1960s onwards, something we shall have considerably more to say about in Chapter 4.

We want here to draw attention to a phenomenon that has arguably had an even greater impact in giving popular identifications a specific shape, namely a civic shape. Paul Voisey (1981) describes civic boosterism as the effort, on the part of local politicians and business leaders, to encourage economic and population growth through promoting cultural activities designed to give their town or city a dynamic "image" in comparison with its competitors. He comments that in the period of settlement in southern Alberta, "boosters searched endlessly for any gimmick to distinguish their town from countless others," in the quest for new settlers and new businesses. One of the most successful ways of spreading a town's name proved to be through semi-professional baseball teams, especially those that won in regional tournaments. Such teams were initially made up of talented locals, but the recruitment of outside stars was soon well established.

Betke (1983) describes these phenomena in Edmonton, circa 1900-1920. Edmonton was competing with other prairie cities to establish itself as the most attractive centre to prospective migrants and businesses; and sporting teams, especially winners, helped to promote the image of a dynamic community. Boosterism was also present in decisions to build theatres and opera halls in frontier cities. However, civic leaders saw that spectator sports were especially popular, and indeed were often seen as one of the major attractions of the new urban culture in the West. They also felt that successful sports teams helped create a sense of "Edmontonness" among the rapidly growing population. It did not matter that as winning teams came to require more and more recruitment of outsiders, the city's "representatives" had increasingly tenuous links with the community. "What mattered was that they be successful and that the whole city be allowed to identify with that success" (Betke, 1983: 54). Certainly the Edmonton Grads, who dominated women's basketball between 1915 and 1940 but who were amateurs and were comprised entirely of homegrown talent, were the pride of the city.

We can see here all the outlines of the civic boosterism that surrounds professional sport today. The acquisition of major league franchises is actively promoted by local elites as a mark of a "big league" city (Ingham, Howell, and Schilperoort, 1988). Successful teams become the focus of much civic pride, especially in relation to local rivals. The war of words between Edmonton (the "City of Champions") and Calgary is a good example. Certainly, life in Edmonton would seem less interesting to many of its citizens without the excitement generated by the Oilers and the Eskimos, and there are those who cannot now imagine Toronto without the pennant fever that surrounds the Blue Jays. Perhaps the best contemporary example of the positive community spirit that can be generated by a professional sports team is the Saskatchewan Roughriders, who produced in their memorable 1989 Grey Cup victory a groundswell of "Rider Pride" all over the province. There were those who remarked that this was "good for" a province that did not have much to cheer about on the economic front.

At the same time, it is important to consider how the meaning of "community" takes on different slants. For instance, hockey remains a focal point for community life in small-town Canada (Dryden and MacGregor, 1989). These are face-to-face communities whose members are friends and neighbours. Players and spectators know each other and the games are occasions for the renewal of personal relationships and socializing. On the other hand, the sense of community mobilized around big-city, big-league teams is very different. Professional players are not from among us; they are our hired representatives. They are usually from somewhere else, and although they often participate in community life they do so as celebrities. Likewise, the fans who are patrons at the Skydome, BC Place, or SaskPlace are only by accident able to socialize with their neighbours. They are consumers of big-city entertainment who briefly share a common passion and then go back to their separate lives. Even though professional sports franchises in North America have prospered by promoting themselves in the language of "community," owners have not hesitated to break their ties with communities in their search for larger markets (see Chapter 5).

Finally, when the particular sense of "us" that the sports media construct around the fortunes of the Oilers, the Jays, or whomever, offers daily reinforcement for a specifically civic identification, the potential of professional sport to symbolize and mobilize other kinds of identifications is effectively pre-empted. In Canadian sport, we have one notable instance of a professional team that was a standard bearer of ethnic consciousness, namely the Montreal Canadiens. Today, Les Canadiens' status as representative of French-Canadian aspirations has been complicated and diminished by the player draft (which disperses Quebec-born players around the league, while Anglicizing the Canadiens), by the relatively new NHL franchise in Quebec City, and by political developments in Quebec. On the one hand, we are fortunate that Canadian sport has not been structured so as to trade on, and hence regularly re-mobilize, religious, ethnic, or class identities. We are thereby spared the violence that has marred soccer in Europe, where it has become a site for acting out deeply rooted structural antagonisms. On the other hand, the structuring of popular identifications in the language of civic boosterism can be seen as one of the important ways in which subordinate group identities are lost in Canada and minority aspirations are incorporated into the Canadian "mainstream" (see Chapter 7). It is also one of the ways in which "culture" is made to appear more apolitical than it ever really is.

Sport, Culture, and Ideology in Canadian Life

The preceding discussion has sought to identify some of the reasons why sport is important to the way of life enjoyed by many Canadians. In this section we want to explore the significance of sport in the construction and diffusion of meanings and values that are dominant in Canadian life. The discussion will begin by considering the place of some sports, both as widely watched spectator entertainments and as popular practices, in our identity as Canadians. It will then explore the place of sport, and more particularly some meanings and values associated with "modern" sport, in reaffirming Canadians' sense of membership in a transnational culture that is by definition not uniquely Canadian. The point is that we typically like to think of ourselves as a culturally distinct society, and cultural forms like hockey reaffirm our sense of Canadian-ness. Yet at the same time, there are important meanings and values that we like to think we share with other modern industrial nations, and participation in international high-performance sport is one of the ways we publicly affirm ourselves as a modern and competitive society. Sport thus plays dual and sometimes contradictory roles in Canadian cultural life, and it is necessary to appreciate both sides of this duality if the full effects of sport in popular culture are to be grasped.

Sport and Canadian Identity

What makes us distinctive? What aspects of our sporting practices and traditions help to constitute a distinctive Canadian cultural identity? It will be apparent from the preceding sections of this chapter that we consider sport to be a legitimate and important part of Canadian life. Put differently, Canadian culture is more than the novels of Margaret Laurence and Robertson Davies, the paintings of the Group of Seven, the Montreal Jazz Festival, and the Edmonton Fringe Festival. Each of these points to what some Canadians are interested in, and each says something about the meanings and values that are important to significant groups of Canadians. Canadian culture is also more than the CBC, *The Globe and Mail*, passenger trains, and medicare, although these are Canadian cultural institutions whose purpose in part has been to make life in the Canadian hinterland viable and to make possible some degree of common ground and knowledge among the disparate communities of this vast country.

Sport arguably provides a common talking point for more Canadians and brings more different kinds of Canadians together than any other aspect of our culture. This is true not only of obvious national events like the Stanley Cup and Grey Cup, but also of many less visible sporting practices, from curling and skiing and community hockey in the winter to cycling and golf and a variety of watersports in the summer. Together, these sporting activities help to constitute the daily and seasonal routines of many Canadians. They also help to constitute community life, especially in many smaller Canadian communities. This becomes more visible when a rink like LaDawn Funk's from Spruce Grove, Alberta, emerges to win a World Junior Curling Championship. Curling, a sport whose heartland is our small cities and towns, is particularly representative even at the level of the Brier, the Canadian men's championship:

> These are not hot-shot professional athletes. They are accountants and railway workers, petroleum engineers and salesmen. They are average Canadians, each one representing his province or territory, who happen to excel at what is basically a club game and who, for a short period, rise to stardom and national prominence. (Strachan, 1989)

The place of sport in the life of smaller communities is illustrated in a different way by the Swift Current Broncos' comeback from tragedy to win a Memorial Cup. After the bus crash that killed four young players in 1986, some outsiders wondered whether the team would fold. However, this underestimates how important junior hockey is to the culture of many smaller cities and towns in the Prairies, to the interior of British Columbia, and to rural Ontario. Rose Shaheen, who managed the hot dog stand at the Broncos' home games, said, "The Broncos mean more to us than the Canadiens do to Montreal. It was like something happened to our family" (Fisher, 1989b). Here she was pointing to a sense of personal involvement, a lack of distance between players and community people that has long since been broken in big-league, big-city sport.

Some of the most distinctively Canadian cultural forms are winter sports, specifically hockey and curling. The practices that surround both of these sports – not just the actual playing and watching, but the travelling to and from arenas in neighbouring communities, the post-game socializing, the many hours of volunteer work that go into organizing events – are simply part of autumn and winter life for many Canadians. To these examples we could add winter carnivals, snowmobiling, and, more recently, cross-country and downhill skiing. These are our counterparts to the rituals of spring and summer that surround baseball in the United States and cricket in the West Indies. We have our own rituals of summer, but they occupy a shorter part of the year and are less distinctively elements in a *Canadian* way of life.

We would also argue that odes to hockey as "an allegory of our life in Canada as Canadians" (Beardsley, 1988:36) overstate the case. To begin with, books like Doug Beardsley's *Country On Ice*, Peter Gzowski's *The Game of Our Lives*, and even Ken Dryden's *The Game* capture very evocatively the place of hockey in the formative experiences of even modestly athletic boys who grew up in Canada before the mid-1960s. They are about a predominantly Anglophone and Francophone Canada that is

part of our simpler past. Certainly, becoming hockey fans has been part of the "Canadianization" of many immigrants, but it is also clear that hockey is no longer the cultural universal it once was in a Canada less multicultural than we are today. Moreover, the childhood associations that hockey conjures up for boys are not usually available to girls. They have their own memories in which hockey, typically, has a different and lesser place. Finally, it is important to note that generalizations about Canadian culture gloss over regional variations. CBC television's *Hockey Night in Canada* did unite hockey fans from coast to coast, and still does to a degree. However, one has only to move from Ontario to the West to realize how much more important CFL football is in the culture of prairie cities than it is in Toronto (or was in Montreal), where it is simply another competitor for the entertainment dollar. Calder and Andrew (1984) give us insight into just how much the Roughriders mean to Saskatchewan, while Stebbins (1987) offers a detailed account of "Canada's second sport" in Calgary. Meanwhile, curling, as noted above, occupies a place in the collective life of rural Canada that is seldom registered in the metropolitan media.

Sport and a "Modern" Canada

An even larger issue that needs to be addressed is: What is now distinctively Canadian about hockey, or indeed any other modern game? Hockey is generally conceded to have been invented here, and climate and tradition gave us a head start, which meant that until fairly recently we were clearly the best in the world. Hockey was a form of excellence that Canadians gave to the world, and until recently we set the standards against which others measured their progress. We were known abroad for our excellence in hockey at a time when few for-

Brian Gavriloff, Edmonton Journal.

Team captains accepting the Canada Cup.

eigners took much notice of our art or literature. Hockey became part of our image of ourselves, which as Dryden (1983) observes is a
good part of why our various series with the
Soviets have evoked such powerful interest and
why defeat becomes an occasion for national
self-examination.

Yet Dryden also points out that several
other nations (Sweden, Czechoslovakia, Fin-
land, the United States) are now competitive
in international hockey, and just as the Soviets
had to learn from us in order to beat us at our
own game, we had to adapt our game (however
stubbornly) to theirs to remain competitive.

The result of increasing contact is that, at the
top levels, the variety there once was in national "styles" is transformed into a relative
sameness, and the *game itself* moves on to new
and more demanding levels of speed, skill, and
tactical versatility (Dryden, 1983). These
changes become felt at all levels of a game and
are reflected in how it is now taught.

To note the increasing similarities one
finds today in sporting practices throughout
the world is to return to the idea that what is
important today about sport in Canadian culture may be less what is distinctively Canadian
than what sport teaches Canadians about being

competitive in the international arena. Both competitive individualism and achievement-orientation are key components of what cultural commentators have called "modernism" and what sociologists have called modern societies. Modernism sees recent human history as a history of tangible improvement and progress. It celebrates the capacity of men and women to make and remake their world, to transform and improve on existing realities: material conditions, ideas, and social institutions. The modernist sensibility supports individual men and women in breaking with the restrictions and limits of traditional ways of doing things. It also supports a profound scepticism toward traditional belief systems. Indeed, the rise and diffusion of a scientific world view is seen as a necessary condition for a modern culture.

Modern people, suggests Berman (1989), celebrate the triumphs and breakthroughs this attitude, especially this commitment to surpass what has gone before, has made possible. We celebrate "progress" in the arts as well as in the sciences, in architecture as well as in the less tangible world of ideas. Berman does not mention sport, but Guttmann (1978) makes it clear that when we are invited to identify with the achievements of modern athletes, we are being invited to celebrate *not only individuals but the social formations that have made these new levels of human achievement possible*. Politician Jean Charest's claim that Canadian athletes "help the modern Canada become better known in other countries" (Fitness and Amateur Sport, 1988: 17) only echoes sentiments expressed by politicians around the world. What this really points to, however, is an increasingly international culture with universal standards of achievement that require individual nations to adapt or fall behind.

The achievements of this modern international culture include remarkable material breakthroughs, such as better facilities and equipment. They also include the economic and political changes that have made the pursuit of athletic excellence a real option for more people. Finally, and perhaps most important, these achievements include those of sport science: breakthroughs in knowledge that have made the production of athletic performance much less a matter of guesswork and guts than it used to be. Together, these developments underline Guttmann's (1978) contention that when we watch an international sporting event we are participating in a thoroughly modern cultural form and celebrating a thoroughly modern form of human excellence.

At the same time, we are also participating in cultural institutions that have lost any national character they may once have had. Rather, they have become arenas in which our modernism is demonstrated. We affirm our stature as a modern and competitive nation when we do well in international sport, even in hockey. We also confirm our membership in this modern, transnational culture when we follow NFL football, Formula One auto racing, and World Cup skiing. From one kind of perspective, this is progress in itself. Guttmann, for example, suggests that international sport today offers entertainment of the highest calibre and that if there are losses involved, such as the loss of popular support for more local and less highly professionalized sport, this is simply one of the prices of progress. In fact, it has been suggested that Canadians' increasing interest in American sports (NFL and U.S. college football, Major League Baseball, NBA franchises) demonstrates that we are becoming more sophisticated in our sporting tastes (Davidson, 1989).

Cultural Domination

English sociologist Stuart Hall (1981: 227-28) offers a sharply different perspective on the process of modernization:

> Time and again, what we are really looking at is the active destruction of particular ways of life, and their transformation into something new. 'Cultural change' is a polite euphemism for the process by which some cultural forms and practices are driven out of the centre of popular life . . . so that something else can take their place.

Hall is arguing not only that cultural change is an integral component of social and economic change, but that in societies where some groups have more access to material and political resources than others, their advantages in establishing their own cultural practices as objects of public attention and interest become an integral aspect of consolidating their leadership role in those societies. He is referring, in particular, to the destruction of working-class culture in twentieth-century England and the long history of the European upper classes' capacity to establish their own cultural practices (from opera to tennis) as "legitimate," while also legitimizing a snobbish attitude toward the cultural forms enjoyed by "lower" classes.

It is also important to recognize that the consolidation of a "dominant culture" can have a gender dimension. If cultural forms that are restricted to men and that celebrate maleness are the objects of widespread public support, then predominantly female cultural forms are taken much less seriously. Cultural domination helps to sustain ethnic and racial privilege, too, where the cultural activities of a dominant ethnic group are treated seriously in the media and in the schools while those of ethnic minorities (whether immigrant or native) are treated as "folkloric" or quaint, if they are attended to at all. Finally, cultural domination and dependence can be said to have a national dimension when people in some countries, usually smaller or poorer countries, think that the cultural forms and products of another country are more interesting and more important than their own. Our interest in American football, professional and college, is arguably a case in point. In a variety of different senses and contexts, then, *cultural domination can be said to exist if any group has come to take a more active interest in the cultural activities of another society (or another group within their own society) than they do in the activities of people like themselves.*

Patterns of cultural domination point to the economic resources required to market sports on a scale that changes cultural habits. This is illustrated in Maguire's (1990) description of the campaign by the NFL to expand its market presence in Europe. This expansion is only one instance of the "globalization" of a U.S.-based "sports entertainment industry" that includes tennis, golf, boxing, and potentially basketball (Davidson, 1989). What is happening here is an active cultivation of markets for global, "world-class" entertainment forms focused (initially at least) on the most lucrative potential markets: Japan, Western Europe, and in Canada the major metropolitan centres of Toronto, Montreal, and Vancouver.

Cultural Hegemony

An even more complex aspect of cultural domination refers us back to the question of dominant meanings and values we discussed earlier. It is striking just how many cultural practices, including many sporting practices that originated outside social elites (e.g., women's sport), have been organized and transformed into institutionalized forms "which support or at least do not contradict other elements within the effective dominant culture" (Williams, 1980: 39). It is also striking the extent to which cultural participation becomes a means of attaching talented subordinate group members (e.g., aboriginal peoples) to the meaning and value system (emphasizing achievement orientation and competitive individualism) of a modern "meritocratic" elite. As Birrell (1989: 213) puts it so aptly:

> Sport as a meritocracy based on skill quietly reaffirms our national common sense: individuals who work hard and have the right stuff will always prevail. Turned on its head, this lesson becomes even more insidious: those who are at the top must have risen to the top through fair means, and thus deserve their position.

Yet seen from Stuart Hall's (1981) perspective, this transformation of playful activities into performance-oriented ones has made it increasingly hard for us to experience alternatives to the meaning and value system we have suggested is promoted by "modern" elites. If we learn our value systems and our "vocabularies of motive" (Gerth and Mills, 1953) through social experiences, and if ideas like self-expression and playfulness or unconditional friendship are seldom given voice, few of us are able to even conceptualize alternatives to the achievement orientation and competitive individualism of the modern market society.

It is in part just such processes that Italian political theorist Antonio Gramsci was trying to address when he developed the concept of *hegemony*. With this concept, Gramsci sought to direct attention to the effects of dominant ideas and ideologies, and especially the effects of meanings and values learned in the course of cultural practices, in the maintenance (or conversely, the challenging) of patterns of power

and privilege in society. Gramsci's concern was to explain how societies characterized by obvious class, ethnic, and gender inequalities hold together, apparently by consent. In his view, the capacity of elites to establish, *as common sense*, systems of meanings and values that apparently justified these inequalities was crucial to maintaining their position of "moral and intellectual leadership." As well, the elites were able to incorporate, within this meaning and value system, practices and activities within which alternative ways of looking at the world might be experienced. Hence the integration of many kinds of playful or leisure activities into meaning structures not inconsistent with productivity and consumption became an important task in maintaining the dominance of what others would call "core" values.

For instance, achievement orientation is inculcated from a very early age in much children's sport (swimming and gymnastics, as well as organized hockey, are examples), until the values of discipline, determination, long-term goals, and delayed gratification are virtually taken for granted by those who stay in sport (Martens, 1978; Vaz, 1982). This is also true for children pursuing excellence in ballet or music, of course, but the very popularity of sport makes it a particularly effective carrier of these values, especially for boys. Indeed, this is often precisely what is meant by the claim that sport builds character (see Chapter 8). Moreover, it is not simply that we learn to be achievers and to honour the pursuit of excellence. We also learn to be competitors and to take for granted the meanings, values, and practices of a competitive society.

Hegemony directs our attention beyond the usual connotations of ideology, i.e., intellectual explanations of the world, or "-isms." It requires us to consider the many ways in which the lessons of everyday experience become part of popular knowledge, a common sense that offers us "normal" aspirations and ways of feeling, as well as orthodox ideas. At the same time, to call this "hegemony" rather than simply "socialization" is to politicize our thinking about culture. It is to suggest that what we are able to formulate as experience cannot really be understood without reference to social structures within which particular cultural practices are privileged, and particular vocabularies of motive are presented not just as right but as natural.

It is finally important to recognize that hegemony does not suggest that we are told what to think; nor does it suggest a universal identification with dominant meanings and values. Clearly no culture, however dominant, wins the allegiance of everyone or succeeds in closing off completely the spaces in which alternative meanings can be experienced. What seems to be equally clear, however, is that when alternatives have difficulty gaining access to institutional resources – to funding, to public spaces and curriculum time, to media attention – experience of them remains confined to very small circles, spread by word of mouth. Thus the most powerful effect of the institutions of the dominant culture, including the institutions of formally organized sport in Canada as well as schools and media, is probably their capacity to limit the range of our likely experience. This renders alternative structures of meaning and practice beyond the effective reach of most individuals and groups.

Summary

In this chapter, we have argued that the significance of sport in Canadian life can only be grasped through an analysis of culture. We showed how sport came to be such an important part of Canadian popular culture and how the cultural meanings and values that are re-enacted every time Canadians participate in sports or watch sporting events help to make us who we are, both as individuals and as a society.

We began by reviewing several influential meanings of "culture" because sport has not always been accorded the status of a cultural form. First, we explored a discourse that equated culture with human refinement; in practice this came to mean that "culture" referred to specific forms of intellectual and aesthetic achievement – the "high arts" – and that the "low brow" entertainments of ordinary people did not count. Then we considered anthropological perspectives on culture. These recognized that cultural production went on all the time, in all sectors of society, and thus made room for the recognition of sport as a cultural form. However, their very inclusiveness made it difficult to distinguish between what was culture and what was not culture, and equally difficult to ask sociological questions about the relationships between culture and social structures, and about the significance of specific cultural practices in social change. We opted for a definition of culture as "the symbolic forms and the everyday practices through which people experience and express meaning." This allowed us to recognize that the cultural forms and practices that become institutionalized in a society are profoundly affected by (and in turn affect) ongoing structures of power and inequality in that society.

With this background, we proceeded to explore the significance of sport as a popular cultural form, both generally and in Canada. We drew attention to sport's capacity to provide excitement in what have become, for many of us, very organized lives, as well as to its capacity to model forms of physical and emotional accomplishment that many of us are able to appreciate. We paid particular attention to sport's capacity to mobilize popular identifications, feelings of "us" and "them," and to the significance of the actual organization of sport, both internationally and within North American professional sport, in mobilizing particular kinds of identification. We went on to suggest, however, that high-performance sport, whether amateur or professional, helps to make "normal," and apparently natural, a set of meanings and values that honours competitiveness and the pursuit of exellence. These have been viewed, alternatively, as core values in an emerging modern society, and as values that reflect and help to normalize new patterns of

power that today cross international boundaries. Either way, our analysis suggests that sport continues to have powerful symbolic and constitutive effects in the making and remaking of Canadians, in our sense of who we are as individuals, and to what larger communities we belong.

Finally, no human product or activity fails to convey meanings. This is as true of sport as it is of clothing or home furnishings. However, the meanings associated with sport, or any other cultural practice, cannot be understood as natural but rather need to be recognized as actively constructed. In most societies, including Canada, some social groups have historically enjoyed a much greater influence over what has "counted" as culture than others. They have enjoyed, as a result, a greater capacity to make their own meanings stick and to render other possible meanings and values in sport difficult to experience and therefore difficult to think about. How did all this come about? In the next chapter, we examine the historical underpinnings of these processes.

SUPPLEMENTARY READING

The role of culture as an interlocutor between society and the individual is a complex and important topic, and our discussion of it in this chapter has also taken us into a number of more sport-specific literatures. On the larger sociological problem, Peter Berger's *Invitation to Sociology*, recommended in the last chapter, offers what is probably the most nuanced treatment of the relationships among individuals, socially constructed experiences, and society, and we

encourage you to continue with it. Berger can usefully be complemented here by Patricia Marchak's *Ideological Perspectives on Canada*, especially Chapter 2.

In the more sport-specific literature, Eric Dunning's essay on sport as "The Quest for Excitement in Unexciting Societies" is now a classic (see Elias and Dunning, 1986); it could usefully be complemented by Richard Mitchell's "Rationalization and Leisure" (Mitchell, 1983, ch. 14). Allen Guttmann's *From Ritual to Record* is the fullest treatment of the development of "modern" sport, and students should read at least Chapters 1 and 2. For more critical analyses of the same developments, and analyses that use the idea of "hegemony" introduced here, see John Wilson's *Politics and Leisure* (especially Chapters 1-3) and David Whitson's (1984) "Sport and Hegemony: On the Construction of the Dominant Culture." For a further development of the comparison between modernization and hegemony, as theoretical frameworks, see Gruneau's (1988) "Modernization or Hegemony: Two Views on Sport and Social Development."

Chapter 3

THE EMERGENCE OF MODERN SPORT

*T*ake a look at the picture on the following page. It shows a group of male snowshoers in 1878 garbed in traditional blanket coats bound firmly at the waist with coloured sashes, blue tuques, and moccasins of moose-skin tramping through the snowy woods near Montreal. The picture does not tell us much about the paramilitary discipline, the male exclusivity, and the importance attached to the "manliness" of these vigorous tramps, but pictures and paintings like these attest to the enormous importance and significance of snowshoeing in the sporting culture of nineteenth-century Canadians. In fact, one of the very early sports clubs in Canada was the Montreal Snowshoe Club, formed in 1840. By the 1880s, snowshoeing was so popular that hundreds of competitors would travel to carnivals in Vermont and New York to compete against the Americans. By the turn of the century, however, snowshoeing was in decline as clubs struggled to attract members and by the 1920s and 1930s only a few diehards competed, as they still do today, in gruelling marathons held over several days.

This is but one example of a sport that has all but disappeared in modern, post-industrial Canadian society, yet which played a very significant role not only in the lives of countless men (and some women) but also in the early organization of sport in such urban centres as Montreal, Toronto, Ottawa, Quebec City, and Winnipeg. How and why did these changes occur?

In the broader perspective, how and why

Courtesy National Archives of Canada, C22233.

A snowshoe outing, c. 1878.

has sport developed in Canada in the way it has? What are the relationships between sport and the broader social determinants of modern Canadian society such as industrialization, urbanization, privatization, and commercialization? How, precisely, has sport been transformed? More specifically, how did very early (eighteenth-century) indigenous and imported game-contests, popular recreations, and pastimes become transformed, if indeed they did, into the recognizable sport forms we know today? How and when did we shift in our soci-ety from a concept of sport based on amateurism to one based primarily on professionalism? The debates were lively and controversial as early as the 1880s.

To what extent, moreover, have Canadian sports become Americanized? Baseball, that quintessential American game, was played in southwestern Ontario as early as 1838, several decades before it became identified as an American sport. By World War One it was played in hamlets, villages, towns, and cities across the length and breadth of Canada. It was, by all accounts, *the* most popular summer recreational and spectator sport. Perhaps it still is. A report on the Americanization of Canada, published in 1905, cautioned that " baseball is becoming the National game of Canada instead of cricket. It has a very deep significance, as has the fact that the native game of lacrosse is not able to hold its own against the southern intruder" (Humber, 1983). These are just some of the questions we wish to consider in the chapter as we reconstruct our Canadian sporting heritage and explain the continuities and discontinuities that mark the past 400 years.

Sport historian Allen Guttmann (1978), in his ode to the achievements and pleasures of "modern" sport, suggests that sports in modern societies are distinguishable from games in traditional cultures by seven characteristics. They are *secular*, in that even though they have their own traditions, the link to the sacred, which in tradition-bound societies serves as a barrier to innovation, is broken. Once games are seen simply as activities rather than as communal rites or customs, people are freer to innovate and to cast aside tradition in the name of "progress." There is also a commitment to what Guttmann calls *equality*, which on further elaboration turns out to mean open and fair competition where skill and determination rather than caste or class are the deciding factors. Others writing in the same vein as Guttmann have suggested that achieved status becomes more important than ascribed status (the status one is born to, as a member of a class or ethnic group), and that achievement itself makes social mobility possible. Third, there is a decisive shift toward *specialization*, as it is discovered that usually the specialist (e.g., the placekicker or the winger) can perform specific tasks better than the all-rounder.

Fourth and fifth, Guttmann cites *rational-*

ization and *bureaucratization*. We have suggested in Chapter 1 that it is more helpful to talk about technical and bureaucratic rationalization as two aspects of the same quest for the efficient production of results. What is important, though, is simply to note both trends and commitments: the increasingly taken-for-granted systemization of training methods in virtually every sport, and the increase in the bureaucracies that surround professional and amateur sport alike. These include the marketing and financial people as well as technical and administrative personnel who make their distinctive contributions to the systematic production of performance. Finally, Guttmann refers to the central place of *quantification* and *records* in the interest that is sustained around modern sports. Quantification in many sports has made the rationalization of training possible. Record-keeping allows many different kinds of comparisons to be made – plus-minus ratings in hockey and earned run averages in baseball, as well as world records and split times in the racing sports.

In this chapter we will describe and analyse the process and struggles by which the pre-modern, traditional sport of early Canada was transformed into the modern, highly sophisticated, and international sport we know today. Where to begin? The history of Canadian sport can be divided into four critical phases that structure not only how sport was viewed by the people of that particular era but also delineate the significant struggles that took place to define the meaning of sport in an evolving Canadian society. The four phases are: sport in early Canada (1600-1850); Victorian struggles and transitions (1850-1920); the development of and resistance to sport as a commodity (1920-60); and the entrance of the state (1960s onwards).

Sport in Early Canada
(1600 - 1850)

Canada's history begins well before 1608 when Samuel de Champlain, considered the founder of New France, erected the first building at Quebec. Aboriginal peoples, including the Inuit of the North, the Iroquois and the Algonquin in the East, the Plains Indians of the Prairies, and the several tribes along the Pacific coast, were here first, and greatly outnumbered the 3,215 white inhabitants, mostly single and male, of New France in 1665. The significance of early Canada to our understanding of modern sport is to ask whether this colonial period was a relatively inconsequential prologue to the rest of Canadian sport history, or did it hold some meaning for the experiences of succeeding generations of Canadians (Struna, 1988)? Unfortunately, we do not have a great deal of historical information to help us answer this question with much accuracy. However, we do know something about the daily lives of early settlers and of the games and recreations of the indigenous native peoples with whom the white intruder came into frequent conflict.

Games, Contests, and Pastimes in New France

As far as we know, all manner of games and contests were important to early native cultures. Some were ceremonial and religious, some transmitted cultural values to the young, some taught survival skills, and others were purely for fun or gambling (Mott, 1989a). But with one exception, namely *baggataway*, or what the white settlers called lacrosse, early colonists were more interested in learning how to survive in an unforgiving wilderness than they were in native people's games and contests. It was particularly the *coureurs-des-bois*, the itinerant fur traders of New France, who adopted native means of transportation – the snowshoe in winter and the canoe in summer. The early trading posts demanded hardy souls able to hunt, fish, paddle a canoe, shoot, and travel from outpost to outpost by snowshoe. By the early 1700s, horses were beginning to replace the traditional snowshoes in winter, which led the governor of New France to complain that the animals "lead to a life of effeminacy, diminishing bodily strength and wholly destroying manliness and courage" (Lower, 1958: 45).

The people of New France were merchants who sought to transform fish, lumber, and particularly fur into handsome profits, colonial administrators struggling to reproduce the political and social structures of France in the wilderness, nuns and priests devoted to imposing a particularly austere brand of French Catholicism on natives and colonists alike, and ordinary *habitants* struggling to carve farms and a new life out of the forest. The settlers' experience varied widely, depending on their social rank and where they lived. Life among the upper classes in Quebec, for instance, was marked by relative comfort and sophistication compared to the hardships and real threats to their existence suffered by the rural *habitants*.

Settlement in the New World diminished the authority that European places and customs could exercise over cultural life. The Catholic Church, for instance, strongly opposed excessive drinking, gambling, and dancing, particularly the latter, which was considered a "mortal sin." "God grant that this may not be a precedent," sighed the head of the Jesuit order after the first official ball took place in Quebec in 1667. Girls and women came under particular censure:

From George Heriot, Travels Through the Canadas (London, 1807).

Carrioling at Montmorency Falls.

However, as the age and vivacity of Mademoiselle requires some diversion and recreation, one can condescend to permit her some modest and moderate dances, but with persons of her own sex only and in the presence of her mother, for fear of license of speech and immodest songs, but not in the presence of men and boys, this mingling of the sexes, speaking properly, is what causes the inconveniences and disorders of ball and dance. (Clark, 1942: 83)

These ecclesiastical edicts did little to prevent the feasts, balls, dances, theatrical performances, luxurious dress, and nudity. Dancing schools in the larger centres taught young people the minuets, cotillions, hornpipes, and country dances in vogue at the time.

Sport in British North America

By 1775, twelve years after the Treaty of Paris when France yielded its colony to England, the population had swelled to 70,000 due to the migration of British Empire Loyalists from America, immigration from Europe, and, of course, an increasing number of Canadian-born residents. The fall of New France ushered in a century of extraordinary change. With the arrival of the British came the military garrisons in such major centres as Halifax, Saint John, Fredericton, Quebec, Montreal, York (Toronto), Kingston, and Niagara, and with the garrisons came the military officers – wealthy, well educated, and imbued with the English private school sporting tradition. Such sports as cricket, horse-racing, and fox hunting, as well as the more socially oriented regattas and sleigh, tandem, and snowshoe clubs, began to flourish. What also became apparent were increasing divisions based on class, ethnicity, and gender. Comprising the dominant class at this time were the colonial estate-holders and landowners, the military officers, and the growing mercantile class (e.g., the retailers, bankers, and exporters), mainly British and certainly all male. Upper-class Englishwomen exercised considerable influence but no official authority. These were the people with the greatest dedication to the new sporting pastimes because they were the ones least constrained by the demands of frontier life.

On the other hand, the "underclasses" emerging in the towns and cities, and certainly the rural farmers and frontier settlers, had neither the time nor the opportunity to participate in regular games or organized physical recreation. In her famous account of pioneer life, *Roughing It in the Bush*, Susanna Moodie, a gentlewoman immigrant from Britain in the 1830s, tells how unprepared she was for manual labour on uncleared farmland near Peterborough in Ontario. Farm life was often dreary and lonely, and always hard.

In the cities and towns, the taverns and inns were the chief places of public amusements. They served as general meeting places and convenient locations for dances, balls, and banquets as well as travelling circuses and amateur theatricals. Numerous sporting clubs and societies were born of the tavern, such as the group of Scottish merchants who met at Gillies

Tavern in Montreal on January 22, 1807, to found the Montreal Curling Club, the first sports club in Canada. There was, noted Anna Jameson in her travel diary from Upper Canada in 1838, much drunkenness at these events and "the means of gratification comparatively cheap, and little check from public opinion." In the town of Niagara she found no booksellers but plenty of taverns, confirming "the dearness of books and the cheapness of whiskey" (Jameson, 1965: 41). Even the logging and barn-raising bees, considered indispensable by the farmers and settlers, came under criticism, again from Susanna Moodie: "they present the most disgusting picture of a bush life. They are noisy, riotous, drunken meetings, often terminating in violent quarrels, sometimes even bloodshed" (Moodie, 1962: 156).

Richard Gruneau (1983) has suggested that the prevalence of heavy drinking and gambling associated with certain rural pastimes, and among the underclasses of the city, was part of a long history of oppositional or "profane" rituals that mocked the dominant classes and contributed to community solidarity among the underclasses. Such an analysis helps us to examine the deeper meanings underlying what appears to be the simple participation in games and sporting practices during this time in Canadian history. Perhaps it was not so simple. Perhaps, as Gruneau suggests further, the values of manliness and conspicuous leisure also served as a means of self-assertion for the dominant class, thereby contributing to a view that stressed the "naturalness" of hierarchy, deference, and class distance. This inevitably led to tensions between the dominant class and the "lower orders" so that by the mid-nineteenth century the cultural practices of subordinate groups in Canada were viewed as a growing social problem that threatened established traditions and privileges.

The moral reform movements of this period, certainly an aspect of the growing significance of religion (especially Methodism) in Canadian society, also represented an attempt to police the underclasses and to control their collective behaviour. For example, legislation was passed in 1845 that sought to encourage agricultural societies in Upper Canada, thereby channelling the energies of rural settlers into supposedly constructive, educational behaviour. The first "game" laws originated in this period because elite groups believed that the insatiable sport hunting of farmers and homesteaders was ungentlemanly and required censure (Simpson, 1987). Regulations were introduced to control the swelling numbers of working-class French Canadians attending the horse races in Lower Canada, long considered the domain of the elite (Guay, 1973). Finally, the Lord's Day Act of 1845 not only prevented the drinking of alcohol on Sunday but also the following:

> . . . nor shall it be lawful for any person or persons to play skittles, ball, football,

Women in riding habits.

From Canadian Illustrated News, June 28, 1873.

racket, or any other noisy game, or to gamble with dice or otherwise, or to run races on foot, or on horseback, or in carriages, or in vehicles of any sort on that day; nor shall it be lawful for any person or persons to go fishing or hunting or shooting, or in quest of, or to take kill or destroy, any deer, or other game, or any wild animal, or any wild fowl or bird or fish, except as next hereinafter mentioned, or to use any dog, gun, rifle or other engine, or any fishing rod, net or trap, for the above mentioned purposes, on the Lord's Day. (8 Vic. Cap 45, March 29, 1845, *Statutes of the Province of Canada*)

Just as there was growing tension between the dominant class and the underclasses, so, too, was their strain between the sexes. Increasingly, women wished to escape the bonds of tradition and to experience at least a modicum of independence and adventure. Some certainly did, whether they were the gentlewomen like Susanna Moodie who accompanied their husbands into the bush or the common folk who settled the land and built the farms. Class cut across gender as it always does. The upperclass ladies of Kingston in 1812, for instance, were admonished by the opposite sex for their innocent summer amusement of swinging:

. . . an exercise which, allowably beneficial to the health when practised in the proper place, loses that merit when a delicate girl mounts a lofty and dangerous swing just after leaving a warm tea room, and at that hour of all others when the chilly dew is most prejudicial to even a strong constitution. (*Kingston Gazette*, April 28, 1812)

The offended ladies wrote a lengthy and witty rebuttal stating that they saw neither criminality nor impropriety in swinging and that "we shall without the least hesitation recommence that favorite amusement, with the season that permits it." This controversy must have seemed ridiculous to the thousands of pioneer women in the countryside whose life was a continual struggle to feed, clothe, and house their children, and often alone if the husband had succumbed to disease or accident. The only time Susanna Moodie mentions any form of leisure, for example, is the time she spent in a cedar canoe exploring the water around her. "I learned the use of the paddle," she boasted, "and became quite proficient in the gentle craft" (Moodie, 1962: 155).

Sport in the Early Schools

The first Canadian private schools appear as early as 1788 with the founding of King's College in Nova Scotia, the first boarding school for boys in the British Empire. By 1850, a half-dozen such schools (all for boys) had sprung up in Quebec, Ontario, and Manitoba. The importance of these schools, as we shall explore further in the next section, was their emphasis on both imperialism and the games ethic. Imperialism in this context meant the acquisition, maintenance, and development of the British Empire to which the British-modelled private schools would contribute by training the statesmen and administrators of tomorrow. And they would do this through encouraging healthy and manly games, and specifically in early nineteenth-century Canada through cricket:

British feelings cannot flow into the breasts of our Canadian boys through a more delightful or untainted channel than that of British sports. A Cricketer as a matter of course, detests democracy and is staunch in his allegiance to his King. (*Toronto Patriot*, July 13, 1836)

Given the atmosphere of rebellion and political strife in Canada in the mid-1830s, it should not be surprising that cricket represented a ritual dramatization of the traditional power of the colonial metropolis and the class interests associated with it (Gruneau, 1983). The social background, for instance, of the participants of a well-publicized cricket match between Upper Canada College and the "gentlemen" of Toronto in 1836, observed one writer, was like "a roll-call of the colonial elite" (Wise, 1974: 103).

Where the private schools emphasized manliness, leadership, and integrity through team games like cricket and rugby football, the newly developed tax-supported free school system emphasized discipline and regimentation through drills and gymnastic exercises (Cosentino and Howell, 1971). Class privilege demanded that the sons of the dominant classes be trained (in large measure through games and athleticism) to lead and develop the nation, whereas the control of underclass "subordination," a product of increasing urbanization and industrialization, as well as young men fit for military service, could best be achieved through discipline and drill. Girls, both upper class and underclass, figured hardly at all in school physical education programs in early nineteenth-century Canada. Schools for young ladies emphasized the genteel arts, strict timetables, and social supervision; even in co-educational academies, they were restricted to subjects deemed suitable to their constitution and their eventual domestic lives.

Rise of the Urban Sports Club

The final legacy of this early period in Canadian sport history is the founding and growth of the urban sports club. We have already mentioned two such clubs – the very first, the Montreal Curling Club (1807), and the Montreal Snowshoe Club (1840). By 1850, Toronto boasted six such clubs: cricket (1827), turf (1828), curling (1835), lawn bowling (1837), and hunt (1843). The taverns and pubs that had originally housed many of these clubs also bred an atmosphere of drunkenness and disorderliness, which led the aristocratic elite to develop their own private club quarters. These clubs were social rather than competitive in nature. Membership was strictly controlled, as existing members proposed new members and those not deemed suitable were excluded (the term was "blackballed"). It went without saying that members of these early Toronto sports clubs would be gentle*men*, white, relatively wealthy, probably Tory in political affiliation, and associated with the ruling Family Compact, a small group of men linked by family, patronage, and shared political and social beliefs to the professional and mercantile upper middle class (Simpson, 1987). Sport at mid-century was firmly under the governance of the social and ruling elite, and the urban sports club was an important institution in the maintenance of this social control.

Victorian Struggles and Transitions (1850-1920)

The period extending from the middle of the nineteenth century to the end of World War One was marked by tremendous economic, political, and demographic changes in Canadian society. By the end of the Great War, a full-blown industrialized society had emerged; rapid urbanization accentuated the growing social problems associated with city life – intemperance, crime, delinquency, and prostitution. Thousands of immigrants provided cheap labour for the swelling factories and sweat shops, thus sharpening class and ethnic differences, and regions in the Canadian West and North were settled and developed. Industrialization brought not only technological changes, such as the railways, the telegraph, and the mass press, but also the concept of regular free time. Working hours were decreased, the Saturday half-holiday was instituted, and the Sabbath slowly became more secularized. Taken together, these changes created the basic conditions for the beginnings of modern sport in an industrialized society. We look now at some of the important sporting developments in this period.

From Sports Clubs to National Associations

The main focus of the early Canadian sports clubs was *social* rather than competitive since there were no regular competitions or leagues and, in some cases, few common rules. These clubs were also for the societal elite and membership was strictly controlled. However, all this was about to change. Montreal in 1860, for instance, had twenty-four clubs in four sports (lacrosse, snowshoeing, cricket, and curling); by 1894 it could boast of 234 clubs in fifteen sports with regularly scheduled competitions, leagues, increasing standardization of rules, and in some sports a so-called "national" association (see Table 1) with which to affiliate (Metcalfe, 1978).

This amazing proliferation of urban sports clubs, particularly in cities like Montreal and Toronto, was due to a number of factors. First, as the mercantile middle class (businessmen, merchants, storeowners, bookkeepers, clerks, and sales personnel) grew, so did the sports clubs, particularly in team sports like lacrosse, baseball, hockey, and football. The original political and commercial elite who had dominated the earlier clubs retreated to their socially oriented golf, tandem, and hunt clubs, leaving the organization and administration of the more competitively focused clubs to the middle class. This rising social group had a strong leaning for order, tidiness, and respectability. In their sport, suggested Wise (1974: 114), they sought "to rationalize it, to reduce it to its fundamentals, to eliminate confusions, to make it conform to rules and regulations."

The Montreal Amateur Athletic Association (1881), for example, was originally a federation of five clubs but by the late nineteenth century it was unquestionably the most powerful sporting body in Canada, and its members were instrumental in the organization and administration of many national sport associations (Morrow, 1981). New segments of society, based on ethnicity, occupation, or religion, were now represented in these sporting clubs, particularly at the playing level though less so at the organizational level. The Shamrock Lacrosse Club, founded in 1868 in Montreal, for instance, was comprised of working-class Irish Catholics. In Edmonton, soccer teams at the turn of the century reflected the city's ethnicity, with teams like the "Callies," St. George's, Sons of England, Sons of Scotland, and Edmonton Welsh as well as teams comprising players from the University of Alberta, the 19th Alberta Dragoons, and employees of the Canadian Pacific Railway and the Edmonton streetcar railway system (Betke, 1983).

These examples should not be taken as evidence that any significant democratization of sport occurred in the latter part of the nineteenth century; rather, they are representative of the central conflict between amateurism and

TABLE 1
Founding of National Sport Organizations (1867-1920)

1864	Canadian Baseball Association (founded again in 1876)	1895	Royal Canadian Golf Association Canadian Jockey Club
1867	National Lacrosse Association *becomes*	1899	Canadian Gymnastic Association National Trotting Association *becomes*
1880	National Amateur Lacrosse Association	1914	Canadian Trotting Association
1869	Dominion of Canada Rifle Association	1900	Canadian Canoe Association
1880	Canadian Association of Amateur Oarsman	1906	Alpine Club of Canada
1882	Canadian Wheelman's Association (Bicycling)	1907	Canadian Snowshoe Union
1884	Amateur Athletic Association of Canada *becomes*	1909	Canadian Amateur Swimming Association
1898	Canadian Amateur Athletic Association *becomes*	1911	Canadian Professional Baseball Association
1909	Amateur Athletic Union of Canada	1912	Dominion Football Association (Soccer) Canadian Motor Cyclist Union
1884	Canadian Lawn Tennis Association Canadian Rugby Football Union	1913	Canadian Squash Racquet Association
1887	Canadian Lacrosse Association	1914	Canadian Amateur Lacrosse Association Canadian Amateur Hockey Association
1888	Amateur Skating Association of Canada	1919	Canadian Amateur Baseball Association
1892	Canadian Cricket Association	1920	Canadian Amateur Ski Association

SOURCES: Adapted from Metcalfe (1987: 101); Schrodt, Redmond, and Baka (1980: 88-91).

professionalism during this period. The Edmonton soccer clubs, for example, belonged to the Alberta Football Association but would not affiliate with the Dominion association because of the latter's insistence that amateurs could not play against the touring professionals from the old country (Betke, 1983).

Gentlemen Amateurs versus Unruly Professionals

Gentlemen players, regardless of class, were expected to play the game for the game's sake, to strive for victory rather than winning itself, and to demonstrate unending courage, perseverance, fair play, and honesty. Sport was an avocation, not a vocation, stressing individual responsibility and honour. This constituted the *amateur code* in the nineteenth century, although the official definitions (see Table 2) were based solely on who was to be excluded rather than included. Quite simply, anyone who earned his living through sport or who benefited financially from sport was not an amateur. By implication, amateurism was defined as the absence of professionalism. Sometimes, as in the 1873 definition laid out by the Montreal Pedestrian Club, members of particular occupational groups (in this case "labourer") or ethnic groups (in this case "an Indian") were excluded by legislation (Morrow, 1986). Amateurism so defined was also very clearly an attempt to preserve a system of class and ethnic discrimination. The issue of whether to allow women as members in these associations or in competitions with men was not to become a problem until much later.

Sport in Canada in the 1880s and 1890s was changing considerably as teams and leagues mushroomed and controlling associations were formed in often futile attempts to impose order on increasing chaos, but most significantly sport was becoming commercialized. Rowing, for instance, was openly professional since successful and popular athletes like Ned Hanlon were offered substantial purses to demonstrate their prowess before admiring spectators. Baseball, lacrosse, rugby football, and ice hockey were becoming increasingly professionalized as sponsors and athletes realized there was money to be made through sport. In individual sports, such as rowing, running, bicycling, and speedskating, separate categories were established for "amateur" and "professional," and absolutely no mixing of the two was sanctioned. The Amateur Athletic Association of Canada (AAAC), formed

Directors of the Ottawa Athletic Association.

Courtesy National Archives of Canada, PA 12248.

TABLE 2
Early Definitions of "Amateur"

The following definitions of an amateur originate with the Amateur Athletic Association of Canada and its successors.

1884: An amateur is one who has never competed for a money prize or staked bet or with or against any professional for any prize, or assisted in the practice of athletic exercises as a means of obtaining a livelihood.

1896 (add): Or who has entered any competition under a name other than his own.

1902 (add): private or public gate receipts . . . who has never, directly or indirectly, received any bonus or a payment in lieu of loss of time while playing as a member of any club, or any money considerations whatever for any services as an athlete except his actual travelling and of selling or pledging his prizes.

1909 (add): promoted an athletic competition for personal gain.

SOURCE: Metcalfe (1987: 123-24).

in 1884, was kept busy investigating charges of professionalism – such as paid jobs, playing bonuses, and outright payments to athletes – within the sports under its jurisdiction. By 1898, the AAAC had become the Canadian Amateur Athletic Union (CAAU) with supposedly seventeen sports within its fold. The issue of amateurs competing with or against professionals, however, appeared to remain insolvable.

The most vociferous defenders of the amateur code were the founders of the emerging local, provincial, and sometimes national organizations. In the early years, many associations were national in name only since they were formed by individuals from just a few clubs, usually located in Montreal, Toronto, and some of the larger Ontario towns. As can be seen from the listing in Table 1, some associations (e.g., baseball and lacrosse) were founded and then refounded several times because either the original organization did not survive or a breakaway group formed another "national" association. It took many years before most of these organizations could claim that they had all provinces under their jurisdiction.

By the turn of the century, the athletic war had heated up considerably, with two national umbrella bodies (the CAAU and the Amateur Athletic Federation of Canada) each claiming jurisdiction over Canadian athletes but split over the playing of amateurs and professionals on the same team or against each other. The matter was finally resolved in 1909 with the amalgamation of the two into the truly national Amateur Athletic Union of Canada. The philosophy of "pure amateurism" had, for the time being at least, finally won out (Morrow, 1986; Metcalfe, 1987).

Why were professionals so abhorred? It's a difficult question to answer, but the athletic administrators of the time believed fervently that sport as work or athletes who made sport their business were completely intolerable. The acceptance of money was to be deplored, and work plus money led to violence, ungentlemanly conduct, and unethical practices (Metcalfe, 1987). Moreover, those associated with professional sport, either as athletes or promoters, of-

Courtesy National Archives of Canada, C25324.

Ned Hanlan.

ten came from different sectors of society than the "old money" of the established clubs, and they represented a challenge to the latter's long-standing authority. Sport, however, was no longer the exclusive preserve of a small elite. It was becoming a reflection of the capitalist, industrial society emerging in Canada in the early twentieth century. The amateur-versus-professional conflict was in many ways symptomatic of a new development in Canadian society, the emergence of commercialized, popular, mass sport and recreation with a very different social and ideological basis.

Sabbatarianism and the Rise of Commercial Mass Sport

The last decade of the nineteenth century, and continuing until the Great War, was marked by the energetic promotion of both participatory and spectator sport. The cities were the natural starting point for this promotion because sports and sport spectatorship were seen as a way to encourage healthful and character-building activity, particularly among the working class, and as a profitable commodity for innovative entrepreneurs. An urban culture was emerging in the major cities and towns across the nation with sports and sports promotion an important aspect.

The urban sports clubs were forced to generate money to survive, which meant the introduction of gate receipts, opening up their facilities for public use, and renting their playing fields, rinks, and pavilions to other users. The end result was to make more facilities available for public use. Local businessmen and entrepreneurs formed joint stock companies to erect needed sporting facilities – covered hockey and curling rinks, race tracks, stadia, and the popular bowling and billiard establishments. As cities grew, public money was used to provide more facilities, slowly at first, but eventually public funding became commonplace. Winnipeg, for instance, made its first move in 1902 to finance athletic facilities when it provided dressing rooms and attendants for outdoor skating rinks. By 1920 the city had used taxpayers' money to build a host of large sports fields, more covered rinks, summer playgrounds, indoor swimming pools, parks with tennis courts and lawn bowling greens, and a public golf course (Mott, 1983).

The rise of mass sport and recreation, as well as the provision of special areas and facilities, fuelled a long-standing controversy over the sanctity of the Lord's day. Urbanization and industrialization had unleashed powerful new secular forces on the Canadian community, but those strongly opposed to any desecration of the Sabbath, mainly Methodists and Presbyterians, were determined to uphold their moral position and enforce a quiet Sunday on their fellow citizens whether they liked it or not. Toronto, whose reputation in the late nineteenth century was that of a progressive, modern, and morally righteous Christian municipality, provides us with two somewhat amusing examples of the serious battle over what ordinary citizens could and could not do on Sunday.

The first controversy raged between 1888 and 1897 among the sabbatarians who were opposed to the streetcars running on Sunday and the commercial interests who owned the street railways (Armstrong and Nelles, 1977). The sabbatarians argued that the Sunday cars would destroy the Sabbath, threatened public morality, worked against the interests of the working class, and were contrary to the interests of Christianity. The streetcar owners, who were eventually joined by labour representatives, argued convincingly that the railway provided an escape for the poor from their unhealthy and unattractive surroundings to the more appealing parks, suburbs, and beaches and that in the end this would lessen class distinctions. It would also strengthen families by carrying more people to church and then on to healthy recreation. It took three plebiscites over a decade but the Sunday car advocates eventually won – on May 23, 1897, the streetcars ran for the first time on Sunday. The ironic twist to this story is that masses of Torontonians took to the new bicycling craze at the same time and abandoned the streetcar, especially on Sundays. And the Canadian Cycle and Motor Company (CCM), the major bicycle manufacturer, was owned by some very influential Methodists who had fought so long and hard against Sunday street-cars (Armstrong and Nelles, 1977)!

The second controversy occurred a few years later when the indefatigable sabbatarians opposed Sunday tobogganing on a fancy new system of public slides in Toronto's High Park (Homel, 1981). The toboggan slides had been built with public money in response to the need for regulation, safety, and improved recreation. The sabbatarians opposed Sunday tobogganing on the usual religious grounds but they also suggested that newcomers, especially immigrants, were less devoted to Sabbath sanctity. Working people argued that the ban was completely unfair and harmful since Sunday was virtually the only day in which they could use the facility. Labour was joined by business, whose interests were in maintaining a contented and efficient labour force that deserved better leisure-time facilities. Despite these protests the by-laws were passed in 1912 and policemen were posted at the slides to prevent their use on Sundays. Enterprising tobogganists simply moved to unpatrolled, unregulated, and less safe areas.

Do these controversies over Sunday activities have any greater significance? Historians Armstrong and Nelles (1977) suggest that the ferocity with which the sabbatarian, middle-class Protestants fought any desecration of the Sabbath revealed a determination to resist any challenge to their social dominance in the community. There was also a certain hypocrisy in their stance since middle-class sabbatarians frequently had recreation opportunities on days other than Sunday. Furthermore, the Sunday by-laws were seen as an institutional means to control the potentially unruly elements in the community, namely Catholics and "foreigners," and to reassert the central place of the English-Canadian middle class in the cultural life of the city. On the other hand, Toronto businessmen were becoming increasingly hostile to the Sun-day restrictions, believing that advancing industrialization required a lessening of class tensions and, more importantly, a satisfied and productive work force. Recreational and sport opportunities, on Sundays if needed, would contribute not only to public health and contentment but also to increased profits. As for the workers themselves, they charged that sabbatarians could not (or would not) comprehend the realities of working-class life that necessitated leisure on Sundays, and were willing to join with business in the pursuit of a common goal (Homel, 1981)

Manliness, Morality, and the Feminine Ideal

Although sabbatarians fought to restrict Sunday activities, these same men of the church recognized and promoted the inherent connections among sport, morality, and manliness. These were not new ideas – the concept of muscular or manly Christianity, which originated with the British novels of Charles Kingsley (*Westward Ho*, 1855) and Thomas Hughes (*Tom Brown's Schooldays*, 1857), had long since made its way across the Atlantic and had become firmly entrenched in the curricula of boys' private schools with their emphasis on producing men of character through athleticism and team sports (Brown, 1988). Historians have also argued that among the early pioneers certain sports and games nurtured the manly qualities of robustness, mental vigour, determination, discipline, fair play, and integrity, and symbolically revealed that true success went to those who possessed these virtues (Mott, 1980). For pioneer Manitobans struggling to establish and maintain British culture in a foreign land, for example, manly games and especially team games like cricket, rugby football, and soccer were easily transplanted to reproduce the Empire. The winter climate also afforded the opportunity to express a distinctly Canadian form of manliness through snowshoeing, curling, and ice hockey. The men of the Montreal Snowshoe Club endured a particularly masochistic form of hibernal manliness: "on crosscountry tramps over hilly terrain under crisp, slippery snow conditions, snowshoes were broken, ankles were fractured, frostbite and blisters were common . . ." (Morrow, 1988: 16). Speeches at annual club dinners repeatedly referred to the "moral bearing, independence and manliness" of snowshoers whereas women "could only aspire to marry a snowshoe man" (p. 29).

In the last decades of the nineteenth century, the notion of Christian manliness broadened considerably to encompass not only physical and moral development but success in later life, particularly in the economic sphere. R. Tait McKenzie, early Canadian physical educator, sculptor, and orthopedic surgeon, wrote about rugby football in 1892: it "cultivates pluck and determination in men." He continued, "the *sine qua non* of a good footballer is grit, and in after life the grit cultivated by the hard knocks will stand men in good stead in the contests of business or professional life" (McKenzie, 1892). Another doctrine in vogue at the time was social Darwinism, the belief that the concepts of natural selection, the survival of the fittest, or differentiation could be applied to both the animal and human worlds. Coupled with muscular Christianity, social Darwinism was entrenched in the private boys' schools of this period where those who survived the Spartan conditions and physically demanding activities were best "suited" to become the economic and political elite (Brown, 1988).

Aside from the obvious role of manly sports in promoting nationalism, rectitude, and later success, why was all this addressed to males, never to females? The answer lies in the strict Victorian dichotomy between *manliness* and *womanliness*. The former, as we have discussed, represented physical virility coupled with a Christian morality ensuring influence and success in the public and economic spheres. Womanliness, on the other hand, embodied a feminine ideal, no doubt stressing an equally impeccable rectitude but also grace and beauty leading to mutual sharing and intimacy in the domestic sphere. Without sport, argued the moralists of the time, boys will become like women, which meant delicate and effeminate. "Flabby muscled boys become pliant men who only talk. Well developed boys become men who will say and act and produce results," intoned the manual for the Canadian Standard Efficiency Tests, a program designed to promote intellectual, physical, religious, and social accomplishments among young boys.

Schools, churches, and other organizations soon began to promote sports participation among male youths in particular. The Protestant churches, increasingly concerned about losing their male youth membership to commercialized forms of recreation, put in place athletic teams, leagues, events, and special programs to attract young men (Howell and Lindsay, 1986). Such organizations as the YMCA, the Boy Scouts, and Boys' Clubs all began to amplify their emphasis on sports by building facilities, hosting events, and developing programs. Boys' private schools already placed what some considered an inordinate emphasis on athleticism, but the public school system was only beginning to attach importance to nutrition, hygiene, and physical exercise. Military drill and discipline were still preferred but more emphasis was placed on organized games and sports by instituting inter-class and inter-school leagues.

We have already mentioned the Victorian

images of manliness and womanliness, one conjuring up physical vitality, decisiveness, and authority in the public setting, the other stressing delicate grace and tact restricted to the private, domestic sphere. Of course, these were caricatures – not all men fit the mould, nor did all women. For the latter, moderate and lady-like forms of exercise were acceptable, and the debates about women's sport were more medical than philosophical. Vitalist theories of human biology held that individuals had a certain amount of bodily energy and that it was absolutely vital to preserve woman's energy for her developing reproductive system and eventual role as a mother. Any drain on this vital source of energy could be disastrous. Thus, the woman who ignored medical warnings regarding athletic activity was challenging the primacy of the uterus (Lenskyj, 1986). Fortunately, many women did.

The introduction of the "safety" bicycle (one with rubber tires) in the 1890s was a major turning point. It not only caused a revolution in women's fashions but was also a vehicle through which women broke tradition and asserted their independence. As the Toronto *Globe* pointed out, "one bicyclist wearing an advanced costume [bloomers] does more towards furthering dress reform than a score of theorists, writers, and lecturers." Paralleling the growth of the many women's organizations that came into being in the late nineteenth century, such as the National Council of Women, the Women's Institutes, and the Woman's Christian Temperance Union, were sports clubs and tournaments exclusively for women. How-

Ottawa cycling group.

Courtesy National Archives of Canada, C24322.

ever, membership and participation were still limited predominantly to the young, the middle and upper classes, and those living in the major urban centres.

Games and sports even began to appear in the Canadian girls' private schools, but athleticism never acquired anything like the same hold it had over the boys' schools. Aggressive nationalism was never a feature of female education, and girls' games were rarely used for discipline since the maintenance of order was not a problem as it was in similar schools for boys. As McCrone (1988: 89) suggests: "games, therefore, were part of a systematic and quasi-social Darwinistic programme of measurement, medical inspection and physical training intended to make students healthier and so fitter for academic toil and ultimately motherhood." Within the public school curriculum, the introduction of calisthenics and limited forms of gymnastics, as well as the plethora of articles, reports, lectures, and demonstrations about physical culture for women, generated much greater public acceptance and even enthusiasm about the value of exercise for the so-called "weaker" sex.

DEVELOPING AND RESISTING SPORT AS A COMMODITY (1920 -1960)

After World War One, most Canadians could scarcely imagine that in twenty years they would be at war again, or that a second war would end the grinding poverty and unemployment of a Great Depression. Post-war Canada, and throughout the 1950s, was marked by a period of economic prosperity, increasing foreign ownership of Canadian industry, rapid techno-

logical change (television made its appearance), and enormous population growth due in part to increased immigration. At the end of this period, Canada was a remarkably different country and so, too, was sport. No longer the pride of a single community, sport teams, both amateur and professional, now contributed to an increasing sense of nationalism. Professional sport was rapidly transformed into big business, where profit reigns supreme. Television became a reality in the early 1950s and, with big business interests, forever changed sport. There were, interestingly enough, at least two groups who struggled against this onslaught of professionalization and commercialization. One was the workers' sport movement, which did not survive; the other was a separately controlled and governed women's sport, which was much more enduring.

Making a Profit from Sport: Private versus Commercial Promoters

Canadian sport in the 1920s was based in individual towns and cities. It was, in other words, a *community* venture. Sports promoters were important men of the community who exhibited as much interest in the affairs of the city as they did in their private businesses. What they promoted were consumer sports like football, hockey, and especially baseball played by paid professional athletes representing the town or city, and such sports generated a paying audience. Semi-professional baseball was particularly successful because not only could it be used to promote the community, but the team and league were participants in a well-established American sports empire (Betke, 1983; Voisey, 1981). In all three sports, amateur and semi-professional teams coexisted in the same community.

At some point, and historians are unsure

Courtesy National Archives of Canada, PA49580.

Boston Bruins, 1929-30.

as to exactly when or how, the *private* sports promoter changed from someone interested in sport for the good of the community to become a *commercial* promoter interested in sport as a means to personal or corporate profit (Hardy, 1986). Let's take hockey as an example. Early hockey entrepreneurs were rink owners who booked games between amateur teams, keeping half or more of the gate receipts for themselves. Professional hockey, certainly well under way before World War One, created a new breed of hockey entrepreneurs who now hired the players and rented the arena, taking the difference between gate receipts and expenses as profit (Kidd and Macfarlane, 1972). These were the

men who founded the National Hockey League in 1917 because they realized that arguments over players and their salaries, gate receipts, rink size, and franchise rights were ultimately counterproductive and threatened the financial success of their new sports business. They formed a *cartel* or joint venture, regulating and restricting their practices so as to maximize their joint profits, thereby increasing their individual profits. Commercial hockey, with a ready source of capital to buy players, prospered over community teams operating on a nonprofit basis, and the men who owned commercial hockey looked toward the United States to expand their market. The first American franchise was sold to a Boston financier in 1925 for $15,000, and the Bruins were born. By 1927, franchises had been sold to New York (Rangers), Pittsburgh (Pirates), Chicago (Black Hawks), and Detroit (Red Wings).

Although the NHL expanded rapidly, the economic realities of the depression reduced it to between seven and ten teams and the league struggled to survive (Simpson, 1989). Community hockey, on the other hand, thrived because for the players it was steady (some were paid), it guaranteed an off-season job, and it did not require leaving your home town (Kidd and Macfarlane, 1972). By 1940 non-profit community hockey (controlled by the Canadian Amateur Hockey Association) once again threatened the profit-oriented NHL. However, World War Two intervened and this time community hockey went into a rapid decline because it lost the base of its players. After the war, the NHL began to develop its sponsorship system whereby every NHL club and affiliate were permitted to sponsor two junior teams, owning the rights to those teams' players. Community hockey never made a comeback.

The story of Canadian hockey illustrates the transformation from civic-minded entrepreneurialism to profit-oriented cartelization and commodification that occurred during this era. Enormous personal and corporate profits (see Table 3) have been made from sport, something we discuss further when we examine the modern-day sports industry in Chapter Five. It is also important to note that Canada's three major professional team sports – hockey, football, and baseball – have very different economic histories. Baseball has always been at least semi-professional and was a willing partner in the early promotion of towns and cities. Until 1969, however, Canada never had a major league team, being a large farm system for the United States: "baseball's top players passed through Canada on their way to somewhere else" (Humber, 1983: 131; see also Morrow,

TABLE 3
Economic History of the Montreal Canadiens

1909	Founded by northern Ontario railway heir Ambrose O'Brien.
1910	Bought by George Kennedy for $7,500.
1921	Sold by Kennedy's widow to three Montreal entrepreneurs for $35,000.
1935	Canadian Arena Company, which owned the Montreal Forum, bought team for $165,000. Colonel Molson was a founder of the company.
1957	Hartland and Tom Molson bought control of the Canadian Arena Company. No purchase price was disclosed but the *Financial Post* estimated its worth at $2.7 million.
1972	Molson family sold their shares to Peter and Edward Bronfman for estimated $14 million in order to avoid a capital gains tax.
1978	Molson Breweries repurchased the club, negotiated a lease-back, leaving title of the Montreal Forum to the Bronfmans. Cost: $22 million.

SOURCE: *Globe and Mail*, February 25, 1989.

1989). In contrast, professional football in Canada was slow to develop a national and standard set of rules, was much more tied to university amateur programs, and did not consolidate or undergo a move to joint profit maximizing until after 1950 with the formation of the Canadian Football League (Cosentino, 1989).

Selling the Commodity: Enter Television

Until the introduction of regular radio broadcasts after the First World War, newspapers were the mainstay of sports journalism and an effective means of sports promotion. One could read regularly about sport in faraway places that often overshadowed local events, matches, and games. Although newspapers still remained an important source of information and promotion, radio (and eventually television) played a central role in allowing corporate sports to develop and refine their particular commodities (Gruneau, 1983). Again, hockey was the exemplar in this context. In 1931, Foster Hewitt, who was to become the voice of the famous *Hockey Night in Canada*, began broadcasting the Toronto Maple Leafs' Saturday night hockey games to CBC listeners. The CBC did not institute a proper sports department until after World War Two, so hockey was the only regularly scheduled sport covered and one of the few sponsored programs.

Television first appeared in Canada in 1951 and the CBC used a variety of sports while testing its television schedule that first year. The first official Canadian televised sports broadcast dates from October, 1952, with the third-period coverage (that's all you got in those days) of a Montreal Canadiens hockey game. A year later, over 10 per cent of the CBC's television programming consisted of hockey and other sports (Nattrass, 1988). By 1960, television viewers were linked across Canada through the proliferation of both government and privately owned stations. Constantly improving technology and the ability to beam a signal to all Canadians created a viable market not only between sports and the media but also between sports and corporate sponsors interested in the medium of television to sell their products. We discuss this "match made in heaven" and the effects it has had on sport in Chapter 6.

Resisting Commercialization and Competition: Socialists and Women

The early commodification of sport and the beginnings of a vast, ever-expanding sports marketplace were by-products of the economic and social changes that came with the transformation to modern, industrial capitalism. Mass sport was now firmly entrenched in a capitalist culture with government, business, church, and youth agencies, acting no doubt from the highest motives, ready to deliver sport programs to ordinary people. Sport entrepreneurs, willing to assume financial risks, provided mass entertainment to appreciative audiences.

Organized labour, itself a product of modern capitalism, initially took no interest in sport, suggesting that workers had more important things to do than engage in such frivolous pursuits (Wheeler, 1978). However, by the last decade of the nineteenth century a workers' sports movement had begun to emerge, primarily in central Europe. In 1913, representatives from Germany, England, Belgium, France, and Austria formed the first international workers' sport association. It did not survive the war but was re-established again in 1920 as the Lucerne Sport International (eventually becoming the Socialist Workers' Sports International). Between the wars it staged three "Workers' Olympiads," in Frankfurt in 1925, in Vienna in 1931, and in Antwerp in 1937, which were deliberate and successful alternatives to the modern Olympic Games. By the 1930s, the Socialists Workers' Sports International could claim two million members.

The workers' sports movement saw itself as a humanistic alternative to the excesses of "bourgeois" athletic competition. Their sports would be open to all, substituting socialist for capitalist values, and emphasizing non-competitive, healthy, enjoyable physical activity like gymnastics, cycling, hiking, and swimming in a positive working-class atmosphere (Wheeler, 1978). The movement, however, was not without its ideological and political divisions. In 1921 a minority of workers' sports organizations broke away to form Red Sport International because they felt that the Socialist Workers' Sports International was insufficiently concerned with the usefulness of sport as a political instrument in the class struggle and as a means to lure youth away from "bourgeois" sport. In fact, the impetus for workers' sport in Canada came from Red Sport International through the Young Communist League, and since workers' sport organizations like those in Europe did not exist in Canada, they had to be created:

Sport, the exercising of the body, and all the mental benefits accruing from sport are an essential part of League work. Baseball should be the most popular, but hikes and runs and boxing and swimming can all be added. But these sports must be turned from commercial antagonistic games into "Red Sports".... They are recruiting agencies because they are beneficial to League membership at large and develop a feeling of comradeship and vitality. (Kidd, 1989: 249)

The Young Communist League acted quickly. Workers' sport associations, encouraging a great diversity of activity including soccer teams, field days, boxing clubs, picnics and hikes, softball leagues, cross-country skiing, and especially gymnastics, were established in seventeen centres (Kidd, 1989). By 1928 the Workers' Sport Association of Canada had been established with twenty clubs affiliated, including the Finnish Workers' Sports Association of Canada, the Ukrainian Labour-Farmer Temple Association, and the Canadian Labour Party. Although the Young Communist League continued to exhort individual workers' sport associations to advance the class struggle through sport, the League paid little attention to their practical needs for equipment, instruction manuals, and leadership courses. For their part, the clubs were proud of their accomplishments, did not like being berated, and sought to "maintain a proper balance between propaganda and serious athletics" (Kidd, 1989). The Workers' Sport Association of Canada campaigned against the pro-Nazi and anti-Semitic 1936 Berlin Olympics and sent five athletes to the ill-fated "People's Games," which were scheduled in Barcelona but had to be cancelled because the Spanish Civil War erupted on the day the Games were to open.

Bowing to pressure from its less radical members, the Workers' Sport Association was soon renamed the Canadian Amateur Sports Federation, and individual organizations were called Universal Athletic Clubs. They operated as non-political and independent units seeking to provide physical training and recreation to all young people irrespective of their nationality or beliefs (Kidd, 1989). However, they in turn were shut down in 1940 because of their continuing ties to the Communist Party of Canada. When the Soviet Union entered the Olympics in 1952, a distinctly Communist in-

Courtesy National Archives of Canada, PA50440.

Edmonton Grads, 1924.

ternational sports movement also came to an end. As a political movement the workers' sports associations had clearly failed, but for a time they had provided alternative sport and recreational opportunities to working people.

After World War One, women benefited from the growing boom in men's professional and spectator sport. It was an era when Canada produced world champion female speed skaters, swimmers, and basketball teams, and dominated women's track and field at the 1928 Summer Olympics. Spectators flocked to support women's basketball and baseball; women's teams were sponsored by industry; radio stations broadcast women's sporting events; and several newspapers employed women sportswriters who wrote special columns on women's sport. Orga-

nizations governing women's sport flourished as women strove for autonomy in this facet of their lives.

But while girls and women were striving to escape the constraints of the past and revel in their new-found physical freedom, many influential voices were sounding the alarm. Among the most vociferous were the newly trained women physical educators who advocated a minimally competitive version of sport for girls and women. The six-player, limited court, two-dribble version of basketball known as "girls' rules" was just that – a modified version of the men's game.

Why did they possess these seemingly reactionary attitudes? Central to their philosophy was their acceptance of the notion of female limitations: menstruation hindered a woman; her lower weight, inferior strength, and lighter bone structure made her more accident-prone; intense physical activity displaced her womb, leaving her barren; and so on. Not only were highly competitive sports harmful to the female, they asserted, she could never do as well as men; hence it was pointless to try. These women found it eminently more sensible to encourage sports for everyone and not just for the talented few. They believed and followed the creed adopted by the Women's Division of the National Amateur Athletic Federation (U.S.): "A game for every girl and a girl for every game." On the practical level, they fought to keep women's sport as unlike men's and as far removed from male control as possible by advocating separate programs, teachers, coaches, and officials. They campaigned vigorously against all championships, tournaments, and interscholastic competitions, branding them "unwholesome." By 1933, the schools in and around Toronto, for example, had effectively banned girls' interscholastic sports competition (Gurney, n.d.). They were particularly incensed at the inclusion of women's events in the 1928 Summer Olympics. They sought alternatives to the competition they so despised by encouraging "play days" or "sports day" where girls from different schools played *with* rather than *against* each other. In sum, they championed what they saw as a more moral and democratic athletic philosophy than men's. Sports for sports' sake was to them morally and socially superior. This philosophy pervaded women's sport until well into the 1960s, and vestiges of it still exist today (see Chapter 7).

What these two examples illustrate is just how pervasive commercialized, commodified sport had become in Canada by mid-century, and how alternatives, or different ways of playing, were pushed to the sidelines. Canadian sport was being transformed into the popular culture practice we discussed in Chapter 2, all of which contributed to Canada's confirmation as a truly modern nation. There is, however, one more step in this process.

SPORT AND STATE: IMPACT OF GOVERNMENT (1960 ONWARDS)

Although we will have more to say about the role of government and politics in Canadian sport in Chapter 4, it is important to appreciate the early beginnings of these now pervasive influences over sport at all levels. In some ways, the Canadian state has always been involved in sport. For instance, one of the earliest national sport organizations, the Dominion Rifle Association, founded in 1869, received substantial support because the government of the day saw the potential to supplement Canada's defence system with well-trained militia. In addition, government statutes, such as the gaming laws and the Lord's Day Acts of the mid-1800s, were direct interventions by the state to police the underclasses and control their collective behaviour, as were the attempts by civic leaders and sabbatarians to control the enjoyment of sport and recreation on Sundays.

In 1846, Egerton Ryerson was appointed chief superintendent of education for Upper Canada. Through his encouragement and efforts, gymnastic exercises, drill, and calisthenics were introduced into the school program. He also promised that the government would provide financial assistance in purchasing the necessary athletic equipment and apparatus. Another example of early government initiative in physical activity was the Strathcona Trust of 1909, established to encourage physical and military training in the schools. Although the money came through the generosity of Lord Strathcona, a wealthy financier, the trust was administered by the Department of Militia. Similarly, but much later, the wartime government in 1943 enacted the National Fitness Act to improve the shortage of physically fit recruits. Through it, a National Council on Physical Fitness was also established.

While they were willing to become involved in physical fitness and recreation, provincial and federal governments prior to the 1960s took a cautious role toward sport, preferring instead to assist sport associations and agencies indirectly, and often questioning whether or not sport should be a government prerogative. In 1932, for instance, 115 of 127 Canadian Olympic team members paid their own way to the Games in Los Angeles, and in 1936 six track and field athletes were sent to Berlin with all expenses paid, while ten others could go if they paid their own way (Kidd, 1988). As early as 1937, there was a call in Parliament for a Ministry of Sport, something that did not come about for another forty years.

Several factors contributed to the Canadian state's decision to involve itself more directly in sport. First, in the years following World War Two, widespread demands were placed on the government to improve labour and welfare legislation. Increasing urbanization and industrialization created a climate of general economic prosperity and the federal government "embarked on a policy of diluted Keynesianism and social intervention" that led to funding initiatives in a number of social assistance programs such as unemployment insurance, mothers' allowances, universal old age pensions, and hospital insurance, but also in the arts, higher education, and film production (Kidd, 1988: 16). Sport leaders began calling for similar assistance to sport.

Second, although in an earlier period many amateur sport leaders would have decried "government interference in sport," and the socialist Workers' Sport Association would have opposed public assistance to "bourgeois" sport associations, these views were rarely aired after World War Two (Kidd, 1981, 1988). With the entry of the Soviet Union into the Olympics in 1952, and the repression of those sympathetic to socialism and communism during the Cold War of the fifties, the critique of the class-biased nature of amateur sports virtually disappeared. In fact, established sport leaders were "prepared to swallow their doubts in the interests of winning teams" (Kidd, 1988: 16). They were, in other words, prepared to accept government financial assistance at the risk of losing some autonomy so that they could build what they viewed as a better sport system for Canada.

Third, Canada's international athletic successes were at an all-time low in the late 1950s. John Diefenbaker, whose Conservative government came to power in 1957, was a strong nationalist who believed that "there are tremendous dividends in national pride from some degree of success in athletics. The uncommitted countries of the world are now using these athletic contests as measurements of the strength and power of the nations participating" (*House of Commons Debates*, 21 November 1960: 39-40). Therefore, given a more favourable political climate, sport and fitness leaders as well as interested politicians lobbied the government to become more involved financially and administratively in sport. With impetus from the Duke of Edinburgh's 1959 speech to the Canadian Medical Association, in which he rebuked Canadians for their low fitness levels, and Prime Minister Diefenbaker's successful visit to the Pan-American Games in Chicago the same year, everything was set in 1961 for the passage of Bill C-131, the Fitness and Amateur Sport Act.

The FAS Act provided $5 million annually for an administrative structure and personnel, federal/provincial cost-sharing agreements, grants to sports governing bodies, the initiation of the Canada Games, and scholarships and research grants to physical education specialists. From this point, voluntary amateur sport would have to work together with the Canadian state, and since the early 1960s there has been a deliberate growth in state intervention in Canadian sport, thus posing a dilemma for the development of genuinely democratic sport. We discuss this process and the issues and problems it raises in the next chapter.

SUMMARY: MODERNIZATION AND HEGEMONY

At the beginning of this chapter, we posed a series of questions about how and why Canadian sport has developed in the way it has. How did indigenous and early imported games become transformed into our modern sport forms? What has been the influence of industrialization, urbanization, privatization, and commercialization? How did a concept of sport based on amateurism shift to one based primarily on professionalism? Have Canadian sports really become "Americanized," or in some cases are they just part of a large North American sports industry? By providing a capsule history of the past 400 years we have described the important processes and struggles through which pre-modern sport forms were transformed into the highly rationalized, international sport of today.

The term most historians use to describe this transition is "modernization," which is an analytical framework or paradigm about how social life has changed in the transition from pre-industrial or traditional societies based primarily on agriculture to industrial societies based on the production and the exchange of goods. Sport historians have found modernization a particularly useful concept to explain the transformation of pre-modern to modern sport forms (Guttmann, 1978, 1988; Adelman, 1986).

However, what ideas are inherent in "modernization" or in what some writers have called a "theory of industrial society"? Richard Gruneau (1988) provides a useful summary of these ideas as they relate to sport. He, in turn, adapted the discussion from British sociologist Anthony Giddens (1982), whom we introduced in Chapter 1.

First, this transition from pre-industrial to industrial society is viewed as a progressive transformation. With industrialization has come considerable affluence, less social ascription, and more equality of opportunity, all of which are reflected in modern sport forms. Despite the problems that continue to plague modern sport (e.g., violence, drugs, excessive commercialization), increased opportunities are now available, especially to the less privileged, women, and minority groups. As well, technological advances ensure a sophisticated scientific approach to training and international competition.

Second, the inevitable stresses and

strains that marked the transition from an agrarian order to industrial society were centred primarily on class conflicts. The early social conflicts in sport – for instance, over the legitimacy of "blood sports" such as cockfighting and bear-baiting, or later, over amateurism and professionalism – were transitory, simply growing pains in the maturation of modern sport. According to modernization theory, class conflicts no longer exist in the institutions, such as sport, of modern industrial societies.

Third, the rise of the liberal-democratic state is essential to the transition from tradition to modernity. The modern state has been fundamental to the more recent development of "voluntary" sport clubs, organizations, and programs. Further, the problems brought about by rapidly expanding urban populations created new functional "needs" for the rational organization of leisure that could be met by the emergence of sport as a modern institution.

Finally, modernization theory promotes the idea that industrial societies, despite cultural differences, become increasingly alike in their basic institutions. Sport, therefore, is basically the same throughout modern industrial societies. What follows is that the modernization of sport translates easily into the "westernization" of sport. It is assumed, therefore, that this particular model of sport would also be the best one for supposedly "underdeveloped" societies.

This particular analytic framework seems to explain the transformation of sport from tradition to modernity. Yet, what seems to disappear in this explanation is the important fact that the history of modern sport, as in all areas of popular culture, is a *history of cultural struggle* (Gruneau, 1988). Modernization theory appears to suggest that this transformation occurred smoothly and naturally from something we abstractly call "traditional" sport to something we know and experience as "modern" sport. However, the historical information we have provided in the preceeding pages demonstrates that little was smooth or natural in the evolution of what would eventually constitute sport in modern Canadian society.

Numerous conflicts and struggles arose over what sporting practices, styles, beliefs, and bureaucratic forms should predominate. Some traditional sporting practices were marginalized or incorporated into more "respectable" and "useful" ways of playing as the colonizers (primarily the British) imposed their particular sports on the colonized. The class-based struggles of the nineteenth and early twentieth centuries over the meaning of amateurism and its alternative, professionalism, led eventually to the emergence of commercialized sport. And there were the inevitable struggles by marginalized groups, such as women and racial and ethnic minorities, to preserve their values and their ways of playing. In sum, the history of Canadian sport is the story of specific struggles of men and women of differing social classes and racial and ethnic groups over different (and often conflicting) versions of how to live, how to work, and how to play.

As we discussed in Chapter 2, privileged groups in our society are able – seemingly by consent – to establish their own cultural practices as the most valued and legitimate, whereas subordinate groups (e.g., natives, women) have to struggle and fight not to have their alternative practices and activities incorporated into the dominant sporting culture. The important aspects of this hegemony are resistance and struggle. It is an ongoing process because alternative cultural forms and practices always pose a threat to the dominant ones. Hegemony provides, in our view, a much more useful analytic framework from which to view the historical development and emergence of "modern" sport in Canadian culture. Sport has emerged in its present form through struggles, negotiations, and compromises, and the process continues. The chapters that follow will provide more specific information and insight into this ongoing, contentious process. Always, however, we need to envision what *could* be.

SUPPLEMENTARY READING

A substantial literature now provides valuable insight into how and why sport in Canada, as well as in Western countries in general, has developed as it has. Most of it, however. is written from a "modernization" perspective. Allen Guttmann's *From Ritual to Record* (especially Chapters 1 and 2) is a comprehensive treatment of the development of "modern" sport. Within the Canadian context, we suggest Alan Metcalfe, *Canada Learns to Play: The Emergence of Organized Sport, 1807-1914*; Don Morrow *et al.*, *A Concise History of Sport in Canada*; and Morris Mott, *Sports in Canada*:

Historical Readings.

For further work on the usefulness of "hegemony" as a concept that explains the development of Canadian sport, we again refer you to Richard Gruneau's (1988) "Modernization or Hegemony: Two Views on Sport and Social Development," as well as to his earlier *Class, Sports and Social Development* (1983). While Gruneau's work focuses on class-based struggles, Helen Lenskyj's *Out of Bounds: Women, Sport and Sexuality* examines Canadian women's efforts to achieve recognition for their sporting activities and practices.

Chapter 4
POLITICS AND THE STATE

On January 4, 1980, Canadian Prime Minister Joe Clark held a news conference to address the issue of a boycott of the 1980 Olympic Games. Clark told the media that Canada was unlikely to withdraw from the Games because such an initiative would have no practical effect on the Soviet invasion of Afghanistan. However, little more than three weeks later Clark announced that Canada would boycott the 1980 Games if the Soviet Union did not withdraw its troops by February 20. Similarly, on March 30, 1980, the Canadian Olympic Association passed a resolution accepting an invitation to participate in the Games, but on April 27 the COA voted 137 to 35 to boycott the Moscow Games. Why did these two dramatic changes of intent occur? What were the reasons for the reversal of previous decisions? The answers to these and other questions about the way sport is structured and organized in Canada can be found in a knowledge of the dynamic and interactive nature of sport and politics.

In this chapter we will focus specifically on the *political sociology* of Canadian sport. We have chosen to use the term "political sociology" because such an approach is centrally concerned with the use of power in a particular social context, in this case, sport. By power we mean "the ability of an individual or a social group to pursue a course of action (to make and implement decisions and more broadly to determine the agenda for decision-making) if necessary against the interests, and even against the

International judging can be controversial.

Brian Gaviloff, Edmonton Journal.

opposition of other individuals and groups" (Bottomore, 1979: 7).

While power, in its broadest sense, is present in most if not all social relationships, the principal focus of political sociology is the phenomenon of power at the societal or state level. More specifically, the focus is on the relationships between states, for example, Canada's actions regarding sporting ties with South Africa, and also on the social movements, organizations, and institutions involved in determining these relations of power. Organizations such as

Sport Canada, the Canadian Olympic Association, national and provincial sport organizations, and social movements such as those concerned with providing equal sporting opportunities for women and those concerned with athletes' rights all fit this latter category. Also relevant, although not as easily demarcated, are those groups that represent business elites and politicians who have used sport to further their own commercial and career interests.

Unfortunately, a good deal of the sociological research falling under the general rubric of "sport and politics" has tended to ignore the concepts and theories of political sociology. In Canada, research has been more concerned with the "machinery of government," with studies focusing on historical accounts of policy development, descriptions of how government agencies have supported sport, and narratives of political incidents that have disrupted many international sporting events. These topics have been largely considered in isolation from their social context and treated in a manner that is for the most part descriptive.

This approach is problematic, because when we analyse sport and its relationship to politics and political action it is necessary to examine the activities of the various social groups involved and their struggles for power. We also need to examine the nature of these groups, the ideologies that unite them, and the ways they engage in political behaviour in order to exercise power. This does not mean that the actions of individuals are unimportant, but rather that the central focus of our analysis here is the social group.

Here we will examine some of the power struggles that have taken place in Canadian sport. First, we discuss in a general way the relationship between sport and politics by examining arguments about both their supposed separation and, obviously, the linkage of the two. Next, we discuss and explain the Canadian state by elaborating its various roles, the fact that it is a welfare state, and that it maintains masculine dominance. Third, we provide a brief chronology of the involvement of one particular arm of the state, the federal government, in amateur sport in Canada. Finally, we examine the impact of state involvement on Canadian sport with specific reference to its impact on sport organizations, athletes, the sports science profession, and domestic and foreign policy.

THE RELATIONSHIP BETWEEN SPORT AND POLITICS

Although perhaps an oversimplification, opinions about the relationship between sport and politics can be divided into two opposing views. First, there are those who see sport and politics as completely separate entities. This view has often been put forward by the media, and by some athletes, sport officials, and politicians. In contrast is the view expressed primarily in the academic literature. Here we find much evidence that, historically, sport has seldom been free of politics, and under advanced capitalism political society increasingly is taking control of sport, an area of social life that for many years was seen as part of civil society and thus beyond the direct control of the state. What is the basis of these two seemingly opposing views?

Arguments about the Separation of Sport and Politics

The idea that sport can be separate from politics is an idealist philosophy, which has its roots in the notion that sport is an advanced form of play, where the players develop a world quite separate from the realities of everyday life. The origins of this conceptualization can be found in the classic works on play by the Dutch historian Johan Huizinga (1955) and the French philosopher Roger Caillois (1961). More contemporary authors (cf. Novak, 1976; Inglis, 1977) have incorporated these ideas into arguments that sport is somehow special, a realm in which the problems and struggles that preoccupy the rest of social life are suspended. They perpetuate the notion that sport is actually separate from the reality of everyday life.

Wilson (1988: 11), on the other hand, in defining politics, suggests that it "denotes the struggle over scarce resources, the domination of one group by another and the exercise of surveillance and control in the interest of social order." Thus, for those who subscribe to the view of sport as a separate reality, its freedom and autonomy must be protected from political interference because intervention will serve to debase or corrupt its very essence (Gruneau, 1981).

Arguments about the separation of sport and politics based on conceptualizations of play as separate from the real world are problematic for sport sociologists. While few (if any) would disagree that play has an essence of freedom, the rules and regulations that separate the activity from society at large

are not spontaneous individual creations, rather they are cultural products that stem from the collective social experience of the participants. Thus while one of the purposes of rules is to separate play from reality, the very act of rule construction has the effect of embedding play deeply in the prevailing logic of social relations and thereby diminishing its autonomy. Play gives the impression of being an *independent* and *spontaneous* aspect of human action or agency and at the same time is a *dependent* and *regulated* aspect of it. (Gruneau, 1983: 21; emphasis in original)

Gruneau goes on to suggest that this "paradox of play" is even more evident in sport. He argues that although we talk of "playing sport," the very nature of such activity is almost completely determined by forces in the political, socio-economic, and cultural environment in which it takes place. A vivid example of this is found in Ken Dryden's *The Game*, where he provides an account of the different ways that hockey developed in the U.S.S.R. and Canada (pp. 213-31). Dryden shows how values and beliefs about rugby, a game brought to Canada by the British, helped shape the original game of hockey. He goes on to show how these values and beliefs became a blueprint for the style of hockey that would develop in Canada. The Soviet game, in contrast, was developed with a logic underpinned by a knowledge of soccer and bandy. Such an example serves to illustrate how play and its subsequent forms are not autonomous but are shaped by their social context.

Beliefs about the separation of sport and politics have also been influenced by liberal assumptions of what constitutes the public and private domains (Allison, 1986). As we noted in Chapter 3, political intervention has often been an important feature of the development of sport in Canada, but until the mid-twentieth century such interventions were periodic and used primarily as a means of controlling growing social unrest among the underclasses. Sport was considered part of the private sphere and government was not to concern itself with any direct and ongoing involvement in such an activity. Prime Minister Mackenzie King exemplified such an attitude when in 1936 he told the House of Commons that "it is doubtful that anyone participating in the Olympic

Games is a representative of the Government of this country" (Kidd, 1981: 240). He reaffirmed this sentiment a year later when his government rejected a private member's bill from one of his own party calling for the establishment of a Ministry of Sport. Even as late as 1957, MP Doug Fisher commented in the House on "the very touchy field of sport and international sport," adding that many people saw this as being "a very frivolous thing on which to spend money" (*House of Commons Debates*, 21 December 1957: 2750, cited by Macintosh, Bedecki, and Franks, 1987: 18). Such sentiments are no longer prevalent among Canadian politicians, and since 1961 the state has come to play an increasingly more visible and direct role in sport. However, sport still is for some an essentially private concern in which the state should have no role.

A final area where arguments have been made about the separation of sport and politics concerns the Olympic Games. As the world's largest and certainly its most visible sporting event, the Games have frequently been the scene of intense political activity. Despite this extensive political history, however, leaders of the modern Olympic movement have consistently denied the relevance of politics to sport (Taylor, 1986). Pierre de Coubertin, founder of the modern Olympics, wanted International Olympic Committee (IOC) members who were free of political ties. Avery Brundage, former IOC president, raged on for decades about the "savage monster" of politics ready to ravage the Olympic movement (Guttmann, 1984). His successor, Lord Killanin, wrote simply that "the International Olympic movement is not a political movement" (Killanin and Rodda, 1983: 13). The Olympic charter itself states that National Olympic Committees "must be autonomous and must resist all pressures of any kind whatsoever, whether of a political,

religious or economic nature" (*Olympic Charter*, 1990: 16).

The basis for the claim that the Olympics are apolitical lies in the structure of the Olympic movement. The International Olympic Committee, the supreme governing body of the Olympics, has over ninety members from around the world. Below the IOC in the structural hierarchy are the National Olympic Committees (NOCs). Originally, it was presumed that the NOCs would be separate from the governments of their respective nation-states. In fact, this was a requirement in order to be recognized by the IOC, and the people who represented their NOC on the IOC were originally those de Coubertin saw as being "of independent means, who were free from governmental influences, who themselves were influential and so could promote Olympism effectively" (Taylor, 1986: 222). As Wilson (1988: 161) notes, however, "this idea was based on the nineteenth-century liberal conception of the supreme importance of private as opposed to government institutions and was much easier to enforce when this philosophy was hegemonic." He goes on to suggest that the period from the founding of the modern Olympic movement in 1896 until the 1952 Games:

> can be defined as a stage of transition in the social organization of sport, during which traditional ties with local life disappeared and ties with local and national governments were still too weak to influence sports significantly. International sports were truly private and amateur, controlled by aristocrats and members of the business elites with the time and money to travel internationally who formed a tightly knit and mutually supportive network of 'old boys'.

The situation began to change after World War Two. The Soviet Union and its Communist allies entered the Olympic movement, and in these countries the NOCs clearly were controlled by the state. Governments on both the left and the right after the war were beginning to realize the political utility of sport, and by the early 1950s many NOCs were linked to state agencies that demanded a say in their affairs.

In addition to the NOCs, individual sport organizations that control the operation and development of their particular sports have in many countries increasingly depended on funding from the state. The extent to which this has occurred in Canada is unique among Western nations. The increasing ties of NOCs and individual sport organizations to the state have resulted in an erosion of the nineteenth-century liberal idea of an Olympic movement separate from politics. Today the movement is characterized by political struggles over "who should hold power within the governing bodies of the Olympic movement and what the structure and relative power of those governing bodies should be" (Taylor, 1986: 220). As well, the high economic impact of the Games and their wide visibility have made them increasingly viable as sites to manifest broader political struggles.

Arguments about the Links Between Sport and Politics

Political theorist Lincoln Allison (1986) suggests that one of the major reasons why sport and politics impinge on one another is because sport creates politically usable resources. Sport is often seen as "character building," or, put more sociologically, as an agent of *political socialization*. Indeed, for such nineteenth-century Canadians as Egerton Ryerson and Lord Strathcona this ideological use of sport underpinned much of the rationale for their promotion of exercise and physical training in schools. As we argued in Chapter 2, governments in modern times see sport as a particularly effective carrier of important values such as achievement, motivation, and competitive individualism. Canadian politicians have recognized the ideological significance of sport and its capacity to confirm Canada as a modern society. Sport is, for modern governments, an important agent of political socialization. We will discuss the general concept of socialization further in Chapter 8.

This preoccupation with political socialization, notes Allison (1986), overlaps with the competition for prestige among politicians in particular. Associating with success in sport can be an important resource that can be used to enhance political power. The many spectators who watch sporting events live or on television, or who follow their progress in the print media, "can become conscious or subconscious recipients of political messages and images while involved as spectators" (Petrie, 1975: 199). Politicians have increasingly realized this fact and have used sport and sports heroes and heroines to further their own political careers and party popularity or to legitimize the actions of their government. Witness, for example, the first Minister of State for Fitness and Amateur Sport, Iona Campagnolo, triumphantly carried on the shoulders of our country's athletes at the 1978 Commonwealth Games, where Canada topped the medal standings. Shortly after the Los Angeles Olympic Games, where Canada did exceptionally well, Fitness and Amateur Sport Minister Jacques LaPierre announced a substantial financial program called "Best Ever" to provide special funding (coaching, scientific and medical support, athlete assistance, training centres, national team programming, and organizational development) to the sports featured at the 1988 Summer Olympics. There was also the "Bravo Canada" poster of our team marching in Los Angeles. Who could forget the spectacle of Fitness and Amateur Sport Minister Otto Jelinek interviewing figure skater Elizabeth Manley on national television immediately following her receiving a silver medal at the 1988 Winter Olympics in Calgary? Finally, in a move he may now regret, Prime Minister Brian Mulroney was quick to phone and congratulate Ben Johnson after his "victory" in the Seoul Olympics.

In a similar manner, provincial politicians have been quick to capitalize on the successes of "their" athletes in major games to enhance their own political power. In fact, some provinces have begun special programs to ensure the greatest representation of their athletes on Canadian teams and to win medals in domestic events like the Canada Games. Such programs as "Mission 76," instituted in Quebec in 1972 to place at least 30 per cent Francophones on the Montreal Olympic team, the Alberta plan to fill 25 per cent of the places on the 1988 Winter Olympics team with Albertans, and the recent "Sask First" program for the 1989 Canada Games are all examples of this type of initiative. Through these programs, politicians have been able to ensure their own "presence" on the victory podium, thus projecting a winner's image as a consequence of their political efforts.

Politicians have also seen in sport the potential to build a national identity and to symbolize both at home and abroad the viability and success of our particular political system. Wilson (1988: 149), although writing about leisure, makes claims about its relationship to nationalism that are equally as applicable to sport. He suggests that:

modern societies now routinely use [sport] to make claims for nationhood, to establish the boundaries of their nation-state, to establish an identity for their people, to deny the claims of other peoples for nationhood, to integrate existing conglomerates into national communities and to symbolize and reaffirm hierarchies of power and status among the nations of the world.

In Canada, political figures have often used differing sporting forms to contribute to the development of a national identity in many of these ways. The victories of early athletes like rower Ned Hanlan and distance runner Tom Longboat were used by late nineteenth- and early twentieth-century civic and political leaders to signal both to Canadians and to the other nations of the world "the growing strength of the young Dominion" (Kidd, 1982: 286). More recently, the state has become increasingly interventionist in directing the efforts of our high-performance athletes for the purpose of enhancing national prestige.

Efforts by politicians to use sport as a means of nation-building are not limited just to the promotion of Canadian nationalism. At times sport has been used to resist this larger nationalism and create and affirm regional autonomy. For example, sport sociologists Jean Harvey and Roger Proulx (1988) have shown how the election success of the Parti Québécois in 1976 brought with it a new ideological approach to sport and recreation, which saw these activities as important elements in the development of a Québécois nation. Quebec Premier René Lévesque's "Quebec 2 Canada 0" quip following Gaetan Boucher's success in Sarajevo served to underscore Quebec's quest for status as a distinct nation. Likewise, the Northern Games and the Arctic Winter Games, which contain a large number of traditional Inuit games, symbolize the efforts of these people to establish their own regional and cultural identity (see Chapter 7).

Sport is also a readily available source of political capital that can be used to build a national identity in the arena of international politics. Our "victories" over the Soviet Union in hockey, our country's support of the boycott of the Moscow Olympics, and our stance against any sporting ties with South Africa are all examples of this phenomenon. Again, we shall have more to say about this particular area in our discussion of sport as an instrument of Canada's foreign policy.

Finally, we would be remiss not to point out that sport has also played a role "in the disintegration of English-speaking Canada as a distinct national community" (Kidd, 1982: 283). The increasing domination of the Canadian economy by the United States has resulted in similar levels of cultural and political domination. American authors, entertainers, politicians, and sport personalities (and teams) are often more readily recognized by Canadians than are our own homegrown products. Let's pursue this criticism a little further.

National Hockey League expansion has had its beneficial side in that cities like Edmonton, Calgary, Winnipeg, and Quebec can now see the very best players perform. However, expansion has also meant that many of the best Canadian hockey players are "now controlled by the richest and most powerful aggregates of capital and sold in the richer and more populous markets of the U.S." (Kidd, 1982: 292). Consequently, a player such as Mario Lemieux, a certainty for stardom with "Les Canadiens" if he were playing twenty years ago when Montreal had preferential choice of French-Canadian juniors, now plays for Pittsburgh. In an even greater blow to Canadian nationalism, Wayne Gretzky no longer plies his trade in the hinterlands of Edmonton but in the glamour of Los Angeles. As a result, many of our youth more easily identify with these American cities than they do with Edmonton or Montreal. Even when an attempt is made to move a struggling American franchise, such as the proposed move of the St. Louis Blues to Saskatoon in 1980, the powerful NHL stopped the move because Saskatoon was seen as having too small a population base and no attraction to American television sponsors. In fact, studies have shown that "despite a small metropolitan population, fan interest levels are extremely high; a tradition of long-distance travel to Saskatoon by a large, affluent hinterland population is strong; and the competition from alternative entertainment forms is minimal" (Geddert and Semple, 1987: 1). Now the NHL is expanding to such hockey hotbeds as San Jose and Tampa, while Canadian hinterland cities Saskatoon and Hamilton, with greater fan support and modern arenas, are passed over yet again.

Canadian football, as Kidd (1982) points out, is somewhat different but the ultimate impact has been similar to that of hockey. The booming post-war economy aided the professionalization of sport, and football saw an increase in the number of American players. Today these players dominate the "key" positions on almost every CFL team; moreover, the league distinguishes between the most outstanding player and the outstanding Canadian player. To its credit, and that of the federal governments which supported it, the CFL resisted a number of efforts by American leagues to move into the Canadian market, although the World League of American Football began play in the spring of 1991 with a team in Montreal. In baseball, breweries have purchased primary interests in the only two Canadian major league teams, which incidentally are almost entirely staffed with American players, so that they can benefit from advertising in the lucrative American markets.

In amateur sport, a number of players in both hockey and football have been lured to the U.S. by college scholarships, so much so that in the 1988 NHL entry draft, thirty-six of the forty-eight players taken from American universities were Canadians and about half of the 600 players competing in major American university hockey programs are Canadians (Christie, 1989a). In basketball, almost all of our men's national team attend American colleges. This exodus by many of our athletes is both a part and a product of American economic power and its domination of many areas of Canadian sport. It is also a phenomenon that undermines Canadian independence and further aids the disintegration of a unique Canadian identity.

Sport in Canadian society clearly has many links to politicians and to politics. Many of these linkages have been strengthened over the past three decades by the increasingly direct and sustained intervention of the Canadian state in sport. We turn now to a brief discussion of the Canadian state.

THE CANADIAN STATE

When we speak of the state we are not referring to one single entity. While the terms "government" and "state" are often used synonymously, the state is more than just government. As Panitch (1977: 6) points out:

the state is not merely the government, far less just the central government. The state is a complex of institutions, including government but also including the bureaucracy (embodied in the civil ser-

vice as well as in public corporations, central banks, regulatory commissions, etc.), the military, the judiciary, representative assemblies, and (very importantly for Canada) . . . the sub-central levels of government, that is, provincial executives, legislatures, and bureaucracies, and municipal governmental institutions.

When applied to sport, the term "state" is usually used to encompass organizations such as federal, provincial, and municipal departments of government, Crown corporations, and what are often termed "arm's-length" agencies of government (e.g., the Coaching Association of Canada, the Canadian Sport and Fitness Administration Centre). There are those who would argue that many of our national and provincial sport organizations are so closely tied to their respective levels of government, both from a resource dependence perspective and from an ideological perspective, that they have become incorporated as part of the state, or what some prefer to call the "state apparatus."

Role of the State

The role of the state in a capitalist society like Canada is essentially threefold. First, the state must create or maintain conditions in which capital accumulation can take place. This is achieved by ensuring a favourable climate for economic growth and by providing subsidies, tax exemptions, and grants to assist private enterprise. The state also controls immigration policies in order to ensure a labour market capable of supporting private enterprise, and plays a vital role in absorbing the social cost of production by providing roads, railways, public utilities, education, and so on, all of which facilitate the accumulation of capital within the private sphere.

Sport and sporting events have also played a role in the state's efforts to foster capital accumulation in Canada. Nick Auf der Maur (1976) describes how large financial gains were made by private industry through construction contracts for the Montreal Olympics. Richard Gruneau (1984: 14) has argued that the prime beneficiaries of these Games were "local and international commercial interests, middle class sports associations and bureaucracies, and the sports professions." More recently, the Calgary Olympics saw public monies expended on the Olympic Saddledome, a facility that would ultimately help ensure the long-term viability of the Calgary Flames, the NHL hockey club privately owned by a group of local businessmen. As a further example, the government of Ontario committed $30 million toward the construction of Toronto's SkyDome, a facility owned and operated by a consortium of large Canadian and multinational corporations.

Second, as well as ensuring the conditions necessary for capital accumulation, the state must also create or maintain conditions of social harmony. This is often referred to as the legitimation of power. As Panitch (1977: 19) points out, legitimation does not refer to "state propaganda or statements by politicians that seek to rationalize capital accumulation in terms of its benefits for the whole community, but rather in the sense of concrete state activities such as welfare measures, anti-combines legislation, redistributive taxation, union protection, and government consultation with labour representatives."

The state's involvement in the provision of sporting opportunities is a component of its legitimation role and is evidenced by the attempts to promote mass, democratized sport in Canada as an aspect of the "good" life (Helmes, 1978). In addition, government poli-cy papers, as well as popular and academic articles, have emphasized the meritocratic character of sport, its integrative nature, and its role in promoting social harmony. Unfortunately, arguments such as these tend to depoliticize the nature of state involvement in sport and present such involvement as the actions of a government acting solely for the benefit of its people. We will return to this critique shortly.

Finally, the state also has a more controversial, coercive role in Canadian society. All states use force to maintain or impose social order. The most recent example in Canada is the ready use of the War Measures Act in 1970 to suppress violence in Quebec. However, by and large we live in a society where the state does not need to rule by direct political coercion. It can do so, as we pointed out in Chapter 2, through ideological domination or hegemony. As McGregor (1983: 127) puts it: "You don't have to carry a gun to rule [Canada]. If you dominate the key institutions, and offices, and media systems, and positions, and hierarchies of control, a stroke of the pen will do."

In Chapter 3 we mentioned several early sport-related interventions by the state, such as the intrusive gaming laws, sabbatarianism, and the introduction of physical and military training into the schools, which in retrospect can be viewed as measures of social control. Similarly, it can be argued that the British Columbia ProRec movement of the 1930s and the 1939 Dominion Youth Training Act, both of which promoted physical activity, were developed in large part to control social unrest among the large numbers of unemployed during the Great Depression. A more recent example is the state's systematic, justified intervention into the working environment of employees and employers through the proliferation of employee fitness and recreation programs in the workplace. The rationale behind these programs is multifaceted: they are less costly than cures; they maintain the work force more efficiently; they make it possible to control people's leisure time; they open up new markets in goods and services; and they respond to demands for a better quality of life (Brodeur, 1988). More specifically, they are designed to increase job satisfaction and productivity and at the same time decrease absenteeism and health costs. Although these new state health and fitness programs, developed in conjunction with business (and rarely the workers), cannot be viewed as "coercive" in the sense of forcing workers to do something they do not want to do, they are an attempt by both the state and private enterprise to reorganize the workplace.

In sum, the threefold role of the state – capital accumulation, legitimation, and coercion – points again to the differences between the state and government, particularly in relation to sport. Not only does the state include government, it also extends well beyond the political and into the bureaucratic and administrative. As Macintosh and Whitson (1990: 13) point out in their analysis of the sport policy-making process in Canada, it is now difficult to demarcate between the political and the administrative:

> The state now includes a range of administrative institutions whose personnel are themselves skilled and knowledgeable agents, who are often highly committed to their own collective projects, whether these are regional development or high-performance sport. The professional staff in the National Sport and Recreation Centre in Ottawa . . . are particular instances of this phenomenon. At the same time, however, all agents of the state, whether politicians or public servants, are subject to political and eco-

nomic constraints that influence them in powerful and often contradictory ways, and place limits both on what they can accomplish and on what they believe they can attempt.

We turn now to two further aspects of the Canadian state: (1) a *welfare state* that produces its own inherent set of contradictions, and (2) women's relationship to a state characterized by *male dominance*.

Sport in a Welfare State

Canada is often described as a welfare state. In other words, it is a society in which governments make available to its citizens a wide range of payments (e.g., unemployment insurance, family allowance, old age security) and/or social services (e.g., health care) for the purpose of providing a basic minimal standard of health and living conditions. The hallmark of the welfare state is that government, rather than private enterprise, usually delivers these payments and services. This form of the state evolved out of the debilitating depression of the 1930s, with the result that there has been an ever-increasing government involvement in the economy. The welfare state not only reduces the economic impact of unemployment, becomes a major employer in its own right, and sets minimum wages for working people, it also provides a form of welfare to business, primarily by such means as tax incentives, development grants, the subsidization of research and development, and marketing assistance.

The modern welfare state, therefore, attempts to do two things: to foster capital accumulation and to reduce stark social inequalities. These two functions are often contradictory because in order to respond to democratic pressures for more and better social services, the state increasingly depends on economic growth (Offe, 1984). Thus, programs established in response to pressure from disadvantaged social groups must often be established in forms that also serve the interests of particular business and professional groups (Macintosh and Whitson, 1990). A good example is the shift in the federal state's involvement in sport from an initial concern with fitness programs and federal-provincial cost-sharing agreements to the encouragement of high-performance sport, which inherently contains greater opportunities for private-sector involvement and private-sector accumulation.

At the provincial level, the Quebec state's initial involvement in sport and recreation was concerned primarily with education and health. However, as Harvey and Proulx (1988: 109) point out: "In essence, recreation was no longer considered only as an area for personal development; it was also assigned a role in the cultural development of the 'Québécois nation'. Recreation became a place for collective emancipation." The 1976 election of the Parti Québécois brought a substantive change. Strongly opposed to federal intervention in sport and recreation and concerned with the distinctiveness of Quebec, the Parti Québécois focused increasingly on high-performance sport. In its quest for nationalism the Quebec state promoted an identification with high-performance sportswomen and men that created contradictions with the social welfare role the state had originally envisioned for sport.

In a more specific example of the contradictions that exist within the state's involvement in sport, Macintosh and Whitson (1990) examine the federal state's sport policy document *Toward 2000: Building Canada's Sport System*. Here the Minister of State for Fitness and Amateur Sport at that time suggested that "if broader social goals (e.g., gender equality, enhanced regional access, Canadian prominence on the world stage, etc.) are to be accomplished *in* and *through* sport, a stronger governmental presence in leadership and financial terms is also required" (Fitness and Amateur Sport, 1988: 29). Macintosh and Whitson (1990) pose the question as to whether Canadian prominence on the world athletic stage is a social goal of the same order as gender equality or enhanced regional access to sporting opportunities. They suggest that these are contradictory aims in that the "pursuit of prominence on the world stage has tended to push issues like gender equality and regional access into the background" (Macintosh and Whitson, 1990: 106).

Sport in a Masculine-Dominated State

In Chapter 7, we take up the issue of gender inequality in more detail. Here, we want to examine briefly the notion of a state that has institutionalized masculine dominance, and what that means for sport. To say that the Canadian state has institutionalized masculine dominance is to argue that the state itself plays a role in the fundamental ways in which men exercise social, political, sexual, and economic control over women's lives (Randall, 1988). For instance, the state has exploited women's labour because it upholds a pervasive sexual division of labour. It maintains many women's economic dependence on men by the entrenchment of men's superior property and inheritance rights in law and marriage. The state itself perpetuates a form of violence against women by allowing men to commit rape, incest, wife assault, and sexual harassment with relative impunity. Finally, through the disproportionate numbers of male versus female politicians, and in the senior positions in the

Brian Gavriloff, Edmonton Journal.

*Canadian team at opening ceremonies, Calgary
Winter Olympics, 1988.*

civil service, the state has remained a bastion of male power.

However, the state itself is often a site of struggle among different social groups, and we often see conflict and contradiction between the actions and policies of the various levels, branches, and agencies of the state (Randall, 1988). One of these areas of conflict and struggle is women's involvement in sport. On the one hand, the federal state (and its branches provincially and locally) legitimates the ideology of masculine superiority in sport by continuing to provide more funds and sporting opportunities for males than for females. At the same time, some state substructures have provided a means to address and rectify gender inequality in sport (Bray, 1988). The federal Women's Program within Fitness and Amateur Sport is a case in point. It was established in 1980 to provide funding to national sport organizations to assist their efforts to improve opportunities for girls and women, to help train women for sport management positions, to liaise with other state structures and organizations assisting women, and to assist with policy development. Canada is among the very few Western nations to have an explicit policy on women in sport (see Fitness and Amateur Sport, 1986). In contradiction, though, the state has recently withdrawn all core funding from the Canadian Association for the Advancement of Women and Sport, an advocacy, membership-based organization whose purpose is to work for changes in the sports system to improve opportunities for girls and women.

The point here is that the Canadian state (and its provincial and local branches) cannot be viewed as a monolithic bloc, nor can we assume that the state acts in a consistent, non-contradictory way. The state itself is a site of conflict and struggle as social groups, whether based on gender, class, race, or ethnicity, seek to change or uphold the myriad state policies, agencies, and processes.

Sport and the Canadian State

The federal government "invests" in the sport system for several important reasons. First, we support sport simply for what it is – part of human nature; a social movement made accessible and equitable through the national sport system. We

also invest in the system because sport forms a part of our national identity and is an expression of our culture and who we are. As well, sport supports individual Canadians as they pursue excellence to the highest levels and provides opportunities for Canadians in general to observe and share in their pursuit and their celebration and to draw important meanings from their performances. Sport as well brings certain physical and health benefits due to the extent and nature of physical preparation needed to participate. Finally, the federal government invests to ensure that certain social benefits and objectives are attended to by the sport community, including bilingualism, gender equity, more favorable regional access and an ethical conduct of sport. (Fitness and Amateur Sport, 1988: 16-17)

The above quotation is the most recent statement as to why the federal government "invests" (now over $70 million annually) in sport. In summary, it suggests five reasons: sport is part of human nature; sport is part of our national identity and an expression of our culture; sport is about pursuing excellence; sport is healthy; and sport is a means to ensure certain social benefits such as bilingualism, gender equity, regional access, and ethical conduct. These have not always been the federal government's reasons for investing in sport. They have evolved through a series of task forces and policy statements, considerable public discussion, and several changes of government. Indeed, since 1976 eleven different ministers have been responsible for the Fitness and Amateur Sport Directorate.

Table 4 presents a chronology of the federal government's involvement in amateur sport since the early 1960s, highlighting what we be-

TABLE 4
Chronology of Federal Government Involvement in Amateur Sport

1961 • Bill C-131, An Act to Encourage Fitness and Amateur Sport, provides $5 million annually for an administrative structure and personnel (Fitness and Amateur Sport Directorate and the National Advisory Council on Fitness and Amateur Sport), federal/provincial cost-sharing agreements, grants to sport governing bodies, the Canada Games, and scholarships and research awards.

1966 • First administrative grants given to sport governing bodies, which became accountable to the government for the use of these funds.

1967 • First Canada Games held in Quebec City with "Unity Through Sport" as the theme.

1968 • Pierre Trudeau promised that, if elected, his Liberal government would establish a task force to investigate amateur sport in Canada (and especially the effect of professional sport, i.e., hockey, on amateur sport).

1969 • *Report of the Task Force on Sport for Canadians* recommends a more interventionist approach by the federal government, through:
• Fitness and Amateur Sport Directorate, which relegates the National Advisory Council to a purely advisory role.

1970 • *A Proposed Sports Policy for Canadians* asserts for the first time that the federal state has a legitimate role in the pursuit of "excellence" in elite sport. It recommends direct administrative grants to sport governing bodies and agencies; in-house administrative reorganization; increased subsidization of travel grants for athletes and officials; and a formal organization for the Canada Games.

1971 • Sport Canada and Recreation Canada are created within the Fitness and Amateur Sport Directorate.
• Also created are two important "arm's-length" agencies: the National Sport and Recreation Centre (Ottawa) and Sport Participaction Canada (ParticipAction).

1973 • Fitness and Amateur Sport Directorate is elevated to branch status and able to have its own assistant deputy minister.
• Annual budget now $11 million.
• Game Plan '76 is formally established as a co-operative effort among the Canadian Olympic Association, the federal government, the national sport organizations, and the provincial governments. Its purpose is to encourage Olympic sports to set specific goals for achieving better performances and records.

1976 • Iona Campagnolo appointed the first Minister of State with responsibilities for fitness and amateur sport.

1977 • Government releases *Towards a National Policy on Amateur Sport: A Working Paper* and conducts cross-Canada public hearings.
• Recreation Canada becomes Fitness and Recreation Canada.

1979 • Government releases *Partners in Pursuit of Excellence – A National Policy*, advocating a partnership of shared responsibility among university resources, business and corporate sponsors, the sport community, the provinces, and a new federal sport structure.

- It also releases *Towards a National Policy on Fitness and Recreation* and seeks public input.
- Liberal government is defeated and these policy statements have little effect.
- Annual budget is now $35 million.

1980 • Formal withdrawal of federal government from recreation, which becomes the sole responsibility of the provinces (Fitness and Recreation Canada now known as Fitness Canada).
- Sport Canada consolidates its athlete support programs under the auspices of the new Athlete Assistance Plan.
- A Women's Program is created to promote more involvement by females in sport and fitness activities.

1981 • A re-elected Liberal government releases *A Challenge to the Nation: Fitness and Amateur Sport in the 80s,* which focuses the federal government's role on the promotion of high-performance sport and fitness.

1982 • Government approves the "Best Ever" program, which provides an additional $25 million to the winter Olympic sports in order to accomplish Canada's best performance ever in Olympic competition.

1983 • Government announces it will help finance national training centres in high-performance sports.
- It also announces a hosting policy for funding major international sport events in Canada.
- The Official Languages Program is established to assist national sport and fitness organizations to acquire a permanent bilingual capacity.

1985 • New Conservative government extends the "Best Ever" program to the summer Olympic sports, providing an additional $50 million in the three-and-a-half-year period leading up to the Seoul Summer Games.
- Sport Canada establishes a Sport Recognition system, which defines the criteria for government funding to national sport organizations.

1986 • Government releases *Sport Canada Policy on Women in Sport,* which sets out the official goal of equality of opportunity for women at all levels of the sport system.
- Government establishes the Sport Marketing Council to encourage sport organizations to gain corporate sponsorship.
- Also established is the Commission for Fair Play in response to a growing concern about the level of violence in sport.
- Annual budget is now $68 million.

1987 • Fitness and Amateur Sport joins forces with the Department of External Affairs to enhance the role of Canada's international relations and to strengthen the international dimensions of Canadian sport policy and relationships.
- Government extends the "Best Ever" program by allocating $32 million to winter Olympic sports over the next five years.

1988 • Document *Toward 2000: Building Canada's Sport System* is released. This is the report of a task force on national sport policy. It is a wide-ranging document with over fifty recommendations concerning the sport system in Canada, high-performance and domestic sport, international sport leadership, high-performance athletes, sport as a component of Canadian culture, and the financing of sport.
- Canadian sprinter Ben Johnson tests positive for anabolic steroids at the Seoul Olympics and the federal government initiates an Inquiry into the Use of Drugs and

Banned Practices Intended to Increase Athletic Performance (Dubin Inquiry).

1989 • The government invites comments and seeks input concerning the task force's report on national sport policy, but the Dubin Inquiry takes virtually the entire year and occupies the attention of Sport Canada.

1990 • Dubin Inquiry report is released in the summer. The government consults national sport organizations and other relevant agencies seeking feedback.

lieve to be the most significant events over the past three decades. From the sport sociologist's perspective, this chronology is the starting point from which to examine the impact of these events and changes on several sectors of the Canadian amateur sport community.

THE IMPACT OF STATE INVOLVEMENT ON SPORT

In four areas the impact of the state has been the most visible and profound. Here, we look at the effect that state intervention has had on sport organizations and also on high-performance athletes. We then examine the state's role in the creation of a sport science profession. Finally, we will describe how sport has become an instrument of domestic and foreign policy.

The Impact on Sport Organizations

The direct and ongoing intervention of the state has resulted in the rationalization of the Canadian sport system with the result that a new, dominant form of amateur sport organization has been created within the sport delivery system. Organizations responsible for delivering amateur sport to Canadians can no longer be characterized by what the 1969 Task Force

report described as "kitchen table administration" since they now exhibit a more corporate style of management. Organizations that once showed low levels of specialization, little in the way of formalized operating procedures, and consensual decision-making with control by volunteers now show high levels of specialization and formalization with most decision-making in the hands of professionals. While there has been a gradual change to this more corporate organizational form, the process in recent years has received impetus from the introduction of the "Best Ever" program (cf. Slack and Hinings, 1987). For the state, the organizational form seen as most appropriate to achieve the goals associated with this program has been the professional bureaucracy. This is an organizational design characterized by high levels of bureaucratization but where control of the organization is decentralized to the level of the professional staff, not the volunteer board as has traditionally been the situation in amateur sport organizations. Although not all amateur sport organizations have adopted this design, and some have openly resisted it, this is clearly the direction in which national and provincial sport organizations are being pressured to move.

Concomitant with the emergence of this new organizational form, there has also been a change in the type of individuals who are the key volunteers in these organizations. Previously a knowledge of the sport was the essential criterion, but now there is a tendency to recruit only individuals who possess particular skills, especially managerial capabilities (Slack, 1985). As Whitson and Macintosh (1988) point out in their study of the "Best Ever" program, one respondent suggested that the criterion for volunteers to serve on the board of directors of a sport organization should be their ability to open corporate doors. This has the effect of excluding certain individuals from the senior volunteer administrative positions in these organizations. Blue-collar workers, for example, are rarely part of the administrative structure. Similarly, women "are not perceived as valuable volunteer administrators because they lack the resources (financial and general management skills, or corporate experience and contacts)" that the organizations now feel they need (Hall, Cullen, and Slack, 1989: 32). We have more to say about who controls amateur sport in Canada in Chapter 7.

The intervention of the state and its push to a more corporate style of management have also necessitated a restructuring of the lines of authority in sport organizations, the result of which is an organization clearly directed by professionals rather than volunteers. The resulting professional control has invariably meant that the focus of the sport organization has been directed to the "systematic production of performance" (Whitson and Macintosh, 1988). This type of focus has necessarily involved power struggles between the new professional elites and the more established volunteers. It has also meant that professionals, because of their central role in an organization's operations, have assumed increasing levels of power while many of the volunteers, who have traditionally managed these organizations, have been marginalized to support roles or have dropped out in frustration over the struggles they faced.

The professionalization of sport organizations has also had the effect of reducing the autonomy of these organizations in several ways. First, the similarity in the training and class backgrounds of professionals in sport organizations with those of government officials often means that they are more closely aligned to state representatives than to the coaches and athletes they presumably represent (Macintosh and Beamish, 1987). Second, the hiring process for professionals, particularly those in key positions, is often constructed in such a way that a Sport Canada official, and at times a member of the state-funded Coaching Association of Canada, sits on the hiring committee. This helps to ensure that only those individuals supportive of the direction of government policy are hired. Third, many of these professionals and the programs they operate are dependent on state funding, so they are limited in the extent to which they can speak out against state initiatives or interventions. Finally, also problematic is the extent to which the rational performance-oriented goals that now dominate these organizations have come to construct our experience of sport at all levels (see Chapter 2). Consequently, many people in sport have lost "touch with the fact that sport can have other meanings and pleasures" (Whitson and Macintosh, 1988: 95).

The Impact on Athletes

The direct and ongoing involvement of the Canadian state in amateur sport has both helped to transform our sport organizations and radically altered the experience of being a high-performance athlete. Sport sociologists Rob Beamish and Jan Borowy (1987: 2) suggest that prior to the 1960s, Canadian athletes participated in international games for rewards of status or social prestige, whereas "the present situation is one in which athletes exchange their specialized capacity for athletic performance for prestige and remuneration with an implicit (if not explicit) contractually defined arrangement." In its quest for athletic excellence, the federal state now has in place a program of financial incentives based on an athlete's performance. In several of the provinces similar programs are also in place.

The first state funding for Canadian athletes emanated from the 1970 policy document, A Proposed Sport Policy for Canadians. The amount available per athlete was from $500 to $2,000 per year and the program carried no specific performance-based obligations. As Beamish and Borowy (1988) note, the proposal for athlete funding was based on the assumption that the majority of Canada's high-performance athletes were students and athletic competition was an ancillary endeavour they undertook while completing university degrees. Over the years, the amount of funding to our athletes through the Athlete Assistance Program (AAP) has increased: "A" carded athletes, individuals who are in the top eight in the world, receive $650 per month; "B," "C," "C-1," and "D" cards receive $550, $450, $350, and $300 per month respectively. Two new categories for team sport, "R" and "J" cards, are for reserve athletes just below the national team level and for junior team athletes. They receive $250 and $150 per month, respectively. As of January, 1989, over 800 athletes were funded through the AAP. Supplements are also available based on need for "extraordinary training costs, child care, special equipment, moving and travel expenses and facility rentals. As well, the program pays for university and college tuition, books and supplies" (Kidd, 1988b: 296). The program is now under the control of Sport Canada, the criteria for funding are more selective, and the requirements placed on the athletes – such as monthly contact with the respective national sport organization, mandatory training camps, random drug testing, and involvement in non-commercial promotional activities if requested by Sport Canada – are most stringent. The enforcement of these obligations is ensured by a signed contract.

Over the years, the state has used the incentive of more funding, albeit still at relatively low levels, to increase its control over "state" athletes. The relationship has been described as akin to that of an employer to an employee. However, unlike many employees, very few athletes have access to any means of expressing their views in a collective manner, and very few have input into decisions made by their national sport organization that directly affect them. As Kidd (1988a: 24) points out, only seventeen of sixty national sport bodies have athletes' representatives and "most of these are appointed by coaches and administrators, not elected."

Two other points are worthy of mention. The first relates to the time commitment an athlete must make to his or her sport. As part of the Athlete Assistance Program, Sport Canada has established rules that govern athletes' training and competitive programs. A survey by Beamish and Borowy (1988) shows that 84 per cent of high-performance athletes travel at least twenty-one days per year with their national team and nearly one out of five spends over 100 days per year in a similar capacity. In addition, 89 per cent of athletes indicated they had to attend compulsory training camps and 97 per cent had to appear for at least one compulsory competition. Such time demands will ensure that the majority of Canadian high-performance athletes continue to come from middle- and upper-class families because most athletes must bear all their training and competition expenses until the point where they can qualify for provincial or federal aid. Even carded athletes incur costs that cannot be met through such aid (Kidd, 1988b).

Our second point, related to the first, concerns an athlete's opportunity to control her or his athletic destiny. What attracts a young person to sport in the first place is the opportunity to experience achievement and excellence, either as an individual or as a member of a team. For many, a part of the achievement itself – and certainly something that made it more meaningful – was related activities such as developing a training program, planning for the competition, "psyching" oneself up for the event, and even, at times, saving up enough money to get to the event. In the past, much of what athletes could achieve was governed by their own decisions, and they were often assisted by family, friends, and volunteers. Athletes were able to exert a reasonable degree of control over their destiny, but the intervention and increasing power of the state have taken much of this away. Today athletes are under the power of coaches, who have through "state incentives and contracts . . . recourse to the utilitarian and instrumental controls characteristic of wage labour" (Kidd, 1988a: 22). Controls may be exercised over such "rights" as employment, place of residence, travelling, sightseeing, dating, and getting married. In addition, athletes are often subject to the demands of sport psychologists, physiologists, sport organization officials, and drug testers. Failure to comply may result in sanctions, such as withdrawal of funding, being sent home from a competition, or even exclusion from a team. As Bruce Kidd argues, Canadian athletes are now "sweat-suited philanthropists, ensuring the careers of hundreds of well-paid coaches, sports scientists, and sport administrators, and subsidizing the ambitions of the federal state" (Kidd, 1988a: 23). For today's athletes, much of their destiny is under the control of others.

The Creation of a Sport Science Profession

At one time a profession was distinguished by the manner in which its members possessed certain traits – lengthy training, a professional association, a code of ethics. More recent thinking about professions has recognized the political nature of establishing such status (cf. Johnson, 1972; Larson, 1977). Professionalization, therefore, involves political struggles to establish control over a body of knowledge, to control admission into the group, and to be self-governing. It is, as Wilson (1988: 15) notes, "a struggle for power, for control over the definition and provision of a service." Such struggles inevitably involve the state.

In sport, the struggle for professional status in areas under the rubric of "sport science," which includes such specialties as exercise physiology, sport psychology, biomechanics, and sport management, began in the early 1970s. As Whitson and Macintosh (1988: 82) point out, "since opportunities for physical education teachers began to shrink . . . physical education departments in Canadian universities have increasingly reconstructed themselves around new 'sciences of human performance'." Such changes became evident as many departments changed their titles from physical education to terms such as human kinetics, sports science, and kinesiology. There are several possible reasons for this shift. First and foremost, the state's increasing emphasis on high-performance sport created a demand for sport scientists and sport managers who could assist athletes and help shape the sport infrastructure in such a way as to achieve performance excellence. Second, and related to the creation of this demand, physical education researchers saw that they could not only supply this new demand, and in doing so generate research grants and publications, but also they could enhance their own status within the university's scientific community as well as the status of physical education (or, more accurately, sport science) in the larger community.

While this shift in focus in physical education departments has helped provide funding for research and jobs for graduates, it has also tended to naturalize rather than problematize the rational pursuit of excellence. There are several important consequences of such actions. First, the preoccupation of sport professionals, both in their training and in the conduct of their jobs, tends to marginalize such issues as gender equity, sport for all, and regional equality. Similarly, the construction of sport as a phenomenon that can only be analysed in a scientific manner minimizes the impact of historical, political, and socio-economic forces on sporting practice. Finally, the creation of professionals in sport and a discourse of sport science also tends to elevate the knowledge of professionals and devalue that of the volunteers.

It is important to remember that the relatively new sport sciences, as well as the professionals who study these subjects, reflect the overlapping interests of universities, the physical education profession, high-performance athletes, and the state in that they represent opportunities "to create political capital out of sporting successes" (Whitson and Macintosh, 1988: 95).

Sport as an Instrument of Domestic and Foreign Policy

The use of sport as a nation-builder is not new to Canadian politicians; however, the direct and ongoing intervention of the state in sport has increased its use as an instrument of domestic and foreign policy. Indeed, much of Prime Minister John Diefenbaker's rationale for Bill C-131 was grounded in our country's poor performance in international sporting events, particularly hockey, and the comparative successes of state socialist countries. Although Diefenbaker first saw the potential that state involvement in sport could have in developing a strong national identity, it was Pierre Trudeau who was to make substantive political capital out of this relationship.

Trudeau came to power in the late 1960s with a vision of a united Canada, and sport was one of the instruments by which he sought to realize this vision. Sport was particularly appealing to politicians of this era because it could be used as an instrument of domestic policy to unite Canadians behind Trudeau's one-Canada ideology. The promotion of nationalism was also an aspect of their objectives within a welfare state. Competitions such as the Canada Games and their provincial equivalents were held in "secondary" cities and relatively remote geographical areas, where there would be some economic benefit and a legacy of new facilities after the competitions had ended. Similarly, the Athlete Assistance Program served as a form of income security (Harvey, 1988). As such, these programs both reflect the logic of the welfare state and the concern with equalizing participation in sport. At the same time, they are clearly an example of the way the state appropriated sport to strengthen Canadian unity. Sport was also appealing to politicians because success in the international sports arena yielded political capital in Canada, in terms of strengthening national unity, and also served to enhance our status among other nations of the world and to advance the state's foreign policy objectives.

In this respect one of the most significant events was the 1972 Canada-U.S.S.R. hockey series. Although it was promoted by the non-governmental Hockey Canada, the Department of External Affairs and the Canadian embassy in Moscow both became extensively involved in the series. The event "was clearly the turning point in the evolution of sport in Canadian foreign policy" (Franks, Hawes, and Macintosh, 1988: 671). The series called into question the practice of leaving the job of improving Canada's performance at international events entirely in the hands of private national sport organizations, and it confirmed the political necessity of further state involvement in sport, particularly as an instrument of foreign policy.

Although there have been many instances over the years where sport has been used by the Canadian government as a form of diplomatic protest, we will examine three specific examples: Canada's China policy and the Montreal Olympics; our policy toward South Africa and apartheid; and the boycott of the 1980 Moscow Olympics.

CHINA AND THE MONTREAL OLYMPICS The IOC had recognized Taiwan (also known as the Republic of China) and not the People's Republic of China as the official entry of China to the 1976 Games in Montreal. Canada, on the other hand, was only willing to recognize mainland China as the official representative, in line with its one-China foreign policy (Olafson and Brown-John, 1986). Under the Trudeau government Canada had sought to distance itself from the United States, especially from its involvement in Vietnam. One way to do this was to support Beijing over the American-backed Taiwan. Canada was also selling quantities of wheat to the People's Republic; consequently, our economic interests were more closely linked to Beijing than to Taipei.

Canada refused to grant entry visas to the Taiwanese athletes unless they agreed to compete under the designation of Taiwan instead of the Republic of China. The IOC was equally adamant that the Canadian position was in conflict with Olympic principles, since the People's Republic was not at the time a member of the IOC. Eventually, a compromise was reached but then was rejected by the Taiwanese, who never did compete in 1976. In future Olympiads, however, they competed as Taiwan. This entire controversy was clearly a victory for the Canadian state over the IOC, and a further reminder of the growing politicization of international sport.

SOUTH AFRICA AND APARTHEID The world-wide sports boycott of South Africa has virtually quarantined the apartheid state: South Africans have not competed in the Olympics since 1960, or in the Commonwealth Games since 1961; many international sport federations have expelled South Africa from membership or restricted its competition; there has not been a major cricket tour in South Africa since 1970 or a rugby tour since 1985, both of which are important white South African sports; many governments bar entry to South African athletes and officials and require their own athletes and sports associations to boycott all sporting contact with South Africa as a condition of funding; and finally, under the United Nations Declaration Against Apartheid in Sports, twenty-seven nations have agreed to bar entry to athletes from other countries who have competed in South Africa (Kidd, 1988c). In sum, while trade, tourism, cultural, and academic exchanges with South Africa continue in the face of minimal sanctions, sporting exchanges have been virtually eliminated.

What is the Canadian government policy regarding sporting contacts with South Africa? Table 5 outlines the current policy. Canada's attitude toward racial discrimination in South Africa changed from one of indifference in the late 1950s to one that openly condemned

TABLE 5
Canada's Policy on Sporting Contacts with South Africa

1. *Sport Events in Canada*

The government will deny entry visas to individuals travelling on South African passports who wish to enter Canada to participate in a sport event or to pursue their sport careers. This policy applies to individuals, including professionals, as well as to individuals and teams representing South Africa.

2. *Sport Events in South Africa*

The government will deny any support, either financial or moral, to any individual, whether affiliated or non-affiliated with a Canadian sport association, whose purpose is to travel to South Africa for sports events or to pursue his or her sporting career. Canadian sports organizations are expected to maintain a policy of non-involvement of any kind in sports events in South Africa. They are expected to discourage participation in any sport event held in South Africa by withholding permits, approvals, and funds and through other effective measures. They are requested to adopt and enforce rules that call for the suspension of athletes and officials who participate in sports events in South Africa.

3. *Sport Events in a Third Country*

The government opposes sporting contacts between Canadians and South Africans in events held in third countries. It will therefore not extend any support (either financial or moral) to any organization or individual for the purpose of participating in sports events in third countries in which South Africans are participating. Canadian organizations are expected to decline invitations, withdraw from, or formally protest South African participation to event organizers and to the international federation on behalf of their members, clubs, etc. Organizations are also expected to deny funding, approvals, and permits to their athletes and officials, affiliated clubs, or teams for any international events or competitions involving South Africans.

SOURCE: Summarized from "Canadian Government Policy Regarding Sporting Contacts Between Canada and South Africa" (June 28, 1989).

apartheid by the early 1970s (Olafson, 1986). In support of its developing foreign policy position, Canada voted for the 1970 IOC decision to expel South Africa from the Games. However, once the 1976 Games were awarded to Montreal, the situation became more acute for Canada. A New Zealand rugby team toured South Africa in 1976, and to protest the alleged indifference of the IOC to the tour and its refusal to bar New Zealand from the Games, thirty-one nations, twenty-nine of them African, withdrew, much to the embarrassment of the Canadian host. Anxious that the same situation should not occur in Edmonton, the site of the 1978 Commonwealth Games, the Canadian government took the lead in persuading other Commonwealth nations to support the 1977 Gleneagles Agreement, by which member states would take all practical steps to discourage sporting contacts with South Africa (Olafson, 1986). The Canadian government announced that it would no longer issue visas to any athletes, coaches, or trainers from South Africa, and it would no longer fund any Canadian athletes who wanted to compete in events in which South Africans were participating. In 1986, the government was again pressured to support a black African boycott of the Commonwealth Games in Edinburgh because of Great Britain's refusal to impose economic sanctions against South Africa. It decided, however, against supporting the boycott and our athletes competed in the Games.

The Gleneagles Agreement was another step in the evolution of the relationship between sport and Canadian foreign policy. First, it had symbolic value in that it accepted that "the withdrawal of the right to participate in major international sporting events is a useful and appropriate foreign policy instrument" (Franks, Hawes, and Macintosh, 1988: 677). Second, it was the first formal agreement, to which the Canadian government was a signatory, that directly tied sport to Canadian foreign policy (Olafson, 1986). Eventually, federal governments have seen the need to maintain a "sports desk" within the Department of External Affairs, and more recently an International Relations Directorate has been established within Fitness and Amateur Sport. Its major purpose is to "strengthen the international dimension of Canadian sport policy and relationships" (Fitness and Amateur Sport, 1988: 6).

THE MOSCOW BOYCOTT The final example of the links between sport and Canadian foreign policy brings us back to the question we posed at the beginning of this chapter: why did Canada boycott the 1980 Olympic Games in Moscow? Over a relatively short period, two policy reversals took place – one involving the Canadian state and the other the Canadian Olympic Association.

At the time the Soviet Union invaded Afghanistan, Joe Clark's short-lived Conservative government was in power, and the Clark administration was clearly more in favour of closer ties with the United States than was the previous Liberal government under Pierre Trudeau (Franks, Hawes, and Macintosh, 1988). Clark's initial stance, that the boycott would have no practical effect, was formulated after U.S. President Jimmy Carter had said a boycott of the Games was not a "priority matter" (Kereliuk, 1982). Carter, on the other hand, was under considerable pressure to pursue the boycott and on January 20, 1980, he announced that unless the Soviets left Afghanistan within one month the Games should be moved, postponed, or cancelled. He also made a personal appeal to Clark, and on January 27 Canada's boycott of the Games was announced. Canada's strong geopolitical and economic ties to the United States, the pressure from Washington, and the Clark government's declared intent to develop closer relations with the U.S. all served to shape the decision. Pierre Trudeau and his Liberal government were returned to power before the Games took place. Although as Franks, Hawes, and Macintosh (1988) point out, Trudeau himself had difficulty with boycotts, and he was anxious to re-establish that Canadian foreign policy was made in Ottawa not Washington, he eventually recommended the boycott to the COA. The COA's decision to change its stance was also influenced by pressure applied by its corporate sponsors, which were Canadian subsidiaries of American companies. In April, 1980, the COA voted not to send a team to Moscow. As to the eventual impact of the boycott, Bruce Kidd (1988c: 661-62) comments:

> It did, I believe, make a significant impact upon Soviet public opinion and demonstrate the world-wide opposition to the Soviet intervention. But it cost many

athletes and coaches the rare privilege of participating in an Olympics, it bitterly divided the international sports community for almost a decade, and it did not get the Soviet Union out of Afghanistan.

These three examples illustrate just how complex and subtle the relationship of sport to Canada's foreign policy has become. When justified, the Canadian government is quite prepared to use sport as a form of diplomatic protest despite the objections of those most affected, be they powerful international sport bodies like the IOC or individual Canadian athletes, coaches, and officials. Further, although private in theory, Canadian sport organizations must comply with the goals and initiatives of the Canadian foreign policy establishment because they depend so heavily on government funding. Finally, through a series of well-planned sport exchanges co-ordinated through the Department of External Affairs in conjunction with Fitness and Amateur Sport, there has been a greater use of our athletes, coaches, officials, and sport scientists to promote Canada's image abroad.

SUMMARY

Any analysis of sport and politics must consider the power relationships that exist not only between nation-states but also among the sport organizations, institutions, and movements within any one state. What is important here is the struggle for power among these various social groups.

We began our analysis by examining the various arguments for the separation of sport and politics: sport is and should be separate from the real world; sport belongs in the private rather than public domain; and the Olympics should be free of politics. Next, we examined the arguments for the linkages between sport and politics: sport creates politically usable resources, especially for politicians; sport can be used as a nation-builder; sport enhances our image internationally; and finally, sport in Canada serves to undermine Canadian independence from the United States.

For obvious reasons, we have focused on the struggles and conflicts over sporting power within the Canadian state, and we showed how the threefold nature of the state (capital accumulation, legitimation, and coercion) points to the differences between state and government, particularly in relation to sport. Canada is a welfare state and, like all states, is characterized by male dominance, factors that both explain and produce contradictions and inconsistencies in state policies and processes.

The federal government now invests substantially in sport, and we traced the evolution of this involvement (some argue intervention) over the past three decades. More important is the impact of this state involvement on the various institutions and social groups that constitute the Canadian sport system. We have argued that the increasing rationalization and professionalization of this system have serious implications (some beneficial, some not) for sport organizations, individual athletes, and sport scientists and for the linkages between sport and Canada's domestic and foreign policy initiatives.

SUPPLEMENTARY READING

The most comprehensive text dealing with the involvement of the Canadian state in sport is *Sport and Politics in Canada* by Don Macintosh, Tom Bedecki, and Ned Franks, a good descriptive account of the major events that have taken place since 1961. We particularly recommend Chapters 9 and 10, which deal respectively with the "Major Outcomes and Consequences" of state involvement and "Issues" that emanate from this involvement. See also Don Macintosh and Dave Whitson, *The Game Planners: Transforming Canada's Sport System*, a further analysis of the role of government in sport. For students who want a shorter, yet informative, discussion of government and sport in Canada, we recommend Chapter 1 of the Dubin Inquiry report, *Commission of Inquiry into the Use of Drugs and Banned Practices Intended to Increase Athletic Performance.*

For a broader overview of the political nature of sport, see Lincoln Allison's anthology, *The Politics of Sport*, which includes several interesting chapters, especially Allison's "Sport and Politics" and two pieces by Trevor Taylor, "Sport and International Relations" and "Politics and the Olympic Spirit."

Finally, for students who wish to broaden their reading in this area, see John Wilson's *Politics and Leisure*. While Wilson's focus is obviously the wider field of leisure studies, he combines historical and sociological material to address such issues as the control of sport, politics and amateur sport, and sport and nationalism.

Chapter 5

BUSINESS AND CAPITAL

*O*ne of the most striking features of modern sport in Canada is its link to commercial enterprise. In the past ten to fifteen years, sport and sport-related activities have become one of our country's largest industries. One has only to pick up a newspaper or popular magazine to realize that sport and business are inextricably linked and that sport is itself a business. We see some male professional athletes being traded for literally millions of dollars. We see cities vying to spend large amounts of public money to host major sporting events. Even a few "amateur" athletes receive large sums to compete, and everywhere we look, sport is used to sell a variety of consumer goods from soft drinks to cars to electronic equipment to cosmetics. The uniforms of minor sports teams are emblazoned with company names and logos, and youth seek peer recognition by wearing the latest and most expensive air-supported sneakers. Recreational skiers, joggers, cyclists, and participants in exercise programs spend millions of dollars on the latest in sportswear fashion.

What is it about sport that makes such people as Peter Pocklington, Pat Bowlen, Charles Bronfman, and the late Harold Ballard want to spend their fortunes to "buy" a winning team? Why do cities like Victoria and Toronto wish to commit large amounts of public capital, most of which they will never recover, to stage world sporting events? Why do companies like Campbell Soup, Purolator Courier, McCain Foods, and Kodak use sport to sell their products? Why, in 1989, did

Brian Gavriloff, Edmonton Journal.

Jubilation at Edmonton's Northlands Coliseum.

Canadians spend close to $4.5 billion on sporting goods and another $3.7 billion to use golf courses, ice rinks, fitness clubs, and bowling alleys (Fennell and Jenish, 1990)?

We focus first on the business of amateur sport, examining the commodification of amateur athletes and how this has led some scholars to suggest that they should be considered employees of the state. We also examine the business of hosting amateur sports events and who gains from these events. Finally we look at state funding and how the state, in its efforts to increase funding for amateur sport, has turned to the private sector. Then we turn to the business of professional sport and consider how professional sport is structured to ensure owners' interests. We look at patterns of team ownership in Canada and at how capital is generated through ownership. We discuss as well who benefits and who loses from professional sport, and lastly we look at the business of gambling and its relationship with sport.

The growth and importance of the sporting goods industry in Canada are also examined, and we conclude the chapter with a discussion of the more recent commercialization of health and fitness. Our major purpose is to examine critically the ramifications and consequences of increasing links between business and sport at all levels.

THE BUSINESS OF AMATEUR SPORT

It may appear somewhat paradoxical to write about the business of amateur sport because amateur athletes are supposedly distinct from professional athletes. Professional athletes compete for teams like the Vancouver Canucks, the Saskatchewan Roughriders, and the Toronto Blue Jays, and they make increasingly large sums of money for being athletes. Amateurs, on the other hand, compete for their local clubs, perhaps for their province, and if they are very good, for their country in a major sports festival like the Olympic or Commonwealth Games. In contrast to professionals, amateur athletes compete not for money but for the love of their sport. Despite its Victorian origins, perhaps there is still an element of truth in this

idealistic notion of the dichotomy between amateurs and professionals because it still pervades much of our popular consciousness. It is important, however, to recognize the extent to which this distinction has become blurred, and how the interests of capital have infiltrated amateur sport, and how it, too, has become very much a business.

The Amateur Athlete as a Commodity

In Chapter 3, we saw how professional sport became increasingly commercialized and commodified throughout the first half of the twentieth century. The predominantly Protestant middle class that controlled sport rejected the ideology of professional sport because it was seen to debase play, to emphasize ends rather than means, to involve passion rather than restraint, and to encourage gambling, drinking, and frivolity. Those who controlled amateur sport maintained a strong ideological belief in the amateur ethos, which meant competing for the love of sport rather than for material gain. The direct and ongoing intervention of the Canadian state into sport, as discussed in Chapter 4, and the emergence of television (see Chapter 6) in mid-century challenged and eventually transformed this fading ideology.

State intervention, particularly the federal state's singular focus on high-performance sport, brought about major changes in many areas of the amateur sport delivery system. Once autonomous, voluntary, and largely self-regulating, amateur sport governing bodies have been transformed into professionally administered non-profit corporations, to a large extent funded and therefore controlled by the state. There have also been significant changes for the high-performance athletes. They must commit themselves full-time to training; there are fewer opportunities to pursue an education or a career at the same time; they must submit to the demands of a national sport organization; and they are less able to control the events that determine their lives. Top-level amateur athletes have, in other words, become increasingly professionalized.

Television has been a significant factor in increasing the visibility and profile of many sports. Corporations quickly realized that sport's mass appeal made sponsoring sports events and individual athletes a logical way to create product awareness. Sport organizations, on the other hand, readily embraced commercial support of their activities because they needed the additional revenue to operate, and the state endorsed it as a logical way to help these organizations achieve their high-performance goals. Indeed, the strong ties that developed between sport and television, along with other forms of commercial sponsorship, did bring financial benefits to a number of sport organizations and to some individual athletes. One estimate suggested that in 1987 Canadian corporations donated $272 million to amateur sport (Wayne, 1988). Another noted that Canadian companies spent $925 million on sports-related advertising, sponsoring events, and endorsing sports stars (Fennell and Jenish, 1990). Such companies as Petro-Canada, Esso, Sun Life, Campbell Soup, Centrum Vitamins, and Nutrasweet have been generous in their corporate support of Canadian sport organizations.

Top-class Canadian athletes have also benefited substantially from corporate sponsorship, increasingly so in recent years. As early as 1984, it was reported that skier Steve Podborski's earnings had probably made him a millionaire (Fisher, 1984). More recently, swimmer Alex Baumann has realized a similar financial status, and if it were not for that fateful urine sample in Seoul, Ben Johnson likely would have made over $10 million in revenue and endorsements (Fennell and Jenish, 1990), and since his return to competition in early 1991 he has certainly capitalized financially. Less well-known athletes, such as runners Art Boileau, Paul and Lynn Williams, diver Sylvie Bernier, and shooter Linda Thom, have been able through their athletic success to win prize money, negotiate endorsement contracts, and earn fees from speaking engagements or by appearing at events (cf. Hunter, 1984; Davidson, 1987).

Clearly, some organizations and individual athletes have done extremely well from lucrative corporate endorsements, sponsorship, and other ventures, but there is another less glamorous side to this story. The association of sport with commercial enterprise has resulted in the *commodification* of athletes. Commodification occurs when something is produced (i.e., an athletic performance) "not to satisfy the producer's needs but to be exchanged in the marketplace for other values (money)" (Rigauer, 1981: 67). Many top-level athletes no longer compete solely for their province or country. They also represent corporate Canada, and as such they become a source of profit, thus facing added pressures to perform. For athletes in sports of high international visibility, such as track and field and World Cup skiing, their corporate connections can become broadly international. As former national ski team coach Currie Chapman noted:

> . . . all of a sudden it's not just them [the athletes] going down the mountain, but it's also a bank, a drugstore, a car parts chain as well. Then comes the phone call or the telex and somewhere there is a little note that says politely 'we'd like to see some results for our money'. (Kidd, 1988a: 23)

The expectations placed on athletes by

Brian Gavriloff, Edmonton Journal.

Olympic silver pays off for Elizabeth Manley.

corporate sponsors, and by the state, have drastically changed the nature of being an athlete. Commercialization has transformed the creative, aesthetic, intrinsically rewarding, and playful qualities of sport, making it a more routinized, quantified, and work-like activity whose rewards are more material than intrinsic (cf. Brohm, 1978; Cantelon, 1981; Rigauer, 1981). As Kidd (1988b: 302) points out, the expectations of corporations and the state have "become so commanding that they, in effect, have blocked expression of older, humanistic, amateur based aspirations of Olympism and other values."

Increasing links between corporations and amateur sport have also tended to encourage uneven patterns of development across sports. High-profile sports and those where there is a mass market to sell equipment and clothing have generally been the ones able to attract corporate sponsors. Included in this list are figure skating, track and field, alpine skiing, and swimming. In contrast, sports such as judo, archery, biathlon, ski jumping, and field hockey have been comparatively less successful in securing corporate capital to assist their development. British sport sociologist John Hargreaves (1986) also suggests that sponsorship may produce uneven development within a sport because there is no guarantee of additional resources percolating down to the lower, grassroots levels.

Finally, in any consideration of the relative merits of commercialized amateur sport, two other points should be noted. First, corporations do not support sport for philanthropic reasons. Not only is sport a relatively cheap and easy way to place a product in front of millions of potential buyers, but money spent on sport or on sponsoring individual athletes can be claimed as a corporate tax deduction. It may also be that the company doing the sponsoring has personal ties to the sport. Ownership and management of the Calgary-based Spruce Meadows Equestrian facility by the Southern family, who also own Atco Industries, is a case in point, as their children are active equestrians. Corporations sponsoring major games and sporting events are often given the best tickets and receive other perks not generally available to the public. As Nelson (1988: 16) noted about the sponsors of the Calgary Olympic Games:

> They get the best hotel rooms. The chairman and chief executive of each corporate sponsor will also get the same white-glove treatment extended to visiting royalty, heads of state and the president of the International Olympic Committee. They will have 24-hour limousine service, access to elegant VIP facilities and

invitations to a swirl of restricted parties, where they can rub shoulders with the princes, dukes, barons and rajahs who run the feudal IOC.

Second, it is not true that large numbers of top-level Canadian amateur athletes are making vast sums of money from commercial sponsorship. A few very talented athletes in certain sports have been able to secure a relatively sound financial future, but as Beamish and Borowy (1988: 3) point out: "Only one in a hundred of Canada's national team athletes enjoys substantial endorsement and performance related income but for the other 99%, the story is a bleak one indeed." In fact, some 65 per cent of "carded" athletes receive no income from employment whatsoever, a situation that would place them below the poverty line were it not for the financial support of their families. The inescapable conclusion is that many high-performance Canadian athletes are underpaid professionals, and as we suggested in Chapter 4, they are no more than "sweat-suited philanthropists" who subsidize the careers of fully paid coaches, sports scientists, and bureaucrats.

The Amateur Athlete as Employee

Given the commodification of Canadian athletes and their highly visible role in state- and corporate-supported events, should they be regarded as employees and should their relationship with the state (specifically Sport Canada) be regarded as one of employees to an employer? The most vigorous argument for such status has come from sport sociologist Rob Beamish and his colleagues in the Sport Research Group at Queen's University, specifically in Q. What Do You Do For A Living? A. I'm An Athlete. Beamish and Jan Borowy (the latter a former national women's field hockey player) argue that athletes meet the requirements normally required to determine employee classification.

First, they argue that Sport Canada determines who will receive government funding (through the Athlete Assistance Program) and as such it has the power to select the workers. In addition, they argue the funding received is a "salary" for meeting performance criteria and selection standards. Through the signed agreement, which lays out rules about competition, training camps, and certain areas of an athlete's lifestyle, Sport Canada is able to control how an athlete's "work" is carried out. Sport Canada can also suspend or dismiss an athlete.

Second, no matter how well or poorly Sport Canada does financially over the fiscal year, it is not the AAP athletes who have to cover the loss, nor do they receive a dividend if there is a profit. Hence, AAP athletes can be considered employees because their financial relationship to their employer is not directly related to the employer's profit or loss status. Finally, Beamish and Borowy argue that Sport Canada is in the business of preparing national teams to represent the country, it builds and/or leases facilities and through the various national sport organizations co-ordinates their use in the development of national teams, and it pays athletes and coaches wages to carry out specific tasks. The athletes in this structure are "clearly working to carry out the business of the employer and do so under the guidance and supervision of superiors such as coaches, NSO officials and Sport Canada officials" (Beamish and Borowy, 1988: 86). They can, in fact, work for no other employer.

The implications of considering athletes as employees are threefold. First, it draws attention to the fact that being a top-class athlete is more than just a hobby or something done to improve fitness. It supports the arguments we have made earlier in this chapter that sport is a business and that athletes are employees in this particular business just as plumbers, carpenters, and electricians are employees in the construction business.

Second, the recognition of athletes as employees means that they "would automatically fall under the protections and rights associated with any one of several labour relations acts in Canada" (Beamish and Borowy, 1988: 88). Two specific rights are cited as being important. The first is the right to form collective bargaining units that can then enter into legal negotiations with the employer. Essentially this would mean that athletes could form a union to bargain collectively with their employer – Sport Canada – for higher salaries, better working conditions, a greater say in the conditions that affect them, and so forth. The second right is that, as employees, athletes could then be covered by employment standards legislation, which would give them protection regarding such areas as minimum wage, workers' compensation, maternity leave, pay equity, and disciplinary measures, including termination. These issues are also addressed by Kidd and Eberts (1982) in *Athletes' Rights in Canada.* As a result of their examination of a number of AAP agreements, which they suggest "bear a strong resemblance to contracts of employment," Kidd and Eberts make a number of recommendations to protect athletes from inappropriate disciplinary measures, including the rights to free speech, to the procedures of "natural justice," and to fair hearings.

The final implication of considering athletes as employees concerns specific protections for young athletes. In sports such as figure skating, swimming, and gymnastics, young athletes work "under conditions that are no less demanding than child workers faced in the nineteenth century" (Beamish and Borowy, 1988:

88). Cantelon (1981), for example, demonstrates how the age of international representatives in certain sports has decreased while the intensity of their training has increased. Given that there are no legal protections for these young athletes, the recognition that their status is that of an employee could help the development of legislation such as that developed for child actors and actresses.

The underlying rationale behind the work of sport activists like Beamish, Borowy, Kidd, and Cantelon is to help to bring about change. Recognition of the fact that amateur sport is now a business that involves large investments of capital, and that athletes are employees in this business, would enable athletes, like others in public service, to receive compensation at a level commensurate with the value they provide.

Hosting Amateur Sport Events

The changing economics of amateur sport have led to the state and private capital combining to host major sport festivals. In the last twenty-five years, Canada has played host to two Commonwealth Games festivals (with a third scheduled for 1994), two Olympic Games, one World University Games, and a host of world championships and major international events. Domestically, the Canada Games are held every two years, provinces stage their own games, and almost every sport has national and provincial championships. The holding of such festivals, particularly the international ones, is usually justified on the grounds that they generate tourist dollars, foster a sense of community pride, create jobs, promote greater interest in sport, leave a legacy of outstanding facilities, and provide many other admirable benefits to the local populace, the city, the province, and the country.

To gain the right to host a major sport festival, a city must compete with other potential sites. Each city wanting to host a particular event is required to prepare a bid, which is submitted to the governing body of the particular games involved, and these bids invariably involve considerable political activity and a substantial financial outlay. In the three years prior to the 1970 IOC meeting that decided the 1976 Olympic Games site, Montreal Mayor Jean Drapeau and his entourage travelled the world meeting with IOC delegates. More than half of the delegates were flown, all expenses paid, to Expo '67, where they were wined and dined. No details and costs were spared in attempting to secure the bid. As Auf der Maur (1976: 13) notes "an IOC delegate couldn't come to a meeting, his wife was ill – and presto, there would be a box of candy, a vase of flowers courtesy of Montreal and its Mayor." It is estimated that Calgary spent some $2.5 million to secure its bid for the 1988 Winter Olympics (Reasons, 1984). Again, officials from the organizing committee travelled millions of kilometres, and IOC members were provided with gifts and expense-paid trips to Calgary. More recently, there was considerable controversy in Toronto over the city's unsuccessful $15 million bid to win the 1996 Summer Olympics. The official bid book alone, a glossy heavy tome outlining in detail the city's plans for the Olympics, cost $700 a copy to produce (Polanyi, 1990). The costs of these bids are in part paid for out of public dollars, with all levels of government contributing substantially. For instance, the Ontario government contributed $3.2 million to the Toronto bid (Westell, 1990).

Once a bid has been secured, public monies are again used to stage the event and as such enhance the accumulation of private capital. In what is probably sport's most celebrated

Brian Gavriloff, Edmonton Journal.

Opening ceremony, Calgary Winter Olympics, 1988.

case of mismanagement, the Montreal Olympics cost that city's taxpayers over $1 billion. In fact, by the time the debt is finally paid off in 1995, Quebecers will have shelled out in excess of an estimated $3.5 billion, many times the original $124 million budget (Picard, 1990). Auf der Maur (1976) shows, however, that well-connected businessmen like Roland Desourdy, the principal contractor in the construction of the Olympic Stadium and the equestrian facilities, made large sums of money from the Games. In Calgary, Cana Construction was awarded the contract for the Saddle-dome concrete without tenders being called. The contract was also awarded on a cost-plus basis, which meant that there was no upper limit on spending; thus the original $4 million contract ended up costing twice that amount (Reasons, 1984). The Olympic downhill ski area at Mount Allen, not originally considered as a site by CODA (Calgary Olympic Development Association) and opposed by environmentalists and taxpayers, brought considerable benefits to private contractors and developers.

The financing of international sporting extravaganzas like the Olympic Games comes from a variety of sources, including broadcast rights, corporate sponsorships, Olympic coin and lottery revenues, ticket sales, and, of course, municipal, provincial, and federal government contributions. The final cost of the 1988 Winter Olympics in Calgary, for instance, was $522 million, of which the federal government contributed $225 million from what are described as "non-tax" revenues: $100 million in lottery revenues and the remainder from marketing Olympic coins and from the seigniorage on the new one-dollar coin introduced in 1987 (Dubin, 1990). The city of Calgary contributed more than $30 million to the Saddledome construction and the province of Alberta contributed more than $100 million to the facilities. The Calgary Olympic Organizing Committee, on the other hand, raised more than $500 million from television rights, sponsorship, ticket sales, and marketing. Similarly, those putting together the Toronto bid for the 1996 Summer Olympics expected that of the $2.52 billion total cost (only an estimate), substantial contributions would be made by all levels of government, not just in cash but in such essential support services as security, transportation, and immigration (Coutts and Polanyi, 1990).

One of the benefits often claimed for public money spent on staging major sports festivals is a legacy of outstanding sport facilities. Although this is certainly true for communities that have hosted, for example, the Canada Games, in reality many of these facilities are of most benefit to professional sport teams. Montreal's Olympic Stadium is now used by the Expos baseball team and was used by the now defunct Alouettes; Commonwealth Stadium in Edmonton is the home of the CFL's Eskimos; and the Olympic Saddledome is the home site for the Calgary Flames of the NHL. The cost of renting these and other similar facilities is usu-

ally so high that it prohibits "their use by elite amateur sport groups and more recreationally oriented community-based organizations" (Macintosh, Bedecki, and Franks, 1987: 166). Some of the most expensive facilities are often for sports that do not have a large participation base in Canada. The Olympic velodrome in Montreal, for example, is now closed, and the facilities built at Calgary's Olympic Park for the bobsled, luge, and ski-jumping events are unlikely to get substantive use by local sports participants. The shooting range and lawn bowling facility constructed for the 1978 Commonwealth Games in Edmonton now function as private clubs primarily servicing their own members (Chivers, 1976). This phenomenon of closing down or under-using facilities is not restricted to those built for international events. A speed-skating oval constructed for the 1975 Canada Winter Games in Lethbridge was ripped up a few years later.

However, as we noted earlier, many smaller communities have benefited from their legacy of facilities after a government-sponsored sporting event. Amenities such as swimming pools, although costly to construct, have provided training sites for elite athletes and developmental programs, and at the same time can offer a number of recreationally oriented community programs. Communities have also benefited from the upgrading of existing facilities such as gymnasia and running tracks, which are often used as training sites or competition venues. Sometimes equipment from games has remained within the community to benefit local groups. We would argue, however, that we do not need to spend vast sums of money to build the grandiose structures that have usually accompanied major games and that only benefit a small segment of the population. Auf der Maur (1976) suggests, for example, that Montreal could have saved more than $600 million with a more conservative building program, and Reasons (1984: 132) notes that the bid for the unique Olympic Saddledome was accepted "despite the fact that other builders offered much cheaper, yet functional coliseums."

The use of public funds to build grandiose and infrequently used facilities often diverts capital away from other, more broadly based civic projects. Kidd (1978: 54), for example, noted: "In Montreal, the colossal Games expenditures forced postponement of long overdue housing, environmental and public transportation projects and sharp reductions in social service budgets." Chivers (1976) highlighted the negative impact that the building of the Commonwealth Stadium would have on several Edmonton communities and the way of life of their residents. This indiscriminate use of public funds has often stimulated the formation of citizens' groups that have lobbied against expenditures on facilities and against the games themselves. Prior to the 1978 Commonwealth Games, a group called Action Edmonton lobbied city council in regard to the proposed site of the Commonwealth Stadium and the Commonwealth swimming complex. In Calgary, citizens formed HALT (Human Action to Limit Taxes) to stop public money being used to build the Saddledome (Reasons, 1984). Neither group received much attention from the organizing committee and neither was successful in its lobby. Most recently, in Toronto, strong opposition to the 1996 Olympic bid came from the Bread Not Circuses Coalition. Arguing that housing, inner-city poverty, unemployment, and environmental concerns were all far more worthy recipients of tax dollars, the group nevertheless was in the minority since apparently 79 per cent of Torontonians supported the bid (Globe and Mail, editorial, February 1, 1990: A6). It can be argued, however, that Bread Not Circuses was an effective lobby in this case, for

Toronto did not win its bid and the successful city, Atlanta, received no negative media attention from anti-bid interest groups.

Those who espouse the merits of hosting major games also point to benefits such as civic pride, international visibility, increased employment, and substantial tourist dollars. Concepts such as civic pride are intangible and hence hard to assess, but certainly the visibility of the host city increases during the games and for several years after. Increased employment resulting from games, however, tends to be relatively small and short-lived. Reasons (1984), for example, estimated that the Calgary Winter Olympics would provide jobs for about 1 to 1.5 per cent of that city's construction force for about three and a half years, and that the overall impact was 0.03 per cent over a six-year period. In terms of tourism, there are obvious benefits during the games to city businesses, primarily in the accommodation, restaurant, and entertainment sectors, and studies suggest that the impact on tourism tends to continue for about two to three years after the event (Board, 1989).

Undoubtedly the major beneficiaries of the games "business" are the members of the organizing committee (usually local politicians and influential businessmen), the developers who secure the contracts to build the major facilities, and of course the corporations who become "official" sponsors of the games. For example, so successful was their sponsorship of the 1988 Calgary Olympics that Petro-Canada, two years later, was still running its drinking glass promotion. Officials anticipated that by the time the promotion finished they will have sold 44 million tumblers – not bad for an oil company! Visa, which also put money into the Seoul Olympics, realized an increase of 18 per cent in the amount charged to its North American credit cards in the year following the games. Sales in the United States topped $10 billion in 1988 for the first time, a fact the company attributed in part to its sponsorship of the Calgary Olympics. Even local companies like Sun Ice and the White Ram Knitting Company viewed their games sponsorship as a springboard to new markets. Sun Ice's exposure at Calgary was in large part responsible for its 1988-89 sales reaching $24.5 million, up from $14.4 million two years earlier, and White Ram expected to expand its production capacity to twice its level prior to the Calgary Games. (Adams, 1989).

Despite the obvious costs to the public purse and the many voices of opposition, Canadian communities will continue to compete for the privilege of hosting sporting events, both relatively small domestic games or championships and extravaganzas like the Olympic Games. For many, it's the pride of showing that their community can do it and do it well; it's also an important form of civic boosterism; and it provides an infusion of capital and tourist dollars. As for the much larger multi-sport games, where there is often substantial community opposition, those promoting the event do so because they believe it will provide a lasting legacy of facilities and leadership, and that it will help to solve at least some of their city's social and environmental problems. Bruce Kidd (1990), former Olympian, sport historian, and activist, puts it this way:

> For most of my adult life, I have defined myself as a "critical supporter" of the Olympics. I make no apology for my belief that much needs to be changed if the Olympic Movement is fully to realize its promise. Some of the current trends in international sport are, indeed, troubling. But overall, when the complex calculation is done, I believe that the Olympic

project has been a plus for humankind. Despite the doomsday scenarios predicted for the most recent Games in Seoul, for example, the Olympic spotlight contributed to an internal process of democratization and an international spirit of dialogue and *glasnost*. I also believe that you don't give up on something important because it's gone wrong. Instead, you join others to work for change.

State Funding and the Privatization of Amateur Sport

As we saw in Chapter 4, the federal state first began funding amateur sport in a direct and ongoing way in 1961 with an original "investment" of $5 million per year. This has risen over the years, with fairly sharp increases in some years prior to each of the Olympic Games, to a current expenditure of more than $70 million per year, most of which goes to support amateur sport. Despite substantial state funding, this funding is not sufficient to realize the state's objectives, nor has it kept pace with the increasing financial requirements of national sport organizations. As a result, the state has turned to the private sector for increased financial support. The high visibility of sport and the tax savings that corporations realize have resulted in the state creating an organization to facilitate this process, namely, the Sport Marketing Council.

The Council originated from the federal government's failure to generate money for amateur sport through lotteries. The federal government originally entered the lottery business to help finance the Montreal Olympics. When the size of the Montreal debt became known, the government, unwilling to provide direct financial aid, created a new lottery corporation called Loto Canada. The monies were to be applied to the Montreal deficit and to any deficit arising from the 1978 Edmonton Commonwealth Games (82.5 per cent), to provincial governments in proportion to tickets sold (12.5 per cent), and to Sport Canada (5 per cent) to assist national programs (Barnes, 1988). However, the lottery fell victim to federal-provincial disputes, and when the federal Conservatives came to power in 1979 they fulfilled an election promise by turning the right to operate lotteries over to the provinces (see also the discussion about legalized gambling and amateur sport in Chapter 9). As Macintosh, Bedecki, and Franks (1987: 111) note:

> Because of the Clark government's action, the revenues from the sport lottery that the Liberal government had intended to use in part for additional funding for Sport Canada were diverted to the provinces. The decision was to have a greater impact on Sport Canada's budget than the federal government austerity program. It made more urgent the need to find private-sector support for elite sport.

Clark's minority government was short-lived. When the Liberals returned to power in 1980, the lottery concept was revised with the creation of Sport Select, which was based on baseball scores and created to help finance facilities for the 1988 Calgary Olympic Games. It lasted only one season, and failed because it was too complicated, had poor payouts, and was unable to compete with existing lotteries (G.J. Smith, 1987). When the Conservative government was returned to power in 1984, one of its first actions was to discontinue Sport Select, and Sports Minister Otto Jelinek began espousing the merits of corporate involvement in sport (cf. Fisher, 1985; Brooks, 1984). In fact, as Macintosh, Bedecki, and Franks (1987: 183)

note: "a 1985 statement from Jelinek called for national sport organizations to obtain 50 percent of their budget requirements from the private sector by 1988."

The vehicle to achieve this aim is the Sport Marketing Council. Its purpose is to ensure that "sport and fitness organizations package their properties (events, teams and programs) as viable, cost-effective additions or alternatives to the traditional advertising, sales promotion and communications media" (Grignon, 1989: 53). It seeks to bring sport organizations and corporate sponsors together to negotiate viable marketing deals. National sport organizations are encouraged to seek funding through Sport Canada's Marketing Support Program in order to compete effectively in the marketplace for the attention of the corporate sector. Funding is available for marketing preparation, marketing implementation, and customer support (Fitness and Amateur Sport, 1987). As Burstyn (1990: 48) comments, the language now used by Sport Canada signals a real change in amateur sport funding: "sport is 'product' and training is 'production'. In this universe, the 'technocratic, production-driven' development of sport is a welcome but still insufficient condition for sport's metamorphosis into a truly profitable corporate venture."

Such proposals to privatize sport are, as Burstyn suggests, problematic. They merely shift control from one master, the state, to another, the corporations. Consequently, instead of serving the interests of the state, some sport could become dominated by efforts to sell commodities. Such privatization "also runs counter to the original intent of Bill C-131, which was to provide sport and fitness opportunities for all Canadians, regardless of regional or economic differences. Depending on the private sector for support will . . . cause substantial inequalities in the ability of different sports to achieve sufficient funding for their endeavours" (Macintosh, Bedecki, and Franks, 1987: 184). Comments by Lou Lefaive, the president of the Sport Marketing Council, support this notion: "I think we're going to have to look at sports like archery, bobsled and luge, ski jumping, the esoteric sports (which cannot attract a sponsor) and say, should they survive at all?" (Kidd, 1988b: 23). Such statements serve to underscore the problems of privatization for a truly democratic sport where participation is equally available to all. As Macintosh, Bedecki, and Franks (1987: 184) note about privatization: "it runs counter to the social-welfare values that have become part of the fabric of Canadian life since World War II. [It] should be resisted by all those who see sport and recreation opportunities as a right, and not a privilege, of Canadians."

The extent to which amateur sport in Canada has actually become privatized is very difficult to assess. What is known, however, is that with encouragement and financial support from the federal government, national sport organizations are busily inventing "revenue generation" plans and hiring marketing co-ordinators to help them find corporate sponsors whose funding ranges from donating uniforms and equipment to sponsoring major international events.

THE BUSINESS OF PROFESSIONAL SPORT

In Chapter 3 we discussed the origins of professional sport in Canada, which can be traced back to the late nineteenth century. The growth of industrialization resulted in increased urbanization, and the relatively large groups of people who migrated to the growing urban centres constituted potential markets for entrepreneurs to stage sports events for profit. Improved transportation and communications both facilitated inter-city rivalries and before long professional teams and leagues were formed. Today professional sport is a multi-billion-dollar industry in Canada. The three major league team sports – hockey, football, and baseball – account for most of this industry; however, sports like golf, boxing, horse racing, tennis, curling, auto sports, and figure skating are all part of this huge financial complex.

In this section, we examine Canada's three most visible professional sports – hockey, football, and baseball. We look specifically at the manner in which professional sport is structured to ensure the accumulation of capital, the patterns of team ownership in these three sports, and the sources of revenue for team owners.

The Structure of Professional Sport

To ensure their ability to maximize the accumulation of capital, the owners of professional sport clubs have created appropriate structural conditions under which to operate. The conditions not only ensure profit maximization, they also help to guarantee the continuity of the owners in their financially advantaged position. As well, the structure limits opportunities for players to negotiate in an open market and makes it difficult to create rival leagues that could compete with the established organizations. It is to an examination of these structural arrangements that we now turn.

CORPORATIONS As sports teams began to enter into mutual financial agreements, it became advantageous for the owners of these teams to incorporate formally. Incorporation is merely a legal procedure whereby a sport team becomes a company just like the Hudson's Bay, Eaton's, or Ford. Corporate status protects team owners in several ways and at the same time allows them the opportunity for further capital accumulation. First, it ensures that the assets of the company are separate from the other assets of the owner(s). As such, team owners are personally protected against any liability for debt that the team may incur. Second, corporate status means that a team becomes a legal entity that can be bought and sold. Finally, corporate status allows owners to sell shares in their companies, if this is allowed by the league. Such a move can permit an owner to keep control of the team by retaining a majority of the shares and can pay him (and it is almost always a him), or more accurately his company, a management fee while providing a substantial infusion of cash. It can also allow an owner to realize capital through the payment of dividends and increased revenues as share prices rise. We have more to say about this when we talk about the revenue from professional sport franchises.

CARTELS Unlike most organizations in the corporate world, a professional sport team that becomes incorporated cannot exist on its own. Teams "are separate entities but are economically interdependent since each requires the presence of viable opponents in order to have an attractive product to sell" (Barnes, 1988: 104). Consequently, leagues are formed, and a natural extension of this is *cartelization*. The purpose of the cartel is to limit economic competition and divide up markets among the teams in the league, thus ensuring greater individual profitability. Each league usually has three types of mechanisms for these purposes, "one dealing with interteam competition for players, another with the location of league

franchises, and a third with the sales of broadcasting rights" (Noll, 1974: 2).

To limit competition among teams for graduating players (i.e., players leaving university or junior teams), all of the major sport leagues have instituted a draft system. The draft "operates by giving first claim on the best graduating player to the team finishing last during the previous season; selections in each draft round then continue in reverse order of league standing" (Barnes, 1988: 113). When a team drafts a player, it obtains the exclusive right to negotiate with that player for a set period of time, which varies by sport. The argument usually made to support this type of player restraint is that it ensures the survival of weaker clubs and creates a more balanced league. This survival, however, occurs at the expense of players by preventing them from selling their skills in a free market, by reducing salary costs for clubs, and by limiting player salaries. Equitable competition benefits the owners because a contest is only attractive for the paying public when the outcome is uncertain.

Cartels such as those created by the CFL, the NHL, and Major League Baseball also restrict competition by limiting the location of franchises, thus guaranteeing each team a viable market area. For example, under the CFL's constitution six of the eight members of the Board of Governors, each representing one of the league's eight clubs, must vote in favour for a new league member to be admitted or for a transfer of controlling interest in a franchise. If a club wishes to transfer outside of its established territory, six votes are also required, and for a franchise to be established in an existing team's franchise area a unanimous vote is required (*Canadian Football League Handbook*, 1989-90). The NHL and Major League Baseball have somewhat similar arrangements. The control exercised by existing owners over the granting of franchises is beneficial to these people because

> . . . it enhances the value of existing teams. This occurs because it reduces competition for fans; causes revenues from national broadcasting rights to be divided among fewer teams; allows the market price of both existing and expansion teams to be higher; preserves a few potentially lucrative franchise sites so that an existing team that begins to fail financially has an attractive alternative site; and, because of the threat of moving, gives a team additional bargaining power when negotiating stadium agreements or local broadcasting rights. (Noll, 1974b: 412)

The final way in which economic competition is restricted is through the sale of television broadcasting rights. By agreeing to let the league negotiate national broadcasting rights, team owners are able to eliminate competition among clubs, ensure higher fees for all their members, and help avoid the economic fluctuations that characterize professional sport. The limiting of franchise locations helps to ensure that owners have maximum leverage in negotiating the sale of local broadcasting rights, which can be highly lucrative.

MONOPOLIES Cartels have important effects on those who provide resources to them and those who buy their product because they introduce *monopoly* and *monopsony* into a product market that would otherwise experience some level of competition (Davis, 1974). Very simply, a monopoly exists when there is only one seller of a particular product, in our case professional hockey, baseball, or football. It is of course possible to argue that the NFL is an alternative to the CFL as a producer of football games, and in part this is reflected in the CFL's relatively weak

financial position. Monopolies are maintained by the conditions outlined in describing cartels; for instance, they control franchise locations and negotiate league broadcasting rights. Since they comprise a monopoly, owners of sports teams enjoy several economic advantages. Competition for facilities, parking, and food concessions is reduced; it allows them to influence the media as to how their sport is covered and thus how it will be marketed; it enables them to determine how long the season will be, the number of exhibition games played, the timing and longevity of training camps, and how post-season play is to be structured (Beamish, 1988). The effects of sport monopolies are threefold. First, spectators are affected because the lack of competition, in terms of the availability of similar sporting events, helps to keep ticket prices high. Second, it allows owners to demand high television broadcast fees because there are no other similar sporting events from which to choose. Finally, it affects players when they negotiate their salaries and contracts because there is only one league in which they can play (Beamish, 1988).

In recent years, there have been challenges to the monopolistic positions enjoyed by two of the major professional sport leagues operating in Canada, namely the CFL and the NHL. In 1974, John Bassett acquired the rights to a World Football League (WFL) franchise that was to be based in Toronto. To protect the CFL, Bill C-22 was introduced into the House of Commons on April 10, 1974, and defended as "a measure to protect national culture and unity" (Barnes, 1988: 29). Although the Bill passed first and second readings, it never became law because of the dissolution of the House in May. By the time the House reconvened, Bassett had withdrawn his proposal to place a WFL franchise in Toronto. On the other hand, a challenge to the NHL's monopoly position was more successful with the creation of the World Hockey Association (WHA) in 1972. Despite several attempts to stop NHL players from jumping leagues, the WHA succeeded in enticing a number of established players to join its teams. The new league survived for seven years but it was beset by financial problems. It folded in 1979 when the NHL accepted four WHA teams into its league, with each club being required to pay a $6 million entry fee. Most recently, an ambitious Global Hockey League is being proposed by a former owner of the Winnipeg Jets, with teams in North America and Europe to begin play in late 1991.

There is little doubt that there could be more professional sport franchises in Canada. Hamilton and Saskatoon could probably both support NHL teams and Vancouver could provide a home for a Major League Baseball franchise. However, the exorbitant fees to enter the leagues and the potential for diluting television revenues mitigate against such a possibility.

MONOPSONY   As well as creating monopoly conditions, cartels also create conditions of *monopsony*. Monopsony occurs when there is only one buyer for a product. For example, as a result of its position, the NHL is the only buyer of hockey players in North America and the draft system restricts a player to signing with only one team. It is of course possible to argue that there are opportunities for hockey players to play in Europe, that baseball players may secure employment in Japan, and that a few CFL players may eventually play in the NFL. For most players, however, these are not really viable alternatives. Under monopsony conditions players have less bargaining power than they would have if two buyers were competing for their services, and in such leagues there is evidence of player exploitation such as lower

salaries, inadequate benefits and pensions, and little player choice in where they play (Medoff, 1976; Scully, 1974). Alternatively, Jones and Walsh (1987) empirically demonstrate how the WHA was primarily responsible for salary increases in the NHL in the 1970s, when two leagues were competing for the same players. Such challenges to existing leagues are rare, and when they do arise, every attempt is made, as was the case with the WHA, by the other league to prevent their development or, if necessary, to take them over to restore the monopsony conditions that are obviously advantageous to owners.

THE RESERVE SYSTEM AND FREE AGENCY   The reserve system began in baseball, and its origins may be traced back to 1879 when National League owners in the United States informally agreed "to 'reserve' the rights of veteran players for particular teams and that no owner would 'tamper' with the players reserved for another team" (Beamish, 1988: 151). Formalized into player contracts in 1887, the system essentially bound a player to one team in perpetuity. In the early 1970s, the Major League Baseball Players' Association was able to negotiate improved salaries, pensions, and benefits, as well as to establish an impartial arbitration panel to help resolve contract disputes. In 1976, such an arbitration panel "undermined the reserve system by allowing pitchers Andy Messersmith of the Los Angeles Dodgers and Dave McNally of the Baltimore Orioles to become free agents after playing a season without having signed a contract" (Drahozal, 1986: 114). As a consequence of this decision, the players' association negotiated a deal that allowed six-year veterans to become free agents. However, a re-entry draft was introduced for these players and teams were allowed to negotiate with the players they chose. As Barnes (1988: 126) notes, "this regime contained clear vestiges of the reserve system but proved unsatisfactory to the clubs as an active free agent market increased players' salaries." Following a fifty-day players' strike in 1981, a Memorandum of Agreement was signed that changed the type of compensation that had to be paid to a team from which a free agent was signed. In the earlier 1976 agreement, a team that acquired a free agent only had to give up one amateur draft choice to the club from which it acquired the player. Under the 1981 agreement, the compensation received varied, depending on the calibre of the player who was lost, and also involved professional players. This system was terminated in 1985 and amateur players once again became the only type of compensation made for free agents. However, as Barnes (1988: 126) indicates: "the main restraint on free agents became clubs' concerted refusal to make any offer to players so long as their present club was interested in keeping them." This collusion was legally challenged by the players in 1987 and an arbitrator ruled that owners had, in fact, conspired to prevent free agency. The arbitrator's decision resulted in a number of players aquiring free agent status, and in the last few years this number has risen, as have players' salaries.

Until 1974, hockey players in the NHL were "employed under a standard player's contract which contained a perpetual reserve clause: movement between teams was possible only if management arranged trades" (Barnes, 1988: 169). Legal challenges to the reserve clause by the WHA resulted in all NHL contracts including the possibility of a one-year extension, after which a player may become a free agent. However, the current collective agreement requires compensation for most free agents. For example, a team signing a free agent who is making over $400,000 annually is required to compensate the club from which he was acquired with two first-round draft choices, both of whom must be in the top seven, in addition to $100,000. Such relatively stringent requirements serve to limit the movement of players between teams.

The CFL is somewhat different from the other two major sport leagues operating in Canada in that following the expiration of their contracts, players can play out an option year and if they are signed following their option year, there is no compensation to the club from which they were signed. Although such an arrangement appears to offer players a relatively free market situation in which to sell their skills, a salary cap of $3 million per team has essentially eliminated any opportunity for players to use such status to their financial benefit. Nonetheless, in 1990 the Ottawa Rough Riders broke the CFL's "gentlemen's agreement" by signing several free agents in order to improve the team's performance both on the field and at the box office.

Patterns of Team Ownership in Professional Sport in Canada

As we noted earlier, commercial sport in Canada began to emerge in the late nineteenth and early twentieth centuries. In these early years, ideological differences between the "promoters and fast-buck artists" who encouraged the commercialization of sport and those who clung to the Victorian ideology of amateurism caused a number of conflicts. The emergence of a corporate orientation to the promotion of sport in Canada can essentially be traced back to the formation of the NHL in 1917. Owners of NHL franchises soon came to understand that profit maximization could only be realized if they instituted the type of structural arrangements for their league that we have described earlier, specifically cartelization and its attendant conditions. In contrast, the CFL "developed more within the ambiguity of amateurism . . . and was in constant contact with university sport programs that maintained an amateur orientation" (Gruneau, 1983: 120). These two differing orientations have in many ways helped shape the patterns of team ownership that exist in professional sport in Canada today. Major League Baseball is a more recent phenomenon in Canada, and since there are only two Canadian-based teams, we do not address their ownership in this section.

The CFL, which did not begin to move toward a corporate orientation until the 1950s, still reflects vestiges of the amateur ethos. Reluctant to commit themselves totally to commercialization, five of the eight teams in the CFL are community owned. The Toronto Argonauts, recently sold by Harry Ornest to the California-based trio of L.A. Kings owner Bruce McNall, hockey star Wayne Gretzky, and entertainer John Candy, the Hamilton Tiger-Cats, owned by David Braley, and the B.C. Lions, owned by Murray Pezim, are privately owned. The community ownership of the remaining five teams in part reflects the difficulty of finding single owners willing to bear the costs, as well as the ideology of boosterism discussed in Chapter 2. This phenomenon of civic boosterism, with its emphasis on community spirit and pride, is in turn more compatible with the amateur ethos that long underpinned the development of football in Canada.

In contrast, the ownership of professional hockey teams in Canada is solely in private hands and as such reflects the corporate orientation that quickly developed with the formation of the NHL. Table 6 lists the owners of the seven Canadian NHL teams. For most of these owners, the controlling interest in a hockey team is, despite frequent assertions about their love of the game, clearly a business venture. Molson Companies Ltd., for example, has attached the Montreal Canadiens "to the most profitable division of the company for tax purposes; it was purchased by the brewing division and is now part of the Retail Merchandising Group which includes Beaver Lumber and Molstar Productions, the producer of Hockey Night in Canada" (Mills, 1990: 4). Molson also produces videos on the Canadiens and sells pennants, sweaters, banners, and other Canadiens' souvenirs through the fifteen stores in its merchandising subsidiary, Le Circle des Etoiles. The late Harold Ballard was even more direct about the purpose of his hockey club when, in his seventeen-minute-long 1985 annual general meeting, he was asked about his team's dismal performance on the ice. He commented: "our shares are all right and we're making money so what the hell do we care" (Mills, 1991). When Edmonton Oilers owner Peter Pocklington's Fidelity Trust collapsed in the early 1980s, and other parts of his business empire began to crumble, he used his hockey team to raise capital. By offering the franchise and players' contracts as security, Pocklington was able to borrow $31 million to reconstruct his food empire and consolidate some of his companies (Mills, 1990).

One anomaly in the corporate ownership of hockey in Canada is the Calgary Flames. Although privately owned, the owners of the Flames retain a low public profile. Team ownership is not motivated by the quest for personal profit; in fact, profits are channelled back into amateur sport. As such, the Flames' owners are not typical of the entrepreneurial capitalism that characterizes the ownership of hockey in Canada. Rather, they are more closely aligned with the logic of civic boosterism more typical of CFL ownership.

TABLE 6
Principal Owners of Canadian NHL Teams

Team	Principal Owner(s)
Quebec Nordiques	Five Quebec groups and individuals: the Quebec Federation of Labour; La Capitale; Marcel Aubut (the Nordiques' president) and Marcel Dutil; Daishowa, Inc; and Métro-Richelieu, Inc.
Montreal Canadiens	Molson Breweries
Toronto Maple Leafs	Harold Ballard*
Winnipeg Jets	Winnipeg Enterprise Corporation
Calgary Flames	Daryl and Byron Seaman, Harry Hotchkiss, Normie Kwong, and Sonia Scurfield
Edmonton Oilers	Peter Pocklington
Vancouver Canucks	Griffiths family

*As we write, the estate of the late Harold Ballard is being contested, and there is considerable speculation over the future of the Leafs.

Sources of Revenue from Owning a Professional Sport Franchise

As we pointed out earlier, one of the ways in which cartelization helps professional sport owners make money is by restricting the sale of broadcasting rights. The CFL, for example, operates an equalization scheme for television revenues: "The league is given the right to negotiate contracts for televising games; revenue received is divided equally among members" (Barnes, 1988: 162). Although the NHL divides network revenue among the twenty-one teams in the league, clubs still negotiate local broadcasting rights, which creates some degree of inequality among teams. Major League Baseball currently has a contract with CBS that ensures each team $17 million per season from 1990 to 1994. Baseball will also receive a further $480 million from ESPN, which will broadcast 175 games over the next four years (Fennell and Jenish, 1990). Individual baseball clubs also negotiate local broadcast rights.

Owners can generate considerable income from ticket sales and related revenues such as parking, concessions, and souvenirs. Their monopoly position allows them to set prices as high as they believe the market will bear (Beamish, 1988). For a team like the Montreal Canadiens, with an average revenue from ticket sales of just under $300,000 per game, a forty-game regular season means approximately $12 million in ticket sales (Enchin, 1989). In the new Toronto Sky-Dome, which houses the Blue Jays and Argonauts, private boxes rent for up to $225,000 annually. Each tenant also pays for installations and the decor, and must buy sixteen tickets for each of the Blue Jays' regular season games at a cost of approximately $23,000 (Gray, 1989). Several box holders are so enraged at exorbitant food prices that they have filed a suit against the Stadium Corporation of Ontario claiming "oppressive exploitation" (*Globe and Mail*, June 15, 1990: A3).

League expansion and league mergers also provide a further means of revenue for owners. In 1977, for instance, Labatt's Breweries, Howard Webster, and the Canadian Imperial Bank of Commerce paid $7 million for the Toronto Blue Jay franchise (Beamish, 1988). The Edmonton Oilers, Winnipeg Jets, Quebec Nordiques, and New England (now Hartford) Whalers each paid $6 million in 1979 to join the NHL when it absorbed the WHA. Not only do league mergers generate revenue for owners, they also restore the monopsonistic position of the league (in this case the NHL), thus helping to keep players' salaries down. In December, 1990, when Ottawa and Tampa proposals were accepted by the NHL, the price of a new NHL franchise was $45 million U.S.

Sports teams also provide owners with considerable opportunities to offset expenses through tax deductions. Players' salaries can be depreciated and thus a considerable portion of this cost can be recouped. Mills (1990: 11) suggests that this was part of Peter Pocklington's financial strategy in the sale of Wayne Gretzky for two players, three draft choices, and reportedly $15 million (U.S.) since he would become a free agent without compensation in 1992, or in Pocklington's words, "an asset worth zero in four years." There were also tax advantages in shedding a large contract that could no longer be depreciated for two smaller ones that could. In addition, owners can depreciate operating expenses such as equipment, stadium rentals, and travel, and as we noted earlier, losses incurred by the team can be used to offset profits in other areas of an owner's total business complex.

Financial gains also accrue to owners through the stock they hold in their teams. Beamish (1988), for example, shows how in 1981 the late Harold Ballard (then the majority shareholder in Maple Leaf Gardens Limited) realized revenue of $2.3 million when the corporation paid dividends of $3.85 per share. He goes on to show how an increase in individual share prices from $14 to $414 netted Ballard approximately $16.2 million in 1984. The increased value of franchises provides yet another means by which a sport team can generate capital for its owner. The value of the Montreal Canadiens, for example, has increased substantially since its founding in 1909 (see Table 3), and this increased value provides equity that owners use to leverage other business deals. Should an owner decide to sell a team, he would of course realize considerable capital from the sale.

The final way that owners generate capital through team ownership is less direct but nonetheless important. Some owners (Harold Ballard and Peter Pocklington are good examples) attain as much celebrity status as their players, or even more. Although it can work against an owner – for example, when Pocklington sold Gretzky there was a movement to boycott the Pocklington-owned Palm Dairies and Gainers meat products – it can also open corporate and political doors that in turn lead to the generation of capital.

Who Wins and Who Loses in Professional Sport?

For many young athletes, professional sport is seen as a lucrative and exciting career to which they can aspire. Whereas ownership of a professional sport franchise can certainly be a lucrative business, a playing career in professional sport may be neither as financially rewarding nor as viable as it is often portrayed in the popular media. Certainly for present and former Canadian athletes like Wayne Gretzky, Mark Messier, Mario Lemieux, Ferguson Jenkins, and Dave Barr, professional sport has provided financial security. However, for the vast majority of Canadian youth there is little chance of fame or fortune in professional sport.

We must also remember that opportunities in professional sport in Canada, and in most other countries, are almost entirely restricted to males. While such athletes as figure skater Elizabeth Manley, tennis player Helen Kelesi, and golfer Dawn Coe have been able to make money from their respective sports, they are exceptions. There are very few opportunities for female athletes to pursue a career in professional sport.

The opportunities for male athletes, while better than their female counterparts, are also limited. For example, few Canadians have played Major League Baseball, either in Canada or in the United States. The Blue Jays opened in 1991 with one Canadian on their roster, Denis Boucher of Quebec, and the Expos also have only one, B.C.'s Larry Walker. While the number of players who have "made it" in football is greater, few Canadians have been able to obtain positions in the NFL. For those who play football in the CFL, the salary cap imposed by the league ($3 million per team) helps keep player salaries low, the average being just over $54,000 in 1988. Even then, the "star" positions, and hence those that pay more, are often occupied by American imports (see Chapter 7). Hockey does provide one avenue where young Canadian males can aim for a career in professional sport. However, the NHL's failure to secure a major U.S. television network contract has kept the average player salary under $200,000, the lowest of the four major North American professional team sports. These relatively low salaries and the small number who make it to the professional ranks, coupled with average career length of less than five years, reduce the attractiveness of hockey as a career choice.

The increased pressures on professional athletes brought about by longer seasons, a greater concern with profit maximization, and litigation to control players have resulted in the suggestion that sport has become a form of alienated labour. As Beamish (1988) notes, this alienation has two dimensions. First, the increased control of sport by owners, managers, and coaches and the concern with the instrumental demands of profit have limited an athlete's opportunity to use sport as a means of creative activity that can lead to self-actualization. The second component of alienation concerns the way in which players find themselves actually creating the structures that work against them. As Beamish (1988: 156) explains:

> . . . the players are the show; they are the real producers, and the owners, with minimal risks, profit from the efforts of the players who risk their careers on every single play of the game.

> In terms of objective alienation, the players not only produce a product that they do not own, they also produce a product which returns high rates of profit, thus further reinforcing the owners' position of power and domination. The players are creating an objective set of structures that stand outside themselves and, in effect, oppose and ultimately control them as athletes.

While player unions such as the Canadian Football League Players' Association and the National Hockey League Players' Association have worked to improve the situation for athletes, such collective action has usually been met with resistance from the owners.

For fans, the growth of professional sport, both live and on television, offers a substantive choice of entertainment. Critics would contend, however, that along with this phenomenal growth has been a deterioration in the quality of the sporting spectacle. The quest for increased profits has led, for instance, to using violence to attract less knowledgeable fans, to referees avoiding penalty calls particularly in close games, to frequent trades and even the sale of whole franchises, and to specialized rules such as the "designated hitter" in the American Leagues, which removes the pitchers from the batting order and thus diminishes the importance of managerial strategy (Lasch, 1979). It can be argued that these changes and others remove the drama from sport and replace traditional values with crass commercialism, the net result of which is a spectacle driven by economics and profit rather than by creativity and athletic prowess (Sewart, 1987).

Sports Gambling in Canada

Sports gambling in the present context refers to wagers made on the outcome of sporting events. Sports betting occurs under a variety of circumstances: a friendly bet on an individual game, an office pool, a legal wager in a Nevada sportsbook, or a bet with an illegal bookmaker. The majority of sports bets are made with friends or acquaintances and involve relatively insignificant amounts of money. A smaller portion of the betting population wagers larger sums (usually a minimum of $100 per game in the larger Canadian cities) with illegal bookmakers (Smith, 1990).

The Canadian Criminal Code prohibits betting on a fight or a single sporting event.

The law is not intended to restrict bets between private parties unless one of the individuals is taking a percentage as a handling charge. The Canadian government's position legislates against bookmaking, not betting. At present, any Canadian province wanting to offer legalized sports betting is stymied, because doing so would require amending the federal Criminal Code (Smith, 1990).

The volume of illegal sports betting in Canada is estimated at $1 billion per year (Campbell, 1989). NFL games attract the most betting action, followed by U.S. college football, baseball, basketball, hockey, and Canadian pro football (Campbell, 1987; Downey, 1986). Surprisingly, indigenous sports like hockey and Canadian football are less appealing to Canadian sports bettors than the popular American sports. In the case of hockey, this may be because bettors prefer pools to team-versus-team bets. As for the CFL, the lack of league parity (the difference between the best and the worst teams in the league may be as high as thirty points) makes bookmakers reticent about taking bets since it is extremely difficult to establish realistic betting lines (Smith, 1990).

An explosion of interest in sports betting over the past two decades is the result of three main factors: (1) the gradual relaxation of community attitudes toward minor vices or so-called victimless crimes such as gambling; (2) the rapid and radical changes in professional sports leagues as evidenced by the formation of new leagues, league mergers, franchise relocations, and league expansions – the number of professional teams has increased, spreading from coast to coast and into Canada, giving virtually every region in North America a team to root for; and (3) the ever-expanding mass media coverage of sport, which provides live broadcasts, detailed statistics, injury reports, and even betting advice to keep gamblers well informed.

Legislators can respond to the issue of sports gambling in one of three ways: (1) prohibit the activity through the criminal justice system; (2) legalize the activity and regulate it through licensing laws; or (3) ignore this "political hot potato" by not implementing new legislation and not rigidly enforcing existing laws. Each of these courses of action results in a variety of social consequences (for a more detailed discussion of the pragmatic and moral arguments for and against sports gambling, see Smith, 1990). With the unqualified success of legalized sports gambling in Nevada, the institution of the Oregon sports lottery, and experiments with sports-based lotteries in western Canada, widespread sports betting in Canada seems inevitable, although perhaps not in the immediate future (see also the discussion in Chapter 9).

New legalized gambling proposals are invariably introduced to meet perceived economic needs. If a provincial government can avoid raising taxes, assist charities, fund worthy causes, or boost a faltering economy through gambling legislation, it is likely to do so. With the interest in horse racing declining in some regions over the past decade (Stock, 1990) and lottery sales stabilizing, sports gambling seems a plausible choice to fill the void. Once it is recognized that sports gambling could help meet government fiscal needs, the challenge will be to find a format that captures the public interest, treats the gamblers fairly, and generates cash for the government. Civil libertarians believe that sports gambling should be allowed simply for the pleasure it provides and for its entertainment value. They note that it is standard practice for gambling legislation to be bolstered by economic or anti-crime thinking, but as Abt, Smith, and Christiansen (1985: 207)

point out, "the argument that individuals have a right to wager on the outcome of these games has never been used to justify sports betting initiatives, even though this would appear to be a logical and forceful argument in a democracy that places a high value on the freedom of individual choice."

With only one jurisdiction (Nevada) in North America permitting head-to-head sports betting, it will be interesting to see if (and when) legalization occurs elsewhere. The most promising areas for legal sports gambling would be those experiencing economic duress combined with a young population base and a record of tolerance for gambling initiatives. In Canada, the four western provinces and the two territories meet these criteria. With their dependency on oil, farming, lumber, and fishing, they have all been affected by declining world prices. In addition, they all currently offer a variety of legalized gambling opportunities. Any proposal to have sports gambling approved would mean pressuring the federal government to amend the Criminal Code. Ordinarily this would be an onerous task, but if all four provinces and the two territories combine to lobby the federal government, it could happen.

What has been the response of the sports world to gambling? North American professional sports leagues adamantly disapprove of legal sports gambling, yet gambling stimulates interest in their product by helping to fill the stands and boost the television ratings. Whenever legal sports gambling proposals arise, league commissioners are quick to denounce them, claiming that public confidence would be undermined. They also assert that the unauthorized use of their copyrighted schedules and trademarks is illegal. If harsh words and the threat of legal action fail, there is always the possibility of coercion. For example, former

Baseball Commissioner Bowie Kuhn said that if the Canadian government went ahead with its baseball pool in 1984, Canadian cities would be excluded from future expansion plans. The NHL is currently suing the Western Canadian Lottery Foundation for using the results of games in a legal betting scheme called Sport Select. CFL and NFL games are also part of the Sport Select wagering package, but the CFL is in favour of this scheme largely because it realizes the promotional benefits to be gained. This is a rare case where a North American professional sports league has publicly endorsed a legal sports betting operation.

THE SPORTING GOODS INDUSTRY

Representing a wide variety of commodity goods ranging from athletic footwear to magazines to bubblegum cards, sporting goods is one of the largest and fastest growing industries in our country. While the names of Nike, Reebok, Cooper, and CCM are well known and well established as a part of the sporting goods industry, other companies not usually associated with this sector are trying to carve out a niche in this lucrative industry. Why is it that companies like Yamaha (golf carts and golf equipment, snowmobiles, and all-terrain vehicles), Timex (specialist sport watches), Provigo (primarily a food distribution company that also owns Sports Experts), and Bata (expanding from traditional footwear markets to athletic shoes) are diversifying their interests to also encompass sporting goods? The answer points to $70 billion per year, the approximate size of the sporting goods industry in North America (the Canadian market makes up about $4.5 billion of this total). Companies in this sector are highly competitive and innovative.

One strategy employed by sporting goods companies is to utilize "off shore" manufacturing plants. Many athletic shoes, for instance, are made in Korea. All of the major North American cycle companies except Huffy Corporation manufacture their products off shore. Through this strategy they are able to employ cheap, usually non-union labour, and ensure the best profit maximization for their product.

Another strategy is to promote goods through high-priced advertising campaigns that emphasize technological innovation (e.g., Reebok's The Pump versus Nike's Air Pressure) and exploit market segmentation by, for example, designing shoes for everything from basketball to windsurfing. The major athletic shoe companies spend over $40 million each per year on promoting their products. They also pay large sums of money to star athletes and other celebrities to act as spokespersons for their products. Nike, for example, has built its Air Jordan shoe (one of the leaders in the athletic shoe market) around the Chicago Bulls' Michael Jordan. Nike also received considerable publicity when Michael Keaton wore boots specially designed by Tinker Hatfield, their creative designer, in the 1989 movie *Batman*. Reebok, in addition to using well-known athletes, has also underwritten human rights concerts featuring such artists as Bruce Springsteen. Technological innovations are also important selling factors for a wide range of sporting goods: Brooks uses HydroFlow, Asics has gel, and Reebok has the Energy Return System. Bike manufacturers are using epoxy-glued aluminum frames and carbon fibre composites used in aircraft construction to build lighter yet strong and durable frames (Sweeney, 1986). Golf club manufacturers like Karsten are building clubs with square grooves on their faces to help control shots (Finch, 1989).

The success of sporting goods companies, particularly those in the footwear and athletic clothing industry, can also be attributed to a strategy designed to sell their goods as fashion rather than athletic wear. Estimates suggest that 80 per cent of athletic shoes are not sold to buyers who have any intention of using them for sport. The emphasis on fashion and the expansion in sporting activities have led manufacturers to a strategy of market segmentation where specifically styled products are designed for selected target markets. To illustrate, Nike now has thirty-four units, twenty-four of which are in footwear, each one designed for a specific sport – cheerleading and windsurfing shoes are among their latest entries into the market (Davies, 1990). Another example is L.A. Gear, one of North America's fastest-growing companies, which began by focusing on the 12-to-25-year-old "valley-girl" set to which it sold rhinestone-studded high-top basketball shoes in pink and white (*Financial World*, November, 1988:14). It is now attempting to capture a part of the men's basketball and running shoe market and has employed such star athletes as Hakeem Alajuwon and Joe Montana to help in its quest (Kerwin, 1989).

For today's young people, and some of the not so young, athletic wear is both fashion and status. Campaigns like Reebok's U.B.U. and Nike's "Just Do It" promote middle-class values of individualism and self-determination. Some have suggested that such promotions lead to the exploitation of the underclasses and to crime; in the U.S. the pressures to have sneakers and others sports apparel, particularly among young males, have been the cause of several homicides (Telander, 1990). Such incidents raise questions about the degree of social responsibility attached to advertising campaigns that have promoted products to the extent that they have the type of symbolic status some will kill for!

THE COMMERCIALIZATION OF HEALTH AND FITNESS

In 1977, *Maclean's* magazine reported that Canadians were in the midst of discovering a new fitness ethic. The article reported a phenomenal increase in YMCA memberships, the astonishing growth of racquet sports like tennis, squash, and racquetball, a revolution in the sporting goods industry, and the advent of corporate-sponsored employee fitness programs. "Fitness," proclaimed the author, "is its own best advertisement – and almost impossible to resist" (Steward, 1977). Over a decade later, the evidence is confusing as to whether the fitness boom continues unabated or is beginning to plateau. The most recent national survey on physical recreation habits, physical fitness, and health status confirmed that as a whole the Canadian population was more active in 1988 than in 1981 (Stephens and Craig, 1990). Important exceptions were young men and women age 20-24, and there was also a significant decrease in jogging. On the other hand, Shephard (1988) reported that admittedly small declines in sales of sports equipment, ownership of recreational equipment, use of national parks, and so forth all point toward a plateau or even a small decrease in interest in physical recreation.

Our collective conscience regarding fitness and health has certainly been altered in the last decade or so. We are no longer complacent about our various addictions – smoking, high-fat diets, and drinking – so that we are exercising regularly, smoking less, and eating more wisely. Not only are we inundated with news and commentary on lifestyle and health, there has been a remarkable commercialization of health and fitness:

> advertising has attached every conceivable product to the changing physical fashion. A cascade of speciality magazines and books flood the market. Almost every major national magazine and network have run features on one or another aspect of the health and fitness revolution. In short, "health" and "fitness" are being manufactured. (Crawford, 1984: 76)

Our various governments, presumably motivated by the escalating cost of health care, are now assiduously seeking new approaches for dealing with the health concerns of the future. One of these is the recent emphasis on "health promotion," which integrates ideas from several arenas – public health, health education, and public policy – and defines an approach that complements and strengthens the existing health care system (Epp, 1986). The Alberta government, for instance, has recently released its vision of future health care in that province (Hyndman, 1989). An important recommendation is that at least 1 per cent of the total health budget should be directed toward health promotion and illness/injury prevention, a not insignificant sum of $30 million. Health promotion advocates argue that there is a direct cost-benefit (both financial and social) for a relatively small proportion of medical spending through reduced demands for medical care, increased industrial productivity, and decreased absenteeism (Shephard, 1990).

Fitness and health promotion have now filtered down to the school and university physical education curricula. Health-related fitness is a major curriculum development in school physical education not only in Canada but also in Britain, Australia, and the United States (cf. Sparkes, 1989; Biddle, 1989; Colquhoun, 1989). Canadian universities have restructured their undergraduate physical education degree programs to provide a steady supply of graduates trained explicitly for the fitness, lifestyle, and health promotion marketplace. Indeed, some physical education faculties have undergone a name change to reflect their increasing involvement in health promotion, disease prevention, and quality-of-life issues. The University of Waterloo's Faculty of Human Kinetics and Leisure Studies, for example, is now the Faculty of Applied Health Sciences.

While there is nothing intrinsically wrong with this relatively new health and fitness consciousness and the movements that stem from it, the uncritical acceptance of state-sponsored programs and centres, and of curriculum changes throughout our educational systems, and the failure of the physical education profession to address how social inequalities affect fitness and health itself are problematic. Our critique is a cultural one that points to health and fitness as social rather than biological constructions that must be deconstructed at the level of ideology, just as we have exposed the ideological underpinnings of other cultural practices.

American political scientist Robert Crawford has introduced the term "healthism" to describe the new health and fitness consciousness:

> the preoccupation with personal health as a primary – often *the* primary – focus for the definition and achievement of well-being; a goal which is to be attained primarily through the modification of life styles, with or without therapeutic help. (Crawford, 1980: 368)

Although "healthists" certainly acknowledge that health problems often lie outside the individual, for example, in our polluted environment or in the North American high-fat, carbohydrate-loaded diet, solutions are seen to be *within individual choice.* The solution rests, in other words, "within the individual's determination to resist culture, advertising, institutional and environmental constraints, disease agents, or, simply, lazy or poor health habits." Although many groups and individuals comprise this new health consciousness, from the primarily private holistic health movement and self-help groups to publicly supported health professionals and programs, what Crawford argues is that the *ideology* of healthism is present in all of them, thus functioning as the *dominant* ideology.

To what exte\ t do individuals internalize this dominant ideology of healthism? In an ethnographic study, Crawford (1984) interviewed sixty adults in the Chicago area. Two contradictory, yet consistent, themes emerge: health as self-control and health as release. For some, health is a goal to be achieved through discipline, self-denial, and will power. Good health is accomplished through health-promoting behaviours such as exercise, weight reduction, abstinence from smoking, and healthy eating. For others, health cannot be achieved through controls or denials or self-discipline because they only interfere with the positive experience of enjoyment. Health, for those who see it as a release, is being able to do what you want, when you want to do it. These individuals resist changing their lifestyle, are critical of health promotion campaigns (e.g., Participaction), and are philosophical about the multiple threats to their personal well-being. Although health is not rejected as a value, it is repudiated as a goal to be achieved through instrumental action. Worrying about one's health will actually undermine one's sense of well-being; it may in fact induce illness; and it will certainly interfere with life's pleasures.

Why is this contradiction between control and release present in our society, sometimes in the same individuals? The first point, and we have made it before, is that ideologies are rarely consistent, and they often contain contradictory elements. Second, our capitalist economy requires continuously high levels of consumption and any attempt to reduce consumption through denial and self-control will be disastrous to those whose livelihood depends on the marketplace. Therefore, one must consume yet at the same time stay healthy. Crawford argues that exercise has become the most popular and visible attempt to resolve individually this tension between control and release. Finally, the new health and fitness conciousness is also an embodiment of this opposition because it emphasizes both control and release, pain and pleasure (i.e., "fitness *can* be fun!").

Critical observers have also argued that the individual pursuit of health and fitness is narcissistic and diversionary, and as an everyday practice it has become increasingly medicalized (Crawford, 1977, 1980; Colquhoun, 1989). Furthermore, wellness or well-being programs, clinics, conferences, and centres, all aimed at encouraging "positive" lifestyles among the Canadian population, are accused of shifting responsibility for good health onto the individual and therefore away from social and environmental concerns (see, for example, Harvey, 1983; Ingham, 1985; Sparks, 1990). Unhealthy "victims" are blamed for their own misfortune. Ronald Labonté (1983: 111) argues that while the new individualized concepts of health are not wrong, they are incomplete and "in their incompleteness sustain rather than confront the social forces that gave rise to ill health." In sum, the critics argue that the net effect of this healthism ideology is

to divert attention away from the hazards to health caused by industrial processes and environmental pollution. Attention is also diverted away from the inequalities that exist in relation to health in terms of social class, gender, and race. (Sparkes, 1989: 61)

The point is clear. If we accept that health and fitness are social and environmental issues, critics argue that we must re-evaluate the role of individual behaviour and lifestyle in determining people's health and fitness. The current emphasis on health promotion, imbued as it is with the ideology of individualism, provides little hope that this reassessment and questioning are about to take place.

SUMMARY: THE EFFECTS OF COMMERCIALIZATION

There is no question that the structure and practice of both "amateur" and professional sport are increasingly shaped by a market rationality. Even amateur sport is a business in the sense that athletes now represent corporate Canada as well as their country, and there are increasing links between corporations and amateur sport organizations for their mutual benefit. For some athletes, this gradual commodification has substantially changed the nature of being an athlete and the need to win takes precedence over everything else. Others, however, such as those in low-profile sports or unlikely candidates to attract sponsors, have hardly benefited at all from this increasing commercialization. Those in the marketplace (agents, sponsors, advertisers, corporations, etc.) in fact dictate their suitability to share in the profits.

Professional athletes, on the other hand, have become entertainers who generate revenues through their performances either for themselves or for their team owner. The issues of income and rights have become extremely important to professional athletes, particularly in team sports. Player associations and unions, which are relatively recent structures, now actively work on behalf of professional athletes to ensure a greater proportion of team profits, better working conditions, and a more secure future in the form of pensions. They now threaten to strike (and sometimes do) to gain what they want. Since the 1970s, the incomes of athletes in such sports as basketball, baseball, football, hockey, golf, and tennis have risen substantially although there is still tremendous variance between and within sports. Amateur athletes do not have access to organizations or unions that will bargain collectively for their rights. However, if amateur athletes in Canada were considered employees of the state, then they would have a greater say in and control over their careers and the conditions of their employment. It is unlikely this will happen until athletes themselves become much more involved than they are at present in the governance of amateur sport and specifically of their national sport organizations. The point is that as the control over the conditions of sport participation and competition moves further away from the athletes, the prospects for minimizing the negative effects of commercialization on sport become less likely (Coakley, 1990).

Commercialization has undoubtedly changed sport into a very unique business. Cities now compete to host major, international sporting events, arguing that the initial financial outlay, the costs of building and upgrading facilities, and the expenditures connected with the event itself will all be recouped through government subsidies, the sale of broadcasting rights, corporate sponsorship, and myriad revenue-producing schemes. Not only has the cost to the taxpayer been substantial when a Canadian city has hosted (or intends to host) a major event, but private businessmen and their companies have also benefited substantially. Municipal governments also subsidize the construction and operation of sports stadia used exclusively for professional sport, promising that a modern stadium will be good for the economic climate of the city, yet little heed is paid to the voices of concern who object to this use of public money. The original estimate for the Toronto Skydome was $150 million, but the final cost came to $532.2 million (Brunt, 1989b). American economists Robert Baade and Richard Dye (1988) question the economic development rationale for stadium subsidies, arguing that the most significant contribution of professional sports to a city is through intangibles such as becoming a focal point for group identification (see our discussion on this point in Chapter 2), rather than any direct economic benefit. For local taxpayers to approve a stadium and then sit back and wait for promised economic growth is, they suggest, naive public policy.

The commercialization of sport has also had an impact on private corporations, which see in sport a profitable way to enhance their image. Sports sponsorship is risky, however, because the rights fee may not be recouped by increased sales or the sponsor may not achieve the "right" image. For example, in 1980 Molson Breweries bought the Montreal Manic, a team in the now-extinct North American Soccer League. Molson was banking on the belief that soccer was the spectator sport of the future. In three years the average crowd plunged from 23,000 to 7,000, and league franchises that had been expected to bring $25 million were being given away by the time Molson got out in 1983, after having lost $10 million on the venture (Maynard, 1987). Air Canada's sponsorship of a 1982 Everest expedition was catastrophic. First the airline was criticized for spending lavishly on a sporting expedition when it was laying off employees and trimming flight schedules. Later, one Canadian mountaineer and three Sherpa guides perished on the climb. The resultant national media coverage associating Air Canada with a tragedy was exactly the opposite image from that which the corporation was hoping to portray. Nonetheless, despite these risks, corporate sponsors continue to seek out viable business opportunities in sport with one motive in mind: profit.

Where is all this heading? Will the corruption and dehumanization of sport that is a result of increasing commercialization and commodification ultimately lead to its destruction? There is really no answer to this question except insofar as cynical fans may begin to leave empty seats in the sports stadia. However, sociologist John Sewart (1987) suggests that by and large the sporting public is ignorant of alternative models of sport where the profit interests of owners, sponsors, and the media are different from what they are today. The public taste in sport, he argues, is shaped by the very commercial and corporate interests who need sport to make a profit; therefore, it is hardly surprising that people express a desire for what they get. The market should not in the end decide the fate of sport.

SUPPLEMENTARY READING

Much more has been written about the economics of professional sport than about the economics of amateur sport. For information on the latter, see Rob Beamish and Jan Borowy's Q. *What Do You Do For A Living? A. I'm An Athlete*, as well as their 1987 article "High performance athletes in Canada: From status to contract."

One of the best sources for specifically Canadian information about professional sport is John Barnes's *Sports and the Law in Canada*. Also useful is Rob Beamish's 1988 article, "The political economy of professional sport," which provides an excellent critical analysis of pro sports in North America, especially hockey. We also recommend David Mills's recent (1990, 1991) articles on the business of hockey in Canada. These can be complemented by Bruce Kidd's monograph, *The Political Economy of Sport*, which contains a good deal of useful historical material.

Finally, more general information about the structure of professional sport (especially employment practices) in North America can be found in Roger Noll's *Government and the Sports Business* and in the more recent *The Sports Industry and Collective Bargaining* by Paul Staudohar.

Chapter 6

MASS MEDIA AND IDEOLOGY

The figures are astronomical and startling. The television rights for the 1996 Olympic Games could fetch as much as $1.3 billion (U.S.). The American network NBC has already paid a record $401 million (U.S.) for the rights to broadcast the 1992 Olympics from Barcelona, Spain. There are fierce struggles among the U.S. networks and cable companies for the right to broadcast professional sports. In 1990, television contracts in the United States alone produced $180 million in revenues for professional basketball, $200 million for football, and $300 million for baseball. National Basketball Association officials estimate that the league's new television contract will raise the *average* player's salary to nearly $1 million by 1991. Without a major U.S. television net-

work contract, National Hockey League players have the lowest salaries (the average is $188,000) of the four major professional sports. Nonetheless, in 1989 Canadian corporations spent almost $925 million on sports-related advertising promotions, event sponsorship, and sports celebrity endorsements (their U.S. counterparts spent $10 billion). Pat Bowlen, an Edmonton businessman who owns the NFL's Denver Broncos, sums it all up neatly: "Leagues and teams could not exist without TV revenues. But where would television be without sports?" (*Maclean's*, April 9, 1990: 44).

What Bowlen is describing is the *economic nexus* that exists specifically between sport and television. A reciprocal relationship exists between sports promoters and mass media execu-

Brian Gavriloff, Edmonton Journal.

Press conference announcing the Wayne Gretzky trade. From left: Peter Pocklington, Gretzky, Glen Sather, Bruce McNall.

tives and advertisers that determines the amount and type of sports coverage conveyed to the public. These interlocking roles can be likened to the legs of a tripod, in that the removal of any one leg causes the whole structure to collapse. Each member's contribution is important, and each gains from the partnership.

Organized sport benefits from the mass media exposure and from the fees paid for the broadcast rights to their events. The mass media profit from this liaison by offering dramatic, unscripted programming that appeals to a wide audience. In addition to covering the live action, the media provide commentary on recently completed sports events. Print journalists especially emphasize detailed statistics, injury reports, trade rumours, rehashed strategy, and insider scuttlebutt. This after-the-fact analysis helps prime the audience for what to expect in upcoming events, and it keeps the sport newsworthy in between events. If sports writers and broadcasters carry out their roles properly, they provide advertisers with an opportunity to deliver their sales pitch to an attentive audience. Sponsors are willing to pay top dollar for commercial time on sports broadcasts and for advertisements in sports magazines because it is good business. They can reach a target audience of mostly well-to-do males in the 18-55 age range, who make buying decisions on varied items such as cars, beer, insurance, computers, and men's toiletries.

While all members of this triad can prosper if they perform as expected, each also assumes a risk. The onus is on the sports league to present a desirable product to consumers. This is done by arranging for the best athletes available to display their talents in suitable venues, under conditions that are intensely competitive. The hazard for a sports league comes if it fails to deliver a product that attracts sufficient consumers. This results in a reduction or possibly an elimination of broadcast revenues – a rather grim prospect, since most leagues depend on these funds for survival. Networks purchase the rights to sporting events because of the prestige and the possibility to advertise other shows. They may also purchase general rights in order to obtain the rights to high-profile plums like championships and all-star games. Once they have the broadcast rights, their primary role is to make the production of the event as entertaining as possible. This means employing skilled announcers and technicians, as well as orchestrating the event with as much pizzazz and excitement as they can muster. The jeopardy for television executives comes if they are unable to sell the advertising slots for more than they spent on the broadcast rights. Advertisers buy commercial time on sports broadcasts anticipating this exposure will be enough to stimulate sales volumes. This may not happen if too few people are watching, or if they are not connecting with the right target group.

Like most ventures in a capitalist society, this intricate three-way compact is motivated by a mutual desire for financial gain. Usually all three players can flourish by protecting and promoting each other's interests, often at the expense of the consumer. This is ironic because consumers could exercise ultimate control, either by not following the sports events or by not purchasing the advertised products. Gener-

ally, however, enough consumers seem content to be swept along in the tidal pull of the sport/mass media economic nexus.

There is, however, a good deal more to the relationship between sport and the mass media than the economic nexus we have just described. Newspapers, magazines, films, television, in fact all aspects of the mass media, are cultural forms and practices through which meaning is produced and reproduced in social life. They are, in other words, both a medium of communication as well as the specific outcome of a wide variety of historical and political struggles (Barthes, 1973). The modern mass media are the primary social institution for the communication of images, symbols, and meanings that are central to our society. We described in Chapter 2 how ideologies become imbedded in all cultural practices; so, too, have the mass media become a site of ideological struggle where dominant and oppositional groups articulate their respective interests and frames of reference for making sense of the world (Gruneau, 1989a). Therefore, just as certain meanings and values in sport (for example, striving for excellence) become dominant and established as common-sense, and alternative meanings (for example, playing for fun) become less and less important, so the mass media organize their representations of sporting events in a way that naturalizes some views of sport while marginalizing, trivializing, or ignoring others.

This chapter explains the relationship between the media and sport. First, we consider the role of the mass media in today's society. Next, we look historically at the relationship between sport and Canadian television, further explicating the economic nexus we described earlier. Third, we examine the major perspectives used currently to study the mass media and we explain why the critical challenge to more traditional research is slowly developing in sport/media studies. Fourth, the important ideological role of the media will be explained and developed. Then we examine and critique the actual construction of sports news through specific media practices. Finally, we focus on the media audience and examine both the indirect and long-term effects of mass-mediated sport.

WHAT ARE THE MASS MEDIA?

In Chapter 2 we introduced the notion of "mass culture" as those entertainment forms, including sport, that had developed with the growth of a mass market for leisure experiences. The mass media are part of this mass culture, and more specifically, according to Lorimer and McNulty (1987: 42-43, citing McQuail, 1983), consist of the following components:

(1) *a distinct set of activities* (creating media content)

(2) *involving particular technological configurations* (television, radio, videotex, newspapers, books)

(3) associated with *formally constituted institutions or media outlets* (systems, stations, publishing firms, and so on)

(4) acting according to *certain laws, rules, and understandings* (professional codes and practices, audience and societal expectations and habits)

(5) carried out by *persons occupying certain roles* (regulators, producers, distributors, advertisers, audience members)

(6) which, together, convey *information, entertainment, images, and symbols*

(7) to the *mass audience*.

In sum, the various components of the mass media create meanings, and in doing so they construct what we think of as "reality."

Based on television ratings, film attendance, and newspaper readership surveys, we can state with assurance that Canadians are avid consumers of mass media information. We tend to use the mass media for three main reasons: information, education, and entertainment. A sports follower may wish to be informed about the score of last night's game, what trades were made, or who is leading the league in scoring. He or she may want to be educated about the pros and cons of banning boxing, why the coach's strategy backfired, or how steroid use affects performance. Lastly, the individual may be seeking entertainment, because for many of us, mass media sports coverage is a source of excitement and stimulation that provides a momentary escape from a humdrum routine. You will recall our discussion in Chapter 2 about the attraction of sport, that it offers excitement in otherwise unexciting societies. The media bring this excitement to more people.

TELEVISION AND SPORT: A MATCH MADE IN HEAVEN

Radio was the primary vehicle for transmitting live sports events until the arrival of television. Radio sports programming was set back initially but has since made a strong recovery, finding its own niche in the sports journalism domain. In Canadian cities that have Major League Baseball, NHL, or CFL teams, a local radio station will broadcast the full schedule of games. In smaller communities the games of the most prominent local team are apt to be broadcast. Often this is a junior hockey team, or in some cases a university football or basketball team. The majority of radio stations provide regular sports updates to keep fans abreast of the latest scores, trades, hirings, and firings. In the larger Canadian cities at least one station features an open-line sports talk show. This format allows the avid fan to question the so-called experts, dispense their own praise or blame to someone in the athletic world, or just listen in to the banter, opinions, and gossip. These sports talk shows also help to sustain the interest in a sport between events, thus making the fan feel more like an insider than a consumer.

Television officially came to Canada in 1952 when the CBC established studios in Montreal and Toronto. Sport was a key element in the programming right from the beginning. The first live telecast of a sporting event was an NHL game from Montreal on October 11, 1952. In the early years of televised NHL coverage the games were not shown in their entirety, only the final few minutes of the second period and the third period. Despite the abridged presentation, NHL hockey soon became the CBC's top ranked show (Nattrass, 1988).

By 1957 the technology existed to allow coast-to-coast broadcasting of the Grey Cup. According to CBC sources, nearly five million Canadians watched the game. While professional hockey and football continued as the essentials of sports programming, boxing and wrestling matches drew sizable viewing audiences, as did telecasts of international sporting festivals. Highlights of the sports and television affiliation in the 1960s included the establishment of a second national network (CTV), the implementation of Canadian content requirements, and the appearance of colour television. Taken together, these developments served to increase the amount of sport shown on television and improved the quality of the telecasts.

The competition provided by the CTV network led to squabbles over the broadcast rights for CFL games. The bidding process enriched the league's coffers but created the possibility that the Grey Cup would not be seen by the widest possible audience. This was a concern to politicians, who constantly stressed the game's importance in strengthening East-West relations. Ultimately, political priorities prevailed and the public interest was served when an agreement was reached by CBC and CTV to share the Grey Cup coverage.

Once the public appetite for sporting events had been confirmed, the networks expanded their coverage to include sports such as figure skating, curling, and golf. Sports variety programs such as *Kaleidosport* and *Wide World of Sports* became standard weekend fare. Though popular, these variety shows were maligned for blurring the distinction between entertainment and sport. Sometimes legitimate sporting events were shown, but spuriously competitive activities such as parachuting, wrist wrestling, and even cheerleading contests often made up the bulk of the programming.

In the 1960s television assumed a different relationship with sport. No longer willing just to cover the games, networks sought to manipulate them. Formats, policies, and sporting traditions were changed solely for the convenience of television. Television moguls dictated game times, interrupted games for time-outs that neither team had called, and lobbied professional leagues to make rule changes that would stimulate viewer excitement. Goldlust (1987) claims that sporting authorities have been overly compliant to the demands of television, so much so that their autonomy has been surrendered. Referring back to our own "triad" analysis, professional sports leagues have become so dependent on television revenue that they make considerable efforts to ensure they get television exposure. Lesser known sports must accommodate the networks because they need the revenues offered by a television contract. The Canadian Interuniversity Athletic Union is an example of an amateur sporting body that over the years has changed cities, venues, and starting times for its championships at the risk of inconveniencing the athletes and alienating the live audience. From the fans' perspective, however, slight modifications in the format or the rules of the game are outweighed by the slick production routines that make sporting events a delight to watch. The use of advanced technical gadgetry such as slow motion, stop-action, split-screen, and instant replay capabilities, combined with strategically located cameras, usually give the television viewer the best seat in the house.

During the 1970s Canadian networks found sports programming a practical way to help meet government-stipulated Canadian content requirements. The CBC was attempting to meet a self-imposed goal of 80 per cent Canadian content and moved closer to this goal by televising more international sporting events, such as the Canada-U.S.S.R. hockey series, Olympics, and Commonwealth Games, and the games of the two Canadian Major League Baseball teams, the Montreal Expos and Toronto Blue Jays (Nattrass, 1988).

The technology of television sportscasts continued to advance in the seventies and eighties. Refinements were designed to improve the total packaging of the product and as a result were not as evident to the viewer. Experiments with sound were tried, such as putting microphones near the boards, or in the players' bench, in an attempt to capture some of the authentic chatter and clatter of hockey. Other modifications included using more cameras and trying different placements, using a camera to isolate a specific player, exploring new intermission formats, and developing the

means to show highlights from other events in progress.

In the past, certain prominent major sporting events have consistently drawn high ratings on Canadian television networks. The Grey Cup game, Stanley Cup playoff games, and major international sports competitions are always among the most watched programs of the year. To illustrate what is possible with a sporting event, the first Canada-U.S.S.R. hockey series in 1972 pulled in an audience of 16 million viewers, more than half of the country's population. In addition, the CBC used what is called an "appreciation index." This was a measure of the audience's degree of satisfaction with the telecast on a scale of 0-100. "The index of appreciation for the last game won in the final seconds of play by Canada, was 97 – an all time record high level of appreciation for any single broadcast" (Nattrass, 1988: 165).

Currently four television networks share the Canadian sports broadcasting market: the government-subsidized CBC, and the privately owned CTV, TSN, and Global outlets. TSN (The Sports Network) is a specialty cable channel that provides twenty-four-hour-a-day sports programming. Seen by market experts as a risky experiment when it started, TSN has carved out a significant viewing audience in just five years of operation to become the most profitable company in the John Labatt Ltd. empire. The numbers, in fact, are staggering: TSN reaches 5.5 million homes on basic cable with an annual income of $60 million from service fees alone; advertising brings in more than $20 million a year; the profit from all this is close to $20 million, or more than 20 per cent of revenue – literally, a money-making machine (Houston, 1990). To keep pace with TSN, the other networks have expanded their sports coverage. For example, in the spring of 1989 the CBC network televised NHL playoff games on twenty consecutive nights. Interrupting its prime-time viewing schedule did not hurt the bottom line, as the hockey games drew large audiences. The three major American networks ABC, CBS, and NBC) are also available to the majority of Canadian viewers through cable subscriptions. The variety of sporting fare they produce gives the sports fan additional viewing options and is a source of vigorous competition for the Canadian networks.

PERSPECTIVES ON THE MASS MEDIA AND SPORT

There are basically two perspectives on studying the mass media and, by implication, their relationship to any social institution, in this case sport. For the sake of simplicity, we label these the empirical tradition and the critical challenge (Wilson, 1986). The empirical tradition, which developed in North America and dominated work in this area until well into the 1960s, is characterized by an accumulation of research findings and was primarily preoccupied with the nature of media effects. Many large-scale audience surveys were conducted to study, for instance, the relationship between violence on television and in society or the amount of television consumption among children and their (in)ability to read. This research was much more within the social psychological tradition than it was sociological, and the focus was more on the individual than on relations between social groups. Studies on sport and the media were (and still are) greatly influenced by this tradition, focusing primarily on the dual impact of television on sport versus sport on television (cf. Smith and Blackman, 1978; Greendorfer, 1981; Rader, 1984; Chandler, 1988).

The critical challenge to the empirical tradition of media and communication studies originated in Europe in the 1960s. What differentiates these two approaches is the focus on *ideology* by those engaging in a critical perspective. Initially, a good deal of the work within this critical challenge centred on the implications of media owned by an economic elite. More recently and productively, the focus has switched to how ideologies become embedded in the media, and how the media organize their representations in a way that reflects the dominant ideologies of our culture. Is the production of a sports telecast, for example, a reshaping, a distortion, indeed a re-presentation of an event such that as an audience we can no longer sort out the real from the ideological? How, for instance, do the media portray sportswomen or racial minorities? Do they do so in a way that promotes sexual and racial discrimination, or do the media present "neutral" images, meanings, and values?

Both the empirical tradition and the critical challenge to this perspective are present in the current sociological work on the sport/media relationship. Indeed, there is some tension between the two approaches (see, for example, Wenner, 1989; Jackson and McPhail, 1989). The point we wish to stress here, however, is that the mass media exert a profound, and perhaps the most controlling, ideological influence in our society (Lorimer and McNulty, 1987). We turn now to a more detailed examination of the ideological role of the media.

THE IDEOLOGICAL ROLE OF THE MEDIA

We have already made the point that the media create definitions of reality and thereby help to shape our perceptions of the social world. These perceptions generally frame and legitimize existing social arrangements such as the relations between women and men, natives and non-natives, or visible minorities and whites. Like all cultural practices, the media have an ideological core or "set of assumptions, procedures, and rules of discourse that come to be taken-for-granted" (Gruneau, 1989a: 7-28). The purpose of this ideological core is to make certain claims to common sense or, in other words, to present a "naturalized" understanding of the social world, in this case the sporting world. For example, Richard Gruneau (1989a) argues that television's various representations of the Olympics present and naturalize sport as highly specialized, committed to record-setting, and dependent on the marketplace. The superbly fit bodies of athletes and the physical excellence they display narrow our understanding of what ordinary people really look like and can do. The associated advertising emphasizes the privatized consumption of sporting goods and commodities that signify "fun" and "sporting."

Gruneau also argues that the purpose of cultural criticism of the mass media is to "crack the codes" through which the media organize their (re)presentations of sport and make their particular claims to common sense. The purpose of this criticism, therefore, is to expose the ideological core of this particular cultural practice. Relatively few studies of this nature have examined the sport media, but the following themes are apparent in those that have: (1) sport is intentionally represented in a way that serves the economic and cultural interests of dominant social groups (i.e., economic elites, men, dominant ethnic groups); (2) certain narratives are emphasized at the expense of others, and the flow, tempo, and rhythm of a sports broadcast are orchestrated to produce a spectacle that will appeal to the widest possible audi-

ence; (3) at the same time, the sports package is presented in a seemingly unbiased manner, so that the consumers are reassured that what they saw was natural and authentic. We illustrate these general points with two specific examples.

Television and the (Re)Presentation of a Sporting Event

It is rather apparent that watching a sports event on television is not the same as viewing it in the stadium. Both the circumstances and what the viewer takes in are different. The home viewer is usually with family or friends in a familiar setting and is susceptible to real-life interventions such as a telephone call or an unexpected visitor. The fan at the stadium has a panoramic view – the athletes, the field itself, the other fans, the pyrotechnic scoreboard, whereas the television viewer is privy only to what the director of the telecast thinks is relevant. At a moment's notice the director can summon the technical wizardry to isolate on a specific player; split the screen so two different aspects of the game can be seen simultaneously; or replay the action in super slow motion so the viewer can see what really transpired. As Birrell and Loy (1979: 13) submit, the use of this technology "enhances the sport experience for the fan rather than diminishing it." While these techniques may stimulate and entertain the viewers, they also reshape the events and provide a very particular view of the proceedings. Gruneau, Whitson, and Cantelon (1988: 276) assert that:

What we see on television is always a representation of even "live" events, a representation which is constructed according to codes which highlight, and eventually naturalize, some themes and

Brian Gavriloff, Edmonton Journal.

The unrelenting media spotlight.

interpretations; meanwhile other possible readings (and questions) are made less available to the viewer.

The case is made that the production of a sports telecast, including the camera angles, the announcers' remarks, and even the content of the pre-game, post-game, and half-time shows, serves to support the prevailing ideology. In his penetrating analysis of the 1984 Olympic Games telecast, Alan Tomlinson (1989) provides examples of how the opening ceremonies were an extravaganza designed to depict mainstream white American culture. Tomlinson speaks of the thinly veiled political, historical, and cultural messages inherent in Ronald Reagan's patriotic address; the blatant commercialization of the torch relay; and how native Americans and Afro-Americans were treated as virtual non-entities. To critical minds the televised opening ceremonies were a Disneyesque paean to goodwill, fellowship, and world peace.

In his case study of the CBC coverage of a World Cup downhill ski race at Whistler Mountain in British Columbia, Gruneau (1989b) shows how specific production values and practices, such as the ways cameras are positioned to make the course look fast, shots composed to emphasize the individual skier, the language and type of questions used in interviews, although accepted as necessary to make "good" television, also create a sense of immediacy and mounting excitement. These practices, as well as others, are used to tell a story and to "make" a spectacle characterized by individual performance, human interest, competitive drama, uncertainty, and risk. From an ideological perspective, these kinds of sports entertainment treat the modern sports/media complex as natural, and as Gruneau (1989b: 152) points out, "they also figure indirectly in winning consent for a dominant social definition of sport ideally suited to a capitalist consumer culture."

Garry Whannel (1989) notes how television organizes our experience of a sporting event in the way that it selects and combines items, and in how music is used to evoke certain moods. The manipulation of these images and effects is designed primarily to heighten the entertainment value of the production. However, it is inevitable in this process that certain chosen cultural meanings are embraced and contradictory messages are downplayed. Therefore, team owners are praised for their benevolence to the community and not a whisper is heard about their shady business deals or their

inhumane treatment of employees. Stereotypically, male athletes are shown to epitomize toughness, overcome debilitating pain, and be imperturbable in defeat, whereas female athletes are seen as fragile creatures, unable to contain their emotions. These and other images from mass-mediated sport eventually become taken for granted as the way things are; they become, as we mentioned earlier, naturalized.

The effect on the audience of this mode of representation is often an unquestioned acceptance of the cultural meanings and myths that are set forth in the mass media sports coverage. Using Whannel's (1984) frame of reference, Cantelon and Gruneau (1988) provide some specific examples of how this process works. One way is in how content hierarchies emerge. Given the emphasis on male professional sports, it becomes difficult to resist the belief that male sports are superior to female sports, and that sports like hockey and football deserve the coverage they get. This is a concern that transcends national boundaries as Canadians are in danger of becoming an American cultural colony. James Davidson (1989) points out how millions of Canadians prefer to watch Americans play American sports. He suggests that we have been influenced by the media to accept the belief that American sports are more sophisticated, skilful, and entertaining products than our own (see also the discussion in Chapter 2). Ultimately our Canadian identity could be undermined if our sports heroes come from another country.

Another instance of how television sports coverage dovetails with our liberal ideology is its concentration on the individual (usually male) athlete as opposed to the team (Goldlust, 1987; Cantelon and Gruneau, 1988). Coaches of elite sports teams repeatedly stress the importance of players submerging their egos for the benefit of the group. In post-game analyses coaches remind us of the contributions of the "grinders" and "hogs in the trenches" whose dirty work allowed the superstars to excel. Sport communicators prefer to dwell on individual feats as they seek to compare and rank players against their own teammates, athletes on other teams, and players from previous eras.

Preferred cultural meanings are also conveyed by sports announcers, whose commentary is spiked with references to rationalism and professionalism (Goldlust, 1987). Media experts are quick to acclaim an athlete they regard as a "real pro" – someone who consistently performs to his or her utmost, never backs down from a challenge, and will do whatever it takes to win, either inside or outside the rules. Team Canada player Bobby Clarke, for example, was revered by the media for his never-say-die attitude. In one Canada-U.S.S.R. series game Clarke slashed Soviet star Valery Kharlamov on the ankle, putting him out for the series. Clarke's media image rose even higher when he admitted the slashing was deliberate; after all, he reasoned, something had to be done to slow him down.

This acceptance of rationalism in sports reporting is seen in the heavy reliance on statistics and in the use of mechanical metaphors to describe male athletic performance (Goldlust, 1987). Statistics supposedly endow the games with meaning for the fans and players because they accentuate exceptional performances, plus they connect past performances to the present and the future. So by quantifying every aspect of a sporting event, the media are creating an abstraction that permits another level of competition beyond the game itself. When Wayne Gretzky was in pursuit of Gordie Howe's NHL scoring record in the fall of 1989, he was trying to help his team win the game, but he was also vying to beat Howe's record. The media hoopla surrounding the record chase often overshad-

owed the games themselves. There is also a tendency for sports commentators to dehumanize male athletes, especially by comparing them to machines. Thus the consummate athlete produces consistently, is driven to seek perfection, has emotional control, and does not break down. When in the groove, the athlete is said to be "clicking on all cylinders." When a super effort is required the athlete is exhorted to "turn on the after-burners"; and when exhausted they are said to have "run out of gas."

In summary, the televised representation of sport has the effect of naturalizing the coverage and minimizing audience awareness of the mediating effect of television. As media studies scholar Garry Whannel (1984: 101) states: "Sport in representation constitutes ground on which ideological themes of nation, gender, class and competitive individualism are articulated in complex and contradictory fashion."

Gender and Sport Representation

Just as sport is a primary arena of ideological legitimation for male superiority, so, too, the media relay and represent many of the crucial features of this dominance. First is the matter of the disproportionate coverage allotted male as opposed to female athletes and sporting events. Second, there is the differential nature of this coverage, and third, there are the ideological messages and themes that frame this coverage and representation.

Females quickly discover that mass media sports coverage is not necessarily about them, although there has been some improvement in the last decade. Still, the actual figures are abysmally low: about 15 per cent of the space in North American newspapers, anywhere from 3 to 7 per cent of the stories in sports magazines, and less than 10 per cent of the television time allotted to sport are devoted to women's sport

(Hilliard, 1984; Rintala and Birrell, 1984; Messner, 1988). The meagre attention women's sports do receive from the mass media tends to be in individual sports like golf, tennis, figure skating, and gymnastics (Duncan and Hasbrook, 1988). These sports are approved for media representation because they display women athletes as suitably feminine, even graceful and beautiful, rather than tough and aggressive. Newspaper and magazine editors as well as network executives argue that they cover what the public wishes to read or see. Canadian males in fact watch more than twice as much sport on television as do females (Statistics Canada, 1988), but the argument is circular in that there is little incentive for women to watch what does not interest them. On the other hand, females purportedly accounted for over half of the viewing audience during the 1988 Winter Olympics in Calgary even though the specific coverage of women tended to emphasize the "aesthetic" (and therefore feminine) sports like figure skating (Coakley, 1990).

The increasing prominence of women's sport means that it is no longer quite so easy for these events and athletes to be marginalized by the media. Women athletes become trivialized when they are portrayed as sex objects and their attractiveness to males is stressed or, at the other end of the scale, when they are presented as sexual deviants whose skills are so exceptional that they must have masculine tendencies, or indeed be lesbians. The efforts and accomplishments of a woman athlete are also marginalized when she is, as Garry Whannel (1984: 105) puts it, "ideologically replaced back into domestic discourse as the woman who 'took time off from husband and the kids' to win an Olympic medal."

Sport sociologist Mary Duquin analysed advertisements appearing in various women's magazines to see how females were portrayed in layouts using a sport or physical activity motif. This research involved comparing the activity levels of the male and female models depicted in the advertisements, as well as an attempt to decipher the ideological messages contained in the advertisements. In summarizing her findings Duquin (1989: 105) noted that:

> Despite the current health and fitness movement, the great majority of ads still idealize women as passive, less powerful and less active than men. Women were seldom seen sporting, and when they were, the ads were rarely exempt from sexual innuendo.

Margaret Carlisle Duncan and Cynthia Hasbrook (1988) have done extensive textual analyses of how television represents male and female athletic events. Their main findings include an emphasis on team play in male sports versus a focus on the individual in women's team sport, and the discovery that male athletes were repeatedly praised for their physical prowess and their heady, perceptive plays, whereas for females there was an emphasis on describing their movement patterns in aesthetic terms, with nary a mention of their savvy or cleverness. The authors go on to note the marked contrast between the presentation of male and female athletes even when they are competing in the same event. In reviewing tapes of ABC's New York Marathon broadcast, for instance, the authors found that males received far more air time, some female competitors were treated as sex objects, there were more commercial breaks during the women's than the men's finish, and a conflicting view of the top women competitors was presented. Male commentators tended to describe women in a negative or prejudicial fashion as compared to the female broadcaster, whose remarks were mostly complimentary.

In a study of how active women (specifically aerobics and bodybuilding participants) are portrayed on television, Margaret MacNeill (1988) shows how camera angles and techniques, accompanying music, and commentary contribute to the sexualization of women's physical activities. She argues that the American television program *20 Minute Workout*, which at one point attracted a million and a half viewers across North America, was an attempt to "feminize" aerobics in the mass media by creating explicit sexual images: "cleavage" shots of women in low-cut leotards; fragmented shots of hips, thighs, buttocks; and the visual caressing of bodies through camera rotation. An analysis of *Sportsweekend*'s coverage of the Women's World Bodybuilding Championship shows how different camera coverage (e.g., direct rather than upwardly tilting angle shots) accentuates the physicality of bodybuilders rather than their sexuality, whereas it is the accompanying verbal commentary that helps reassure viewers that despite their muscularity, these women can still attract men. The point of this research is to show how televisual representations of active women often reaffirm (rather than challenge) traditional notions of femininity while intentionally obscuring images of female physicality.

Finally, what other ideological messages about gender are framed and encoded in the media representation of sport? One is that sport offers a prime site for the ideological construction of gender difference (Willis, 1982; Whannel, 1984). Earlier we discussed the rational need in sport for statistics, records, and measurement, which constantly offer a particular kind of evidence that reinforces common-sense logic: men perform better than women. The facts that in some sports women are literally catching up to men (see Dyer, 1982) and that the top women professional golf and tennis players would easily challenge a good many male professionals are quite often ignored. The strength of the ideology is that it forces people to make the comparison in the first place and establishes male performance as the yardstick for *all* sport, including women's (Whannel, 1984). The media reinforce this ideology by treating women's sporting accomplishments as not very newsworthy, or by perpetually comparing women's performances to those of men. There is, however, no getting around the fact that the major professional team sports (i.e., the "money" sports) are defined largely according to the most extreme possibilities of the male body (muscular bulk, height, weight, and explosive power used aggressively). If women chose to compete *with* men in these sports, not only would they be at a distinct disadvantage, but their performances would be compared to those of men (Messner, 1988).

Another ideological message related to gender is the unquestioned relationship between sport and masculinity. Whannel (1984) points out that many film representations of sport engage precisely with this relationship, and certainly do not challenge it. For example, in films like *Raging Bull* and *Chariots of Fire*, "femininity is inscribed as distinctly outside and separate from the sporting world, just as masculinity is intrinsically bound up with it." Also often unquestioned are the relationship between masculinity and violence in sport and how the media contribute to the construction of this relationship without ever challenging it (see also our discussion about sports violence later in this chapter, as well as in Chapter 9). For instance, in an interesting analysis of the media response to a specific, violent sporting encounter, Nancy Theberge shows how media accounts framed the event in such a way that a critique of violence never received a full airing. The episode in question was a game between the Canadian and Soviet teams at the 1987 World Junior Hockey Championship in Czechoslovakia, where a fight broke out that escalated into a bench-clearing brawl. Both teams were eventually suspended from the tournament. Rather than providing a critique and analysis of violence in hockey, the ensuing media coverage, with a few notable exceptions, "offered a powerful affirmation of both the 'naturalness' and legitimacy of violence as a masculine practice" (Theberge, 1989a: 254). The players were mostly exonerated for their behaviour ("they did what any red-blooded Canadian would have done"), and the incident was primarily framed as a technical failing that could have been prevented had certain individuals acted responsibly. As a result, argues Theberge, "the opportunity to initiate meaningful change in one of the cultural bases [i.e., sport] of hegemonic masculinity was lost" (p. 255).

We turn now to a brief discussion of how the sports media actually practise their craft. We do so to show how and why the representation of sport along the lines we have just discussed will not likely change very much in the future.

MEDIA PRACTICES

How do sports journalists actually do their job? What journalistic practices are central to the construction of sports news in particular? The purpose of this section is not to provide an in-depth examination of the Canadian sports journalism profession (see, for example, Smith, 1976; Smith and Valeriote, 1983; Garrison, 1989), but rather to examine some of the institutional practices and social relationships that are important to the construction of sports news and the representation of sporting events. Earlier we discussed the specific production practices of televised sport. Here we wish to focus more on the newspaper and magazine coverage of sport.

Before the days of television, sportswriters were mainly promoters for the teams and the players with whom they travelled. Rick Telander (1984), a senior writer for *Sports Illustrated*, tells how, in the pre-television era, sportswriters made heroes out of athletes by ignoring their private lives and reporting only their athletic exploits. Radio commentators simply reinforced these larger-than-life images. All this changed with television in the 1950s because the media could no longer just give the score and describe the action; people could see this for themselves, and the press was forced to take a different approach. Now the primary responsibility of the sports journalist was not only to report the results of sporting events but also to provide behind-the-scenes information on athletes, coaches, and teams, thus offering an insider's viewpoint that would help the reading public interpret the sports they saw on television. This new, more comprehensive coverage, focusing especially on the players and their lives, thereby created serious tensions in player-press relationships (Telander, 1984). Telander points out that players became increasingly less willing to talk to the press, until promoters and team owners, very aware of the necessity of the written media for marketing their "product," were forced either to fine the players who refused to talk to the media or to provide them with training sessions on how to handle the media articulately and effectively.

Moreover, television commentators and announcers, rather than sportswriters, now assumed the role of "promoter" for teams and their events. Indeed, many teams hire their own radio and television commentators, and at the same time provide them with certain guidelines for their broadcasts (Bain, 1990).

Announcers, for example, are requested to be as positive as possible by both the teams and the networks. Dave Hodge, CBC's *Hockey Night in Canada* moderator, was relieved of his duties when he criticized his own network on air for interrupting a game in progress and switching to a political convention. Again, in December, 1989, Hodge was banished by team owner Harold Ballard from announcing Toronto Maple Leafs' games on the Global television network because of his editorializing (Brunt, 1989c). Although Hodge was merely reporting the Leafs' record of ineptitude during the last decade, a matter of public record, he was replaced on the telecasts under the rights of the agreement that gives the hockey club a say in the choice of on-air personnel.

The big difference between a sportswriter and a television commentator is that the sportswriter's job is to provide information to a reading public, whereas the commentator's main role is to entertain a viewing audience and to "sell" sports events. Unlike pre-television days, sports reporters are no longer mere extensions of the teams and players they cover; they no longer depend on the teams for money and favours; and they cannot be bought as they were in the past (Koppett, 1981). In the modern world of sports journalism, they are supposed to be objective. Several factors, however, mitigate against complete objectivity and, sometimes, against good investigative reporting. Leonard Koppett (1981), a well-known and respected American sportswriter, points out that the judgement of many reporters is distorted by very subtle aspects of their jobs. For example, to be effective, it is essential that reporters maintain some distance from the people and events they cover. This is very difficult because, to get their stories, sportswriters must interact regularly with the athletes, coaches, and team management, who, as we pointed out earlier, wish to use the writers for publicity purposes. Furthermore, the close proximity of reporters and players makes it difficult for a journalist to be critical of an athlete one day and expect to interview him or her the next.

Finally, if and when sportswriters are assigned investigative reporting, they are unlikely to be able to probe topics in depth. Koppett argues that along with deadlines to meet and editors to please, they ultimately have to put their stories in forms that are "inescapably superficial." Another problem is that sports journalists generally do not have the sophistication and background to do justice to investigative, in-depth reporting on a wide range of issues. Few Canadian sportswriters have attended university, and fewer still have any professional training; they learn primarily on the job (Smith, 1976). Craig Neff (1987), a *Sports Illustrated* reporter, despite having a solid liberal arts education, tells of finding himself over his head in dealing with complicated off-the-field issues like environmental concerns, legal arguments, Korean politics, AIDS, and gambling. A problem specific to Canadian sports journalism is that often the better sportswriters are too busy covering the American World Series, the Super Bowl, or even baseball spring training to pay much attention to Canadian issues (Fisher, 1989a). A notable exception was the coverage and editorial comment in Canadian newspapers allotted to the Ben Johnson "affair" and subsequent inquiry into the use of drugs and banned practices.

We conclude this section with a brief comment about some of the media practices that make it difficult for women's sport to receive fair and adequate coverage. In their study of a typical (American) newspaper sports department, sport sociologists Nancy Theberge and Alan Cronk (1986) came to the conclusion that this unequal coverage was due primarily to four factors. First, there is simply more standardized information available to reporters about men's sports events because it comes regularly over the wire services, supplied by sports information directors and others employed by men's teams to generate publicity. Second, men's sport has traditionally been defined as "news," and sports reporters automatically cover men's sports as part of their assigned beats. Women's sports, on the other hand, are more likely to be treated as "soft news" or as special-interest events, and sportswriters may or may not cover them, depending on their time and interest. Third, virtually all sportswriters are men, and those who do the hiring (usually the sports editors) are men. However, simply increasing the number of women in sports journalism will not necessarily eliminate sexism in the sports news. Female sportswriters would have to approach their stories differently, and work in different ways from men, which would be extremely difficult given male journalists' beliefs about the makeup of sports news and the practices they follow to uncover this news. Finally, since a good deal of women's sport is neither professional nor elite, both of which are the major focus of any newspaper sports section, it is no wonder it is covered so inadequately. For instance, through a content analysis of two major Canadian newspapers (Toronto's *Star* and Montreal's *La Presse*), Gelinas and Theberge (1986) show how disproportionate the coverage of recreational physical activity is compared to elite and professional sport. Although infrequent, both papers did a good job of providing information and instruction on participation in physical activity, but neither provided much coverage of sport among underrepresented groups such as women, blue-collar workers, the disabled, and the aged.

MEDIA EFFECTS

There is a widely held belief that the mass media are influential, powerful, and persuasive. Age-group coaches, for example, bemoan the fact that the media promote violence and glorify harmful attitudes like winning at all costs. Do the mass media really have the power to change attitudes, opinions, and behaviours? Despite volumes of research on mass media effects, there are few clear-cut answers. What researchers generally agree on is: (1) the media message does not influence the audience uniformly; (2) the effects of the media are difficult to gauge; and (3) media effects are understood to be subtle, indirect, and not immediately recognizable.

The Indirect Effects of Mass-Mediated Sport

Two examples of the roundabout way the media can be influential are identified by Wilson (1986) under the rubrics of "agenda setting" and "the spiral of silence." Agenda setting, in the context of mass media sport, refers to the way sporting news and issues are brought to the public. The implication is that the media can mould public opinion simply by how the information is treated. To illustrate, regular viewers of a nightly five-minute sportscast soon discern that some sports get far more attention than others, both in terms of time allotment and in their order of appearance. Sooner or later the emphasis on male professional team sports and its ultra-competitive ethos becomes unquestioned and is seen as part of a natural state of affairs.

The spiral of silence is based on two interrelated assumptions, that individuals are reluctant to express unpopular beliefs and that individuals ascertain the popularity of public opinions via their use of the mass media. Presumably, if people think they hold the majority view they will not be shy about voicing an opinion, but if they perceive they are in the minority they will likely remain silent. Eventually this media-aided spiralling process results in one opinion being dominant. This process mutes dissenting viewpoints and has the potential to turn popular opinion into a self-fulfilling prophecy. Examples of media-supported opinions that may have become entrenched are: a city is second rate unless it has a domed stadium; fighting in hockey is acceptable because it acts as a safety valve that helps to prevent more malicious forms of violence. We turn now to this second example because of its prominence in the Canadian sport media.

Long-term Effects: The Example of Sports Violence

Most mass media impact studies in the sports realm have dealt with the problem of violence. It seems there are four possible effects of mass-mediated sports violence: (1) it has no discernible impact; (2) it acts as a catharsis; (3) it reinforces violent behaviour; and (4) it causes or creates violent behaviour. Of these four outcomes, the weight of the evidence suggests that being exposed to sports violence in the mass media is not cathartic, nor does it normally cause the viewer to be violent. Viewing sports violence may, however, reinforce patterns of violent behaviour in individuals who are already prone to violence.

Numerous laboratory studies have shown that when subjects view a film or television program depicting violence, they are apt to display a similar kind of behaviour if given the opportunity. Whether this modelling behaviour occurs, however, is dependent on a host of critical factors. Some of these include whether or not the violent act was novel, whether it was realistically presented, whether the person who perpetrated the violence was rewarded, and whether the subjects had been angered (Smith, 1983; Russell et al., 1989). The validity of laboratory studies on this topic has always been suspect because, first, we do not know if the conditions that apply in this artificial setting will transfer to real life, and second, the laboratory studies deal with immediate effects, whereas in everyday life the chance to respond aggressively to a stimulus is not as readily available. Despite the fact that violence in the media does not seem to induce hostile behaviour in the viewer, it does not rule out the possibility of a few individuals copying violent acts they have seen in a sporting event.

Media sports violence comes in many forms, including, for example, the explicit, within-the-rules mayhem of a kick-boxing match; the illegal but expedient antics of Philadelphia Flyers' goalie Ron Hextall using his stick as a weapon; and the psychological aggression of tennis pro John McEnroe tongue-lashing an official. Ostensibly, the media persist in spotlighting sports violence because it has entertainment value. A study by Bryant et al. (1981) revealed that the enjoyment of watching a football telecast increased in accord with the amount of brutality and violence in the game. Also affecting viewer gratification was the type of commentary accompanying the action. If the announcers stressed items such as how rough the action was, how bitter the rivalry was, or how important the game was, viewer enjoyment was enhanced (Bryant et al., 1982). One would surmise there is a limit to how far this line of reasoning could be extended. Highly aggressive play featuring contact and combat seems acceptable to the public as long as serious injury does not occur regularly.

An important point to consider in this discussion is whether the media cover sports violence as a newsworthy item or whether they deliberately promote it to attract viewers and readers. Several authors suggest the latter as they pinpoint various ways that the media exploit sports violence (Young and Smith, 1989; Bryant and Zillman, 1983). Examples of how this is done include the use of melodramatic headlines; articles on violent teams or athletes that show them in a favourable light; and violent action in the video clips used to promote upcoming games. At the very least, by condoning the actions of the perpetrators, the media are endorsing the violence (see also our previous discussion about violence and masculinity).

Summary

There has been a dual focus to this chapter. On the one hand, we have described and explained the complex economic nexus comprising the sports promoters, mass media executives, and advertisers. We have seen how each component benefits from the other so that today television could not exist without sport, nor could commercialized sport as we know it today exist without television. On the other hand, broadcast codes and production practices always re-present a sporting event so as to naturalize certain values and meanings, at the same time making alternative values and meanings less available to the viewer. Presented in this way, however, both the sport/media economic complex and the re-presentations of televised sporting events seem overly deterministic, and neither really acknowledges the possibility of an active, thinking viewer.

There are two primary approaches to studying the mass media. The empirical tradition with its focus on media effects has been most influential in North American research, whereas European research has produced a critical perspective that recognizes the importance of decoding the ideological significance of media messages. We have seen that these two approaches are also represented in studies of the mass media and sport, with the critical perspective more prevalent in studies conducted in Britain and Canada than in those carried out by American researchers. It is, however, a little more complicated than we have suggested here.

First, the empirical tradition has moved beyond the old-style audience surveys, with their monolithic conception of "the viewer" and simple-minded notion of "effects" on a passive viewer, to a much more active conception of the audience. Research on viewers' "uses and gratifications" is now in vogue. The theory behind this research is that viewers use the media, among other resources in their environment, to achieve their goals and to satisfy certain needs (cf. Blumler and Katz, 1974; Rosengren, Wenner, and Palmgreen, 1985). Here the audience (or individual viewer) is seen as active and able to choose among media experiences to satisfy personal desires (for suspense, or romance, or laughs). Viewers are also seen as active and sometimes sceptical "readers" of what programmers and advertisers present us with rather than being the passive recipients of encoded messages. For instance, a study by Gantz (1981) investigated the motives among university students, as well as their experiences and feelings, when viewing televised sports. The students' motives of "thrill in victory" and "letting loose" were accompanied by feelings of nervousness, excitement, anger, and happiness.

Second, the European critical tradition of media research has also readjusted its focus over the years. Central to this research is the notion that the media (especially television) construct ideological messages. The focus of these studies has been primarily on the "text" (i.e., the encoded messages) of specific television productions. Now, however, there is a greater recognition that the social relations within which viewing takes place have to be brought more directly into focus if the audience's choices of, and responses to, their viewing are properly to be understood (Morley, 1986). Television viewing, for instance, is seen as less isolated and more social, whether we do our viewing with friends or with family members. Therefore, the activity of "watching television" has to be understood, analysed, and explained in terms of the particular setting and social relationships in which it takes place. David Morley's (1986) study of this activity within different types of families (e.g., unemployed, single-parent, middle-class, wealthy) is a good example of this research. He found, for instance, that gender was directly related to power and control over program choice, program preferences, viewing style, planned and unplanned viewing, and television-related talk, regardless of the family situation.

The difference between this sort of critical research and the "uses and gratifica-tion" research is that the former challenges the assumption that viewers can always make a rational choice about their television viewing when, in fact, everyday domestic and social settings influence our viewing habits, and often our responses to what we do view. The notion of individual choice, which is assumed in "uses and gratifications" research, is qualified by the assumption that these choices are typically made in social situations (i.e., the individual is not "autonomous") and that what we are likely to want and choose is likely to be a product of our particular life experience (as an educated woman, for example, or as a blue-collar worker). At this point we can only suggest a few examples of research projects along these lines about watching televised sport because none has been conducted. Ethnographic studies are needed, for instance, of men watching televised sport with other men; of the place of watching televised sports within different family settings; and of how different members of a family offer critical commentary on broadcast codes (e.g., how women are portrayed, display of violence) in sports programming.

Finally, it is important to remember the context of North American commercial television in which all sports programming must compete for a mass audience. This competition, where enormous sums of money are at stake, places an inexorable pressure on media executives, especially television producers and directors, to produce enjoyable entertainment. Those involved in sports programming must strive to make it as exciting and full of drama as possible in order to enhance its entertainment value. They must, in other words, make spectacle.

SUPPLEMENTARY READING

A good book to begin with is John Goldlust's *Playing for Keeps: Sport, the Media and Society*, particularly Chapters 3 to 6, where he traces the history and issues that develop from the relationship of sport and television in the United States, Canada, Britain, and Australia. This can be complemented by several of the articles in *The Olympic Movement and the Mass Media*, a compilation of papers given at an international conference held at the University of Calgary in 1987 (see especially the articles by Alan Tomlinson, Garry Whannel, and Richard Gruneau).

A useful and recent reader is *Media, Sports, & Society*, edited by Lawrence Wenner. See especially the introductory essay by Wenner and articles by Sut Jhally and Richard Gruneau. Finally, for good overviews of a "critical" approach to sports television and especially the unique characteristics of television as a medium for the production of culture, see "Method and media: Studying the sports television discourse" by Richard Gruneau, David Whitson, and Hart Cantelon (1988) and Cantelon and Gruneau's (1988) "The production of sport for television."

Chapter 7

SOCIAL INEQUALITY AND CONFLICT

We live in a country of incredible wealth and plenty. Many of us enjoy the "good life" – good education, potential for a rewarding job, nice home, regular vacations, and eventually we can ensure that our children and grandchildren have much the same, perhaps more. Paradoxically, we also live in a country where a quarter of the population lives below the poverty line, less than 2 per cent earn nearly one-third of the total income, aboriginal peoples exist largely outside the labour force and educational institutions, and systematic differences in access to power and privilege exist between groups such as Anglophones and Francophones, men and women (Marchak, 1988). Inequality is a fact of life, something most of us take for granted in a country that offers so much. If we do recognize inequality, it is often attributed to individual differences – "he's not very smart; she comes from a poor family; he's native; she's an immigrant" – or, we accept that imperfections in our system have something to do with history and leave it at that.

Sociologically, *social inequality* is an important focus of study. It is concerned with the unequal ordering of society along dimensions such as class, gender, race, ethnicity, age, or region. Sociologists are interested in explaining inequality as a structural feature of societies rather than as a character or attribute of a person or groups of people. We want to distinguish here between a psychological approach to inequality, which attributes it to characteristics of individuals, and an approach that focus-

Alberta Northern Lights.

Wheelchair basketball – increasing access to sport.

es on how social structures serve to reproduce patterns of inequality. By social structures we do not mean concrete institutions like sport or education, but rather patterns of *relations* between people that extend across a great many institutions and, in doing so, effectively structure the lives of individuals. We will focus our attention in this chapter on class relations (between rich and poor), gender relations (between men and women), and ethnic and race relations. We do so partly because they are standard sociological categories but more importantly because they are categories that structure virtually everything we do. We are poor or wealthy, male or female, white or black or native, in every relationship we enter into, and what we are constructs how others treat us in every circumstance. Before analysing these

structural inequalities, however, we need to introduce some basic data to illustrate that participation in sport is not evenly distributed among Canadians.

WHO PARTICIPATES?

The information in this section is based on national surveys of the sport and leisure patterns of Canadians in addition to several secondary analyses of these surveys. The national surveys are Kirsh, Dixon, and Bond (1973), Statistics Canada (1978), Canada Fitness Survey (1983), and Stephens and Craig (1990); the secondary analyses are Milton (1975), Curtis and Milton (1976), Curtis and White (1984), Curtis and McPherson (1987), and Boulanger (1988).

What these studies show is that relatively few adult Canadians (less than 15 per cent) are regularly involved in *sports* activities while low-cost and convenient *exercise* activities like walking, gardening, swimming, bicycling, and dancing are much more popular (between 30 and 60 per cent), and these latter activities have become increasingly popular during the past decade.

This research has also consistently established that active participation in sport is a reflection of age, education, and occupation in addition to other social characteristics such as marital status, sex, and region (see Table 7). For the Canadian adult population, we can summarize it like this: young, well-educated, white males who belong to the professional or managerial occupational categories, and who have relatively high incomes, are the *most* likely to participate in at least one sport. Conversely, those *least* likely to participate are either not in the labour force (e.g., homemakers or those retired) or in low-status jobs, as well as those whose education is minimal and who are female. We now discuss some of these social characteristics in more detail, paying particular attention to the interaction of the various indicators.

Age

After adolescence, active participation in sport and physical activity is inversely proportional to age (see Table 8). However, as McPherson (1984) points out, this particular pattern of less involvement with successive age is more pronounced among the less well educated, those with lower incomes, those who live in rural areas and small towns, females (especially if they are married and have preschool children), and blue-collar workers.

Information such as that presented in Table 8 is obtained through *cross-sectional* studies where the activity levels of people from different age groups are compared at the same time. It tells us that active participation does vary with age. However, in order to understand and explain the changes that occur with aging, we would have to study the same people *longitudinally* over a considerable period of time. For instance, although the cross-sectional data in Table 8 indicate that those sixty-five and over report as much or more involvement as some younger age groups, this does not imply that older adults are becoming more physically active in their later years. What this does tell us, especially when we compare these data with earlier cross-sectional data, is that older adults in Canada are more active now than was a similar cohort fifteen or twenty years ago. The data also suggest that there may be increased specialization with age, as older adults adjust the nature of their sport and physical activity participation to what they feel is appropriate and what they are able to do (Curtis and White, 1984).

Sex, Ethnicity, and Race

Males and females are now equally active in low-intensity exercise activities, and in some activities like walking, social dancing, and home exercise women are considerably more active (see Figure 1). More males, on the other hand, opt for golf, jogging, and gardening. The major sex differences occur in sport activities, where except for bowling and volleyball, which are socially and competitively oriented, the majority of the small percentage who do participate are male. Males and females now spend about equal amounts of time on physical recreation, but males more often engage in physical activities that are more intense in terms of energy expenditure (Stephens and Craig, 1990).

TABLE 7
Social Characteristics of Active Versus Sedentary Canadians

		active	moderate	sedentary
Age	15-19 years	68 %	24 %	7 %
	20-39 years	54	37	8
	40-59 years	47	37	13
	60+ years	53	23	21
Education	Elementary	41	31	25
	Some secondary	53	33	12
	Secondary and more	56	34	8
	Certificate or diploma	58	33	7
	University degree	63	31	5
Occupation	Manager/professional	60	34	6
	Other white collar	53	36	8
	Blue collar	48	38	10
Marital Status	Single	63	27	8
	Married	49	37	12
	Other	55	24	19
Sex	Male	57	32	9
	Female	55	30	13
Region	Atlantic	52	34	12
	Quebec	51	31	15
	Ontario	55	32	11
	Prairies	61	32	7
	B.C.	65	27	7

SOURCE: Compiled from the Canada Fitness Survey (1983). "Active" was an average of 3+ hours per week for 9+ months of the year; "moderate" was less than 3 hours per week for 9 months *or* average of 3+ hours per week for less than 9 months; "sedentary" was less than 3 hours per week for less than 9 months of the year. The balance of each row consists of unknown activity levels averaging from 1 to 3 per cent.

As we discuss later in this chapter, Canada is increasingly a multicultural society, yet we know virtually nothing about the similarities and differences in sport and physical activity patterns of the many ethnic and racial groups that now constitute this country. Using 1976 data, White and Curtis (1990) found that although there was no significant difference be-

TABLE 8
Participation in Physical Activities by Age

	Scheduled[a]	Directed[b] or Coached	Competitive[c]	Casual[d]
Total, Age 10+	45%	22%	17%	41%
Males, Age 10+	46	17	23	42
10-14	60	52	42	37
15-19	62	46	44	39
20-24	45	≤15	24	42
25-44	49	≤10	22	41
45-64	36	≤10	≤10	43
65+	23	≤15	≤15	51
Females, Age 10+	43	27	12	40
10-14	70	70	37	19
15-19	60	49	28	33
20-24	39	18	≤15	41
25-44	43	25	≤10	40
45-64	34	13	≤10	45
65+	28	16	≤15	51

[a] Activity scheduled at a specific time.
[b] Activity directed by an instructor, coach, or supervisor.
[c] Involvement with organized teams, leagues, or races.
[d] Activity that was freely scheduled.
SOURCE: From Stephens and Craig (1990: 58).

tween Anglophones and Francophones in their general sport participation, both male and female Anglophones were more involved in competitive sport than Francophones.

Education and Occupation

Whether or not someone is in the paid labour force is a strong predictor of active involvement in sport and physical activity. On the whole, those not in the labour force (e.g., homemakers, retirees, unemployed, disabled) are inactive in sports, although some may be quite active in exercise activities like walking, swimming, and gardening. The type of occupation is also a good predictor of involvement (see Table 7). Salaried professionals and managers with good educations and high incomes are far more likely to be involved in individual sports that cost money, such as downhill skiing, indoor tennis,

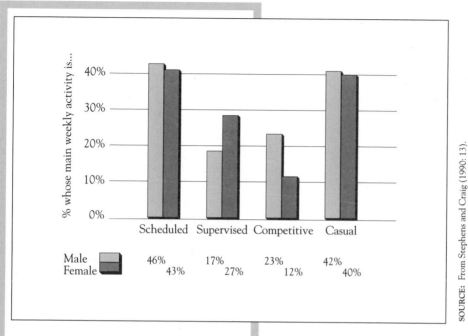

Figure 1 *Characteristics of Weekly Activities by Sex (Age 10+)*

SOURCE: From Stephens and Craig (1990: 13).

squash, windsurfing, golf, sailing, and equestrian sports (Boulanger, 1988). Due to considerable professional autonomy, they are also more likely to be involved in sports requiring extensive preparation and training, such as marathon running (McTeer and Curtis, 1984). Again, age and sex are important factors, with younger males being the most active. Male blue-collar and white-collar workers, who generally have less education and lower incomes, tend to seek out more social situations for their sporting activities, notably bowling, baseball or softball, hockey, and fishing. Working-class women, on the other hand, display little or no interest in sport, or even in physical activity, most likely because of such insurmountable barriers as in-

adequate child care and a lack of money. In making these connections between education, occupation, and social class, we are returned to the first of the structural inequalities we alluded to at the beginning of the chapter.

SOCIAL CLASS AND SPORT

The classes continually invent new ways of differentiating themselves and putting distance between themselves and others in order to mark their positions in the social structure. If sport is no longer, as it was in the recent past, the exclusive privilege of the upper classes, neither is it today a universal, democratized activity. (Boulanger, 1988: 264)

In our introductory remarks to this chapter, we discussed how social inequality in a liberal democracy is inevitable, and often taken as "natural." We then examined who participates in sport in Canada, and we have seen how important socio-economic privilege (reflected in one's income, education, and occupation) is to understanding the distribution of all kinds of social experiences and opportunities. The same is true for sport: we expect those with more income, higher education, and more secure employment to have the money, knowledge, and flexibility to incorporate sport and physical activity into their lives. We also expect those with expertise, organizational resources, and prestige to be running our sport organizations and making important decisions. This is all very well, but investigating who participates (whether focusing on social class, gender, race, or ethnicity) tells us very little about *why* these particular distributions occur in the first place.

Defining Social Class

To talk of a "class society" is normally to refer to a society in which a relatively small group of wealthy people hold most or all of the power. In feudal societies, "class" was directly related to the possession of land. The landed classes (royalty, and other "gentry" with large family estates) were in a position to derive substantial income from their property and from the labours of those who worked that property. Those who didn't own land had to work for landowners; and since what they produced (largely agricultural products) belonged to the landowners, it was difficult if not impossible to change this relationship and to move from one class to another.

In the contemporary world, money (or capital) is a mobile form of property that is convertible into economic power anywhere. Money buys land, constructs manufacturing plants, and creates jobs for others. Money, in other words, buys a choice of opportunities to make more money, along with opportunities for consumer spending. However, the complex distribution system of modern economies and the growing importance and hence the saleability of new kinds of specialist knowledge each created new opportunities to make a good living without ever becoming "owners of the means of production" in the classical Marxist sense. These new ways of making one's way in the world have constituted avenues of social mobility for many individuals who did not start life with the advantages of property; and together these kinds of individuals – traders and salespeople, technicians, professionals, administrators – make up the "middle class" that has become a characteristic feature of modern capitalist societies.

Inequalities, of course, continue to exist in these societies, within the middle class as well as between the really wealthy and the very poor (Marchak, 1988). However, some scholars prefer to describe this as a system of *social stratification* rather than as a class system. In this account, disparities in standards of living are theorized as rather like a ladder. Those on higher rungs are more privileged, of course; but the ladder metaphor suggests both that individuals can climb up (or slip down) and that the rungs are close enough together to make this a real possibility. Real hardship can be ameliorated through the political system, but economic inequalities are seen not only as inevitable but as a useful incentive system that keeps individuals working and makes the society as a whole more productive. Indeed, even poorer people are seen as having an objective interest in a productive society in which living standards can rise even for those on the bottom rungs. "Class," if it is used at all, becomes equated with social "status" rather than having anything to do with power.

When we use a class analysis, we are suggesting that the relationship between the upper "rungs" of society and the rest is a power relationship, not simply one of difference or even status (Darroch, 1986). When we talk about class structures, we are pointing to the ability of those with economic power to organize social life to their own advantage, and to the relationships between economic power and privilege in virtually all the "official" institutions of society. In the economic sphere itself, money is able to make more money and to reap dividends from the productivity of others. This has the effect of increasing concentrations of wealth, and widening the disparities between the very wealthy and the rest, even when absolute living standards rise. In the political sphere, since investment in factories and businesses creates jobs for many others, the interests of the investment community are deeply embedded in our politics and in the everyday practices of our governments. Large businesses routinely use the threat of relocation or closure to make governments take their interests seriously, even when these conflict with those of other groups or the "community" in general (for example, with respect to the environment).

At a more personal level, those who are relatively rich are able to purchase, for themselves and their families, access to opportunities for personal development that are not as readily available to poorer people. Education is the most important of these; but opportunities for summer camp, for travel, and for the development of sporting and artistic talent all develop not only specific skills but a more general confidence that can open other doors as well (Shot-

ter, 1984). Finally, we noted in Chapter 2 that the dominant groups in society are more able to establish their own cultural practices as objects of public attention and support.

Taken together, then, we can suggest that a *class* society is one in which there remain significant inequalities of wealth – even when the class structure becomes more differentiated and movement between classes more open – *and these translate into many other kinds of inequalities*: in political influence, in access to developmental opportunities, and in many kinds of personal relationships. Here, we allude to what Sennett and Cobb (1972) call the "hidden injuries" of class, injuries that derive from a dominant ideology that says that poor people and their cultural practices are less important, less interesting, and less worthy of respect.

The Canadian Class Structure

The popular vision is of Canada as a classless society, or, if we admit to a class-based society, most of us probably think we belong to a huge, largely undifferentiated middle class. The fact is that the Canadian class structure is very complex, not only because we are a relatively young and recently settled country, but also because so much of our industry is owned outside the country. Thus a hereditary "ruling class" whose wealth is literally "grounded" in real property (as in Britain, for example) does not reside within Canada (Marchak, 1988). Conversely, although we have poor people in Canada and we certainly have workers, the idea that we have a "working class" – Canadians who are both poor and collectively powerless, and who therefore have a common interest in fighting a system that has exploited them for generations – is not as readily descriptive of Canadian society as it has been in Europe. Indeed, this is why workers from many European countries have experienced Canada as a "land of opportunity."

However, we want to suggest that wealth still structures Canadian society in important ways. At the political level, the "needs of industry," first resource industries but subsequently manufacturing industries, have always been taken very seriously by Canadian governments at all levels. Here, economic power can be seen to yield enormous political power; indeed, "good policies" were often (and still are) seen as precisely those that promoted and supported economic development. At a more personal and concrete level, there is ample historical evidence of business leaders seeking to influence politicians. We can also see why it has often appeared to be in everyone's interest to have people with business experience in government and in the public service. Thus there has been a frequent movement of individuals back and forth between the senior ranks of government and industry. It is not unrealistic, therefore, to talk about a Canadian "power elite" who wield influence more effectively than other groups of individuals (Porter, 1967).

Below this group, we have suggested that most Canadians think of themselves as either members or potential members of a middle class that constitutes most of the population. However, other than being somewhere in the middle of either being very rich or very poor, this group is far from undifferentiated. It encompasses such wide differences that these may seem more significant than what is shared, namely, some access (however limited) to the "good life" of the consumer society. At the very least, this group encompasses: middle management and technical personnel working in the corporate sector, independent professionals (doctors, lawyers, etc.), professionals working in the public sector (in the education and health care sectors, in Crown corporations, as well as the civil service itself), self-employed business people,

sales people, clerical personnel, and skilled production workers. None of these people exercises the kind of political and economic power that the leaders of large corporations and important governments can. Yet all, or most of them, earn sufficient incomes (especially in a two-income family) that they can aspire to a reasonably comfortable lifestyle. Clearly, however, they do not think of themselves as the same and they are not. They are likely to have different educational levels, different tastes, different political opinions, and different lifestyles (including different interests with respect to sport and leisure).

Differences in Sport Participation among the Social Classes

French sociologist Pierre Bourdieu (1978), in an important article about the relationship between sport and social class, argued that the distribution of sporting practices among and within the social classes was determined by three factors. The first and most important of these, not unexpectedly, is *economic capital*. Historically, the significant distinction was between those sports that required property and purpose-built facilities and those that could be played in unimproved public places. Thus golf and tennis, for example, were for a long time available almost exclusively through expensive private clubs, and as a result were primarily upper-class pursuits. Conversely, team games that could be played with simple equipment on empty fields or roads or on stretches of frozen river were more accessible to ordinary people and quickly became popular sports among "the people" (for example, cycling and road racing, as well as hockey and baseball). A corollary of capital, in the early days at least, was *spare time*. Long ago this meant time to play, and thus some sports were really pastimes of the leisure classes. But in the contemporary era, rising standards in almost all sports have required that successful athletes practise long hours over many years, and even though public recreational facilities (e.g., rinks) have helped democratize sport to some extent, young people who must take part-time jobs or leave school for full-time employment have less chance to develop in sport than those with genuinely free time.

Finally, Bourdieu introduces the interesting notion of *cultural capital*. By this he draws our attention to the fact that some kinds of knowledge are much more socially prestigious than others. We alluded to this idea in Chapter 2 when we suggested that the knowledge that goes with appreciating classical music has traditionally been more respected than knowledge of jazz, let alone sport. Bourdieu extends the idea by pointing to distinctions among sports. Some sports (e.g., golf, racquet sports, sailing, equestrianism) may still be largely confined to the upper and upper-middle classes. Bourdieu's point, however, is that knowledge of these sports has greater social "currency" than knowledge of cycling, for example, or football. It becomes itself a badge of "class" that, displayed smartly, can be converted into other kinds of advantage.

Moreover, argues Bourdieu, what also distinguishes working-class activities from those of the privileged classes is the relation to one's own body (*body habitus*). The privileged classes are more likely to treat the body as an end in itself and therefore engage in activities designed to improve the health and appearance of the body (e.g., jogging, exercise programs, aerobic classes). They are also likely to be those most concerned with nutrition, diet, smoking, and so forth (remember our earlier discussion about the ideology of healthism in Chapter 5). The working classes, suggests Bourdieu, are more likely to use their bodies to achieve some other

end. Their choice of sports and physical activities will require "a considerable investment of effort, sometimes of pain and suffering (e.g. boxing) and sometimes a *gambling with the body itself* (as in motor-cycling, parachute jumping, all forms of acrobatics, and, to some extent, all sports involving fighting, among which we may include rugby)" (Bourdieu, 1978: 838). Perhaps in Canada we would want to include ice hockey in this list.

In an interesting study that empirically tests some of Bourdieu's theories, sport sociologists Suzanne Laberge and David Sankoff (1988) examined the relationship between physical activity and body habitus (relation to one's body) among a group of women from various social classes. Body habitus was determined by asking the women about their concerns and behaviours regarding their bodies, health, beauty care, and hygiene. Four different groups became apparent: (1) those concerned with the discipline of the body (check their weight regularly, diet if need be, do not smoke, avoid fast foods); (2) those whose body care involves primarily cosmetics (they buy beauty-care products, read beauty magazines); (3) those who engage in good health practices (exercise regularly, eat nutritiously, have medical examinations); and (4) those who have the luxury not only to engage in good health practices but also to eat very well, obtain regular dental check-ups, and employ domestic help. The researchers also identified four social class categories among their sample: working class, middle class, intellectual bourgeoisie, and upper class.

As expected, working-class women showed the least interest in physical activity whereas middle-class women (such as primary school teachers, secretaries, nurses, and librarians) demonstrated the most, especially in activities like swimming, aerobics, or "jazzercise."

These two groups also had very different attitudes toward their bodies: middle-class women focus on health and discipline (dieting and frequent, regular physical activity); working-class women look almost exclusively to cosmetics and beauty-care products to enhance their bodily image. Women in the intellectual bourgeoisie expressed dislike for intense physical activity (like aerobics) and engaged in activities that provided relaxation and body awareness (yoga, for example). Finally, upper-class women, able to afford a lifestyle of comparative luxury, engaged in sports like golf, tennis, and downhill skiing, often with friends or family.

Therefore, as Laberge and Sankoff suggest, members of various social classes engage (or do not engage) in sports and physical activity because they can or cannot afford it (economic capital); they do or do not have the time (spare time); they do or do not have the appropriate knowledge (cultural capital). Probably more important, however, is that their participation may or may not fit with a particular view they have of their bodies and lifestyles (body and class habitus). For some social classes, therefore, regular participation in sport and physical activity is an important aspect of their lives, while for others it is viewed as a waste of time.

Democratization and Canadian Sport

Over the past 100 years there has been a gradual process of "levelling out the class bias and exclusionary nature of a variety of sport-related aspects of social life" (Gruneau, 1975: 152). More people today, regardless of class background, participate and compete in physical activity and sport than ever before. And yet, as we have shown, sport is not entirely *meritocratic*. It may be much less exclusionary, but the distribution of resources and rewards in the

sporting world is still not solely based on an individual's merit or abilities. This will become abundantly clear when we discuss the importance of gender, race, and ethnicity.

Gruneau (1976) investigated the social class background of Canada Games athletes and found that the athletes' fathers were overrepresented in the professional and white-collar occupational categories and underrepresented in the blue-collar and primary industry (mining, fishing, logging) occupations. In a more recent study of Canada's national team athletes, Beamish (1990) found they were still far more likely to come from upper-income families where the father held a white-collar, managerial, or professional occupation. He makes the point that even though the federal government set out in the early 1970s to establish sport programs that would reduce, if not eliminate, the effect of social class background on sport participation, these inequalities still persist twenty years later. In a similar study that examined the social class backgrounds (based on occupation of father) of approximately 1,800 high school athletes in Ontario, Macintosh (1982) found that they were more likely (56.8 per cent) to come from the "professional" class and less likely to be from the "clerical" (11.4 per cent) or "labour" (31.8 per cent) class. The same relationship held true for both male and female athletes and for those participating on out-of-school teams. Finally, based on a sample of over 200 Ontario families with a registered competitive swimmer or swimmers, Eynon, Kitchen, and Semotiuk (1980) found that, based on educational level and income of the parents, these families were overwhelmingly "upper middle class."

As we discussed in Chapter 4, amateur sport in Canada is organized and administered by officials in provincial and federal governments, hundreds of full-time coaches and sport administrators, and even greater numbers of volunteers who comprise the presidents, directors, and committee members of national and provincial sport associations. The middle class is overwhelmingly represented in voluntary associations in general and sport is no exception. When the leading volunteers in twelve national sport associations were asked to describe their "social class background," nearly 90 per cent of the females and 85 per cent of the males placed themselves in either a "middle" or "upper middle" social stratum (Hall, Cullen, and Slack, 1990). No matter what indicator is used to measure socio-economic privilege (income, education, or occupation), the research shows unequivocally a direct relationship between socio-economic level and participation in voluntary sport associations (as with all other kinds of voluntary associations). For example, Table 9 contrasts the occupations of sport exec-

TABLE 9
Occupational Categories of Sport Executives Compared to Labour Force Percentages, 1975 and 1988

Occupational Category	1975 Execs. N=218	1971 Census	1988 Execs. N=258	1981 Census
White Collar				
Managerial	21.6 %	4.3 %	30.6 %	6.8 %
Professional and technical	59.2	12.6	44.6	15.1
Clerical	2.8	15.9	1.9	18.3
Sales and service	7.8	20.7	6.6	21.5
Blue Collar				
Manufacturing and mechanical	1.8	17.7	1.6	17.5
Construction	0.0	6.6	2.3	6.4
Primary				
Agricultural	0.5	5.9	0.4	4.2
Logging	0.0	0.7	0.4	0.7
Fishing, hunting, trapping	0.0	0.3	0.0	0.3
Mining	0.0	0.6	0.0	0.6
Transportation and communication	0.5	3.9	0.4	3.8
Homemaker	3.6	—	9.8	—
Unknown	2.2	10.3	1.4	4.8
Totals*	100.0	99.5 *	100.0	100.0

* Total does not add up to 100% because of rounding.
SOURCES: Hollands and Gruneau (1979), for 1975; Darroch (1986), for 1971 and 1981; Hall, Cullen, and Slack (1990), for 1988.

utives in 1975 and in 1988 with the percentage of these occupational categories in the total labour force. There are two important facts to note here. One is that in both 1975 and 1988, approximately 80 per cent of a representative sample of sport executives were from the managerial, professional, or technical occupations. The second point is that there has been no change in this distribution over a very long period of time (see our discussion about the history of amateur sport organizations in Chapter 3, as well as Hollands and Gruneau, 1979, for data as far back as 1955). Therefore, study after study has confirmed that volunteer executives are well educated, usually hold jobs in the managerial or professional sector, and earn well above average incomes (see Beamish, 1985, for a good summary of this research).

In sum, these findings and others do not corroborate an image of a classless and generally meritocratic sport system with universal access. The question remains, however, will there ever be? Richard Gruneau (1976: 132) offers this conclusion:

Until the situation occurs when well-placed families are no longer in a position to confer differential advantages and a broader range of life chances to their children, a high degree of social self-recruitment will continue freely from one generation to the next.

GENDER AND SPORT

Organized sport, as a cultural sphere defined largely by patriarchal priorities, will continue to be an important arena in which emerging images of active, fit, and muscular women are forged, interpreted, contested, and incorporated. The larger socioeconomic and political context will continue to shape and constrain the extent to which women can wage fundamental challenges to the ways that organized sports continue providing ideological legitimation for male dominance. (Messner, 1988: 208)

Gender is a major social and theoretical category just like class, race, and ethnicity. It is also an analytical tool that helps us to understand better major societal changes involving relations between males and females. Unfortunately, "gender" is often translated to mean only "women," which means that courses, symposia, and texts with the label "gender and sport" are considered for females only, and the issues discussed relevant only to women. Later we will discuss why gender relates as much to males and masculinity as it does to females and femininity.

Gender is also a system of institutionalized relations between females and males. The term *gender relations* is the most common one used to describe this system of relations structured by gender. In the same way that class and race relations deal with domination and subordination and in themselves have a history, so, too, do gender relations since they are characterized by male dominance and female subordination. Gender, then, is a set of power relations whereby "men, as a social group, have more power over women than women have over them; they are not fixed, rather they are subject to historical change and they can be transformed" (Hall, 1990: 226). We want to examine several questions concerning gender relations in sport. How did sport come to embody and recreate male power and domination? Why does gender inequality in sport persist? How does sport contribute to the reproduction of existing relations between (and within) genders? Can sport contribute to bring-

Brian Gavriloff, Edmonton Journal.

Co-ed sport.

ing about equality between women and men? In asking such questions, we want to move from an emphasis on the distributional issues (relative absence of women in different levels of sport) discussed previously to underlying relational concerns. These questions are, according to Whitson (1990: 20), "of more far-reaching significance, both theoretically and in practice, than the distributional issues (though they are not, of course, disconnected)." This is also what Bruce Kidd (1987: 255) means when he writes:

The effect of sports is also to perpetuate patriarchy by powerfully reinforcing the sexual division of labour. By giving males exciting opportunities, preaching that the qualities they learn from them are "masculine," and preventing girls and women from learning in the same context, sports confirm the prejudice that males are a breed apart. By encouraging us to spend most of our creative and engrossing moments as children and our favorite forms of recreation as adults in the company of males, they condition us to trust each other more than women. By publicly celebrating the dramatic achievements of the best males, while marginalizing females as cheerleaders and spectators, they validate the male claim to the important positions in society. . . . Sports contribute to the underdevelopment of the female majority of the population and the undervaluing of those traditionally "feminine" skills of nurturing and emotional maintenance essential to human survival and growth.

Gender Inequality in Canadian Society

Although much has changed for the better for Canadian women, especially in the last thirty years, they still occupy an unequal position compared to men in our society. Just a few facts about some of our major social institutions – education, labour, family – will suffice.

Although the teaching profession, certainly at the lower grades, is dominated by women (95 per cent of all kindergarten teachers are women, 70 per cent of all elementary, and 33 per cent of secondary), they are underrepresented in teaching at the higher grades and they seldom occupy administrative positions (Gaskell, 1981). In universities, only 17 per cent of the academic staff are women, and the vast majority of these are in the lower academic ranks – just 6 per cent are full professors (McKie and Thompson, 1990). However, more females than males graduate from high school. But in university undergraduate programs women are still underrepresented in engineering, forestry, dentistry, architecture, computer science, law, business, science, and medicine; at the same time, they are overrepresented in household science, nursing, and rehabilitative medicine. Unfortunately, too, women are still underrepresented and portrayed in traditional ways in textbooks, teaching materials, films, and readers, something the relatively new women's studies courses and programs are attempting to offset.

The Canadian labour force, as far as women are concerned, is characterized by occupational segregation into low-status and low-paying jobs. In 1988, 73 per cent of all working women were employed in clerical, sales, or service positions, teaching, or health services, mostly nursing. A few additional facts: women earn on average 66 per cent of what men do; two-thirds of all minimum-wage earners are women; only 20 per cent of working women are unionized (40 per cent of men are); and only 5 per cent of those employed in managerial and administrative positions are women (McKie and Thompson, 1990). Women have, however, made particularly substantial inroads into what traditionally have been male-dominated professions (for example, as veterinarians, pharmacists, biologists), although they are still significantly underrepresented in the most prestigious and highly paid professions.

Increasing numbers of elderly women live in poverty because they live longer (about eight years) than men, they have worked all their lives in the home, and they have no work-related pensions of their own. Today, however, 54 per cent of married women are in the paid labour force compared with 38 per cent in 1975. The continued movement of women into the labour force and the increase in lone-parent families, most of which (87 per cent) are headed by women, make for a growing demand for child care. Nonetheless, unlicensed child care still predominates in Canada.

There is no question that feminism and the women's movement have had a major impact on Canadian society, just as they have in most modern, industrialized, Western nations (cf. Adamson, Briskin, and McPhail, 1988).

The goals of the women's movement have been to allow women to speak for themselves, to break their isolation, and to set up a network of groups and organizations across the country to help them do this. There has been an explosion of women's culture in the form of women's writing, publishing presses, film, music, and theatre. Society is gradually being restructured – not fast enough for some, too fast for others. Everyday relations between women and men have changed and no doubt will continue to change, but fundamental change in a society so intractably structured around gender inequality is still a long way off.

Gender Inequality in Sport: Defining the Problem

There is no reason to believe that sport is any different from any other aspect of society insofar as it is characterized by gender inequality. Earlier, we noted that Canadian men and women are now equally active in low-intensity exercise activities but that men are much more active in competitive sports generally and they are more intense in their participation. This, however, does not tell the full story.

Certainly girls and women have benefited from a steady growth of opportunities for participation and competition: greater access to coaching and facilities; government policies and funding; the health and fitness movement; increased publicity given to women athletes and greater recognition of their achievements; and considerable feminist advocacy, specifically in sport. However, after reviewing a number of reports and studies from across the country, sociologist Helen Lenskyj (1988: 72) concluded that there are still more opportunities for "males to engage in a wide range of competitive team sports, while in programming for girls and women there remains a strong emphasis on fit-

ness and recreational activities, and, overall, a much narrower range of options in sport." This is true at the school, university, and community levels, something we explore more fully in the next chapter. Girls and women are continually denied access to the full range of sports. This is also true even at the very highest levels of competition, such as the Olympic Games, where the number of events available to women is still about half those available to men (cf. Hargreaves, 1984; Coakley, 1990).

Not only are females denied access to sporting opportunities, they are often treated as second-class citizens. In some circumstances, they are still routinely given the least convenient practice times, the worst facilities and equipment, the least experienced teachers, trainers, and coaches, and less funding and sponsorship, and in some sports they receive no media attention at all. During the last decade this has led to a marked growth in sports clubs, leagues, and programs organized by and for women – self-defence courses, fitness classes for the overweight, and outdoor and adventure programs, all for women only.

Another reason for the growth and development of women-only sport programs and opportunities is because the structure and control of traditional sport remains firmly in the hands of men. Women are underrepresented as sport leaders in Canada just as they are everywhere else in the world. In fact, women comprise approximately one-third of the volunteer sector in Canadian amateur sport, but they are virtually absent from positions of higher responsibility, and thus of power, in the decision-making processes of sport. There is, however, a tremendous variety among sports, with some associations being predominantly female, some predominantly male, and most others mixed. Women obviously take stronger leadership roles in such predominantly female sports as synchronized swimming and field hockey, but even in competitive swimming and basketball, for example, which have large numbers of female participants, women are grossly underrepresented at the leadership levels.

How do we explain this underrepresentation? Most studies have merely documented and described the problem rather than addressing the *gender structuring* of sport organizations, the organizational processes and dynamics that structure gender, and the relations of power between women and men within an organizational context. However, based on some relatively new and more theoretically informed research (see especially Theberge, 1984a; Hall, 1987; Whitson and Macintosh, 1989; Hall, Cullen, and Slack, 1989, 1990), the explanations for the underrepresentation of women can be summarized as follows:

- Women face stereotypical notions about their competence despite their formal qualifications, organizational resources, and technical expertise.
- Women are assumed (in actuality or in the perception of themselves and others) to lack the proper training, motivation, and skills to succeed.
- Women must prove themselves and work their way up the sport hierarchy whereas the competence of men is often taken for granted.
- Women who choose to enter a primarily man's world must learn the language, symbols, myths, beliefs, and values of that male culture. They sometimes become "honorary" men.
- Women's family responsibilities are a "given" and beyond the control or interest of the organization. Child-care facilities and arrangements, for example, are generally of no interest to the organization.

- A strong and informal male network (and a weak female network) exists that enhances men's (and discourages women's) opportunities.
- Male elites ensure the maintenance of the status quo, and their own power, by selecting those individuals most like themselves.
- Women both perceive and experience discrimination in greater numbers than do men.
- Most sport organizations usually see no need to initiate any sort of "affirmative action" program or structure to address the needs of women, although some organizations do and have.

Women are also badly underrepresented in all levels of coaching, from volunteer positions in elementary schools and youth sport programs to national team coaches (Lenskyj, 1988). Not only do women coach less than men, their percentage decreases further as the level of competition increases. At the university level, for instance, the number of full-time coaching positions held by women has actually decreased over the last decade despite the increase in female athletes (Inglis, 1988).

The same pattern is reflected in the declining numbers of women physical education teachers employed in the secondary schools. With the gradual introduction of co-educational physical education into the school curriculum, more male physical education teachers are now teaching both girls and boys. Since female physical education teachers leave the school systems at a faster rate for a variety of reasons (pregnancy, husband moving), men have been taking over these jobs. In contrast to earlier practice, it is not seen as a problem for men to teach girls in physical education, particularly with co-educational classes. However, it is still often considered inappropriate for women physical education teachers to teach (or coach) boys (Hall and Richardson, 1982). One consequence is that girls do not have sufficient exposure to appropriate role models. A similar problem exists in university physical education departments, where women represent approximately 25 per cent of the academic staff yet most undergraduate degree programs in physical education have equal numbers of male and female students (Hall and Richardson, 1982).

Finally, it is important to recognize the extent to which women's sport is trivialized and often ignored, thus contributing further to gender inequality. In Chapter 6, we discussed media representations of women's sporting events, including the lack of coverage compared to men's sports and the often biased portrayal of women athletes. Sometimes more discussion focuses on the female athlete's appearance and marital and maternal status than on her training, performance, and achievements (Lenskyj, 1986; Blue, 1987). However, as Messner (1988: 205) argues for the North American situation:

> I would speculate that we are now moving into an era in which female athletes have worked hard enough to attain a certain level of legitimacy that makes simple media marginalization and trivialization of female athletes appear transparently unfair and prejudicial. The framing of female athletes as sex objects or as sexual deviants is no longer a tenable strategy if the media are to maintain their own legitimacy.

Women have also tried to create their own media outlets to increase the coverage and lessen the reporting bias of women's sport, but they are usually forced to adopt an approach necessary to compete with women's magazines emphasizing fashion and beauty (for example, the American magazine *Women's Sports and Fitness*). If they try to treat women's sport seriously (for example, the now defunct American magazine *The Sportswoman*), they find there is no market and the outlet quickly disappears.

The problem of gender inequality in sport, as we have elaborated it here, is one of not being taken seriously, fewer competitive opportunities, underrepresentation in leadership, and male control of sporting structures. These, among others, are often described as the "barriers" to full and equal participation by females in the sporting world. Still, this merely describes a situation of unequal resources and rewards we all know exists; it does not contribute much to explaining why these patterns persist and why they are so difficult to change.

Reproducing Gender Relations through Sport

Specific social and cultural practices accomplish the physical and ideological exclusion of women from sport. We have shown that females are often excluded from enjoying the same opportunities in sport as males and that the control of sport rests generally in the hands of men, but *why* and *how* does this occur?

Let's take a specific example – the integration of girls into boys' sport. One recent case was that of Justine Blainey, who in 1985 was chosen to play on a first-class boys' hockey team in the Metro Toronto Hockey League but was barred from playing by the Ontario Hockey Association. She fought her case through the courts (as have several others before her) and two years later finally won her right to play. Justine wanted to play boys' hockey because of the bodychecking and slapshots, both of which are not allowed in the girls' league. The case consumed much media attention and thousands of dollars in legal costs, and garnered a phenomenal amount of public debate and discussion. Why so much fuss over a thirteen-year-old girl who wanted to play on a boys' hockey team?

Sport traditionally has been a "male preserve," a powerful cultural arena and an important site for the construction (and preservation) of male solidarity. In Chapter 3 we discussed the role of games and sport in encouraging Christian manliness among nineteenth-century male youth, particularly those who attended private schools. Two themes emerge: the equation of physical prowess with moral strength (the "muscular Christian"), and a clear concern to maximize the differences and distance between men and women (Whitson, 1990). Michael Messner (1988), an American sport sociologist, has argued that the twentieth century has seen two periods of crisis for masculinity – each accompanied by significant feminist movements – where organized sport has been a crucial arena of struggle over conceptions of masculinity and femininity. The first crisis, extending from the 1890s through to the 1920s, was marked by significant societal changes, including a weakening of the male breadwinner role, the rise of female-dominated public schools, urbanization, and the closing of the frontier, all of which led to a defensive insecurity among men that became manifested in an increased preoccupation with physicality and toughness. The second crisis, he argues, began in the post-war era and continues until the present, when sports, particularly American football, have become increasingly important to males because they link men to a more patriarchal past. Finally, British sport sociologist Eric Dunning (1986) argues

that men responded to the continuing emancipation of women by forming male sporting enclaves (rugby, for example) where they could at least symbolically mock, objectify, and vilify women.

Today, as the Justine Blainey case and other similar cases (see Hall and Richardson, 1982) make clear, sport as a proving ground for masculinity can only be preserved as such if girls and women are excluded. Sport in our culture is still viewed by many as a "masculinizing project," a cultural practice where boys learn to be men and male solidarity is forged. This explains, we believe, the resistance not just among men but also among women to sex-integrated sport. It also explains why men who are threatened by such changes, as well as the larger societal changes in gender relations, proclaim the importance of all-male institutions and in particular defend the importance of toughness, confrontation, and aggression in sport (Whitson, 1990). In addition, it explains why, when women actively participate in the symbols, practices, and institutions of sport, what they do there is often not considered "real" sport, nor in some cases are they viewed as real women (Young, 1979).

Our second point concerns the role of sport in the reinforcement of common-sense ideologies that represent males as *naturally* superior to females. In seeming praise of Justine Blainey's hockey prowess, she was probably told many times over: "You play just like a boy." Although meant to be a compliment, the statement reflects the ideology that physical and skill differences between the sexes are natural, and that boys and men are naturally more skilled (Willis, 1982). Obviously, in some sports (those requiring speed, height, or bulk) most males *are* more skilled, and the performance differences are greatest, but there are also many sports (those requiring endurance or flexibility or aesthetics) where the performance differences are minimal or indeed the scale tips in favour of females. Also ideological, and therefore taken up into popular consciousness, are the myths surrounding female athleticism (for example, they will damage their reproductive organs or they are more susceptible to injuries) used to justify their exclusion. Research (see Lenskyj, 1988, for an excellent summary) has shown how these myths have no basis in fact and yet they still remain a part of popular common sense used to reaffirm male dominance in sport. It is a strange paradox that one rationale for the age-old prohibition against contact sports for females is that they will irreparably damage their *naturally* protected reproductive organs, whereas the fact that the exposed male genitals *have* to be protected is never considered problematic! Through sport, the ideology of naturalness is an essential ideological tool for producing and reproducing the domination of men over women (cf. Willis, 1982; Lenskyj, 1986; Jennifer Hargreaves, 1986; Birrell, 1988).

Our third and final point concerns the significance of physicality, sexuality, and the body in the reproduction of gender relations. Justine Blainey wanted to play boys' hockey, and not girls' hockey, because she wanted to be more physical:

> I love it when you hit somebody. Even if you get hit, you can take someone down with you. I once bodychecked a guy who was so big . . . he fell on top of me. That was a mistake. He was only 13 but he must have weighed 200 pounds. (Davidson, 1985)

Physicality, or the sensuous experiencing of strength and skill, has often been denied to females because it has never been readily associated with women or with femininity. Alternatively, physical masculinity seems natural, almost never requiring explanation. Through their childhood and adolescent involvement in sport, young males learn that force, skill, and competence, which together constitute power (the capacity to achieve ends even if opposed by others), are the embodiment of physical masculinity (Connell, 1983). Young girls are often denied this experience, and, as Young (1980: 146) observes, women have more of a tendency than men to greatly underestimate their bodily capacity: "a woman frequently does not trust the capacity of her body to engage itself in physical relation to things. Consequently, she often lives her body as a burden, which must be dragged and prodded along, and at the same time protected."

The link to gender relations, argues Theberge (1985a), is that sport reproduces gender inequality by translating women's supposedly inferior physicality into social inferiority. She argues further that "sport as a male preserve has contributed to the oppression of women through the objectification and domination of their physicality and sexuality" (p. 93). Men control women through controlling their bodies in other more blatant ways (for instance, rape, domestic violence, pornography), yet sport is also a place where women's bodies have been (and still are) controlled, objectified, and defined. Increasingly, women are experiencing their bodies as strong, powerful, free, *and* physical, and yet there is still a good deal of ambiguity. Female bodybuilding, for example, is fraught with tensions between traditional perceptions of femininity and a new muscularity for women (see the film *Pumping Iron II: The Women*). Women are also spending more time on the management and discipline of their bodies as they flock to aerobics, jazzercise, and similar exercise programs; undergo liposuction and cellulite management, sometimes at risk to their health; and abuse their bodies through such eating disorders as anorexia and bulimia. Women are clearly attempting to control and define their own bodies (and their lives), yet many still feel they must do so within the existing hegemonic definitions of femininity.

There is an ongoing struggle over the control of women's sport, the structures and mechanisms required, and the most effective strategies and policies. We can label this the "politics" of gender relations in sport, and it occurs among women, among men, and between women and men as participants, competitors, teachers, coaches, professional or volunteer leaders, policy-makers, academics, and activists. Some of these individuals are also feminists, yet their approaches to bringing about change are quite diverse. Some, for example, are working within the male-dominated governing structures of sport while others are resisting this domination by creating totally women-centred sport forms and structures. Some argue that girls' and women's sport programs should be combined with and modelled after similar programs for males; others maintain that women's sport must be separate and autonomous (cf. Birrell and Richter, 1987; Jennifer Hargreaves, 1986; Lenskyj, 1985; Theberge, 1985a, 1985b, 1987, 1989b; Williams, Lawrence, and Rowe, 1985). We will return to this discussion at the end of the chapter.

RACE, ETHNICITY, AND SPORT

Sports activities were, and were seen to be, deeply embedded in the ethnoculture, and ethnic associational life was rarely seen as complete, if space in the form of a gym or a picnic site with playing fields were not provided within the group's own ambiance. So in this sense, organized sports, far from being a novel North American challenge to the immigrant, were one of his [or her] resources, a catalyst of fellow-feeling and a natural medium for transmission of the many small things of the ethnoculture. (Harney, 1985: 8)

Canada is a culturally pluralistic society – this statement reflects the belief that the survival of racial and ethnic groups as separate groups in Canadian society is socially useful and desirable. Our various governments support a policy of *multiculturalism* or *cultural pluralism* that originates from the early 1970s, when Prime Minister Pierre Elliott Trudeau announced:

Every ethnic group has the right to preserve and develop its own culture and values within the Canadian context. To say that we have two official languages is not to say that we have two official cultures and no particular culture is more "official" than the another. A policy of multiculturalism must be a policy for all Canadians. (*House of Commons Debates*, October 8, 1971)

Today, multiculturalism means that people of various cultures and languages who make up Canada can live and interact with one another in a spirit of mutual respect and intercultural understanding. In our everyday lives, we are proud to celebrate our cultural diversity through festivals such as the annual Edmonton Heritage Day extravaganza or Toronto's famous West Indian Caribana. Most institutions try to be multicultural: city newspapers run features on ethnic neighbourhoods; television hires individuals from "visible" ethnic and racial groups; school curricula incorporate "multicultural education" into the teaching of all subjects; ethnic and racial representatives are sought to serve in community organizations; and supermarkets stock their shelves with "ethnic products" presumably in response to local demand.

What must be remembered, however, is that multiculturalism (or cultural pluralism) is an ideology, that is, a popular conception of what is good and desirable in our society, specifically about ethnic and racial survival. It is also important to remember that ideologies change over time. During a period of large-scale immigration of culturally diverse groups to Canada in the late nineteenth and early twentieth centuries, the Canadian government supported a policy of *assimilation*. After a period of adjustment, immigrant groups were supposed to disappear as distinct groups and blend into the host society, thus promoting equality and social harmony. Too much ethnic diversity, it was argued, would pose a threat to societal cohesion.

Today, multiculturalism has its opponents. Many Anglo-Saxons fear a threat to their way of life and express concerns about Canada's immigration policies. On the other hand, French Canadians are apprehensive that multiculturalism will undermine their efforts to maintain their own culture and distinct society. Nonetheless, multiculturalism and cultural pluralism seem firmly entrenched in Canadian government policy and Canadian life in general.

As an important facet of Canadian society, multiculturalism, both as ideology and as government policy, must impact on sport. Racism and "ethnicism" are also present in sport, as they are in all aspects of social life. The central question here, however, is how do we examine these phenomena sociologically and what do we learn when we do?

Bias or Discrimination Models

The easiest way that sociologists have found to explain racism (or "ethnicism") is to describe the social interaction between members of different racial and ethnic groups. They have used the concepts of prejudice and discrimination, which can be easily operationalized and quantified. Considerable research is implicitly framed within a bias or discrimination model.

The most current research, on a subject certainly with the longest history in Canadian sport sociology, is that pertaining to discrimination against French-speaking Canadians in the National Hockey League. Studies point to the phenomenon of *stacking* in the NHL, whereby relatively large numbers of Francophones are goalies, many are forwards, but very few are defencemen (Lavoie, 1989). Why?

At least four theses have been put forward to explain the empirical evidence (Lavoie, 1989). The *style-of-play* thesis states that Francophones are too offensively oriented, reluctant to fight, and lack a work ethic. Obviously these are stereotypes and do little to explain the stacking phenomenon. The *reservation wage* thesis posits that Francophone players have to be paid more than Anglophones to induce them to play professional hockey due to the higher language and cultural costs associated with emigrating from Quebec. Only very good Francophone players, who can command high salaries, choose to pursue a professional career; mediocre players, by this thesis, choose not to play professional hockey. Although this seems quite convincing, it does not explain why the cultural and language adjustment costs should be substantially larger for Francophone defencemen than for forwards. The *linguistic fluency* thesis suggests that Francophone (or European) players not fluent in English require a linguistic investment on the part of clubs, which they are not prepared to expend on marginal players. However, this thesis cannot explain why performance differentials are so large for defencemen and so small for goalies.

The thesis most consistent with the facts is *discrimination*. Coulombe and Lavoie (1985, cited in Lavoie, 1989: 27) state it best:

> Where uncertainty or subjectivity is high, barriers to entry against minorities are high: Only the very best members of the minority group gain entry and therefore performance differentials in their favor are substantial. Where certainty and objectivity prevail, the participation rate of the minority is high and performance differentials are null or feeble. In the case of hockey, the position of defense is presumed to be the most difficult to assess whereas that of goalie is presumed to be the easiest. Forwards occupy an intermediate spot in this hierarchy. Performance differentials, stacking, and their correlation, are thus all explained within this discrimination thesis.

Why is there discrimination against Francophones? Lavoie (1989) suggests that while few in the game are ready to concede the existence of an overt dislike of Francophones, it is generally acknowledged that the primarily Anglophone club management (scouts, coaches, and general managers) will prefer an Anglophone player to a Francophone one if their talent is equal. On the other hand, the two Quebec-based teams have a preference for Francophone players.

These particular researchers have also suggested that hiring discrimination will be reflected in salaries (Grenier and Lavoie, 1988). Francophone defencemen are significantly underpaid, to the tune of 10 to 15 per cent, whereas no pay discrimination is found against Francophone forwards and goalies. Therefore, not only are the skills of Francophone defencemen uncertain and underestimated, they are also underpaid. But for the forwards and goalies, whose skill assessment is more certain and where entry discrimination is less prevelant, there was no discrimination in salary. The discrimination thesis, the researchers conclude, is the only one not contradicted by the facts.

Similar research within a bias or discrimination model has focused on the underrepresentation of French Canadians in major international competitions. French Canadians (usually defined as a persons with a French-sounding name and/or whose first language is French) currently represent approximately 28 per cent of the Canadian population. Yet, as Boileau, Landry, and Trempe (1976) showed in their study of Francophone participation (athletes and support staff) on Canadian teams at major international games, they were seriously underrepresented in terms of their numbers in the population. Prior to the 1976 Summer Olympics, Francophones had rarely accounted for more than 10 per cent of the total Canadian representation at these games. A similar pattern existed for the Winter Olympics (average Francophone participation of 8.2 per cent), as well as for the Commonwealth Games (10.1 per cent) and the Pan-American Games (9.3 per cent). Certainly some sports had a higher Francophone representation: weightlifting (43 per cent), men's gymnastics (31 per cent), cycling (23 per cent), fencing (18 per cent), boxing (15 per cent), and wrestling (10 per cent). Nonetheless, prior to 1976 the overall average for these three international games was 8.2 per cent Francophone participation.

As for the reasons behind this underrepresentation, Boileau, Landry, and Trempe were cautious in applying a discrimination model, suggesting instead that sport had not been important to Quebec culture, that there was a distrust of anything foreign, and that the late arrival of sports and physical education programs to the school system all contributed to a general indifference toward the demands of amateur sport.

When Montreal was awarded the 1976 Summer Olympics, the Quebec government created Mission '76, the purpose of which was to increase the Francophone participation on the Canadian team to 30 per cent. By and large this succeeded, as the total representation was 28 per cent, although in sports such as men's basketball, women's canoeing, women's gymnastics, judo, men's trapshooting, and women's volleyball there was still no Francophone representation. Although Canada boycotted the 1980 Summer Olympics in Moscow, a Canadian team was still named. In a study comparing black participation on U.S. Olympic teams and Francophone participation on Canadian teams, Kjeldsen (1984) reported that Francophones comprised only 14.9 per cent of the athletes and 7.7 per cent of the coaches for the 1980 Summer Olympics team (17.6 per cent and 3.6 per cent respectively for the Winter Olympics team). Our own research shows that Francophone representation on the 1984 Canadian Summer Olympics team was 12 per cent and on the 1988 team it was marginally higher, at 12.7 per cent.

The question remains: Why are French Canadians still greatly underrepresented on our international teams in comparison to their proportion in the Canadian population? Is it because French Canadians place less value on sport in their culture, thus creating a smaller pool of athletes (see White and Curtis, 1990a, 1990b)? Is it because of the underdevelopment, until the 1980s, of amateur sport in Quebec? Is it because of the lack of physical education and interscholastic sport programs in many parts of the province (see White and Curtis, 1990b)? Or is it because of prejudice and discrimination against French Canadians by those selecting the teams? Voluntary sport associations in Canada are overwhelmingly Anglophone, with Francophones consistently underrepresented. Again, little has changed over the years. Data show that in 1955, 8.6 per cent of executive positions were filled by Francophones; 7.8 per cent in 1975; and approximately 10 per cent in 1988 (Beamish, 1978; Hall, Cullen, and Slack, 1990). Unfortunately, we simply do not know how to answer these questions – it is quite plausible that all of these factors explain the underrepresentation.

Another major focus within a bias or discrimination model has been centrality, stacking, positional segregation, and the salaries of blacks and other minorities within American professional football and baseball. Not many studies have been conducted in Canada, but in a study published in 1972 Smith and Grindstaff found that although the position of the black athlete in the Canadian Football League (CFL) had improved between 1954 and 1969 in terms of numbers and leadership positions, these players were discriminated against both socially and occupationally, and generally were not given equal treatment with the white players. Twenty and more years later, the situation of the black athlete in Canadian professional football and baseball has improved considerably. Concern now, however, focuses more on the lack of blacks and other visible minorities in the management structure of professional sport (see Fabiano, 1984) and in the administration of Canadian amateur sport (see C. Smith, 1987; Christie, 1989b).

Even more interesting within the Canadian context is the practice of excluding Canadians from certain positions in the CFL. In 1979, Jamie Bone, a Canadian college quarterback who unsuccessfully tried out with the Hamilton Tiger-Cats, complained to the Canadian Human Rights Commission that the CFL's designated import rule discriminated against him on the grounds of national or ethnic origin because it prevented Canadians from being hired to play quarterback. The Commission investigated his complaint and concluded that it was always in a team's best interest to select the most talented quarterback regardless of his national origin, and that although a particular CFL coach may mistakenly perceive the designated import rule to favour hiring imports to play that position, the rule itself does not. Donald Ball (1973) found that Canadians in the CFL (as opposed to American imports) were stacked primarily on defence, and in supporting and reactive positions. Even those with American college experience were excluded from the more rewarding and desirable positions (e.g., quarterback). This differential treatment was also reflected in the lower salaries they received compared to those of imports. Still today, most Canadian-trained quarterbacks are converted to defensive halfbacks while teams opt for quarterbacks from American colleges. Roy McMurtry, a senior CFL executive and former commissioner, is strongly in favour of encouraging the development of Canadian quarterbacks in the league through more co-operation with the Canadian Interuniversity Athletic Union (Christie, 1990).

The problem with all these studies that use a bias or discrimination framework is that they are merely descriptions of what exists. Discrimination and prejudice are concepts that don't really draw out the *power* of racial or ethnic majorities to define other groups in ways that appear to constitute "reasons" for their exclusion from socially desirable positions. Neither do they capture the qualitative character of the oppression felt by blacks, visible minorities, and some ethnic groups. They tell us, in other words, what exists, but they do not tell us *why* the situation persists.

Assimilation Theories

Assimilation theory predicts the gradual dilution of cultural traits among ethnic immigrants through a cycle of initial contact, then conflict leading to accommodation, followed by eventual assimilation into the dominant culture. Groups or individuals as yet unassimilated are seen as culturally deprived. A variant of assimilation theory is the cultural pluralism model, which allows ethnic groups to maintain their cultural, linguistic, and religious autonomy yet integrates them into the dominant political and economic systems.

Sport, from an assimilationist perspective, is seen as an important mechanism by which ethnic groups (and their individual members) are assimilated into mainstream society. In one of the few Canadian studies in this area, Day (1981) used ethnic soccer clubs in London, Ontario, in an attempt to measure the degree of assimilation of their members into the "core" society. His finding was that the London clubs, which were originally formed to help ethnic groups preserve a sense of their cultural identity, now actually promote assimilation because of the intensely competitive nature of the league and the necessity of recruiting from several cultural groups. In an earlier study, McKay (1975) examined the effect of sport involvement on the assimilation of Italian amateur soccer players in metropolitan Toronto. He found that, like the clubs in London, the necessity of recruiting from outside the Italian community promoted assimilation and inter-ethnic contact rather than the preservation of ethnic identity and solidarity.

One problem with defining ethnicity and race in terms of a subjective identity is that they are accepted as being natural. In other words, these categories are never questioned. We rarely ask how it is that people come to be classified as racially or ethnically different in the first place? If we do, then we are forced to recognize that race and ethnicity are really social categories (just like class and gender) that define not subjective identities but the social processes whereby relationships between dominant and subordinate groups are maintained on racial and ethnic grounds. Social practices determine racial and ethnic categories, not vice versa.

The second conceptual problem with the assimilation model is the lack of distinction between race and ethnicity. Race is often regarded as a biological category and ethnicity as a cultural one. On a simplistic level this works well, but if race and ethnicity are combined, as is so often the case, then this will obscure the differences within various racial groups. Blacks and aboriginal peoples in Canada, for instance, are as diverse ethnically as are whites.

Finally, if race and ethnicity are understood as social categories then the analysis of race and ethnic *relations* and sport must "move beyond the treatment of race [and ethnicity] as a descriptive variable and address ideological questions of the production of race [and ethnic] relations and the specific forms such relations take in particular times" (Birrell, 1989: 218). More specifically, it is important to determine the role of sport in the construction of race and ethnic relations, which are often characterized by unequal relationships between dominant and subordinate groups. This brings us to a discussion of an alternative perspective.

Critical Analyses of Race and Ethnic Relations

On one level, Canadian society can be described as a complex network of relations among various racial and ethnic groups that occupy unequal economic, political, and social positions. Identifiable ethnic and racial relations revolve around three major axes:

- relations between *natives* and *non-natives*;
- relations between *French* and *English*;
- relations between the *colonizing* or "charter" groups (French and English) and *other immigrants* and their descendants.

These relations are relevant not only to the private experience of individuals, but they also structure debates over some very public and divisive issues, such as aboriginal rights and land claims, linguistic rights, provincial powers, immigration policy, multiculturalism, racism, and so on. As we have already stated, these relations are characterized by unequal relationships between dominant and subordinate groups. They arose through our particular history, they continue in the present, and, more important, they are often a source of societal conflict. Here we are specifically interested in the role of sport, if any, in the reproduction or change of race and ethnic relations in Canadian society.

RELATIONS BETWEEN NATIVES AND NON-NATIVES
Research on the role sport plays in the relation between natives and non-natives has focused on three areas. The first is primarily historical in that it examines the evolution and role of sport and games within traditional native cultures prior to, during, and after European contact. Gerald Glassford's (1976) study of the importance of games and sport to a transitional

Courtesy National Archives of Canada, PA50294.

Tom Longboat.

Eskimo culture and Salter's (1972) study of the changes that occurred in the original North American Indian game of lacrosse as a result of European contact are two examples of this sort of research.

The second area is the study of the native athlete within mainstream Canadian sport. Bruce Kidd's (1980, 1983) studies of the famous Indian runner, Tom Longboat, and Zeman's (1988) biographical stories of less well-known native athletes are examples. By its nature this research is historical, but it does, according to Paraschak (1989), point to three major themes that have characterized the relations between natives and non-natives in the modern sporting context: racism, exploitation, and ethnocentric distortion.

We mentioned in Chapter 3 that many early Canadian sport clubs barred native people ("Indians" specifically) from their membership, particularly in sports in which they excelled, such as lacrosse, snowshoeing, and running. In an ardent defence of Tom Longboat, who dominated Canadian running in the decade prior to World War One, Kidd (1983) argues that racist characterizations of Longboat – "having all the waywardness and lack of responsibility of his race" – have gone unchallenged. They were, as the historical record shows, simply untrue. Tom Longboat was exploited by the sports clubs and officials who fought regularly to use him as their symbol or commodity, as were earlier native lacrosse players whose prowess was used to promote the novel "Indianness" of the game on international tours and at the box office at home. As the novelty wore off, natives were pushed aside and the amateur aspect of the game at least became totally white-dominated. The native athletes in Zeman's *To Run With Longboat* all describe incidents of racism as well as the enormous difficulties of adjusting to life off the reserve and how little attention is paid by the mainstream of Canadian sport to their very considerable accomplishments.

Most accounts of the native sport experience have suffered from ethnocentric distortion; in other words, the bias of viewing *their* experience from the perspective of our primarily white culture and experience. As Paraschak (1989) points out, non-natives have clearly used a Western brush to paint their perception of natives, whether in condemning gambling in native sport practices, or in imposing Western concepts on a traditional native game (e.g., the name change from baggataway to lacrosse), or in presenting ideological distortions of the accomplishments of native athletes.

The third focus of research concerns the mix, sometimes a clash, between traditional native (northern) sports and mainstream (southern) organized sport. The clash of northern and southern values has produced the inevitable cultural tensions:

> the desire to preserve an autonomous native culture while claiming to become part of the "mainstream" or dominant culture; the potential contradiction between the social role of native games and the social structure of "Western" sport; the evocation of an anti-modern or at least pre-modern past and yet the exploitation of modern technology such as aviation and tele-communications. (Mrozek, 1987: 35)

In Chapters 2 and 3 we discussed the differences between "pre-modern" and "modern" conceptions of sport. The elements of modernity in sport are secularism, equality, specialization, rationalization, bureaucratization, quantification, and record-setting. The "modern" ways of sport have provided new competitive structures to northern native peoples such as the Northern Games, a yearly festival held to celebrate traditional recreational activities, and the Arctic Games, held every second year as a form of regionalized Canada Games. The competitions contain a mixture of Inuit contests (e.g., high kick, whip contest, rope gymnastics, hand tug-of-war, the Eskimo drum dance) as well as mainstream, southern sport. As both Paraschak (1982) and Mrozek (1987) suggest in their critiques of this transplantation of organized sport into the North, all this seems so removed from the spontaneous play and games of an indigenous culture. Moreover, as Mrozek (p. 38) puts it so aptly: "the consciousness of having to preserve the culture fundamentally alters what is preserved – turning it into a museum piece."

RELATIONS BETWEEN FRENCH AND ENGLISH The history of French-English relations in Canada is characterized by recurrent power struggles for the control of the economic, linguistic, and cultural dimensions of their respective societies. In all provinces except Quebec and New Brunswick, Francophones constitute a small percentage of the total population, frequently smaller than that of other ethnic groups. From the perspective of Francophones, there are two approaches to resisting the obvious inequality in relations between dominant and subordinate ethnic groups. One is federalism, where the struggle has been to increase the presence of Francophones in federal institutions in order to secure their influence in defining national goals and in allocating national resources. In sport, for instance, six out of the ten federal Ministers of State for Fitness and Amateur Sport (the position originated in 1976) have been Francophone. For many Francophones, however, an alternative way of resisting inequality has been to support separatism by creating a society – with something approaching complete political autonomy – that would be predominantly, if not exclusively, French.

To some extent, these two political approaches have been reflected in sporting institutions and structures because sport is viewed by both French and English, federalists and separatists, as an important symbol of cultural struggle. In the 1968 federal election campaign, for example, federalist Pierre Trudeau, facing the growing threat of Quebec separatism, grasped at sport as a symbol of national unity. The task force to investigate amateur sport in Canada, which Trudeau set up immediately after his election victory, lauded the Canada Games as an "excellent unifying force" and decried "how scant is the involvement of the government in encouraging the development of so potentially influential a psychological nation-builder" (Task Force Report, 1969: 13). On the other hand, as we noted in Chapter 4, Quebec's separatist Premier René Lévesque is purported to have quipped: "Quebec 2, Canada 0" when speedskater Gaetan Boucher won his two gold medals at Sarajevo in 1984.

Does sport contribute to Canadian unity or disunity? Sociologically we cannot say whether it does or does not, since there is no way to confirm or deny such a direct causal connection. On the one hand, the structures of Canadian sport do not allow for French-English antagonism to surface since we usually compete internationally as one nation, not two. Our professional teams are organized around cities with our loyalties supposedly determined by locale, not ethnicity. As Dunning and Sheard (1979) have pointed out, sport has a unique quality of fostering local and regional rivalries, but subsequently unifies these rival factions around a common national sport endeavour. On the other hand, since the early 1970s, the government of Quebec has very determinedly developed a Quebec sports elite intended to enhance its image not only nationally but also internationally (Harvey and Proulx, 1988). What we can say, therefore, is that sport continues paradoxically to operate as an important symbol both for those whose focus is Canadian unity and for those more interested in Quebec nationalism.

RELATIONS BETWEEN COLONIZERS AND IMMI-GRANTS Canada has seen a decline in the British ethnic group over the past eighty-five years and an increase in the non-English and non-French population, now estimated at 30 per cent and representing some thirty-five different cultural backgrounds. The majority of these ethnic minorities are European, with Asians, native peoples, and blacks constituting the racial minorities. Most of the population increase among the ethnic and racial minorities has resulted from changing immigration patterns, especially in the post-war years of industrial expansion.

What is the significance of play, games, and sport for ethnocultural persistence as well as individual and group ethnic identity in Canada? Have sports played a role in "making" Canadians, whether through school and neighbourhood-sponsored teams or by creating popular enthusiasm for the Blue Jays or the Edmonton Oilers? Are sports, as Harney (1985) asks, a vehicle of acculturation and individual mobility, or a trusted handmaiden of ethnic persistence? Again, little research is directed toward answering these questions. For instance, except for Hershfield's (1980) historical survey of the contributions of Jewish athletes to the sporting heritage of Winnipeg, we know nothing about the place of sports within the Canadian Jewish community. Significantly, we know virtually nothing about the all-black baseball teams that dominated the Canadian game in the 1930s and 1940s, many of whose heroes are still alive today (Humber, 1983). Aside from Chamberlain's (1983) study of the role of soccer in the Italian-Canadian culture, no accounts exist of early Italian-Canadian soccer clubs and their contribution to ethnic survival.

The information we need is buried in the documents and files of ethnic sport clubs, associations, leagues, and special events. A recent (1985) issue of *Polyphony*, written from the perspective of immigrant narrators, provides only glimpses of autonomous immigrant sports traditions in Canada and their struggle to preserve them in a host society. As the editor of the issue reminds us:

> serious study of sports organizations and their sponsors could enrich our understanding of the problems of immigrant integration in Canadian society and of the constant encounter of immigrants and their values with the host society and its ways, encounters which constitute the backdrop and engine of the ethnicization process. In fact the formation of any sports team, or the events and rituals surrounding any organized game, contain those elements of a cultural artifact in which a good ethnographer can read a narrative and can carry on the sort of deep textured analysis which show ethnicity to be a complex process and a negotiation, not just a hard fact acquired from the census or from looking at someone's surname. (p. 10)

SUMMARY: RESISTANCE TO INEQUALITY

We began this chapter by pointing out that social inequality in Canadian society, although often admitted and accepted, is frequently attributed to individual differences in motivation and achievement. Liberalism, the dominant ideology in Canada, assumes that we are all equal in our opportunities, that if we become educated and work hard we will succeed. Yet, for society at large and for sport specifically, many inequalities exist among those of differing social class backgrounds, between males and females, and within the various ethnic and racial groups.

No matter how we choose to look at it, one's background, sex, colour, language group, and immigrant status *do* matter when it comes to the opportunities and power available in our sport structure.

It is simply not possible to lay the blame for an unequal distribution of rewards and resources in sport on individuals when these very patterns are connected to factors over which individuals have no control – their family background, their sex, their racial or ethnic background. In other words, these inequalities are structural and are embedded in the very fabric of our culture. Those who compete for Canada will continue to come from primarily high-income, privileged families because only these families can provide a broad range of life chances and opportunities for their children. Women will continually struggle to enter the power structure of sport because they must also have children and raise families, and probably work full-time as well. Francophones, aboriginal peoples, and immigrants, as minority groups in Canada, will continue to struggle with the Anglophone majority over their right to maintain their own values, customs, and cultural practices.

Resistance to inequality produces struggle and conflict, both of which are as inevitable as inequality itself. People protest their unequal position, opportunity, or power as being unfair and unjust. They may also take action in one of two ways: they either work within the "system" to bring about changes, or they opt out of the system and try to work for change from the outside. The first is a more liberal, reformist position; the second is a more radical, perhaps revolutionary stance (see also the discussion in Chapter 10).

Let's take as an example feminist attempts to change sport. The liberal feminist strategy makes extensive use of the state to bring about the abolition of sex discrimination. In Canada, "women and sport" policy statements have been developed by the federal government, a few of the provinces, and a very small minority of the seventy or so national sport organizations. Such policy statements all address issues of structures and systems, allocation of resources, opportunities for participation and competition, leadership opportunities, as well as promotion and public education. Governments, or government-funded bodies, promise to initiate, assist, support, provide, and encourage "equality," meaning access to the fullest opportunity for individuals to exercise their potential, and "equity," meaning justice and fairness in providing for the physical activity needs of girls and women. These strategies have won women unprecedented admission to the world of sport but in terms very different from the ideals envisioned by earlier women's sport leaders who fought against integration into a male-defined and controlled institution (Theberge, 1989b).

The liberal strategy is to ensure that women have just as much of the resource pie as men, but the radical perspective wants as little as possible to do with "men's" sport in order to create alternative women-centred activities. Take, for example, Birrell and Richter's (1987) discussion of a women's summer recreational softball league in the United States where a group of feminists tried to transform their sport by making it more process-oriented, collective, inclusive, supportive, and infused with an ethic of care.

Through conscious intervention and counterhegemonic practices, they were transforming their game into an experience that had meaning within their own lives. This approach is both radical and separatist, providing for women an opportunity to use sport as a site of resistance to patriarchal domination and control. Advocacy groups such as the Canadian Association for the Advancement of Women and Sport must continually negotiate a fine line between liberal, system-oriented interests on the one hand and, on the other hand, more radical strategies that would fundamentally change the system.

The point is that there will be considerable resistance to social inequality, which in turn will produce the inevitable struggles and conflict. It is important to recognize that different groups and sectors will have differing views as to how best to bring about change toward a more egalitarian and socially just society. We cannot afford to be judgemental about strategies with which we may not personally agree, because in the end they may make sense to someone else.

SUPPLEMENTARY READING

To understand the nature and extent of social inequality in Canada generally, the reader might begin with Michael Czerny and Jamie Swift's *Getting Started on Social Analysis in Canada*, a well-written, easy-to-read exploration of social injustice in Canada. Also see Patricia Marchak's *Ideological Perspectives on Canada*. The literature specific to sport and social inequality is not located in any one collection; nonetheless, for a more complete understanding of the historical basis of both class and gender inequality in Canadian sport, we again suggest Richard Gruneau's *Class, Sport and Social Development* and Helen Lenskyj's *Out of Bounds: Women, Sport and Sexuality*.

Although written in 1982, Ann Hall and Dorothy Richardson's *Fair Ball: Toward Sex Equality in Canadian Sport* still contains useful information. By far the most complete source of Canadian information about women in sport is *Women, Sport and Physical Activity: Research and Bibliography*, compiled by Helen Lenskyj. There are also some worthwhile essays on sport and gender relations in Mike Messner and Don Sabo's *Sport, Men, and the Gender Order: Critical Feminist Perspectives*.

Bruce Kidd's *Tom Longboat* and Brenda Zeman's stories about Canadian native athletes, *To Run With Longboat*, are both interesting and informative. So, too, is the special issue of *Polyphony* – 7, 1 (1985) – on ethnic sport in Canada, a fascinating collection of essays written from the perspective of immigrant narrators.

Chapter 8
YOUTH AND EDUCATION

*F*or virtually all young people, physical play, which involves discovering what can be done with one's body, is an important and almost inevitable part of growing up. In the informal games of street and schoolyard, children pursue the mastery of familiar physical skills until these become unself-conscious pleasures. When they are ready, and indeed sometimes before they are ready, young people find themselves testing the limits of what they have done before. Girls and boys try a new "move" with a puck or a skateboard or on figure skates, and when they succeed, and have practised until they can repeat these successes with some confidence, they are "empowered." A natural talent has been transformed into a skill that can be used and enjoyed when appropriate (Shotter, 1974). With failure

the consequences may simply be the absence of these positive experiences, and the incentive to try again. More negatively, they may include physical pain, from scrapes and bruises to more serious injuries. And failure may also include the social pains, often acute in childhood, of embarrassment in front of peers.

At least as important as its role in developing physical skills, streetcorner and schoolyard sport provide many opportunities, informal but nonetheless highly charged, for the development of social skills (Devereux, 1976). How we react to others' failures and successes (as well as our own), how we negotiate disputes, how well we sustain the group feeling that keeps the game going – all these are among the interpersonal skills that get subsumed under la-

Brian Gavriloff, Edmonton Journal.

Sport is about extending our limits.

bels like "leadership" and "getting along with others." These and other qualities are learned in the informal games that children organize for themselves, despite the presence sometimes of bullying and the use of force. Critics of organized youth sport, such as Edward Devereux, suggest that when adults take over the responsibility for managing the situation – by deciding who will do what, by calling the offsides and stopping the arguments – important opportunities for this kind of social learning are sacrificed.

Nonetheless, children's sport today is highly organized. There is a long history of games, and subsequently physical education, organized under the auspices of adults as part of the educational program of the schools. There is also a tradition of children's sport organized originally by other bodies, such as the YMCAs and churches, but now characteristically by sport-specific clubs and by provincial and national sport associations. This history is shorter, but today minor hockey and soccer, as well as gymnastics and swimming, are important features of childhood for many Canadian boys and increasing numbers of girls. The decision to put a daughter or son into gymnastics or hockey, or to keep children out of organized competitive sport, is also seen as an important one by many families.

Adult interest in children's sport can in part be attributed to a belief in the value of physical fitness. This is found first in expressions of concern about the physical state of young men recruited to fight at the time of war. In more contemporary times, fitness has come to be seen as a health issue, important to the individual and society alike (see Chapter 5). For the individual, the physical education profession's belief that the habit of regular sport or exercise contributes to a healthier and therefore happier life is manifest in the Canadian Association for Health, Physical Education, and Recreation's frequent campaigns to have "quality daily physical education" institutionalized within the provincial school systems. For society, improved fitness among the population, instilled when one is young, will presumably translate into savings in health care expenditures.

Another recurring theme in parents' and educators' beliefs about the positive value of organized sport for children is access to better coaching and teaching, and hence the faster and more systematic development of sports skills. Again, from the perspective of the individual child, clearly a case can be made that proper instruction not only makes activities safer but also makes for success and mastery. Learning to hit a golf ball powerfully and accurately can be empowering, while shanking it into the rough creates frustration. Moreover, where parents foresee the possibility of a career in professional sport, early and intensive coaching may be actively sought for obvious reasons. The importance of proper coaching is also stressed by sport leaders whose concern is the development and future of their specific sport. The concern here is less with the development of individuals than with what is perceived to be a national objective or societal good, although this distinction is not always acknowledged.

The most important reason behind adult organization of children's and youth sport, however, has to do with "socialization," that is, the inculcation of what are seen as important values, attitudes, and habits. Traditionally, this belief that sport builds character has given sport such a prominent place in our school systems, as well as in the recreational and competitive leagues that are now the basis of children and youth sport outside the school environment. Therefore, our purpose in this chapter is to explore the development of sport inside the schools and of youth sport outside the schools, as well as the relationships and tensions between them. We also discuss the role of sport within Canadian universities and the issues this raises. First, however, we more fully examine the notion of socialization through sport.

SOCIALIZATION: A CRITIQUE

It will doubtless have occurred to some readers that the idea that "sport builds character" obscures a series of beneath-the-surface questions: What kind of character is built by the lessons and practices of competitive sport? Who is it appropriate for, and what kind of society results when this character is celebrated and held up for emulation? It is apparent that the character said to be developed through sport has historically been seen to be male, and this has been used as a reason for keeping some sports closed to girls and women. Yet clearly some of the qualities believed to be developed through the practice of sport – determination and discipline, commitment to long-term goals, poise under pressure – are not gendered qualities at all. They are to be valued in individuals of either sex. Other qualities, such as aggression and competitiveness, are arguably dysfunctional in many other kinds of social relationships.

Our point is that there is more to "socialization" than the mutually beneficial and "natural" process depicted in theories about the "functions" of play, games, and sport. On the surface, socialization is a necessary part of growing up for every child. We need to know how to get along in the world. Conversely, it is in society's interest to bring up young men and women to be able and willing to fulfil the demands that will be made on them as adults: as workers, as family members, as citizens. Thus, activities that teach boys and girls "appropriate" skills, and the structures of feeling and attitude that accompany them, serve the interests of individual and society alike. However, British sociologist Anthony Giddens (1979) reminds us that societies do not have interests of their own, certainly not independent of the interests of the groups who constitute a given society. Likewise, American sociologists Peter and Brigitte Berger (1974) remind us that societies are human constructions and that the reproduction of a particular social order (for example, where the rich are

honoured and in which men have all kinds of privileges) has to be seen in terms of the reproduction of ideas and norms and values that make these relations seem natural and right.

The challenge becomes to understand how specific "socialization" practices serve the interests of dominant groups in our society by making their privileges seem either natural or deserved. Here we connect the analysis of social inequality and the power structures of Canadian society developed in the last chapter with the analysis of culture (i.e., as meanings and values and practices) developed in Chapter 2. We will need to look at the specific values and "vocabularies of motive" (see Chapter 2) associated with the teaching of sport, in and outside the schools, and at how and where these have changed over the years. In recognizing historical changes in values, we need also to appreciate that the "official" meanings and values at any given time are neither neutral nor natural. Instead, they articulate and thereby popularize the beliefs of dominant groups in society, and in doing so they point to the capacity of dominant social groups to "define the situation."

Finally, in identifying contemporary issues in school sport and in youth sport outside the schools, we will want to relate pressures for change (and resistance to it) to struggles between different interest groups. At one level, these are struggles between groups with very direct stakes in an institution like minor hockey: for example, the interests of parents in their own children, of minor hockey officials whose commitment is to "the game," and of physical educators who want to change how hockey is taught are likely to be quite different. At a deeper level, it is also possible to see (and again minor hockey provides some of the best illustrations) the defensive resistance of many men to social changes they perceive as threats to "normal" gender relations (see Chapter 7).

We have introduced the idea that "socialization" is *more* than just a routine or natural process whereby individuals learn skills, traits, values, attitudes, norms, and knowledge associated with a particular "social role" because we find it noticeably absent from much of the research and literature on sport and socialization. The approach usually adopted is that of a *social learning* perspective, where it is argued that social learning occurs via imitation and modelling of significant others encountered in one or more "social systems" (e.g., family, school, church, peer group) to which the individual is exposed (McPherson and Brown, 1988). A long tradition and a great deal of research now exist concerning two categories of social learning: socialization *into* sport and socialization *through* sport. In the first instance, individuals are socialized both formally and informally into specific sport roles such as recreational participant, competitor, coach, retired athlete, sport consumer, etc. Socialization through being in one of these roles involves the learning of skills, values, attitudes (e.g., sportsmanship, teamwork, discipline, aggressiveness), and specific knowledge associated with that role (McPherson and Brown, 1988). This literature is replete with such terms as "socializing agents and agencies," "role learners," "sex role socialization" (see Chapter 7 also), and "social environments" (cf. Coakley, 1986; McPherson, 1981, 1986).

We are critical of this theoretical perspective and empirical research because, quite simply, after an enormous amount of time and effort on the part of researchers, the results are contradictory and confusing, and there appears to be no discernible relationship between sports participation and subsequent attitudes, values, self-conceptions, or behaviour (cf. Fishwick and Greendorfer, 1987; McCormack and Chalip, 1988; Stevenson, 1975; Theberge, 1984b). There are many debates about apparently inconsistent findings, but the presuppositions behind this research are highly problematic. First, social learning theory, which is essentially a psychological rather than sociological approach, places more emphasis on the individual than the social context, yet rarely recognizes the individual as an active rather than passive participant in the socializing process. Second, sport is often thought to provide a context for unique processes of socialization, when obviously it is impossible to separate the experiences of sports participation from an individual's other life experiences. Competitiveness and an achievement orientation, for instance, may be learned regardless of one's participation or lack of participation in organized sport. Third, sporting environments are often treated as if they were all the same when indeed they are not. There is considerable difference, for example, between the experiences of young children learning their skills informally on the playground and those involved in highly organized, adult-controlled sports clubs, leagues, camps, or programs.

The approach we are taking here, while not entirely ignoring the sport socialization literature, is to examine some of the historical roots or precursors of children's and youth sport in Canada with a view to explaining contemporary developments and issues in these often controversial areas. There are also large differences between Canada and the United States, where a good deal of the sport socialization literature originates, and it is important to recognize that both the historical precursors and current issues are quite different as a result.

SCHOOL SPORT: EMPHASIZING THE EDUCATIONAL

The Private School Legacy

In the English private schools of the late nine-teenth century, as we observed in Chapter 3, sport had become an integral part of the educational program, and contests between these schools had become traditional fixtures and often objects of public interest (Mangan, 1981). British educational historian Anthony Mangan indicates that games were promoted out of an almost missionary belief in their educational value. Physical fitness and hardiness were virtues in their own right (see also Barman, 1984, on boys' private schools in British Columbia). But even more important were the moral and social lessons that could be taught through the medium of games: lessons to do with self-discipline, loyalty, fairness, honour, and respect for rules. This "muscular Christianity" could, with some justification, be accused of neglecting the intellect and, indeed, of encouraging an anti-intellectualism that survives in some corners of the jock sub-culture even to-day.

However, these headmasters saw themselves as crusaders for the education of the "whole man" in the context of an educational tradition that had been narrowly scholastic. Their case was that "in the playing fields boys acquire virtues which no books can give them; . . . and all that 'give and take' of life which stand a man in such good stead when he goes forth into the world" (cited in McIntosh, 1979: 28). Mangan (1981: 39-40) cites another headmaster who believed that sport "prepares boys for that knowledge of men and manners which in practical utility" was more important for the next generation of leaders than extensive academic knowledge. In another school, the headmaster compared the "vigorous man-hood, full of courage," which he claimed was developed through games, with "the languid, lisping babbler about art and culture" (Mangan, 1981: 56). Here, anti-intellectualism is made explicit. Several other features of athleticism, as an ideology and a set of practices having to do with class and gender relations, warrant further discussion.

The first bias has to do with leadership and class, and the extent to which sport in these private schools, catering to upper-class and aspiring middle-class families, was about developing "leadership" qualities in boys who were expected to become leaders. In the most established of these families, sons would simply inherit positions of authority in family companies or estates. In other families of this class, sons were expected to make careers as officers, colonial administrators, or leaders in the church or in business. In any event, parents wanted their sons to develop leadership qualities: decisiveness, poise, skill in the "handling of men," qualities not reducible to book knowledge, and that constituted a class-specific model of male authority in the careers these young men were being pointed toward. We will see shortly that a very different kind of justification was constructed by the advocates of sports for boys who were not expected to become leaders. And even the elite classes did not want their daughters to learn the habits of command. Girls' early private schools were places where young women learned to be deferential: the headmistress of one such school rejected the introduction of games precisely because the "republican spirit of independence" they appeared to foster in boys was inappropriate for young "ladies" (cf. Fletcher, 1984; McCrone,

1988; and our discussion in Chapter 3).

In the boys' schools, this approach to games gave considerable organizational responsibility to the boys themselves, placed most decision-making and leadership responsibilities on team captains and "house" captains, and correspondingly less emphasis on the teaching and development of sports skills. Indeed, "games masters" were not intended to be physical education specialists or coaches so much as role models, in their enthusiasm for the game and their attachment to the "amateur" values discussed in previous chapters. These were not "free schools"; they were places where respect for authority was expected and where academic teaching was often highly authoritarian. Sports were explicitly constructed as an area where boys were to learn to make their own decisions (and hence their own mistakes), in a framework that gave some credence to the leadership development claims discussed earlier.

It is also worth noting that "every boy played every game" (Barman, 1984: 241). This was important, first of all, because games were the centrepiece of these schools' character-building strategies. They were, therefore, too important to exclude some children from (because of ineptitude) or for others to opt out of. Schools fielded as many teams as necessary to give everyone a game. This contrasts, of course, with the structure of tryouts and cuts that most of us take for granted today. It is also noteworthy that team games were viewed as much more valuable than individual sports. Activities like track, boxing, and swimming were seen to embody their own particular lessons. Through being part of a team, however, one learned things like "give and take," leadership, and, conversely, subordinating one's own ambitions in the name of "esprit de corps."

Physical Education: Education through the Physical

Today, of course, much of this will sound old-fashioned. Physical education and inter-school sport now have established places in the public school systems of every Canadian province. Physical education is part of the curriculum from the primary level through to grade twelve, although PE specialists (now recognized, however grudgingly, *as* specialists within the teaching profession) continually have to press the case that "the physical" is an important aspect of everyone's education, not just a frill. Physical education now typically encompasses a much broader range of activities: non-competitive activities like dance and outdoor pursuits, as well as all manner of individual sports, and gymnastics and exercise programs whose purpose is to provide a basic foundation of fitness and psychomotor skill. Most of this is done in the name of offering positive and empowering experiences of physical activities to *all* children.

The most significant change, of course, has been the gradual, though always contested, legitimation of physical activity for girls. Helen Lenskyj's (1989) account of the struggles to establish physical education for girls in Ontario schools is a chronicle of ideas that seem bizarre today but were widely believed in their time. Some of these concerned the threats that vigorous physical activity supposedly posed to the female anatomy: arrested female "development," impairment of the menstrual function, harm to the reproductive organs. Harder to address, because they were ultimately matters of social prejudice, were views that vigorous physical activity, especially competitive sport, promoted "masculine" character traits. Thus Lenskyj describes girls' physical education as initially restricted to gentle exercises and rhythmic activities where the point was graceful display

Brian Gavriloff, Edmonton Journal.

Children enjoying a sack race.

rather than competition. When females did achieve access to competitive sports, these advances were typically compromised by "women's rules" (for example, in basketball) and by clothing that was "feminine" rather than functional.

Today, girls and boys usually have equal rights in access to school physical education programs. This does not necessarily mean, however, that they also have equal opportunities "to learn and express themselves through physical activity" (Talbot, 1989: 15). Official curriculum guides, and indeed PE teachers themselves, often have stereotypical notions about the performance capabilities of girls vis-à-vis boys: girls don't like contact sports; girls have more rhythmical ability; boys hate dance; etc. These ideas become reified and consequently they perpetuate differences in the expectations we have of girls and boys. Co-educational physical education, now the norm in Canadian schools, is considered to confer equality of opportunity. Considerable evidence, however, now suggests that co-education actually detracts from rather than enhances girls' performance in physical education: girls are less active; boys actively harass and ridicule girls; their behaviour is more polarized; and boys take over and girls become more subservient (Talbot, 1989). These findings have led some physical educators to design programs, policies, and practices to bring about equity (the opportunity for successful and full participation, instruction, and learning) in the gymnasium (see Griffin, 1989). Finally, some school physical education, especially when it emphasizes competition and team games, simply does not meet the needs of young women living in a male-dominated society. Female adolescents often resist physical education, and certainly they choose it less often as an option when they have a choice (see Butcher, 1982). Sheila Scraton (1986, 1987) argues within the British context that young women's negative responses to physical education can be interpreted as a sub-cultural resistance to male institutions (e.g., team games) and male values like discipline, control, and conformity. In contrast, she argues, physical education for girls needs "to develop a new programme geared to assertiveness, confidence, health, fitness and the capacity to challenge patriarchal definitions of submissiveness, passivity, dependence, etc." (Scraton, 1987: 182).

More generally, the discourse of inclusion and "something for everyone," as the official rhetoric of physical education, has often been belied by the behaviour of teachers who have concentrated their attention on the skilled and competitive. This has unfortunately turned many boys and girls off physical activity completely. In this, of course, physical education teachers should not be seen as different from other teachers. Just as math and language teachers usually respond to the best pupils, so, too, have PE teachers been taught that their job is the production of "excellence" in their own

field. Our point, however, is that the historical development of physical education, as well as current issues within it, cannot be adequately understood without some attention to developments in sport outside the schools and to developments in public education, each of which need to be seen in the light of transformations in class and gender relations.

However, it is also fairly easy to see that the discourse of "education through the physical," which originated in the boys' private schools, helped to legitimize ideas about the potential of sport in personal education that were subsequently applied in the public schools. In the first half of the century, "progressive" physical educators promoted the practice of sport among girls and among working-class youth, and skill development was less an end in itself than something that offered experiences of mastery, confidence, and self-esteem. In the sixties, the idea of education through the physical coincided easily with a belief in "humanistic education" (see Hellison, 1973). Here, structured introductions to self-directed physical activities (dance and outdoor activities as well as the traditional individual and team sports) were advocated, and indeed widely accepted, as part of a core curriculum whose object was "living and learning" (see, for example, the *Hall-Dennis Report*, 1968).

The ideas underlying "Quality Daily Physical Education" were to give all young people positive experiences of physical activity, to introduce habits of physical activity that might be sustained into adult life, and to introduce students to a variety of activities out of which they could choose favourites to develop into lifelong interests. Sports that had "carry-over" potential, especially ones that men and women can enjoy together as adults, tended to be promoted more actively than the body-contact team games that most adults find difficult to stay involved in after they leave school. Sometimes these official "messages" of school physical education conflict with the actual behaviour of PE teachers, who take great interest in the best athletes and ignore others. Sometimes, too, students will experience conflict between the ideals espoused in physical education and the traditions and priorities still enshrined in inter-school sport.

School Sport Today: Issues and Controversies

School sport in Canada is a provincial responsibility, like education itself. Each province has a provincial secondary school athletic association that establishes playing and eligibility regulations and organizes provincial playdowns and championships. Just like other programs within the public education system, there have been pressures to cut back or at least do the same job with fewer resources.

School sport has always officially sought to distance itself from the "excesses" of youth sport, which we will discuss shortly. Seasons are shorter, and students are often encouraged to play several sports. Especially in the individual sports, teacher/coaches often make a real effort to encourage boys and girls who are *not* stars. Even where there is a strong competitive tradition, the single-minded focus of youth sport organizations on winning and on talent development is typically tempered by some concern with broader educational objectives. Historically, sport organizations have not wanted to rely on inter-school competition for the development of their respective sports, expressing reservations about the lack of specialist coaching and the low quality of competition that often result from the schools' educational priorities. On the other hand, some school districts have decided to exclude club competitors

above a certain level from inter-school competition (for example, in hockey and swimming) in order to maintain relatively balanced and satisfying competition for the majority of students who are non-specialists. Some schools, conversely, have actively recruited good players, using a tradition as a good basketball school, for example, to encourage boys (and it usually has been boys) to transfer. This has led to the introduction of more stringent eligibility rules in some provinces, including rules that required transfer students to sit out for a year unless there were academic or family reasons for the transfer. In Ontario, the OFSAA (Ontario Federation of Schools Athletics Association) transfer rule has been challenged in the courts, with much controversy about tensions between individual rights, the rights of school coaches to run high-performance programs, and the ultimate purposes of school sport (Macintosh, 1989a).

Differences in participation rates between the sexes is still very much an issue in school sport. Most provinces still fail to recognize its importance because they do not keep statistics based on participation by gender. In Ontario, where statistics have been kept regularly, females comprised 39 per cent of inter-school athletes in 1977-78 and 38 per cent in 1987-88 (Macintosh, 1989a). Most provinces suggest that the differences in participation rates can largely be accounted for by the large numbers of males who play football and ice hockey (Hall and Richardson, 1982; Macintosh, 1989a). In the past several years, there has been an increasing emphasis on fitness and individual-oriented activities, with less emphasis on competitive and structured physical activities. In addition, inter-school sport programs show male participants moving away from football and wrestling to rugby and soccer, while there has been a dramatic increase in girls' soccer, sometimes at the expense of field hockey (Macintosh, 1989a). Liability and safety concerns have also reduced participation in high-risk sports like gymnastics and football. Finally, the steady influx of immigrants into the large metropolitan areas over the past decade has also been a factor in the rise of popularity of sports like soccer at the expense of traditionally North American sports like football and basketball.

Another issue concerns the supervision of school sport. Traditionally, leadership has been provided by physical education teachers, and PE teachers were expected to coach. Many teams, however, were still handled by "other subject" teachers who were sometimes expert but more often were "games masters" in the traditional sense; in other words, they gave much time and enthusiasm and often wisdom, but were not trained in physical education. But as teachers' workloads have continued to increase, significant numbers of teachers have withdrawn their voluntary services, making it necessary either to use volunteers from the community or to cut programs. Macintosh (1989a) reports that the use of non-teachers to coach inter-school teams in Ontario rose from 3 per cent in 1975-76 to 14 per cent in 1987-88. Some have emphasized the positive side of this, that it gave opportunities to unemployed physical education graduates and often raised the technical standard of the coaching. However, the use of coaches who do not have class contacts with the pupils and are not part of the broader educational project of the school is regarded by others as increasing the likelihood that educational objectives are subordinated to the more visible success of having a winning season.

The temptation that is always there to make school sport more like youth sport – to teach skills rather than teaching girls and boys, to pursue results, and to concentrate on the development of the elite players – is given a fur-

ther push in Sport Canada's recent policy document *Toward 2000: Building Canada's Sport System* (Fitness and Amateur Sport, 1988). What is envisaged in Sport Canada circles is "better" (i.e., more technically qualified) coaching in school sport, increased collaboration between schools and clubs, and elite school leagues that would provide better competition for promising young athletes. The document proposes a closer integration of the club system and the school system in an overall "Canadian sport system." It is clearly intended that the schools should become more professional in their approach to talent development, rather than that the club system should take on broad ideas like "education through the physical."

YOUTH SPORT: FROM CHARACTER-BUILDING TO SPORTS SKILLS

Early Precursors

The sponsorship of sport and physical recreation for young men (and it was only males to begin with) outside the auspices of the school system had its origins in beliefs that sport was character-building and that the offer of enticing activities would attract young players into a sphere of positive social influences. In such programs, a genuine concern for individual boys came together with equally genuine concerns about social order and Christian values, in what has been variously termed the "social gospel" tradition and the "rational recreation" movement. This movement was not any single organization but rather a collection of organizations that shared concerns about the future of the new industrial societies if they did not help urban working-class youth to lead constructive lives. They included such national and ultimately international organizations as the YMCA, the Boy Scouts, and the established churches. The Protestant churches, for example, sponsored sport as a means of keeping young Christian men involved in church activities and of bringing others under Christian influence (Howell and Lindsay, 1986). Such organizations also included local initiatives ("settlement" or "neighbourhood" houses), in which groups of reform-minded citizens attempted to do "social work" through the provision of organized sport and recreation.

Consistent with these objectives, church leagues and YMCAs sought to include everyone who wanted to play, with the continuing exception of girls. The dominant ethos, not surprisingly, was one of character-building rather than the teaching of sports skills. Sporting activities were a means to a more important end rather than an end in themselves. Yet, that "character" seldom extended to include the development of leadership qualities and skills. What it did mean was respect for authority, punctuality, and the acceptance of external discipline. The virtues of following rules were explicitly emphasized, but there were few opportunities for the self-organization and leadership that were central to what character-building meant in the private schools (cf. Cavallo, 1981; Hardy, 1982). These were boys not seen as destined for leadership positions in society, so the meanings of "character-building" were recast to suit different social objectives.

There were also other "players" in the arena of youth sport. One that we have already mentioned in Chapter 3 was the Workers' Sport Association. The WSA was active primarily in a few smaller cities in northern Ontario and the West, but its members saw themselves as competing for young men (in an era when most working-class youths quit school as soon as possible) with YMCA and factory-sponsored teams. Their project was to teach a set of values and loyalties explicitly opposed to those of "bourgeois" culture. However, just like their bourgeois competitors, they offered organized sport as a "carrot" to attract boys into an environment where a set of social values and allegiances could be taught (Kidd, 1989). A more widespread and arguably more poignant and complex instance of this general project is represented by the ethnic sports clubs, the purpose of which was the preservation of ethnic identities (see Chapter 7). Harney (1985) describes how many of these ethnic clubs competed with the schools and other dominant culture institutions (including the Ys) for boys' time and allegiance.

In each of the above instances, sport was seen by the organizers primarily as an instrument for teaching values. This, rather than the teaching of sports skills or the production of sporting excellence, was the primary purpose of early youth sport. However, in order to "win" boys, all of these organizations, whose larger purposes were moral and ideological rather than sporting, still had to compete with each other to attract boys into their programs. They did so through better coaching, better facilities, better uniforms and equipment, better organized and more "attractive" competitive programs. This reality produced debates between those prepared to emphasize the sport and those for whom the moral teachings were never far from the surface. The YMCA movement, for example, embodied a compromise between physical and spiritual purposes that satisfied most, although not all, church people (Howell and Lindsay, 1986).

Not surprisingly, the organizations that were able and willing to provide good sporting experiences without too much moral baggage attracted the most young people, while the more sectarian and evangelical organizations found themselves struggling for members. The YMCA and, in some cities, the YMHA (Young Men's Hebrew Association), were probably the most important institutional organizers of sport for young people in the period between the wars. But with the growth of municipal recreation and, hence, the availability of public facilities, inter-community competition began to be organized, under the auspices of city parks departments where they existed. More typically, local businesses were enlisted to sponsor teams and local service clubs organized the volunteers who actually put on the programs.

Here we have the precursors of Canadian "youth sport." However, the highly organized youth sport we know today is more a product of events occurring after the Second World War. Gordie Howe, as Dryden and MacGregor (1989) observe, played for three teams when he was fourteen but still got less organized hockey than most bantams today. The post-war period saw the growth of minor sport organizations independent of the education system and the growth of a minor sport "sub-culture" in which the dominant values were drawn more from adult sport (i.e., professional sport) than from the education system. Indeed, some authors make the point that, in the United States, youth leagues developed precisely because of the negative attitudes toward competition that held sway among physical education and recreation professionals at the time (Fine, 1987; Berryman, 1975). When these professions declined to organize competition on any scale, or when the programs they did organize downplayed the competitive aspect, the enthusiasm for inter- and intra-community competition was such that volunteer organizations found themselves with a lot of takers. Little League baseball in the United States had its counterpart in minor hockey in Canada.

Post-War Developments

The evolution of youth sport into the highly organized and sophisticated phenomenon we know today is primarily a post-war development, a product of unprecedented prosperity in Canada and also of the rise of new ideas about childhood and parenthood. The "Memorial" arenas and pools that sprang up across the country were one of the most visible signs of post-war affluence in Canada. Municipal recreation provision was an established feature of Canadian cities before the war. After the war, new levels of prosperity and a new consensus that "good communities to live in" had not only well-equipped hospitals and schools but opportunities for recreational and (especially) sporting participation together meant a dramatic growth in such facilities. In the rural areas, government commitment to make available at least some of the public services that were now "normal" in cities meant subsidies and grants toward arenas in many small towns and villages. Everywhere, new high schools that once had contained just gyms and fields now were built with pools and tracks as virtually standard facilities. All of this meant more sports facilities to use, more school-sponsored sport, and many more public facilities available for rental by service clubs and other groups organizing games for young people.

Also connected to the dramatic growth of youth sport was the commitment of many post-war parents to involve themselves in the lives of their children and to give them every opportunity to "be the best you can be" (Dryden and MacGregor, 1989). On the one hand, this may conjure up images of parents pushing a child, screaming at coaches and referees, wanting the child to succeed even more, perhaps, than the child does. If we think about this sociologically, however, a more complex and perhaps under-

Minor hockey can be fun.

Brian Gavriloff, Edmonton Journal.

standable picture emerges. First, few post-war parents had known anything like these marvellous new facilities, or the opportunities for coaching and for "real" games and trips, in their own childhoods. They were also living in a period when the conventional wisdom in psychology, spread not only through the schools but through the popular media and self-help books, emphasized the benefits of an early introduction to skill development and learning. Organized children's sport fit right in with early childhood education, learning toys and games, educational television, and lessons in everything from dance to piano. With hindsight, and recognizing the extremes to which some families took it, some critics now call all of this the "erosion of childhood" (Suransky, 1982). But Dryden and McGregor suggest that for 1960s parents, and indeed for many parents today, organized youth sport looked very good to those who wanted the best for their children.

Finally, organized youth sport is also a product of the increasing post-war sophistication of high-performance sport. We need only to recognize the impact of the National Hockey League and the CAHA, and of the national and provincial sport associations in the Olympic sports, which were becoming increasingly (even if indirectly) involved with talent identification and development (see Chapter 4). This increased the sense, from the perspective of parents and young aspirants, that whatever the real effects of coaching, a young person needed to get into the "system" early and be noticed. This was less true in some sports (basketball, track) than it was in others (hockey, gymnastics, swimming). However, the overall effect of more systematic "talent development" has undoubtedly meant more organized sport and at younger ages.

Youth Sport Today: Issues and Controversies

Today, approximately 2.5 million Canadian youths between the ages of six and eighteen participate and compete in sports clubs, community leagues, minor league programs, and developmental programs (e.g., field hockey's Grasshopper program) in both Olympic and non-Olympic sports. Nearly three-quarters of these youths are male, with females involved in individual sports in greater numbers than in team sports. The ten most popular sports (not taking gender into account) are hockey, soccer, baseball, softball, figure skating, football, basketball, lacrosse, volleyball, and swimming (Valeriote and Hansen, 1986). It is important to recognize that there is no *one* youth sport system in Canada. As our historical information shows, there are really several systems – one in the schools, those in the service agencies like the Ys, those sponsored by the provincial and national sport organizations, those in private clubs – all of which developed under different auspices and have continued to operate quite independently until fairly recently. Throughout this history, there have been a number of recurring issues that continue to be debated today.

PURPOSES OF YOUTH SPORT The most basic of these issues concerns the ultimate purposes of youth sport, whether within the education system or elsewhere. The private school legacy, which is still visible in some of the discourses of contemporary physical education, emphasizes the value of sports in the education of the individual. From the perspective of sport organizations, however, we are more likely to hear about "talent development, or "the future of the sport" as the basic issue. This becomes "natural" when youth sport is understood as a feeder system in which future professional or Olympic athletes are being developed. It happens most frequently outside the schools, as the Canadian experience of minor hockey (or swimming, or gymnastics) suggests. It can also happen inside school systems, as American college and high school football and basketball illustrate.

A corollary of this issue concerns the relative emphasis to be placed on the systematic teaching of sports skills. At first glance this is a non-issue because almost everyone would agree that some level of skill mastery is a prerequisite for enjoyment. However, those whose concern is with the aggregate development of talent (in other words, with the "level" of Canadian basketball, for example) and those physical education teachers who see their *raison d'être* as the teaching of sports skills find themselves pitted against teachers and coaches whose pleasure and satisfaction lie in watching young people grow and develop, emotionally as well as physically. The larger issues are whether teaching and coaching are about "education through the physical" or about the "production of performance," and whether demonstrably successful ways of achieving the latter (new training methods, for example, or particular game tactics) are to be tempered by philosophies of humanistic education.

EXCLUSION THROUGH TALENT DEVELOPMENT Related to the above are issues of access and structures and traditions of exclusion. The most fundamental instance, of course, has been the

Brian Gavriloff, Edmonton Journal.

Determined young speedskater.

historical exclusion of girls from youth sports, long after girls' physical education was institutionalized in the schools. This is connected, however, to an emphasis on performance and winning in much of youth sport that focuses attention and rewards on the most promising players and progressively discourages and eliminates most others (Orlick and Botterill, 1975). The connection is that where youth sport is seen as a feeder system for elite levels (whether the NHL or the national swim team), the adults involved are less likely to be interested in making available *to any child who wants to play* the positive experiences that are available in their particular sport.

To develop this issue a little further, we would also argue that where the primary concerns are talent development and winning, youth sport becomes something quite different. In the results-oriented environment that Canadian national sport organizations now have to work in, it is not surprising to find staff saying they have neither time nor resources to "waste" on those who are not likely to make it to the international level. Recreational sport is someone else's responsibility. For those who do "make it," moreover, whether in AAA bantam or midget hockey or into the most competitive levels of swimming or gymnastics, they are no longer playing the game for fun. The emphasis on skill development, which will have begun even earlier in most instances, is now complemented by a new emphasis on fitness and mental discipline and by training regimens that are very demanding on families as well as on the young people themselves (Dryden and MacGregor, 1989).

AN OVEREMPHASIS ON WINNING   The emphasis on skill is also complemented by a "professionalization of attitudes." More than twenty years ago, American sociologist Harry Webb (1969) conducted a study suggesting that the longer a young person had participated in organized competitive games the more likely he or she would say that winning was more important than playing well or simply having fun, and that "good penalties" and the use of intimidation as a tactic were all part of the game. Webb suggested that all of these represented a "professionalization of attitudes." Despite some methodological criticisms (see Coakley, 1986; Greer and Stewart, 1989; Knoppers, 1985; Knoppers, Zuidema, and Meyer, 1989), several studies of highly competitive inter-school sport as well as youth sport, in both Canada and the United States, have confirmed Webb's general point (Albinson, 1976; Mantel and Vander Velden, 1974; Vaz, 1982).

Undoubtedly an important influence here is the professional sport that young players see in the arena and especially on television. When popular heroes quite clearly do whatever is necessary to win and when the moral construction that commentators and other hockey people put on such behaviour is almost uniformly admiring, it is scarcely surprising that young people come to believe this is what the game is about. Another factor is simply that a single-minded commitment to winning and a willingness to do whatever is necessary to win are routinely commended by coaches (Albinson, 1976; Orlick and Botterill, 1975; Vaz, 1982; Fine, 1987). Conversely, a happy-go-lucky attitude or a failure to take the results sufficiently seriously is held against even the most talented young players and can prove to be a barrier to progress through the system. In this early teaching of the values and norms of professional sport (or elite Olympic sport), the transformation of youth sport from a vehicle for the teaching of Rotarian civic values to a form of "anticipatory productive labour" is now complete (Ingham and Hardy, 1984; Cantelon, 1981).

DROPPING OUT OF SPORT   It should not be surprising, in these circumstances, that many boys and girls who have progressed into elite programs have started to find sport more work than fun and have dropped out (cf. Brown, 1985; Orlick and Botterill, 1975; Watson and Collis, 1982). This happens especially in the teen years, when sports interests compete with new demands at school, new friends, and new interests in other aspects of teen culture (Dryden and MacGregor, 1989). Dropouts have become a source of increasing concern, especially in Canadian minor hockey in recent years. In Quebec, François Bilodeau has documented that 56 per cent of the boys who had registered as "Atoms" (ages ten-eleven) in 1983-84 had dropped out by 1987-88 and that overall registrations had declined by 24 per cent (Thérien, 1988). In Alberta, the 1990 Minor Hockey Week tournament attracted less than 400 teams, well down from the 900 teams that used to compete in the early 1970s (Brownlee, 1990).

The dropout phenomenon in youth sport is not particularly new. Some of it can be attributed to the many more choices in consumer entertainment available to contemporary teens and to the fast-food jobs they need in order to take their own places in consumer culture (Johns, Linder, and Wolko, 1990). At the same time, only the most complacent would suggest there are no problems within minor sports. Critics such as sportswriters John Underwood and Martin Ralbovsky began saying publicly in the 1970s what many American boys and their families already knew, that youth sport in Little League baseball and Pop Warner football was becoming so serious as to take the fun out of the game (see Martens, 1978). In Canada, sport psychologists Terry Orlick and Cal Botterill (1975) drew attention to all the same issues, citing dispirited young players and parents who were disillusioned with minor hockey in particular.

Parents and children alike complained about coaches who play their best players most of the time, leaving the others on the bench. They complained about the "win at all costs" philosophy and about a value system that "normalized" instrumental violence, that turned winning and losing into tests of character and personal worth, and that produced great pressure even on the successful kids. Dryden and MacGregor (1989) offer a useful counterpoint to these criticisms in their chapter on "The Playing Fields of Scarborough." Focusing on the story of the captain of the Toronto Marlboro peewees, they remind us that success in minor sport can be the source of a quiet personal confidence, of feeling completely at home with one's body, of the experience of what can be accomplished through perseverance and discipline. Aniko Varpalotai's (1987) study of ringette underlines that girls, too, can get the same positive, even "empowering," experiences from the pursuit of sporting excellence. Dryden and MacGregor also point out, however, that for the boy who dreams of an NHL career, and his family, this intensive preparation for the work world of professional hockey becomes necessary simply because others are doing it. "Minor hockey," argue Dryden and MacGregor (p. 87), "has become largely an exercise in prodigy creation, driven by the needs of the elite player, by the competition, driven by the dream." We would suggest that the same point can be made with respect to "talent development" in such sports as swimming and gymnastics.

As Dryden and MacGregor suggest, these are also mass activities, affecting many children who are never going to be elite athletes. If sports have valuable lessons to offer the growing child, should they not be run so that "every kid can win" (Orlick and Botterill, 1975): girls as well as boys, small as well as big, the late developers as well as the highly co-ordinated prodigies? Dryden and MacGregor suggest that elite sport will survive because the dream will always be attractive to the few with the talent and desire to make it to the top. However, they also propose that if minor hockey is not to continue to lose popularity, it is going to have to be restructured to offer positive experiences to the many who will not "make it" rather than focusing its energies and commitment on the elite. The point is equally applicable to the Canadian system in the Olympic sports. As Dryden and MacGregor point out, "being the best you can be," the slogan popularized in much Olympic-related advertising in Canada, is a notion easily abused. Once it had to do with being the best person you could be, and sports offered one arena, along with school, a part-time job, and voluntary activities in the community, for personal development. Now it has come to mean being the best *at something*, opening the door to a very different set of aspirations and a different set of lessons.

CONTROL OF YOUTH SPORT Finally, there are recurring issues surrounding who "controls" youth sports in Canada. Struggles over control, and over whose definitions and purposes will prevail, can pit physical education professionals against volunteer coaches and administrators. National sport organizations face off against school or university sport organizations, and government objectives for sport as embodied in Sport Canada and the Coaching Association of Canada often are at loggerheads with the traditional volunteer culture of many NSOs (see Chapter 4). These struggles find individuals or other interest groups against minor sport organizations in the courts; this is illustrated by the OHA's resistance to admitting girls into organized competitive hockey (see Chapter 7). Also illustrated here, however, is that in public institutions like schools, "traditional" practices can be more readily subjected to review and challenge. In the case of nominally independent organizations, even ones that have a substantial public role, it becomes more difficult to invoke equity or human rights issues, or even public interest issues (like violence in minor hockey) that challenge the traditional values of the dominant groups in a sport.

We have outlined in the preceding sections how youth sport today has become something quite different, in its objectives and ethos, from its precursors in the schools and in the settlement house and YMCA movements. We have also outlined how a critique of youth sport has thrown into relief its preoccupations with winning, with skills development, and with potentially elite performers. Much of this critique has come from the physical education profession, and models of "alternative practice," to the extent that they exist in Canada, are most likely to be found in physical education programs and in school sport programs that are run in a consciously less intensive way. We return now to the educational system and examine the role of sport within Canadian universities and colleges.

University Sport: Providing for Elite Aspirations?

Sport in Canadian universities dates back to before the turn of the century when students formed teams, challenged other university teams, and inaugurated leagues. The older universities – McGill, Toronto, Queen's – were the originators of much inter-university sport. By 1906 there was sufficient interest among colleges and universities across the country to form the Canadian Intercollegiate Athletic Union (now the Canadian Interuniversity Athletic Union, or CIAU for short). Today, Canadian university sport is no longer organized and controlled by student organizations, and it has grown and developed into a large bureaucracy run by professional athletic administrators, coaches, and marketing personnel.

Throughout the years there has been much debate and discussion over the place (and purpose) of sport within Canadian colleges and universities. What is the best organizational structure? How should it be financed? Should it be a broadly based program or should it emphasize high-profile (and therefore male) sports like football, basketball, and hockey? What is its relationship to the development of high-performance and Olympic athletes? (See Macintosh, 1986, for a useful summary of these debates.)

In our discussion here, we take up just three of the more important issues because they link with our earlier discussions about the tensions and conflicts between school sport and youth sport, and specifically between physical educators versus those outside the educational systems. These issues – athletic scholarships, the role of universities in high-performance sport, and equality of opportunity for women – reverberate at the university and college level in their own particular way.

Athletic Scholarships: Pressures for the American Model

Clearly the young prodigy, and indeed every aspirant to elite status, at some stage has to commit him/herself to an environment where specialist coaching and top-class competition are regularly available, and where other aspects of one's life are organized around training and competitive objectives. Canadian tennis player Carling Bassett, for example, made this kind of commitment when she moved to a tennis school in Florida. Generations of young hockey players have made this commitment when they have moved away from home at age fifteen or sixteen to play junior hockey. Young Canadian football players who have developed their talent within the Canadian high school and university system typically have a much less intensive preparation for a football career than have their American peers. Obviously this raises, for all young athletes, a set of questions concerning their own dreams and prospects. Do they want to commit themselves to an environment where sport clearly comes first, even if this means that getting a good education is rendered more difficult? Or, recognizing that "many are called but few are signed," do they

try to cover themselves by choosing schools where sport is taken seriously, but where education still comes first?

A factor in this choice, historically, has been the availability of athletic scholarships at American universities, scholarships that have not been offered openly at Canadian institutions. The scholarship route is attractive to many athletes for a variety of reasons. First, it offers financial assistance. When access to higher education is as costly as it is, and when these costs must be met through personal and family savings or through student loans, athletic scholarships can make it possible for athletes from less privileged families to attend college. Second, the range of entry standards at American institutions is broader, and even these are often flexible for athletes that a university wants to recruit. University entrance is therefore available to students who might not be eligible at Canadian institutions. Finally, the place of athletics in many American universities is such that the athlete can usually expect much more intensive training than is available at Canadian schools.

The well-known downside to this is that scholarship athletes at American universities are apt to be treated as if they were semi-professional athletes. Obviously, there are differences between schools, between sports, and indeed between individual coaches. However, the norm is that the athlete is an employee; and especially where the athletic program is "big business," athletes are expected to organize their lives around the demands of training and competition. For some, this suits their own priorities, and in hockey at least, the American college system provides opportunities to combine hockey and education more readily than in Canada, where one or the other has to be sacrificed to a considerable extent (see Christie, 1989a; Heinz, 1988). Still, there are many tales

Brian Gavriloff, Edmonton Journal.

Canadian university basketball.

of abuse in the U.S. system (see Chapter 15 in Coakley, 1990, for an excellent discussion).

Some of the same issues are now being raised with a new urgency in the Canadian university system. The tradition in CIAU universities has been that student-athletes were students first and athletes second. This has meant that athletes have had to meet the normal admission standards at their universities and that athletic departments have not been able to offer either scholarships or easier academic demands. Although this has continued to be official policy, it has been infringed at the margins by schools that have offered relatively small amounts of assistance to varsity athletes and that have been prepared to exercise some "discretion" in their admissions policies. Such policies are not uncommon even at leading Canadian universities. Explicit recognition is made of the time and money demanded by the pursuit of excellence in athletics; but there is also a serious commitment to the concept of the student-athlete and to the athlete's academic progress. Infractions of these principles are not unknown, but they have tended to be in some of the smaller universities where a winning tradition in basketball, hockey, or football has become a spectator draw in towns without professional sport.

Those who argue for the status quo – in other words, no significant athletic scholarships in Canadian universities and with the primary emphasis on the education of the student-athlete – maintain that this *is* the best approach for Canada. Others, however, argue that a greater move toward scholarships would facilitate more Canadian athletes staying in Canada, more student-athletes able to attend university, better calibre of athletes, more media attention on university sport, and athletes more able to focus on their sport careers (Pooley, 1987). They also recognize the problems this may bring: greater disparities between universities, more time and money on recruiting, more pressure on athletes, greater costs, and so forth, but they maintain that the benefits outweigh these costs. This, of course, leads to the question of who would finance an American-modelled athletic scholarship program? Some have argued that the federal government, specifically Sport Canada, should, which brings us to a discussion of the role of our universities in Canada's high-performance sport system.

High-Performance Sport: Pressures on the Universities

Pressures have been placed on Canadian universities through the initiatives of Sport Canada and some national sport organizations to develop "centres of excellence" at selected universities and to "upgrade" the competitive level of at least some inter-varsity sport. These proposals would involve government-supported scholarships to NSO-designated athletes, NSO subsidy of coaches and other support staff (for example, athletic therapists), support for sport-related research activities, and sometimes substantial capital contributions to new and improved facilities. In some sports, moreover, "super leagues" were proposed to raise the level of competition by separating out those schools prepared to run a serious competitive program (for example, in basketball) from those who remained committed to the traditional "education through sport" concept.

From Sport Canada's point of view, all this would facilitate keeping Canada's best athletes at home and together, instead of dispersed at U.S. colleges or in European leagues. It has long been an objective of Sport Canada to centralize Canadian national teams under the supervision of a national coach. This is only realistic if the Canadian team program can offer comparable opportunities, educational and financial, as well as competitive opportunities, to those available elsewhere. From the universities' point of view, Sport Canada funding constitutes an important potential resource at a time when all university programs are under severe funding pressures. The opportunities for research funding also provide physical education faculties with opportunities to buttress their standing among their academic peers. Finally, from the athletes' point of view, the availability of scholarships at home partially addresses the access issues raised earlier, while also circumventing the problems some have experienced when the demands of their university sport programs have conflicted with national team fixtures. On the surface, everyone is a winner.

However, as Zeigler (1989) notes, to move in these directions is likely to change the nature and objectives of university sport in Canada. It will certainly mean that resource allocation decisions are more often made with the needs of elite athletes in mind. This means not only spending decisions but other decisions about who uses facilities when and who is hired for coaching and other instructional positions. The losers in this are typically other students: genuine student-athletes who would make varsity teams if semi-professional athletes were not on campus, students who make teams but whose experience is different because of results-oriented coaches, a student body that has fewer opportunities to understand how educational sport can be. Zeigler also suggests that although university PE departments are richer financially for their collaboration with Sport Canada, they will lose their autonomy as the NSOs have before them (see Chapter 4). Finally, as university physical education gets increasingly involved with the production of sporting performance, the discipline itself changes until it becomes virtually divorced from its traditional concern with "education through the physical" (Whitson and Macintosh, 1990).

Gender Issues: Achieving Equality

Canadian universities are now more than ever faced with shrinking resources, which means that athletic departments must increasingly look outside the university for money to support their programs or they must cut back on the breadth of their offerings. When seeking new sources of finance, whether through corporate sponsorships, television revenues, or by selling goods, women's sport traditionally has not been as attractive as men's (Macintosh, 1986). Therefore, in a time when there is increasing pressure on universities to improve the gender balance in all areas, there is virtually no money to do so. Increased emphasis on high-profile male teams such as football, basketball, and hockey means that women's sport will continue to struggle for recognition and support.

Also mitigating against improving sport opportunities for university women is an administrative and policy-making structure dominated by males (as is the case in all areas of the university). In fact, women have lost a good deal of ground over the past twenty years in terms of *significantly* declining numbers of female coaches and athletic administrators in Canadian universities (see Lenskyj, 1988, for a good review of the evidence). This is all the more disturbing because the number of university-level athletes is actually increasing. In part, this trend can be explained by the combining of separate governing organizations for men's and women's university athletics and the amalgamation of university athletic departments. It is also possible that an increased emphasis on high performance and increasing numbers of high school-trained women athletes have made positions coaching women more attractive to men because there is greater emphasis on competitiveness and winning (Macintosh, 1989b). Alternatively, universities have often been extremely reluctant to hire full-time coaches for women's sport, male or female. Whatever the reasons, policy and resource allocation decisions in university sport are now primarily in the hands of men, thus making equity an even more distant prospect.

Summary

The original connections between sport and education were institutionalized first in the boys' private schools and subsequently in physical education in the public schools. Sporting excellence was not an end in itself but a means to personal education. This use of sport to teach other lessons and to accomplish other social purposes was also characteristic of the first "youth sport" in North America, sponsored under the auspices of religious, cultural, and civic organizations. In the post-war period, youth sport expanded dramatically and the concern with moral lessons steadily gave way to an emphasis on the teaching of sports skills, as well as on the pursuit of victory. If character development was still an issue, and some believed it was, then the character of a "winner" became the role model and the norms and values of professional sport were the objects of direct teaching. Youth sport, in other words, became oriented toward the professional aspirations of young players and their families and toward the needs of the professional system.

Throughout most of this growth period, physical education still sought to reiterate the *educational* value of sport and to promote the enjoyment of physical activity not just among elite athletes but among as many young people as possible. As part of this campaign many new sports were introduced into physical education curricula, which moved away from traditional body contact games and toward co-educational activities and sports with "carry-over" potential. This was not always reinforced by the allocation of resources in inter-school sport, which continued to favour the traditional male team sports. Even here, though, educational values took priority over the production of performance, with the result that school sport rarely served the needs of those whose purpose was elite development. Schools, for their part, introduced eligibility rules to preserve school sport for the student-athlete.

In 1988, Sport Canada proposed that the "sport system meet the school system" and that school sport be upgraded so as to provide more effective talent identification and coaching as the basic tier of a national talent development system (Fitness and Amateur Sport, 1988). Critics of this argue that if school sport (in our universities as well as our high schools) becomes integrated into Sport Canada's efforts to improve our standing in international games, the strong institutional base of "sport as education" will be lost and Canadian young people will have lost their major opportunity to participate in sport for fun and self-realization. In any event, these proposals raise again the basic issues that have been posed repeatedly throughout this chapter:

- What are the ultimate purposes of sport for young people?
- Can differences of purpose be reconciled within a common institutional framework?
- Who are youth sport and school sport for?
- How can issues of access and resource distribution be most effectively addressed?

SUPPLEMENTARY READING

The fullest available discussion of youth sport, and the issues surounding it, is Rainer Martens's edited collection, *Joy and Sadness in Children's Sport*. Written for the student audience, it includes contributions by former professional players, journalists, coaches, and parents, as well as academics. Terry Orlick and Cal Botterill in *Every Kid Can Win* give many of the same issues a Canadian accent. The basic intellectual framework for each of these books, however, is social and developmental psychology rather than sociology. More sociological and more contemporary are Gary Alan Fine's (1987)

study of Little League baseball and Ken Dryden and Roy MacGregor's chapter on youth sport in *Home Game*. The latter, while not drawing on academic sociology, does an excellent job of situating minor hockey in Canada in a social and cultural context.

One small book, *The Role of University Athletics: A Canadian Perspective* (edited by A.W. Taylor), is virtually the only available discussion of the issues facing university sport in Canada, and Don Macintosh's essay there is very worthwhile. An adequate treatment of school sport in Canada remains to be written.

Chapter 9
ISSUES AND CONTROVERSIES

In the summer of 1986 the Honourable Otto Jelinek, who at the time was Minister of State for Fitness and Amateur Sport, established the Commission for Fair Play primarily in response to a growing concern on the part of Canadians about the level of violence in sport (specifically ice hockey), but also with a focus on cheating, drug use, and any form of exploitation in an effort to win. "When elements such as these are introduced," said the announcement, "the true competitive spirit is lost, and there remains no purpose for sport." The goals of the Commission were to ensure that fair play *can* thrive and that those who participate in sport have the right "attitude." Through an advertising, promotional, and educational campaign, its specific objective was the promotion of integrity,

sportsmanship, and honesty, and more specifically still the reduction of violence in sport. The program began with a great deal of fanfare and enthusiasum: posters were designed and distributed; Fair Play awards were initiated; television commercials were aired; educational materials went to schools; information/media kits were produced; discussions took place with provincial governments and sport organizations; agreements were signed with other countries. Two years later, Canada looked a little silly when Ben Johnson tested positive at the Seoul Olympics, although the Commission for Fair Play continues its work primarily by developing marketing strategies to generate private-sector sponsorship for its advertising and public relations campaigns. Most recently, the sport

Brian Gavriloff, Edmonton Journal.

Boxing can be a brutal sport.

bureaucracy has been consumed with the Commission of Inquiry into the Use of Drugs and Banned Practices Intended to Increase Athletic Performance (Dubin Inquiry).

What is "fair play" in sport? Moral and political philosophers have debated this question for centuries. Peter McIntosh (1979: 2) states it this way:

Fairness is an idea, perhaps an ideal implicit or explicit in human relations. Fair comment, fair price, fair deal, by fair means or foul, and other phrases in the English language show that "fairness" is not confined to sport and fair play. Fairness is related to justice and justice is fundamental not merely to an ordered society large or small but to the very survival of the human species. (1979: 2)

In *Fair Play*, McIntosh traces the links between morality and sport from the ancient Olympics in Greece to the present, asking whether sport has any moral basis at all. His conclusion is that it does, and he goes on to examine competition, cheating, and violence in physical education and sport, and at the same time addresses their implications for the education of young people.

What are the most important moral and ethical issues in Canadian sport today? Canada's Commission on Fair Play focuses primarily on violence, specifically hockey violence. The Dubin Inquiry was about "drugs and banned practices," of which there is now a growing list from anabolic steroids to masking and blocking agents to urine substitution. Others suggest that money and cheating are ruining sport. We have chosen three issues and controversies to discuss in this chapter: violence in hockey, the use of drugs and banned practices to enhance athletic performance, and perhaps a little surprising, the policy of financing amateur sport with gambling dollars.

Hockey violence has been the subject of numerous books, editorials, and commissions, and despite being under the magnifying glass all this time it exists in much the same form it did over fifty years ago. In fact, the game was probably a violent sport at its inception; even the name "hockey" may have emerged from the brutal nature of the game. Legend has it that the game, as it was "first observed by European settlers in North America, was played by Iroquois Indians who cried ho-gee! (it hurts!) when they were slashed by errant swipes of the stick" (Ronberg, 1975: 10). We will assess the scope of hockey violence, why it exists, and what possibly can be done about it. Our discussion will centre mainly on the NHL because of its influence on all other levels of hockey.

The widespread use of drugs and other banned practices to improve sports performance began in the 1960s and was considered

threatening enough that drug testing for Olympic athletes was first introduced in 1968 at the Mexico City Games (Mottram, 1988). As one of the first countries to formulate a comprehensive drug use and doping control policy, Canada was viewed as a world leader in operating "clean" athletic programs until the events in Seoul. We will examine the conditions that forced the Dubin Inquiry, the evidence presented, the report itself, and what impact it may have.

The practice of using gambling revenue to support amateur sport programs gained prominence in the 1980s, particularly in western Canada. On the surface this appears to be a rational policy because it has resulted in improved facilities, coaching standards, and travel opportunities for young athletes. There is, however, an ironic twist to this policy because often these gambling monies are extracted from the poor, the welfare recipient, and the criminal element. We will explore the implications and consequences of this policy both for amateur sport and for society at large. The overall intent of this chapter is to probe more deeply into three specific issues, to examine why they occur and why they persist, and to offer some suggestions for change.

Violence in Hockey: Is "Goonery" Gone?

What matters is that fighting degrades, turning sport into dubious spectacle, bringing into question hockey's very legitimacy, confining it forever to the fringes of sports respectability. (Dryden, 1983: 190)

Hockey at its best can be the world's fastest, most exciting team sport. It is a fierce and

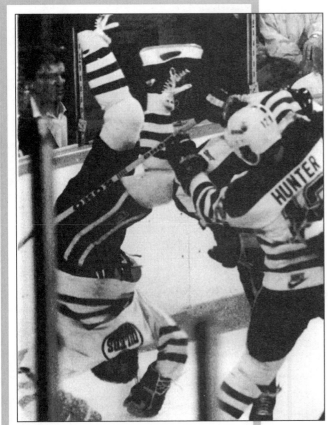

Brian Gavriloff, Edmonton Journal.

Up-ended.

frightening spectacle that combines both grace and brutality. Some of its appeal is ever-present danger: razor-sharp blades that propel players around the ice, sticks that can be used as weapons, and a rubber disc fired at over 100 mph. The game is also "polluted" with gratuitous violence: vicious stick fouls, charging the goalie, blasting players from behind, and the use of "goons" to rough up opponents are standard features of the sport. If we accept the cliché that hockey is a reflection of our national character, what does it say about us? Are we bloodthirsty yahoos who prefer watching mayhem to slick passing and fancy stickhandling? This approach to the game has been anything but successful: Canada's senior national teams have not won a gold medal in World Championship play in over thirty years, and since the mid-seventies our national team's record against the Soviets is 1 win, 18 losses and 3 ties.

TABLE 10
A Hockey Violence Typology

Relatively Legitimate

Brutal Body Contact

Conforms to the official rules of hockey, more or less accepted. Hard body checks are the best example.

Borderline Violence

Violates the official rules of hockey and the law of the land, but widely accepted. An obvious example is hockey fights between equally willing and capable opponents.

Relatively Illegitimate

Quasi-Criminal Violence

Violates the official rules of hockey, the law of the land, and to a significant degree informal player norms; more or less not accepted. Hockey examples include fights between mismatched opponents, cross-checking a player from behind, hard body checks into the goal post, or hard body checks in the open ice aimed at or below knee-level.

Criminal Violence

Violates the official rules of hockey, the law of the land, and players' informal norms; not accepted. Hockey examples include deliberate attempts to injure such as stick swinging, butt ending, spearing, and kicking; also, invading the stands to settle a score with a fan, or physically abusing an official.

SOURCE: Adapted from Smith (1983: 9).

What Is Meant by Hockey Violence?

The terms "violence" and "aggression" are often used interchangeably to signify behaviour intended to harm someone. Canadian sport sociologist Michael Smith (1983) sees aggression as a broader term that encompasses both physical and psychological harm, whereas he delimits violence only to the physical. Confounding matters is the way the terms are used by sports journalists. To be labelled "aggressive" on the sports pages is a positive attribute (for males anyway); it connotes readiness, intensity, stout-heartedness, and an eagerness to engage in hard physical contact within the rules. The aim of aggressive play is to smother the opposition, to overwhelm them, but the element of hostility is missing. Violence is normally used as a pejorative, alluding to physical actions meant to frighten or injure opposing players. Usually these physical actions are outside the rules, but not always: for example, whistling a slapshot at the goalie's head is not illegal but it could be considered a violent action if premeditated. Typically, hockey violence refers to stick fouls, illegal body contact, and fighting. Smith (1983) has devised a typology of sports violence consisting of four categories that range from tolerable to intolerable acts, or in other words, from relatively legitimate to relatively illegitimate (see Table 10).

While violence is commonplace in hockey, only a few players use brute force on a regular basis: in the NHL only 2 per cent of the players account for over 90 per cent of the fighting penalties (Strachan, 1990). On a typical twenty-player NHL roster, there are one or two "goons" or enforcers (players who are expected to start fights if need be, or at least to stand up to the opponent's tough guy); eight to ten "grinders" (players who will fight if provoked, but who don't ordinarily fight); and the remaining seven to ten who seldom, if ever, resort to fisticuffs. Generally, a team's best scorers are not fighters and a team's enforcers are not scorers. A few of today's leading scorers have earned a "tough guy" reputation for their fistic prowess (Cam Neely, Mark Messier, Rick Tochett, for example), while pure scorers like Wayne Gretzky, Steve Yzerman, and Denis Savard refrain from fighting; in fact, they are sometimes given "enforcers" to create space for them to manoeuvre. Team management prefers the scorers to avoid scuffles because they are too valuable to risk injury, suspension, or penalty time, whereas enforcers are deemed expendable.

Occasionally an entire team will manifest a violent personality, as was the case with the Philadelphia Flyers in the 1970s. Nicknamed the "Broad Street Bullies," the Flyers' belligerent style helped them win two Stanley Cups. There were four components to the Flyer philosophy: maximum effort, structured positional play, bone-jarring physical contact, and a cheerful willingness to do whatever it took, either inside or outside the rules, to unhinge their opponents. To implement this system the Flyers sought players with the size, courage, and temperament to absorb and dish out the pounding in the corners and the crease area. Their ultimate aim was to win games by provoking teams into losing their composure while retaining their own, and it worked for the better part of a decade (Ronberg, 1975).

The 1980s saw a reduction in the strategic use of overt violence and an increased emphasis on fluid skating, nifty passing, and precise shooting. This trend occurred for several reasons: the influx of talented European players who are less inclined to be violent; the introduction of rule changes and stiffer suspensions to control the most flagrant forms of violence; and the fact that winning teams like the Edmonton Oilers, Calgary Flames, and Montreal Canadiens relied as much on speed and finesse as they did on ferocity. Despite a general downturn in professional hockey violence, teams still employ their requisite goons and violent incidents continue to happen.

Explanations for Hockey Violence

In *The Game*, former goalie Ken Dryden talks about the "NHL theory of violence." It goes, according to Dryden (1983: 189), something like this:

> Hockey is by its nature a violent game. Played in an area confined by boards and unbreakable glass, by players carrying sticks travelling at speeds approaching 30 miles per hour, collisions occur, and because they occur, the rules specifically permit them, with only some exceptions. But whether legal or illegal, accidental or not, such collisions can cause violent feelings, and violent feelings with a stick in your hands are dangerous, potentially lethal feelings. It is crucial, therefore, that these feelings be vented quickly before anger and frustration explode into savage overreaction, channelled towards, if not desirable, at least more tolerable, directions.

Dryden makes the point that this "explanation" is really just Freud's "drive-discharge" theory of human aggression, and in the case of hockey there are only two possible channels for this discharge: fighting or stick-swinging. Mass brawling and "goonery" have been largely eliminated, thus leaving fighting as the most tolerable channel; stick-swinging, infinitely more dangerous, is dealt with through expulsions, fines, and suspensions. According to Dryden, the NHL's theory is *wrong*: it is "nothing more than original violence tolerated or accepted, in time turned into custom, into spectacle, into tactic, and finally into theory" (p. 190). A more realistic explanation, says Dryden, is that *violence is learned and repeated.* The social psychological literature clearly supports Dryden's view: sports violence is a socially constructed and learned behaviour that serves to legitimate and foster more violence (see Smith, 1983, for an excellent review of this research).

Within the game situation itself, hockey violence can usually be traced to one of four causes: frustration, perceived injustice, desire for extrinsic rewards, or game strategy. Frustration-induced violence stems from a player's shot being blocked, or a missed pass – when an expected outcome does not occur, anger is aroused. It can also result from a person's own actions, like missing an easy scoring chance, or more commonly when the opposition is dictating the play. A perceived injustice can also be frustrating, but it arises when players sense they have been unfairly treated according to the rules of the game. The distinction between frustration and perceived injustice is that "frustration involves a discrepancy between one's goals (or expectations) and what actually happened, while perceived injustice involves a discrepancy between what one believes should have happened and what actually happened" (Mark, Bryant, and Lehman, 1983: 86). Typical perceived injustices in hockey result from an official's inconsistency, obvious bad calls, or failure to notice blatant penalties.

The relatively few players who participate in violence for extrinsic rewards are usually seeking approval from peers, management, or fans. Players whose violent antics make the team more successful may receive tangible rewards such as money (a long-term contract) or status (being known as the king of the enforcers). Strategic violence is calculated to produce an advantage for one team over another, in either the present game or one in the future. Examples of strategic violence include attempting to take out the opposition's key player through injury or penalty and starting a fight to change the tempo of a game (usually to spark lacklustre play) or to send a message for an impending game, that being, come prepared to do battle.

What is it about our culture and the structure of Canadian society that caused hockey to evolve to its present malevolent state; and why is there such resistance to curtailing the violence in the game? Our belief is that hockey violence persists in North America almost solely because NHL executives believe that violence helps to sell tickets, especially in American cities where fans are less attuned to the subtleties of the game. This conviction was never more in evidence than in the late 1960s when the NHL expanded from six to twelve teams. Marketing strategies in such new franchise cities as Atlanta and Los Angeles focused on the speed and roughhouse aspects of the game on the theory that fans might not understand the game, but they would be drawn toward the elemental struggle of two combatants "fighting" it out.

When fights do occur, NHL executives often shrug them off with comments such as "it's part of the game"; "no one ever gets hurt"; or "the players are just letting off steam, far better they do it with their fists than their sticks." As Ken Dryden (1983: 198) puts it: "A league, through its referees, sends messages to the game, the players react, the game takes on its form." Two government inquiries into hockey violence both attributed much of the blame for the problem on the NHL (cf. McMurtry, 1974; Neron, 1977). They were pessimistic about prospects for change in this area, suggesting that the NHL must forgo its laissez-faire, non-interventionist approach or that changes be forced on the sport from outside.

The Legality of Hockey Violence

The most likely external source that could do something about hockey violence is the state, through its criminal justice system. Up till now governments have taken the position that hockey teams and leagues should be able to maintain order themselves. The reasoning for this approach is twofold (Eitzen, 1985). First, league officials should know better than judges and lawyers whether a particular act violates the standards of the game and puts other players at risk. Moreover, the league should be able to reach a verdict faster than the courts ever could. The league also wields considerable power in that it can ban and suspend players, thus affecting their livelihoods. Second, contact sports like hockey sanction aggressive play. The game is fast-paced, intense, and pressure-filled, all of which make the hockey milieu much different from what ordinary citizens face in their daily lives. This being the case, proponents of league control argue that athletes in contact sports be given some relief from a strict application of assault and battery laws.

In theory, a league administering its own justice seems to be a sensible option, but in practice it is ineffective for two main reasons. First, it is inappropriate for any organization to act as "accuser, judge and jury" (Eitzen, 1985: 103). Under this system, a player's rights may

not be protected to the same extent they would be in the public realm. Second, disciplinary action against excessive violence in hockey has sometimes been lax and erratic. For example, in the 1989 Stanley Cup playoffs, Philadelphia goaltender Ron Hextall charged across the rink to level Montreal player Chris Chelios with his stick, but Hextall was suspended for only twelve games.

The criminal court system has always had the authority to punish hockey violence, inasmuch as the laws pertaining to assault and battery do not differentiate between the sports arena and the street. Over the years, several celebrated hockey incidents have been tried in court; only one resulted in a conviction. In that case, assault charges were filed against Dino Ciccarelli, then with the Minnesota North Stars, for an incident that took place during a game in Toronto against the Maple Leafs. Ciccarelli swung wildly with his stick, whacking Luke Richardson twice on the head and then punching him in the face. Richardson was wearing a helmet and was unharmed. Ciccarelli was ejected from the game and suspended by the NHL for ten games. In Toronto Provincial Court, Ciccarelli was fined $1,000 and sentenced to one day in jail. This was a landmark case because it was the first-ever successful criminal sanction in professional sports (Carroll, 1988). It was also noteworthy for the comments made by the judge during the sentencing. He reckoned that professional hockey's acceptance of violence had a negative influence on the youngsters who idolize NHL players; consequently, he wanted to send a message from the courts indicating that unprovoked violence would not be tolerated. His sentence (though unduly permissive in the minds of some observers) was intended to warn the NHL to clean up its act or expect further legal intervention (Harris, 1988). Nonetheless, efforts to control hockey violence through court action have largely been a dismal failure.

New Directions: A Change for the Better?

While the solution to curbing hockey violence has not been found in the criminal justice system, or in the NHL's own disciplinary procedures, certain cultural and economic counterforces perhaps signal a change for the better:

- A high percentage of boys drop out of youth hockey programs (see our discussion in Chapter 8). One reason for this is the parents' perception that there is too much violence in their child's league (McPherson and Davidson, 1980). Vaz (1982) explains how professional hockey aspirants must ultimately make a commitment to a violent sub-culture as they move through the ranks. This means a willingness to engage in violent play or at the very least tolerate the use of violence as a possible game-winning strategy. Players not seeking a professional hockey career, those who eschew violence on philosophical grounds, or those who are just plain frightened usually turn away from the sport, perhaps to re-enter at a later stage to play in the increasingly popular no-hit, no slapshot leagues.

- There is evidence of a feminist backlash against the masculine ideology of sport, particularly as it is expressed in sports like hockey with its emphasis on virility and violence. In her critique of the media coverage of the brawl between the Canadian and Soviet teams at the World Junior Hockey Championship, Theberge (1989a: 254) showed how "public response and interpretation of the events offered a powerful affirmation of both the 'naturalness' and legitimacy of violence as a masculine practice." Feminists also contend that hockey violence helps to sustain a masculine hegemony and it may desensitize us to blatant forms of male-female violence such as wife beating, rape, sexual harassment, and pornography (Messner, 1990).

- The accustomed path taken by prospective NHL players has changed considerably over the past decade. Previously, the vast majority of NHL players were products of Canada's three major junior leagues. Nowadays, European leagues and American college leagues are just as viable breeding grounds for new talent (Christie, 1989a). Junior hockey programs still offer the best facsimile of the NHL style of play because of their emphasis on toughness and intimidation. The European and American college players are well versed in the basics but less inclined to fight because they learned the game in a system where discipline was stressed. The interweaving of the two approaches has, however, had the wholesome effect of mitigating violence in the NHL. Journalists covering the 1990 playoffs commented on the absence of bench-clearing free-for-alls and assaults that have characterized past playoffs. There is an optimism in the air that clean, high-speed, hard-hitting hockey will become in vogue in the 1990s (Strachan, 1990).

- In addition to changes in player recruitment patterns, there has been a similar, though less conspicuous, transition in the coaching ranks. Coaching in the NHL used to be a closed shop, reserved for individuals who had played in the league or who had served a long apprenticeship in junior or minor professional outposts. Generally these coaches had little formal education, and their hockey knowledge was limited to what they had gleaned from the coaches they played under.

This inbreeding created a restrictive atmosphere where new ideas were looked upon as heresy. There was a breakthrough in the eighties as several coaches were hired who held university degrees and who had coaching experience in university and European leagues. Coaches from these non-traditional backgrounds are less likely to advocate the old style rockem-sockem hockey. One of these coaches, Boston's Mike Milbury, has teasingly been called "Coach Gandhi" for teaching his players to absorb cheap shots and not retaliate. While the old guard may initially resent these new methods, they are quick to copy them if it looks like they will be successful.

- Hockey players are the lowest paid athletes of the four North American team sports (see the discussion in Chapter 5), and their players' union has been timid in negotiating better working conditions. This situation is due to two main reasons: hockey players' lack of formal education – 58 per cent of NHL players have high school diplomas and 9 per cent hold university degrees (Blann and Zaichkowsky, 1987); and the iron-fisted control of the players' union by Alan Eagleson, who often has seemed to side more with management than with the players. More recently, the players themselves have adopted a more militant stance, and Eagleson is to be replaced. This new, contentious attitude might lead to player demands for ways to temper hockey violence. If players can be convinced that the physical destruction of opposing players is dehumanizing and not part of the game's basic nature, more of them may respond by speaking out against violence (as Wayne Gretzky has recently), or by boycotting games to dramatize their opposition to violence (as Bobby Hull did in the 1970s).

- Two attempts at passing sports violence acts were made in the United States in the 1980s. One bill died in committee because the legislative session ended before it was introduced and the other was voted down, primarily because of the professional sports lobby "who argued that such a bill, if passed, would change the nature of contact sports" (Eitzen, 1985: 110). We may see more of these bills in the future, especially if the leagues and the courts cannot curtail the gratuitous violence.

- The NHL faces a dilemma: eight of its present franchises are in Canada where the game is immensely popular, while the remaining sixteen teams are American-based, where there is a constant struggle to gain public and media recognition. Hockey rarely gets high-profile space in American newspapers and the television rights are owned by Sports Channel, an expensive pay-TV service that reaches only nine million viewers (Alaton, 1990). One reason for hockey's second-class status in the U.S. is that it is seen by discerning sports followers as being more akin to roller derby than a real sport. Respected publications like *Sports Illustrated* continually mock the NHL for its apathy in not controlling brawling and bullying. With league expansion in the 1990s, the NHL will need an image make-over. Toning down the violence would be a positive first step in winning over new fans and obtaining credibility with the media gatekeepers.

Concluding Remarks

A substantial reduction in hockey violence seems inevitable although not necessarily right around the corner. Speeding up the process would require a change in attitude on the part of league executives, coaches, players, fans, and media personnel. The first step would be to expose the dogma that has guided league decisions over the years. There does not seem to be a shred of evidence to support the view that fighting is needed as a safety valve to guard against vicious stick attacks. Hockey is the only team sport that makes allowances for fighting; athletes in sports much rougher than hockey, such as football and rugby, have learned not to fight because they face immediate expulsion from the game. Perhaps the best illustration of the fallacy of the safety valve theory is that most NHL players don't fight. If fighting provides such an emotional outlet, would not all players resort to it on occasion? Some players have spent ten-year careers in the league with nary a serious fight.

The most difficult hurdle to clear may well be the myth that fighting is a show of manliness: if you refuse to fight you are branded a coward. This idea is drilled into the minds of young hockey players until it becomes orthodoxy. This is an overly simplistic view of courage that elevates the physical over the moral and denies the value of good judgement. Sometimes it takes moral courage to resist the temptation to fight, and it is common sense for a player to steer clear of an obvious mismatch where he stands to get clobbered.

Perhaps there is wisdom to be gleaned from the words of former "goons" who look back on their careers with a twinge of regret. Dave Schultz (1981) admitted that it did boost his ego to be known as the most feared enforcer in the league. However, along with this recognition came several major drawbacks: the constant paranoia (the fear of being hurt or embarrassed) of being knocked off by an opposing team's top gun; having to face the sarcasm of teammates who joke about your inferior hockey skills and forever typecast you as a "goon"; and coping with the abuse of opposing

fans. "I could deal with adults, or at least I thought I could, but seeing the angry faces of youngsters bothered me no end. There seemed to be something morally wrong when a performer like me could inspire elementary school kids to vilification with the worst x-rated epithets" (Schultz, 1981: 141).

Back in 1972, Bruce Kidd and John Macfarlane wrote an insightful book, *The Death of Hockey*, in which they decried the fact that "sportsmanship, skill and beauty had been sacrificed for profit" (p. 20). Today, the NHL product is about to change – largely against the league's will – because of an infusion of new ideas and because of evolving cultural and economic patterns. It probably won't be a radical change, because the greedy profit motive will still reign supreme, and the competition will still be dog-eat-dog, but violence will subside, thus allowing artistry to move to the forefront.

DRUGS AND BANNED PRACTICES: DUBIN AND ITS IMPACT

The evidence in this Inquiry establishes that for many years in many of the Olympic events, Canadian athletes have resorted to performance-enhancing drugs and other banned practices, thereby gaining an unfair advantage over those who did not do so, and most of the cheaters have gone undetected. Those who have cheated have threatened the very future of sport and tarnished its reputation, perhaps irreparably. Thay have also unfairly cast a cloud of suspicion over the majority of athletes, who abide by the rules, and have threatened their future financial support from governments, corporations, and the general public. (Dubin, 1990: 517)

Drugs used by Issajenko, 1979-88

Anabolic steroids

Estrogol
Anavar
Dianabol
Winstrol
Deca-Durabolin
Primobolin
Testosterone
Depo-Testosterone
Aqueous Testosterone
Proprionate

Human growth hormones

Somatropin
Crescormon
Primabolin

Other drugs

Butazolidin:
Anti-inflammatory drug
L-Dopa:
Encourages release
of growth hormones
Diuretics:
To help mask steroid
presence
**Vitamin B-12 complex
Inocene:**
To supplement B-12 shot
Norflex: a muscle relaxant
**Calcium tablets
Potassium tablets
Other vitamins**

Sept. 1988

Aug. 1979

Toronto Star, March 17, 1989. Courtesy The Toronto Star Syndicate.

Angela Issajenko, 1979 and 1988.

As the above quotation indicates, the links between drugs and sports are not a recent phenomenon. Rumours of athletes using some form of anabolic steroid have circulated since the 1950s (Todd, 1987). Although a Canadian athlete was disqualified from competition for steroid use as early as 1981, on September 27, 1988, drug use became a central issue in Canadian sport when the IOC disqualified Ben Johnson from the Olympic Games in Seoul. Only a few days earlier Johnson had become a Canadian hero when he had beaten his arch-rival Carl Lewis in what many people consider the "blue ribbon" event of the Games, the 100 metres. In the words of one sports journalist, Ben went from "hero to zero" after his disqualification and hasty departure from Seoul. In addition, four Canadian weightlifters never reached Seoul because they failed to pass a drug test, and several track and field athletes left the Games under suspicious circumstances after the Johnson disqualification.

Prior to 1988, the Canadian government had taken a fairly prominent and proactive stance in regard to the use of drugs and banned substances in sport. In 1986, Minister of State for Fitness and Amateur Sport Otto Jelinek had addressed the Council of Europe Sports Ministers Conference on the need for a worldwide doping charter. As a result of this, as well as subsequent initiatives, the First Permanent World Conference on Antidoping took place in Ottawa in June, 1988. The increased financial resources the federal government had put into sport throughout the 1980s (see Chapter 4), and its leadership position on issues such as doping meant that it was anxious to claim "the lion's share of the credit" for Canadian sporting successes. However, the Johnson scandal "threatened to tear the whole system apart," and the problem now was "to avoid the lion's share of the blame" (MacAloon, 1989: 6). The response of the government was to establish the Commission of Inquiry into the Use of Drugs and Banned Practices Intended to Increase Athletic Performance, what is commonly called the Dubin Inquiry.

The Dubin Inquiry

The request for an inquiry was initiated by Ben Johnson himself. When he returned to Canada from Seoul, he asked (through his lawyer) for "a thorough public inquiry as to all circumstances surrounding his disqualification" (Dubin, 1990: xviii). The Commission of Inquiry was formally established on the recommendation of Prime Minister Brian Mulroney by an order-in-council. When incidents such as the Johnson affair create enough public pressure to force the government to act, Part 1 of the Inquiries Act permits the establishment of a commission to investigate the issue (Beauchesne, 1990). The individual placed in charge of the Commission was the Associate Chief Justice of Ontario, the Honourable Charles Dubin. Between January 11 and October 3, 1989, Mr. Justice Dubin and his team of lawyers heard from over 100 witnesses whose testimony filled nearly 15,000 pages. The cost of the Commission was close to $4 million, and it resulted in the publication in June, 1990, of a 638-page report. The report itself is a lucid, often fascinating, account containing seventy wide-ranging recommendations relating not only to the events in Seoul that prompted the Inquiry in the first place, but also concrete proposals pertaining to the use and abuse of drugs and banned practices in sport. From a sociological perspective, the most interesting questions raised by the report are those that focus on the purpose of the Commission, as well as its impact in both the short term and the long term. We turn now to these specific issues.

QUESTIONS OF PURPOSE To most observers, the purpose of the Dubin Inquiry was to examine the use of performance-enhancing drugs and practices used by Canadian athletes, and more specifically to investigate the situation surrounding the disqualification of Ben Johnson at the Seoul Olympics. However, as Beauchesne (1990: 16-17) points out, commissions of inquiry also serve a number of political purposes: (1) "to dissociate the government or government bodies from scandal"; (2) "to convey the impression of taking action to remedy the problem"; and (3) "implicit in the trial format itself, to expose the guilty and to affirm the power of sanction as the best means to deter the situation."

The Dubin Inquiry was commissioned, as many previous public inquiries have been, when the government's popularity was at a particularly low ebb (Brodeur, 1979). In this case, the proposed Free Trade Agreement with the United States had aroused considerable concern over the government's interest in preserving national identity. It had also raised the issue of Canada's ability to compete with our much larger and more powerful neighbour to the south. Johnson's victory gave Prime Minister Brian Mulroney the opportunity to expound on Canadian nationalism, and to interpret Johnson's success explicitly "as evidence that Canada could compete internationally (meaning particularly with the U.S.) under a regime of free trade, private initiative and government coordination, precisely his election platform" (MacAloon, 1989: 10). Johnson's subsequent disqualification challenged these assertions and, to some extent, the credibility of the government and its re-election bid. As MacAloon points out, the ensuing Commission of Inquiry served to deflect blame from the government and place it on others. Most notably, these were: sport organizations (e.g., weightlifting,

track and field) that were seen as lax in their attention to issues of doping control; other countries who implicitly condoned drug use; and something called "today's sport culture" corrupted by an overemphasis on winning, media hype, and commercialism. In particular, Mr. Justice Dubin challenged the moral character of those who cheated while he affirmed "the real heroes of the lengthy battle to eliminate the use of performance-enhancing drugs and other banned practices in sport . . . those coaches and athletes who refuse to engage in such practices" (Dubin, 1990: 488). By adopting this approach, the Inquiry deflected blame from the state, which through its growing emphasis on high-performance sport had helped create the structural conditions (see our discussion in Chapter 4) that had contributed to the Johnson affair. Instead, responsibility was placed primarily on individuals who "by their failure to abide by the rules – by their cheating – they have displayed a lack of ethics that has brought dishonour to themselves and to Canada" (Dubin, 1990: 511).

As well as dissociating the government and its agents from a scandal, public inquiries can also create the impression that they will help to correct the problem. The idea is that "experts and eye witnesses expose the facts, and knowledge will automatically lead to change" (Beauchesne, 1990: 18). However, as Beauchesne argues, such change is rare because most details exposed are predictable, the type of information presented is limited, and commissions usually have such a narrow mandate that new knowledge is rarely produced. Such was the case with the Dubin Inquiry. While it investigated what had already taken place, it did little to challenge this situation. By placing the most blame on individual cheaters, little attention was devoted to examining the broader, contextual conditions and forces that helped precipitate drug use in the first place. The information placed before the Commission on these points was given by two senior government bureaucrats who "were presented as the neutrals, as the only ones with complete and authoritative knowledge of the system, capable of dispassionately understanding and explaining it to the public" (MacAloon, 1989: 18). With the exception of sport historian and activist Bruce Kidd, the work of Canadian scholars who have critically examined our sport system was not presented at the Commission, nor were any of these individuals placed on the Sports Expert Panel assigned to assist the Commission.

The third purpose of the Commission, as we mentioned previously, was to expose the guilty and to affirm the deterrent power of sanctions. The Inquiry fulfilled this function by exposing Johnson, his coach, doctor, and therapist, along with a number of other Canadian athletes. It also recommended appropriate sanctions against these individuals. However, such actions merely affirm the guilt of specific individuals and thus limit public perception of the problem as one that is reducible to individual values. They do little to challenge or change the structural conditions (media pressures, economic rewards, state pressure, overemphasis on winning, etc.) that underlie the situation. Mr. Justice Dubin (pp. 501-02) not only failed to address these issues in any substantive way, but he actively dismissed them as causal factors when he noted:

> While acknowledging the existence of all those factors and their undoubted effect on Canadian athletes, there can be no justification for athletes to cheat in order to win. The pressures and temptations are the same for all athletes, yet most do not succumb. Those who do show a lack of character. Sport is intended to build character; cheating destroys it. I agree

with those who say the problem is not educational, not economic, and not social – but moral.

We can see, then, that the Dubin Inquiry presented almost a facade of addressing the problem of doping. By attributing blame to the moral character of individual athletes and those around them and endorsing sanctions against them the Inquiry served the purposes of the state. While such an approach may be politically useful, it does little to enhance our understanding of the factors that created the problem in the first place.

Finally, it would be wrong to leave the impression that responsibility for the doping problem lies entirely with pressures from the state, commercial interests, or the media. As the Dubin Report makes apparent, officials from both the Canadian Weightlifting Federation (CWF) and the Canadian Track and Field Association (CTFA) clearly avoided taking steps to address the problem despite pressure from Sport Canada, and in the case of the CTFA from within the organization itself. Moreover, the leaders of these national sport organizations (and others) have often uncritically embraced an "ideology of excellence" (Kidd, 1988a). Any analysis of the Johnson affair cannot place blame solely on the "cheaters" or on the performance pressures that emanate from external factors, because the situation is far more complex. The events that took place reflect the interplay of the broad socio-economic and political forces that have surrounded NSOs in recent years, the internal power structure of these organizations, and the aspirations of athletes, coaches, trainers, officials, and administrators, both paid and volunteer, as they seek to enhance their own power and prestige through athletic successes. The Dubin Inquiry, in the quest to serve its political purposes, reduced these complexities to a question of individual choice.

THE IMPACT OF DUBIN Despite its wide-ranging recommendations, it is doubtful that the Dubin Report will have any substantive impact on the direction, organization, and administration of the Canadian amateur sport system. The federal government has initiated a set of responses to the Report in the form of a discussion paper, "Doping Related Matters" (Fitness and Amateur Sport, 1990). The central purpose of the discussion paper is to outline the structure of an expanded Canadian Anti-doping Program, which would include an agency "at arm's length from government, to co-ordinate the anti-doping campaign, and serve as the principle agency responsible for doping controls in Canada" (p. 38). The discussion paper does not question the central aims and objectives of our sport system. Any mention of initiatives such as those found in Mr. Justice Dubin's first recommendation (a call for the federal government to fund a broader range of sporting opportunities) and his fifth recommendation (a call for the federal government to examine the focus of its relationship with sport) is noticeably absent from the document.

Such recommendations are unlikely to be considered because they would involve a substantive reorientation of the sport system, as well as a restructuring of its infrastructure. Both are unlikely to take place because, as we noted earlier, not only does a complex network of political, economic, and social forces influence the sport system, but the system itself is resistant to such changes. The focus on excellence has been embraced by most of its constituents – athletes, coaches, administrators, and volunteers. Moreover, the possibility that dominant groups and individuals would lose power, the fact that there would be substantial

costs, and certainly that a loss of legitimacy would occur in the international sports arena all mitigate against any restructuring of the system. The last two decades have seen an increased emphasis on the rational production of performance, and any deviation from this focus does not seem plausible.

Proposals for Change

We conclude this section with further comments concerning the government's response to the Dubin Report along with a few suggestions of our own.

- Educational programs and campaigns directed at drug abuse in sport should receive increased attention and funding. The Dubin Report focuses primarily on the use of drugs and banned practices by elite "amateur" athletes, which represents only a small portion of the overall problem. It is generally accepted that the use of drugs to enhance athletic performance is not uncommon among some male professional and intercollegiate athletes (e.g., football players). Dubin himself notes that the problem has trickled down to high school athletes. He was also convinced that competitors involved in strength and power sports (weightlifting, powerlifting, and bodybuilding) have been using anabolic steroids and other drugs, such as growth hormone, for some time. The government's discussion paper gives some attention to the need for an educational campaign and proposes linking it to the Commission for Fair Play.

- A more balanced focus is needed in the Canadian amateur sport system. It would be naive to suggest that high-performance sport should no longer be central to the system. But as a former sports minister, John Munro, noted twenty years ago, the pursuit of excellence must be put into proper perspective "as a consequence and not as a goal of mass participation" (Munro, 1970: 23). While producing such a balanced focus will not be easy, it could begin with the federal government. The recent requirement of NSOs to produce a domestic sport plan is certainly a step in the right direction; however, the relative lack of funds attached to this directive means that it will not be a high priority for most NSOs. The provision of block funding rather than designating funds for specific programs (usually high-performance oriented), plus an infusion of funding to domestic competitions, regional games, and indigenous sports, would also help to bring about a more balanced focus.

• Whatever procedures are put in place for enhanced doping control, they must ensure confidentiality and the protection of every athlete's human rights. Every effort must also be made to use education and rehabilitation as sanctions when rules are broken.

THE GAMBLING AND AMATEUR SPORT CONNECTION: A MARRIAGE OF CONVENIENCE

Any discussion of Canadian gambling policies must first recognize that conditions vary widely from province to province. As a starting point, however, any provincial regulations pertaining to gambling must be in accord with the Criminal Code of Canada. This means that Parliament enacts the laws, but each province has the choice of opting in or out of the various legal gambling opportunities. The Criminal Code authorizes provinces to operate gambling schemes if the beneficiaries of these games are charitable or religious groups. In recent years the letter of the law has been stretched to include bingos, raffles, sports pools, "pull" tickets (you break it open to see if you have won a prize), casinos, and slot machines under the rubric of a lottery scheme. So far, Alberta, Manitoba, British Columbia, and Quebec have been the most liberal in terms of permitting new forms of gambling or allowing the expansion of existing forms. Several questions arise whenever an activity like gambling is made legal. Does gambling lose its stigma through legalization, or does the perceived immoral nature of the activity discredit the policy-makers who legalized it (Skolnick, 1978)? What, if any, economic, political, and ideological considerations arise when there is state intervention into gambling?

Whenever gambling is legalized, certain tradeoffs must be made so the activity can be reconciled in the public mind. The Canadian experience suggests that gambling is most acceptable and easiest to rationalize when proceeds go to "sports, cultural, recreational and other community-oriented events" (Beare, 1989: 187). As a result of this arrangement, millions of dollars of gaming monies are available to enhance amateur sport and recreation programs in Canada. This funding is derived from two main types of legalized gambling: lotteries and gaming activities (the latter include bingos, casinos, raffles, pull tickets, sports pools, and slot machines). The money from lotteries is essentially a form of government subsidy. Lottery revenue is first collected by the government, and then either it is passed on to agencies that direct it to various qualifying organizations or it goes into the province's general account to be doled out to authorized groups according to an agreed formula. Gaming monies are different because they are earned directly by the sponsoring groups, which supply volunteer staff to administer the casinos, bingos, raffles, and sports pools (Smith, Williams, and Pitter, 1989).

Canadian amateur sports groups have access to gaming revenue because they fall under the broad definition of a charitable organization. In the legal sense, a charity must fit under one of four categories: (1) the relief of poverty; (2) the advancement of education; (3) the advancement of religion; and (4) a catch-all category described as "other purposes beneficial to the community" (*Dominion Law Reports*, 1983). Amateur sport fits into the fourth category. Its inclusion as a legitimate charity is justified in two ways. First, the promotion of amateur sports under controlled conditions purportedly improves health and physical fitness. Second, participation in organized competitive amateur sports is deemed educational in the sense that it helps to train and discipline the body, and the interaction of athletes from different regions and cultures is believed to be a broadening experience (*Dominion Law Reports*, 1983).

Each province has a slightly different format that must be followed for groups seeking to conduct gaming events. The Alberta system, which has been lauded as being "light years ahead of all other jurisdictions in gaming control" (Robinson, 1983: 124), is provided as an example. The first step for a group is to apply to the Alberta Gaming Commission for a licence. The group must demonstrate its credibility, which means it must have a charitable registration number, a constitution, an executive, a membership list, and proof that it keeps accurate financial records. Once a group's trustworthiness has been established, there are different application procedures, depending on the type of gaming licence desired. To give the reader a sense of the dollars involved, the 1988 year-end totals for legalized gambling in Alberta

are presented in Table 11.

Without question, legalized gambling has been a tremendous boon to many Canadian amateur sports groups. It is not unheard of for some enterprising organizations to realize over $200,000 a year from this source (Smith, Williams, and Pitter, 1989). Through gaming events, groups can raise more money in a shorter time span, and with greater ease, than by using traditional fund-raising methods. All other funding schemes pale in comparison to the rate of return for the hours worked. Car washes, bottle drives, chocolate sales, and skateathons are now obsolete – gaming is the new, slick way to raise money.

The Politics of Legal Gambling Initiatives

Despite the expansion of gambling opportunities in Canada, legalized gambling remains a politically sensitive issue. "Revisions to the gambling sections of the *Criminal Code* have tended to occur on the basis of executive-level arrangements negotiated between federal and provincial bureaucrats in the absence of informed public debate or input" (Campbell and Lowman, 1989: xviii). Canadian politicians seem very reticent to align themselves with any pro-gambling legislation. At the recent (1988) First National Symposium on Lotteries and Gambling, politicians representing the various levels of government were asked to comment on Canadian gambling laws and policies; only one, an opposition party member from Alberta, agreed to participate (Campbell and Lowman, 1989).

The present gambling policies are not so much a result of prudent planning as they are a reaction to deteriorating economic conditions and intense lobbying by special interest groups (Smith, 1987). Despite the *ad hoc* nature of

TABLE 11
Dollars Realized from Lotteries and Gaming in Alberta in 1988

Gross Revenues *	
Gaming activities (bingos, casinos, etc.)	$ 475 million
Lottery sales	$ 300 million
Profit Realized	
Gaming activities	$ 76 million
Lotteries	$ 101 million
Profit Breakdown by Game	
Bingo	$ 32 million
Pull tickets	$ 19.7 million
Casinos	$ 13.4 million
Raffles	$ 10.7 million
Percentage of Each Dollar Wagered That Is Returned to the Consumer	
Lotteries and raffles	45.0%
Bingos	73.2%
Pull tickets	73.7%
Casinos	79.0%

* Horse-racing revenues are not included here because, unlike the two other major forms of gambling, the proceeds do not go back to qualifying charitable or religious groups.
SOURCE: Alberta Gaming Commission *Annual Review*, 1988.

provincial gambling policies and the aura of secrecy surrounding their implementation, gambling restrictions have been relaxed for three main reasons. First, gambling schemes are seen by government authorities as effective and relatively trouble-free ways to generate public monies. In some areas of Canada, the funds go toward necessities like environmental concerns and health care, while in other jurisdictions the funds are channelled to worthy causes sponsored by religious, cultural, or recreational organizations. Second, there is a general belief that a more tolerant approach to legal gambling will weaken, if not eliminate, unlawful gambling operations. Third, the moral stigma associated with gambling appears to have diminished over the past decade. There is a growing public perception that individuals in a free society should have the right to gamble, with the condition that it occurs in a regulated environment that mitigates against damages to both the players and society.

The Economic and Social Impact of Legalized Gambling on Amateur Sport

Through their access to gaming profits, sports groups have the opportunity to stabilize their budgets and improve the quality of their programs. Gaming funds are used by sports organizations in four ways: for technical improvements; for facilities and equipment, for outreach programs; and for travel opportunities. Some amateur sports groups have been able to recruit internationally renowned coaches and officials to give workshops, and in some cases have persuaded them to accept full-time positions in Canada. With an abundance of gaming funds, some sports groups have built their own state-of-the-art facilities, while those not owning private facilities can at least rent ones that meet their requirements. To illustrate, gaming funds have been a blessing for a sport like figure skating, which in the past was strictly a seasonal sport. Elite athlete development in this sport has been accelerated because ice time can now be rented on a year-round basis. Gaming event proceeds have also been used to subsidize travel costs. Initially it was intended that gaming monies be used only for within-province travel, but some provinces are now allowing national and international trips under certain conditions (Smith, Williams and Pitter, 1989).

The lottery funds allotted to amateur sports tend to go to larger projects or to provincial sports governing bodies rather than to individual sports organizations. In Alberta, for example, lottery funds were instrumental in allowing the province to host three major international sports festivals in a ten-year period: the Commonwealth Games in Edmonton in 1978; the World University Games in Edmonton in 1983; and the Winter Olympics in Calgary in 1988. These festivals have left a legacy of sports facilities that are unrivalled for an area of comparable population density.

Campbell and Ponting (1984) submit that provincial gaming policies are intended to serve accumulation and legitimation purposes (remember our discussion about the purposes of the state in Chapter 4). By allowing charitable, religious, and community groups to raise funds through gaming activities, the state is promoting accumulation at the community-level rather than in the private sector. Through this policy the government is seen as "facilitating an increase in recreational, cultural, and social amenities which contribute to the enhancement of neighborhood property values" (C.S. Campbell, 1988: 354). When communities are provided with public facilities such as golf courses, playing fields, ice arenas, bicycle paths, and so forth, the residents benefit by having new facilities at their disposal and their property values go up. The legitimation purpose of state gambling policies works on two levels. First, the expanded gambling opportunities offer hope to the mostly low-income players who are less likely to acquire wealth by orthodox means. Second, the charitable and community-based groups that sponsor and run the gaming events are being "rewarded for their self-initiative" (C.S. Campbell, 1988: 354). Ostensibly, all three interest groups can benefit from the government gaming policy: the gamblers get "action" (the chance to play games that had been forbidden); the charity groups can earn money for their good works; and the government is seen as responding to the needs of the community (Campbell and Ponting, 1984).

There is, however, a downside to all this. The patrons of casinos and bingo halls are drawn disproportionately from the lower socioeconomic strata, the elderly, and various ethnic minorities. There is also a strong suspicion that a fair percentage of the money that passes through casinos comes from welfare cheques, drug and prostitution deals, and the sale of stolen property. As one police officer commented: "How else do you explain the fact that there are a number of casino regulars who gamble heavily yet are unemployed; or if they do work it is usually in low paid, menial jobs"

(Smith, 1987: 31)? This does not mean that the upper strata of Canadian society are not gamblers; some are, but they prefer to gamble under different circumstances. They go to Nevada, the Caribbean, and Europe, presumably because they fancy the excitement and luxury of these surroundings over the austere atmosphere of most Canadian gambling venues. These venues, by and large, are unpretentious and an inordinate number of players smoke. Observers of this scene are struck by a situation that is doubly ironic. First, a group of coughing, wheezing smokers (people who are obviously unfit) is supporting programs for robust young athletes. Second, individuals who from outward appearance can least afford it are subsidizing sporting activities that are most popular among the middle and upper classes (Smith, 1987).

Another detrimental effect of legalized gaming is the way the gamblers and sponsoring groups are thrust into an adversarial position. This can have a dehumanizing effect on both parties. On the one hand, feelings of hostility and alienation emerge from the narrow self-interest of the charitable groups that run the gaming events. Their goal is to maximize profits; thus the gambler is not seen as a person but merely a wallet to be emptied. As a result, gamblers are held in contempt and often called names like "degenerates" or "addicts" behind their backs. The gamblers, on the other hand, seldom have an appreciation of the causes or projects their bets are supporting, and they could care less as long as the game is available (Smith, Williams, and Pitter, 1989).

Policy Implications: Resolving the Conflicts

On a more positive note, the provinces are sanctioning an activity that has obvious public appeal. Moreover, most provinces have built in safeguards (for example, no credit wagering, moderate betting limits) that have kept problems to a minimum. There has not been a major Canadian gambling scandal, nor has there been any evidence of intrusion into legal gambling by organized crime interests. Finally, by allowing gaming monies to fund important social programs, the provinces are reducing the strain on their own budgets. Nonetheless, the system needs revamping, and in this regard, we raise the following issues and concerns:

- The provinces operate in a conflict of interest that arises from their "dual role as both operator and regulator of the gambling industry" (Singer, 1989: 287). Government first creates the conditions allowing gambling to flourish, but then it must do an about-face and develop rules that protect citizens from the evils associated with the activity. This raises two issues. First, should provincial governments be inducing people to gamble? "Far from taking a passive approach, governments have chosen to maximize the revenue generating potential of lotteries by sponsoring massive promotional campaigns. Governments are not simply satisfying a pre-existing demand for gambling; they are creating it" (Singer, 1989: 282). Second, to avoid the present conflict of interest, should gambling be privatized? That is, the government would license and regulate commercial operators who would run the gaming activities (see McMillen, 1989, for an excellent discussion of the pros and cons of this approach).

- There needs to be some way of taking account of public opinion in developing gambling policies. In the United States referenda are used to gauge public opinion on gambling issues, and in Australia decisions on gambling are made by "impartial experts and committees of inquiry" (McMillen, 1989: 389). In Canada the policies are still made in private by politicians and bureaucrats with virtually no public input.

- All forms of legal gambling in Canada are "regressive"; that is, money is extracted from those who can least afford it to pay for the programs and facilities used by those who are more fortunate. Provincial governments need to work harder to ensure that a greater portion of gaming funds gets to the people who need it most.

- Excess and wastefulness are common in the distribution of gambling monies (see, for example, Smith, Williams, and Pitter, 1989). Charitable groups should not be allowed access to gaming revenues that exceed their reasonable requirements; there also needs to be greater government acuity in discouraging extravagant grant payments and to eliminate dubious expenditures.

- A neglected segment of this whole system is the gamblers themselves. The gamblers are an unprotected consumer group who are victimized by the unfair practices of the gambling industry. Lotteries are particularly unsporting because of "the inequitable distribution of prizes and the lack of information regarding relative odds" (Singer, 1989: 280). Unfairness also resides in the fact that legalized gambling opportunities put an emphasis on luck over skill. The one form of gambling for which the public has expressed a desire, which is not regressive, and that allows the bettor a reasonable chance to win – sports betting – is illegal in Canada.

- If governments are going to benefit from legal gambling initiatives, they have an obligation to provide treatment and education for those who cannot control their gambling impulse. Pathological gambling is recognized as an addictive disorder that affects about 3 per cent of those who gamble (Lesieur, 1989). While Gamblers' Anonymous chapters exist in major Canadian cities, there is not one treatment centre for pathological gamblers in Canada.

- Recently there have been indications that provinces themselves can become addicted to gambling. In both Ontario and Alberta, bills have been passed that give the provincial government discretionary power over the distribution of accumulated lottery funds. When lotteries were legalized in the early seventies, it was agreed that proceeds would be directed to sports, fitness, culture, and recreational endeavours. But when the demand for lottery tickets far eclipsed expectations, governments were able to meet their obligations to these groups and still establish huge reserve funds ($1.6 billion in Ontario and over $200 million in Alberta). This stockpiling of lottery funds was an embarrassment to both governments, hence the legislation to free lottery dollars from their original purpose (Brunt, 1989a). In Ontario, lottery funds will now also be used to fund health care and environmental projects (Vincent, 1990). Sports and cultural groups are afraid that once these lobby groups get their foot in the door, they will no longer receive their fair share of lottery proceeds.

SUMMARY

Violence, drugs, and gambling have been a part of sporting culture since the time of ancient Greece. Through the ages, various control mechanisms and strategies, ranging from complete prohibition to a laissez-faire attitude, have been tried. Yet despite over 2,000 years of practice, we are still in a quandary over how to deal with these irritants. In modern-day Canada hockey violence is still tolerated, less so (after Dubin) are performance-enhancing drugs and practices, and there seems no end to the money available to amateur sport through gambling proceeds. Hockey violence endures, however, often because team owners think it will help them win games and fill arenas, and because it plays an important role in the reproduction of masculinity. Steroid use is condoned by athletes, coaches, and administrators strictly for the competitive advantage it produces. When sport changed from a predominantly social to a highly competitive endeavour, a new ethic emerged based on free enterprise maxims: "What would the traffic bear? What was necessary to get the job done? What would work? All's fair in love and war. Don't get caught" (Cosentino, 1990: A7). The ends, in other words, always justify the means.

Using gambling dollars to subsidize amateur sports organizations is also about ideals and ethics. Critics of gambling say it fosters greed and material gain, dampens the desire to work, and erodes family ties (Braidfoot, 1985). While we take the position that gambling is a legitimate recreational pursuit, engaged in under tightly regulated conditions, we nonetheless question the present arrangement in Canada whereby gambling schemes are used to pry money from the underprivileged to benefit more prosperous citizens. In our view, provincial governments must take measures to minimize the social costs of gambling. This means not allowing avaricious charity groups to prey on the disadvantaged, providing games with fairer odds, and investing in treatment facilities for those unable to control their gambling impulse.

A permanent solution to any of these problem areas will require a major restructuring of our social and economic relationships. Those who influence our sporting culture (government officials, team owners, sports journalists, coaches, and athletes themselves) must share the responsibility for ensuring that integrity and human dignity are not sacrificed for the expediency of winning games or entertaining spectators. If that ever happens, sport may transcend political manipulation and vulgar merchandising and imbue us with the merriment, joy, and connectedness with one another that we always thought was possible. Fair play will truly have returned.

SUPPLEMENTARY READING

Although the sporting world has certainly changed in the intervening decade since it was published, Peter McIntosh's wonderfully informative and nuanced discussion of ethics in sport and education in *Fair Play* (especially Chapters 5 through to 13) remains the best analysis of ethics in sport available.

As for the specific issues discussed in this chapter – violence, drugs, and gambling – numerous books and articles are useful. With regard to hockey violence, we again recommend Ken Dryden's *The Game* and his more recent (co-authored with Roy MacGregor) *Home Game*. Michael Smith's *Violence and Sport* contains a good analysis of the social psychological literature, with many examples drawn from hockey.

For a thorough account of drug use (and other banned practices) in the Canadian context, we suggest the Dubin Report, in particular Parts Four, Five, and Six. With regard to the gambling and amateur sport issue, we recommend the several articles written by sport sociologist Garry Smith.

Chapter 10

CONTINUITY AND CHANGE

"It is the best of times, it is the worst of times, it is the age of wisdom, it is the age of foolishness . . . ." For many of us, this slight paraphrase of Charles Dickens's introduction to A *Tale of Two Cities* may aptly describe the current state of sport in Canadian society. It is the best of times for many reasons, among them the technological advances that have raised the limits of athletic performance. Yet it is the worst of times because an emphasis on technocratic rationality has reduced, if not removed, many of the playful, aesthetic, and creative components of sport. It is the best of times because now more people than ever before participate in sport or some form of physical activity; yet it is the worst of times because barriers to participation still limit the involvement of women, visible minorities, and the poor at the same time that the "fit" lifestyle is presented to the public as a personal responsibility. It is the age of wisdom as we see more and more information generated about sport; yet it is the age of foolishness as some universities reduce or eliminate their social science courses on sport and concentrate on those sciences more directly related to the rational production of performance.

As Canadians, both individually and collectively, the process through which we have arrived at our present situation has been one of continuity and change. It has been a process shaped by our own lived experience and that of those who have preceded us. These experiences help shape the way we understand and

Brian Gavriloff, Edmonton Journal.

The sporting future – expect the unexpected.

live the present, and, in turn, the way we construct our future. But seldom do we examine our lived experiences or those of others and ask how they relate to broader social issues. It is, as C. Wright Mills suggests, necessary for anyone who wishes to understand the changing nature of sport or any other significant feature of social life to relate the personal troubles of individuals' lived experience to the public issues of social structure. That is to say, it is necessary to link these personal experiences to broader social structures that limit the capacity of some individuals while allowing those already advantaged to maintain or enhance their position. To encourage students to practise this type of thinking has in many ways been the central fo-

cus of this book. As we have worked our way through the preceding nine chapters, we have challenged what we see as some of the dominant assumptions that pervade Canadian sport. By deliberately examining what is often taken for granted, we can better understand the social structure that we and others have created, and in turn understand how these structures contour the limits and possibilities for a more democratic form of sport. Like Mills (1959: 174), our interest "in social structure is not due to any view that the future is structurally determined. We study the structural limits of human decision in an attempt to find points of effective intervention, in order to know what can and what must be structurally changed if the role of explicit decision in history-making is to be enlarged." As Mills (1959: 174) also suggests, we study the history of our own lived experience and that of others "to discern the alternatives within which human reason and human freedom can now make history. We study historical social structures, in brief, in order to find within them the ways in which they are and can be controlled. For only in this way can we come to know the limits and the meaning of human freedom."

In the concluding chapter of this book, we will examine briefly some of the issues we believe will be important to the future development of Canadian sport. We will look at the way in which the trends of the past will continue, the way these trends have shaped our present situation, how this situation is problematic, and how we may work for change. We focus, as Mills suggests, on the structures we have created in order to discern how these may, if necessary, be changed. We focus not only on the concrete institutional structures of sport but also on the less tangible structures of ideology, which may also limit our capacity to imagine alternatives.

Have We Reached the Limits of Athletic Performance?

One of the most central issues in Canadian sport over the past half century or more has been an overriding concern with increasing performance levels. Today the times and distances of great Canadian athletes like Percy Williams, Bruce Kidd, Elaine Tanner, and Jean Wilson are routinely bettered by many of our top performers. In team games like hockey, elite athletes are generally regarded to be stronger, faster, and technically more efficient

than their predecessors. Not that this in any way minimizes the performances of our former athletic greats. Rather, it highlights the emphasis that commercial promoters and governments, coaches and sport scientists, and indeed fans and athletes themselves have placed on the rational production of performance. This more systematic approach to pushing back the frontiers of athletic performance has had at least four dimensions worth citing here: time, knowledge, equipment, and money.

In the first instance, the basic point is obvious. The more time athletes can spend in training and allied activities and the less time they have to spend in other tasks that tire or distract them, the better they are likely to become. This is why full-time professionals are normally better than part-time amateurs. It is why, even in the nominally amateur sports, Canadian athletes have had to find ways of making time for more and more training in order to remain competitive internationally. Today, athletes in Olympic sports that were once seasonal (track and field, water sports, skiing) now must do some kind of training virtually throughout the year. They must also have done so since their early teens, in order to have access to the coaching and competitive opportunities that are now part of "talent development" in almost every sport. Today, athletes in professional sports like hockey, who once took summers "off" and whiled away many an afternoon during the season itself in pool halls and bars, now put a great deal of off-season and off-ice time into working out: on weights and running and in health clubs (Heinz, 1988). If they don't, they risk being pushed out of their jobs by stronger and fitter athletes.

In almost every sport, moreover, improvement has been accomplished not just by more training but by smarter and more scientific training. In the more technical sports like gym-

Brian Gavriloff, Edmonton Journal.

Former Canadian decathlon champion Dave Steen, bronze medal winner at Seoul Olympics.

nastics and the field events of track and field, there have been dramatic advances in technique and indeed the development of quite new techniques. Often the way toward technical innovation has been outlined and established by research in biomechanics, with researchers increasingly working directly with coaches and athletes. A second major area of advance has involved new knowledge of how to produce highly specific kinds of strength and endurance. As recently as the early 1960s, runners brought times for events from the 800 through 10,000 metres down dramatically by working to very detailed schedules that combined speed and endurance work in precise proportions and sequences. When the experiments of athletes and coaches with what the human body could take were augmented by research in exercise physiology, further advances became possible. Finally, peak performance in virtually every sport involves mental and emotional qualities that can be actively developed, and recognition of this has brought sport psychology increasingly into the picture. The development of knowledge, and indeed of new "sport sciences," has become central to the systematic production of performance.

Third, in some sports it is clear that developments in equipment have been central to performance improvements. This is perhaps most evident in an event like the pole vault, where fibreglass and then carbon poles virtually transformed the event. Some observers of athletics have noted that although all distance runners have access to the same knowledge of training, times for the longer track events (5,000 and 10,000) have come down much faster than marathon times; they have attributed this to the advent of resilient, rubberized track surfaces. In a different area of sport, the development of lightweight yet strong synthetics has made a big impact in both downhill and cross-country skiing. An interesting issue, however, is raised here. There is an important difference between developments in competitive facilities (whether running tracks, playing surfaces, or pools) that improve conditions for all competitors and developments in personal equipment that give an edge to those with the new material or the breakthrough design. This is partly why in sports like skiing and sailing (and before, in the pole vault) competitors and managers kept a proprietary watch over their equipment.

Finally, we come to the impact of money in the rational production of performance, for money makes possible full-time training, funds research in the sport sciences, produces breakthroughs in equipment, and provides expensive new equipment to athletes. Producing perfor-

mance costs money, and we have proposed throughout this book that both private entrepreneurs and governments have had reasons that were quite valid, from their own distinct perspectives, for putting more and more money into sport. Team owners and sport promoters, collectively, have tried to put a "professional" entertainment product on the field, since not many of us would regularly pay to watch true amateurs, although we might honour amateurism in theory. Governments have had different reasons for seeking to produce top-level performance, which we addressed in Chapter 4; but we noted also that there is little question that the advent of this money has radically changed the Olympic sports in Canada.

Basically, we suggest that the lowering of records in the last fifty years is unlikely to continue at the same rate over the next fifty. We say this for two kinds of reasons. The first concerns the limits of the human body, for no matter how much the ideology of "pushing back the frontiers of human performance" may appeal, research shows that even the best-trained and fittest body requires cycles of rest and recovery. We have gone far beyond the era when training systematically was "not quite cricket" and we now know, fairly accurately, just how much training of various sorts athletes can take. We have also created the structures, the financial supports, and the access to coaching and to state-of-the-art facilities and equipment that permit our most likely athletes to train as hard as they can in pursuit of sporting excellence. Therefore, further improvement will come more slowly and gradually. This prediction can be qualified in several ways. Some sports, like sailing and cricket, have been slower to institutionalize year-round training (especially fitness training), and we might expect some dramatic improvements when they do. Likewise, professional hockey and some other team games have been notoriously slow to approach fitness training systematically.

More generally, the East European dominance of women's events in the post-war period has showed what women could achieve when they trained as hard and as systematically as men (see Dyer, 1982). Their achievements have been clouded by the issue of drug use, of course. However, what is demonstrated nonetheless (for drug use in sport was certainly not confined to East bloc women) is that when the social and ideological constraints on women's pursuit of physical achievements are set aside, their performances can and will improve dramatically. Finally, phenomena like drug use and blood doping bring us back to the fact that we are approaching in most sports the limits of what the human body can do without artificial assistance. Progress will be made in sports that have not yet rationalized the production of performance, and more people may be able (and indeed encouraged) to pursue their personal limits. However, to raise the issue of gender here, as well as questions of access and of the use of artificial aids, is to point beyond the question of bodily limits to what Hirsch (1976) called, in another context, "the social limits to growth."

Hirsch was talking about the social costs of the unbridled pursuit of economic growth, but the idea can serve to remind us that the further rationalization of the pursuit of sporting performance is also a social question, involving our priorities as a society. Evidence given to the Dubin Inquiry suggests that there are some in the sport community who simply take it for granted that if the purpose of sport is winning, and the purpose of training is altering the body and mind in order to achieve that end, steroid use is simply a logical extension of a system that supplied them with vitamin supplements and sport psychologists. Against this view, Mr. Justice Dubin several times observed that this kind of evidence itself suggested that Canadians were getting sport out of perspective; and this more critical viewpoint was echoed in letters to various newspapers across the country. Some Canadians, at least, are troubled by the results of our quest to produce performance. And while drug use became the focal point of this disquiet in the wake of Seoul, there is also concern among many parents about the performance-oriented focus of youth sport, discussed in Chapter 8. If we take the fun out of sport, critics say, we lose what is most important about it. Thus it may be that our "sport system" may divide even more clearly than at present between recreational leagues, sponsored perhaps by schools or community organizations or even local businesses, and talent development leagues sponsored by professional sports, by NSOs, and indirectly by government.

WHAT ROLE SHOULD THE STATE PLAY?

What is also raised by speculations about the future of Canadian sport is the question of how much Canadians want our governments to spend on sport, and for what purposes. We tried to show in Chapter 4 that the state's push for national organizations to focus on the production of excellence cannot be considered in isolation from broader issues relating to the increasing presence of the state in civil society and the symbolic use of sport to confirm the vitality of our sociopolitical system. At one level, we have to look no further than the events of the 1988 Seoul Olympics to see that whatever the merits of sport science and state funding of sport, they can produce Frankenstein-like results.

Yet alongside this we have to consider what an event like the 1988 Winter Olympics meant: and not just to the athletes and others directly involved in the sports community, but to the citizens of Calgary, to those who were touched by auxiliary events like the cross-Canada torch relay, and to those who were inspired by seeing (even on television) new forms of human excellence, for example in speed skating or ski jumping. We might consider the thoughts of a Colombian journalist, not a sports fan, on her country's participation in the 1990 World Cup.

> It is difficult for North Americans to grasp the significance, for a small developing country, of taking part in an international championship. When daily life is a struggle to survive for most people, there is little time or energy for even the talented to hope to develop their athletic prowess. (Rodriguez, 1990)

Our point here is that whatever else it does, a publicly funded high performance system makes it possible for poorer Canadians to discover, and aspire to develop, their talents. The Ben Johnson saga illustrates this, too. And pursuing the argument developed above, if money is a factor in making the pursuit of excellence possible, it follows that any cutbacks or reallocations of monies designated for sport are likely to have consequences.

It appears, as this book is being written, that the Canadian government continues to be committed to sponsoring a high-performance sport system. However, several shifts of emphasis also can be predicted with at least some confidence. First, in keeping with its broader strategy of privatization and cutting back on government spending, federal government expenditure on sport will not rise nearly so steeply as it did between 1968 and 1988. The

desire to showcase Canadian winners will probably mean another round of "game plan" type funding for selected NSOs. The long-term trend is almost certainly that NSOs will be required to raise increasing proportions of their budgets from corporations and from their memberships. In the first instance, even though there is some history of corporate sponsorship of mass participation events (e.g., Hoechst's involvement with the Canadian Ski Marathon), the natural desire of corporate sponsors for publicity tends to place the more popular and high-profile sports in a much stronger position than smaller and less highly publicized ones. Even with the former, it often favours sponsorship of newsworthy events like national championships rather than ongoing programs like clinics for junior athletes.

Raising the costs of membership can also have complex consequences. On the one hand, it clearly makes "official" participation in a sport more expensive, though clearly thousands of Canadians run and play hockey without paying dues to Athletics Canada or the CAHA. On the other hand, those who pay dues usually expect services, and there are already signs of demand (in track and field, for instance) that Athletics Canada should provide more services for the many members who are road and cross-country runners and who are Masters, rather than devoting all its resources to the national team. Skiing (both alpine and cross-country) has done more than most sports to sponsor Masters and mass participation events, and swimming has also taken initiatives in this respect. Nonetheless this is clearly an issue of the future if sports organizations want to raise any more of their funding from their memberships.

The issues of funding and of the relationship of national and provincial sport organizations (PSOs) to their memberships surface again in the struggles for control described in Chapter 4. In general, the increasing "systematization" of sport in Canada has led to greater control by technical and administrative professionals. Technical expertise has become necessary, as the knowledge involved in the production of performance has become increasingly sophisticated. Administrative expertise has also become necessary as organizations have grown and as raising and managing money have become increasingly central to the success of the whole enterprise. The result has been the growth of small "sports bureaucracies," not only in Ottawa but in all of the provinces that fund their sport organizations. These professional bureaucracies, like most others (for example, in social services and education), take for granted that what they are doing is desirable in Canadian society and that professional expertise is necessary for it to be done properly. They can be expected to resist (as indeed would social workers or teachers) any suggestion that the system be cut back drastically, that it should do different things (e.g., have a recreational rather than a high-performance mandate, for this might best be accomplished by professionals with different skills), or that effective control over their activities be restored to volunteers.

At the same time, we have seen and are likely to continue to see considerable changes in the volunteer "base" of Canadian NSOs and PSOs. The traditional sources of recruitment for coaches, referees, and officials and helpers of various sorts were former players who wanted to stay involved and, of course, parents. Today, however, many former participants in highly competitive youth sport know the demands and opt out. Others are deterred by the increasing pressure (largely coming from professionals) for the certification of coaches. Men and women who feel they "know" a sport and are prepared to give up a couple of evenings a week to coaching can balk at being asked to also attend a series of courses. Parents, for their part, are still absolutely necessary in youth sport as drivers and fund-raisers, if not as coaches and officials. And many parents still fill these roles with enthusiasm, as Dryden and MacGregor's (1989) discussion of minor hockey makes clear. However, one does not need to talk to many parents in our more intensive youth sports (hockey, swimming, gymnastics) to hear resentment at the time demands and at how things are run, as well as their desire to help their children succeed at something they like.

Our point here is that when being a volunteer becomes almost a "career" in itself, some individuals drop out because of the demands, while other very dedicated individuals give up out of frustration with the high-performance system and its professional bureaucracy. The result of volunteer alienation is that some PSOs, in particular, are almost "shell" organizations, their grassroots virtually non-existent. This is true, moreover, even when the sport might be quite popular as an informal or unorganized activity. Some sports recognize this problem and are making real efforts to create meaningful roles for former players and other adults who show interest in helping out. Others are actively seeking volunteers for their financial skills and corporate connections rather than for their knowledge of the sport. There are still some in the sports bureaucracy, however, who see dealing with volunteers as a nuisance, and who continue to work to reduce the volunteers' role in making and implementing policy. These structural tensions between professionals and volunteers are likely to continue.

These tensions are intimately connected to questions about the purposes of government funding of sport. The Dubin Inquiry raised explicit questions and stimulated many Canadians inside and outside "the system" to think, to voice criticisms of what has become the official thrust of Canadian sport policy, and sometimes to propose alternatives. What appears likely in the mid-nineties, however, are small shifts in emphasis rather than any marked changes of direction, let alone a dismantling of the system. Federal government statements indicate a renewed concern with "domestic programming." But "those who are familiar with previous federal government statements about its intent to support mass participation programs . . . will probably want to see some concrete evidence before they are convinced that this is indeed the intent of the government" (Whitson and Macintosh, 1988: 85).

How Far Can the Market Expand?

In the booming sports industries, too, we can probably expect more continuity than change. Professional sport is likely to continue to occupy a major place in Canadian popular culture, even though free trade with the United States and a more general "globalization" of the entertainment industries will probably mean that this culture is less distinctively Canadian. The World League of American Football, which in 1991 included the Montreal Machine, is a case in point. With teams in Barcelona, Munich, and London, as well as in North America, this new "minor" league's *raison d'être* appeared to be to extend and test the market reach of the National Football League.

Expansion in the National Hockey League has placed another franchise in Canada – the Ottawa Senators – for the 1992-93 season, and also one in Tampa, Florida, where natural outdoor ice for skating has never existed. Retired Canadians, though, may support the Japanese-financed Tampa NHL entry.

The most interesting future developments in hockey may well surround changes in the structures of international competition. The political and economic transformations in Eastern Europe already mean that Czechoslovakian stars are seeking NHL contracts when their careers are still ahead of them, and top Soviet players may soon be in a position to follow suit. At the same time the growth of hockey as commercial entertainment in Scandinavia, Switzerland, and a booming Italy is beginning to mean that leagues in these countries can offer salaries attractive even to established NHL stars. This competition is not serious yet, for most European leagues still have import restrictions. However, the integration of the Western European economies, as well as their manifest prosperity and their enthusiasm for spectator sport, together lend substance to talk of a European "super league" and even regular competition with North American-based teams.

Other ownerships, not now part of the National Hockey League cartel, are likely to attempt to stake claims in this market. If the threat of competition for players (and fans) ever becomes serious, it is highly probable that the established ownerships on both sides of the Atlantic will quickly move to institute their own structures of international competition. The major beneficiaries stand to be the players, whose salaries will rise closer to those in other major professional sports. The major casualties will be the existing structures of international competition and those non-commercial organizations that run them. In Canada, hockey will continue to be our most popular television attraction, even if private networks outbid a privatized CBC for the rights to *Hockey Night in Canada*.

Elsewhere in team sports, it appears unlikely that the NFL will expand into Canada or that Major League Baseball will add new Canadian franchises. Indeed, in baseball, Montreal may lose the Expos if dwindling fan support continues and American players still resist being traded into a city whose language they don't understand and which they describe as uninterested in baseball. In football, the CFL is not able to compete financially with NFL teams, and the NFL to date has refrained from serious consideration of Canada, though one must wonder with the new Montreal franchise in the WLAF. Almost certainly the establishment of an NFL franchise in one of the major CFL markets (i.e., Toronto or Vancouver) would mean the death of the CFL. However, the NFL is now actively cultivating European markets for its game; and the marketing success of the Blue Jays is likely to mean renewed overtures from Toronto promoters, overtures that may be harder to resist in the context of free trade. What all this will mean for the future of Canadian football as an independent game is difficult to predict. Finally, it is certain that the staging of soccer's World Cup in the United States in 1994 will mean major efforts to sell the game as mass market entertainment throughout North America. Today, soccer is one of the fastest growing youth sports in Canada, with the growth in girls' soccer especially noteworthy. Soccer is also played in ethnic leagues in major Canadian cities. Professional soccer, however, has failed to displace any of the more traditional team games as an object of mass spectator interest, despite substantial investments; and it is difficult to imagine the conjuncture of changes – in media coverage, in the production of homegrown stars, and in the reconstruction of fan allegiance in such places as Toronto, Edmonton, and Montreal – that could turn this around.

In individual sports there is perhaps more scope for change, and indeed one of the striking things about the last twenty-five years has been the enormous upsurge of interest in a great variety of individual sports across the developed world. Golf, tennis, skiing, and auto racing always had their followings. However, the commercial promotion of these sports – by a combination of television interests, players' associations (e.g., the PGA, the WTC), facility owners, and equipment manufacturers – has created huge new audiences in populations that once took only passing interest. The global interest created by "world circuits" (for example, "world class" tennis and golf coming to Toronto), even though very few Canadians have ever competed successfully in these sports, is noteworthy. It is also worth noting the role of sports "magazine" programming, on all the major American and Canadian networks, in creating audiences not just for the mainstream sports mentioned above but for "emergent" sports from snooker to surfing. Here we refer back to our discussion in Chapter 6 about the processes through which sports programming actively seeks to cultivate new audiences for entertainment products that are packaged in ways carefully constructed to appeal to them.

One of the most significant success stories, indeed, has been the creation of commercially significant audiences for women's tennis, golf, skiing, and figure skating. The top women in these events are now popular culture "celebrities" in much the same sense as their male counterparts. They are also able to earn celebrity incomes, not just from prize monies but from endorsements, too. However, as we noted in Chapters 6 and 7, top female athletes have had to succeed against a tradition of media coverage that sometimes has been openly sexist and at other times subtly so. The coverage of women's sport is arguably getting less sexist; and today stars like Martina Navratilova and Florence Griffith Joyner can afford to ignore the sexually loaded persona the media create around them. But it also remains the case that television has not even seriously tried to create audiences for women's basketball and women's hockey, despite the manifest popularity of the male professional games. Here we see principles of equity and the real efforts of pioneering supporters running up against the logic of commerce, and behind this the ideologies of gender that structure a still patriarchal society.

Thus far here we have focused on spectator sport; but before concluding our discussion of the future of the sports business, it is also important to consider sports participation, and changes in the sports equipment business. Probably the most far-reaching change here has simply been the production and marketing of sports equipment and clothing for women. Once sports equipment was made for and sold to a male market; but the success of Reebok in making shoes to fit women's feet and marketing them to women through aerobics instructors has not been lost on other sportswear manufacturers. Other lessons learned by the sporting goods industry are the importance of niche marketing (in addition to women, the youth market in particular) and the erosion of the distinction between sportswear and fashion (Davies, 1990). Sportswear used to be designed for function, in "sensible" colours, and outdoors wear, in particular, used to be predictable for its homespun appearance. Today, companies from Patagonia to the Vancouver-based Mountain Equipment and Quebec's Haute Chlorophylle, from L.L. Bean to Eddie Bauer, all demonstrate that sports clothing need not be dull to be good. This trend will doubtless continue, though it also should be observed that turning sports clothing into fashion items brings with it the cost dynamics of the fashion industry. The new sportswear has a distinctly "yuppie" cost to it, though as always, high-quality originals very soon spawn mass-market imitators (in fleece jackets as well as running shoes).

In addition, the development of new and lightweight materials has helped to create new markets in backpacking and camping, in cross-country skiing, and in canoeing and windsurfing. In the former case, lightweight yet water-proof materials for tents, sleeping bags, and apparel together make backcountry travel on foot not only possible but easy enough to be fun. In the case of cross-country skiing, the development of strong yet light skis helped to make winter travel easier and more enjoyable, while the development of no-wax bases made learning the sport a much faster and less frustrating experience. In both instances, purists often prefer traditional constructions, but the development of new ones has helped to increase participation in these sports. Similarly, fibreglass and later kevlar increased the marketability of canoeing, while the development of windsurfing and mountain-biking as sports would have been virtually inconceivable without breakthroughs in materials technologies and design.

In the growth of such sports we can see evidence of the market's potential to cater to old and new demand, and also to create demand for products that once no one thought of. On the one hand it is important to recognize that the market thus creates new possibilities for pleasure and enjoyment. Indeed, in the growth in the use of the outdoors for recreational purposes, many Canadians in very different social circumstances gain access to leisure choices that were once available only to highly skilled, fit, and well-to-do enthusiasts. It is also fair to argue, as does Wilson (1990), that through the boom in "wilderness sports," private equipment manufacturers and "adventure" tour operators recognized and responded to what were genuine yet latent public interests, both in the natural environment and in non-competitive forms of physical challenge. At

Nordic skiing in Canada's mountain wilderness.

the same time, the target markets for most forms of outdoor equipment and travel remain the relatively affluent; in other words, these are not yet "mass-market" items.

Significantly, the growth of a large new constituency of backcountry users places new pressures on the backcountry itself as it is made more accessible. The presence of large numbers of people in these areas erodes the very "wilderness" experience that many users seek.

Furthermore, it creates problems of "demand management" for the managers of our national and provincial parks. Parks staff and politicians alike must balance the claims of the environment and of those who want spaces left for low-cost, low-impact activities against demands from the recreational industry that more and more backcountry be opened up to higher-impact but more profitable forms of recreation like downhill skiing and "destination" resorts

(Sax, 1980). This conflict is likely to increase and to create growing problems for governments caught between "development" and "conservation" lobbies (Bella, 1987).

Finally, the capacity of entrepreneurs to respond to currents in public concern and desire, yet at the same time to give a particular shape to how those desires will be fulfilled, is illustrated in the burgeoning health and fitness industry. On the one hand, advertising and the cumulative public presence of fitness-related talk and equipment have helped to legitimize the very idea of physical activity and regular exercise. In addition, better designed shoes, new forms of exercise equipment, and sports medicine have all prolonged the possibility of pain-free and enjoyable exercise for a great many middle-aged men and women. And the promotion of non-competitive forms of exercise (including aerobics, tai chi and yoga, dance, and martial arts) has opened up new possibilities of empowerment to many women and some men.

At the same time, the associations between fitness and fashion and between fitness and sexual attractiveness, associations that the industry actively trades on, reinforce "standards" of appearance that are impossible for many people of both sexes. Again, too, the actively promoted rowing machines and other specialized exercise paraphernalia are clearly "up market" items; indeed, the pervasive promotion of purpose-built clothing (e.g., different jackets and pants for every sport) obscures just how much exercise can be enjoyed without specialty clothing or accessories, with little or no expenditure at all. Perhaps the most problematic effect of this is that the practice of fitness becomes integrated into the popular imagination with a consumer lifestyle, even an expensive lifestyle. Fitness has taken on a distinctly middle-class image that may create some prob-

lems for the future. The fitness boom may be fairly described as a great thing for all of those who have been able to "buy in." However, in its forms, its costs, and its dominant imagery, the fitness boom has arguably excluded others, and this creates problems for those concerned with health promotion as a social (i.e., rather than a commercial) challenge and for those who see health inequities as an important social issue.

Discussion of wilderness and of fitness leads us, finally, to some observations about the relationships among public, commercial, and private institutions in the provision of a range of sporting possibilities to Canadians. In the case of the wilderness, the successes of the outdoor equipment industries have helped to create a much greater demand for public facilities (parks) accessible to the more urban communities where most of us live. This in turn creates economic demands on governments and political problems for governments, which must mediate between different publics and different economic interests (Butler, 1989).

In the case of fitness, the interests of "the industry" in selling equipment and advice and venues (squash clubs, etc.) mesh to some extent with those of the government in "health promotion." However, there are limits to this coincidence of interests and arguably there are responsibilities peculiar to government. The industry's interest, naturally enough, is in those sectors of the population that can afford what they produce. Governments, on the other hand, have some obligation to be concerned also (and perhaps especially) with those who cannot afford what is available in the shop windows. This does not mean the provision by the state of personal equipment. It does mean, however, the provision of public facilities at low cost and the preservation of public spaces where sports and other forms of physical recreation (like walking) can be enjoyed outside the market framework.

Likewise, with respect to gender and ethnicity, it can be argued that only government is likely to defend the interests of disadvantaged groups or provide for minorities. In Canadian sport, Sport Canada's initiatives in encouraging women to qualify themselves for leadership roles and in requiring NSOs to address gender issues specifically in their plans for human resource development point to both the promise and the limits of government intervention. Progress has been made in some sports, and enough pressure has been generated that even more progress seems predictable. However, resistance to these changes is also endemic, so it is also predictable that further progress for women in NSOs (and indeed in sport) is inseparable from a broader struggle to change the ideologies and the concrete social arrangements that together structure relations between men and women in Canada.

SPORT, SOCIAL CHANGE, AND SOCIOLOGY: SOME FINAL REMARKS

For most of this chapter we have been talking about the future as if it is something that simply unfolds in a manner that is perhaps predictable but largely independent of our aspirations and efforts. We want to conclude by qualifying this view of history to re-emphasize some themes we have sought to develop throughout the text – about the nature and significance of power in understanding social institutions and about the significance of ideology (or dominant ideas) in either maintaining or challenging institutional-

ized patterns of power. We must remember, too, that many people involved in Canadian sport have had a positive influence – on others, on local institutions, on national institutions – but specific examples are less important than thinking about the *different* ways in which making a difference can be achieved.

The most immediate and arguably the most effective way is to work "within the system." To do this requires accepting for the time being its limitations – its barriers to women and natives, for example, or the domination of minor hockey by the interest of the NHL – while establishing enough credibility and acquiring enough power and influence to change it gradually. This carries with it very real dangers of being absorbed or co-opted into the very system one sets out to change, yet it remains the most likely route to real personal influence and the path followed by the most widely known agents of change.

Another option is to involve oneself in "oppositional" groups that work outside official institutions, criticizing them and trying to reorient the directions of official policy by presenting research at hearings and trying to mobilize public concern about the effects of existing policies. These public interest groups are now active players in the Canadian political process and, in the case of environmental groups, they can constitute the most articulate and effective opposition to the plans of economic and political elites. In sport, examples are the Canadian Association for the Advancement of Women in Sport and the Bread Not Circuses Coalition, the group formed to oppose Toronto's bid to spend large sums of public money to stage the Olympics (as well as plans to build a new opera house) instead of on housing and more basic services. Sometimes these groups achieve very visible successes: stopping a pulp mill or a stadium, or winning funding (e.g., for women's programs or native programs) that had not been forthcoming through more normal political channels. More typically, however, their successes involve pre-emptive concessions intended to ward off more broadly based public opposition, or having parts of their agenda incorporated into official plans (e.g., more future public housing included in plans for an Olympic Village).

A third possibility is simply to ignore the politics of official institutions and concentrate one's energies on working with other like-minded people to create alternatives. These alternatives may involve quite fundamental challenges to dominant norms and values: for example, the "co-operative" sports and games movement (see Orlick, 1978) and "feminist baseball" (Birrell and Richter, 1987). Such initiatives involve infusing sport with radically alternative values and practices, and they typically encounter at least some hostility, even when they are personally satisfying to the participants. In their very difference from what is "normal" they encounter problems in getting access to facilities, to public funds, and so on. However, the growth in non-competitive forms of physical activity illustrates that the proponents of alternatives are not always doomed to failure.

Finally, certain connections between knowledge and social action need to be considered here. We argued in Chapter 2 that to see sport as a set of cultural institutions and practices is to begin to appreciate just how intimately changes in sport have been bound up with broader changes in social relations. To say this is not simply to say that sport reflects the power of dominant social groups to showcase their own achievements and to give symbolic expression to meanings and values they cherish. Clearly, our discussions about sport and masculinity, and of the institutionalization

of sport by the Victorian upper and middle classes, illustrate that this has been historically true. To see sport as culture has also served to highlight how struggles to legitimize different sports and different approaches to sporting practice have been a part of broader changes in social relations: struggles to "modernize" class and gender relations, and struggles to establish new bases of national identification and solidarity. We suggested that culture was about the expression of meaning in everyday life, and we reiterate the significance of sport, as a very *popular* cultural form, in the construction and dissemination of meaning. Our earlier discussion emphasized the various advantages enjoyed by dominant social groups in establishing their own meanings as official and "normal." However, the work of those who seek change, whatever their strategy, is primarily about helping people to think freshly by holding dominant meanings up for critical examination.

Here we return to Mills's suggestion that we study society in order to find effective points of intervention. At least potentially, it is liberating to realize that what we have always thought about sport and indeed other established institutions is largely a product *of* those institutions. If we are able to reflect on our own ideas and on where those ideas come from, we are likely to find ourselves freed to think both more critically and more imaginatively about our personal experience of sport and about the public (or more general) issues raised by sport. In this freedom we develop what we called the sociological imagination. As Anthony Giddens has suggested, it is precisely by revealing and understanding social practices, which often appear to us as natural or inevitable but which are really products of history, that sociology can play an emancipatory role in human society.

REFERENCES

Abt, V., F. Smith, and E.M. Christiansen (1985). *The business of risk: Commercial gambling in mainstream America*. Lawrence: University Press of Kansas.

Adams, J. (1989). "Games sponsors reaped millions from promotions," *Calgary Herald*, February 12, p. C8.

Adamson, N., L. Briskin, and M. McPhail (1988). *Feminist organizing for change: The contemporary women's movement in Canada*. Toronto: Oxford University Press.

Adelman, M.L. (1986). *A sporting time: New York City and the rise of modern athletics*. Urbana: University of Illinois Press.

Alaton, S. (1990). "Stanley Cup fever pits a lone Canadian against cool New York," *Globe and Mail*, May 24, p. A12.

Alberta Gaming Commission (1988). *Annual Review*. Edmonton: Government of Alberta.

Albinson, J. (1976). "The 'professional orientation' of the amateur hockey coach," in R.S. Gruneau and J.G. Albinson, eds., *Canadian sport: Sociological perspectives*. Toronto: Addison-Wesley.

Allison, L. (1986). "Sport and politics," in L. Allison, ed., *The politics of sport*. Manchester: Manchester University Press.

Armstrong, C., and H.V. Nelles (1977). *The Re-*

venge of the Methodist Bicycle Company. Toronto: Peter Martin.

Auf der Maur, N. (1976). *The billion-dollar game: Jean Drapeau and the 1976 Olympics.* Toronto: James Lorimer.

Baade, R.A., and F. Dye (1988). "Sport stadiums and area development: A critical review," *Economic Development Quarterly,* 2, pp. 265-75.

Bain, G. (1990). "Sportscasters risk jobs for telling it like it is," *Maclean's,* August 27, p. 48.

Ball, D.W. (1973). "Ascription and position: A comparative analysis of 'stacking' in professional football," *Canadian Review of Sociology and Anthropology,* 10, pp. 97-113.

Barman, J. (1984). *Growing up British in British Columbia: Boys in private school.* Vancouver: University of British Columbia Press.

Barnes, J. (1988). *Sports and the law in Canada* (2nd ed.). Toronto: Butterworths.

Barthes, R. (1973). *Mythologies.* London: Paladin. (Original work published in 1957.)

Beamish, R. (1978). *Socioeconomic and demographic characteristics of the national executives of selected amateur sports in Canada (1975),* Working Papers in the Sociological Study of Sport and Leisure, Vol. 1, No. 1. Kingston: Queen's University.

Beamish, R. (1985). "Sport executives and voluntary associations: A review of literature and introduction to some theoretical issues," *Sociology of Sport Journal,* 2, pp. 218-32.

Beamish, R. (1988). "The political economy of professional sport," in J. Harvey and H. Cantelon, eds., *Not just a game.* Ottawa: University of Ottawa Press.

Beamish, R. (1990). "The persistance of inequality: An analysis of participation patterns among Canada's high performance athletes," *International Review for the Sociology of Sport,* 25, pp. 143-53.

Beamish, R., and J. Borowy (1987). "High performance athletes in Canada: From status to contract," in T. Slack and C.R. Hinings, eds., *The organization and administration of sport.* London: Sports Dynamics.

Beamish, R., and J. Borowy (1988). *Q. What do you do for a living? A. I'm an athlete.* Kingston: The Sport Research Group, Queen's University.

Beardsley, D. (1988). *Country on ice.* Toronto: PaperJacks.

Beare, M.E. (1989). "Current law enforcement issues in Canadian gambling," in C.S. Campbell and J. Lowman, eds., *Gambling in Canada: Golden goose or Trojan horse?* Burnaby, B.C.: Simon Fraser School of Criminology.

Beauchesne, L. (1990). "The Dubin Inquiry's political purpose," paper presented at the "After the Dubin Inquiry: Implications for Canada's High-Performance Sport System" Conference. Kingston, Ontario, September.

Bella, L. (1987). *Parks for profit.* Montreal: Harvest House.

Berger, P.L. (1963). *Invitation to sociology: A humanistic perspective.* Garden City, N.Y.: Anchor Books.

Berger, P.L., B. Berger, and H.H. Kellner (1974). *The homeless mind: Modernization and civilization.* New York: Vintage Books.

Berman, M. (1989). "Why modernism still matters," *Tikkun*, 4, pp. 11-14, 81-86.

Berryman, J.W. (1975). "From the cradle to the playing field: America's emphasis on highly organized competitive sports for preadolescent boys," *Journal of Sport History*, 2, pp. 112-31.

Betke, C. (1983). "Sports promotion in the western Canadian city: The example of early Edmonton," *Urban History Review*, 12, 2, pp. 47-56.

Biddle, S. (1989). " 'Innovation without change' and the ideology of individualism: A reply to Sparkes," *British Journal of Physical Education*, 20, pp. 64-65.

Birrell, S.J. (1988). "Discourses on the gender/sport relationship: From women in sport to gender relations," in K. Pandolf, ed., *Exercise and Sport Sciences Reviews*, Vol. 16. New York: Macmillan.

Birrell, S.J. (1989). "Racial relations theories and sport: Suggestions for a more critical analysis," *Sociology of Sport Journal*, 6, pp. 212-27.

Birrell, S.J., and J.W. Loy (1979). "Media sports: Hot and cool," *International Review of Sport Sociology*, 14, pp. 5-19.

Birrell, S.J., and D.M. Richter (1987). "Is a diamond forever?: Feminist transformation of sport," *Women's Studies International Forum*, 10, pp. 387-93.

Blann, W., and L. Zaichkowsky (1987). *Career-life transition needs of National Hockey League players: Spouses perspectives.* A final report prepared for the National Hockey League Players' Association.

Blue, A. (1987). *Grace under pressure: The emergence of women in sport.* London: Sidgwick & Jackson.

Blumler, J.G., and E. Katz, eds. (1974). *The uses of mass communication.* London: Sage.

Board, M. (1989). "Tourist gold legacy of winter Olympics," *Calgary Herald*, February 12, p. C10.

Boileau, R., F. Landry, and Y. Trempe (1976). "Les Canadiens français et les grands jeux internationaux (1908-1974)," in R.S. Gruneau and J.G. Albinson, eds., *Canadian sport: Sociological perspectives.* Don Mills, Ont.: Addison-Wesley.

Bottomore, T. (1979). *Political sociology.* New York: Harper and Row.

Boulanger, R. (1988). "Class cultures and sports activities in Quebec," in J. Harvey and H. Cantelon, eds., *Not just a game.* Ottawa: University of Ottawa Press.

Bourdieu, P. (1978). "Sport and social class," *Social Science Information*, 17, pp. 819-40.

Braidfoot, L. (1985). *Gambling: A deadly game.* Nashville: Broadman Press.

Bray, C. (1988). "Sport and the Canadian state: Gender and class issues," *Resources for Feminist Research*, 17, 3, pp. 75-77.

Brodeur, J.P. (1979). "L'ordre délinquant – Les commissions d'enquête sur la police comme instrument politique," *Déviance et Société*, 3, pp. 1-22.

Brodeur, P. (1988). "Employee fitness: Doctrines and issues," in J. Harvey and H. Cantelon, eds., *Not just a game*. Ottawa: University of Ottawa Press.

Brohm, J.-M. (1978). *Sport: A prison of measured time*. London: Ink Links.

Brooks, J. (1984). "Jelinek wants business to spend more on sport," *Montreal Gazette*, December 1, p. C4.

Brown, B.A. (1985). "Factors influencing the process of withdrawal by female adolescents from the role of competitive age group swimmers," *Sociology of Sport Journal*, 2, pp. 111-29.

Brown, D.W. (1988). "Social Darwinism, private schooling and sport in Victoria and Edwardian Canada," in J.A. Mangan, ed., *Pleasure, profit, proselytism: British culture and sport at home and abroad 1700-1914*. London: Frank Cass.

Brownlee, R. (1990). "Youngsters' depleted ranks a growing concern," *Edmonton Journal*, January 12, p. F1.

Brunt, S. (1989a). "Making money is no lottery for Ontario," *Globe and Mail*, March 17, p. A8.

Brunt, S. (1989b). "SkyDome's financial saga makes baseball a sideshow," *Globe and Mail*, July 14, p. A13.

Brunt, S. (1989c). "Hodges firing a rational business decision, if not moral," *Globe and Mail*, December 15, p. A12.

Bryant, J., P. Comisky, and D. Zillman (1981). "The appeal of rough-and-tumble play in televised professional football," *Communication Quarterly*, 29, pp. 256-62.

Bryant, J., D. Brown, P. Comisky, and D. Zillman (1982). "Sports and spectators: Commentary and appreciation," *Journal of Communication*, 32, pp. 104-19.

Bryant, J., and D. Zillman (1983). "Sports violence and the media," in J. Goldstein, ed., *Sports violence*. New York: Springer-Verlag.

Burstyn, V. (1990). "The sporting life," *Saturday Night*, March, pp. 42-49.

Butler, R.W. (1989). "The future," in G. Wall, ed., *Outdoor recreation in Canada*. Toronto: John Wiley.

Butcher, J. (1982). "Student satisfaction with physical education," *CAHPER Journal*, 48, 5, pp. 11-14.

Caillois, R. (1961). *Man, play and games*, M. Barash, trans. New York: Free Press. (Original work published in 1958.)

Calder, R.L., and G. Andrew (1984). *Rider pride: The story of Canada's best-loved football team*. Saskatoon: Western Producers Prairie Books.

Campbell, C.S. (1988). "Casino gambling and the peripheral state," in W.R. Eadington, ed., *Gambling research. Proceedings of the Seventh International Conference on Gambling and Risk Taking*. Reno: Bureau of Business and Economic Research, College of Business Administration, University of Nevada.

Campbell, C.S., and J. Lowman, eds. (1989). *Gambling in Canada: Golden goose or Trojan horse?* Burnaby, B.C.: Simon Fraser School of Criminology.

Campbell, C.S., and J.R. Ponting (1984). "The evolution of casino gambling in Alberta," *Canadian Public Policy*, 10, 2, pp. 142-55.

Campbell, N.A. (1987). "Horse racing bookies no longer fans' favourites," *Globe and Mail*, May 19, p. A11.

Campbell, N.A. (1989). "Say it ain't so: Gambling threatens to take over major league sports," *Globe and Mail*, July 22, p. D1.

Canada Fitness Survey (1983). *Fitness and Lifestyle in Canada*. Ottawa: Government of Canada.

Cantelon, H. (1981). "High performance sport and the child athlete: Learning to labour," in A. Ingham and E. Broom, eds., *Career patterns and career contingencies in sport. Proceedings of the 1st Regional Symposium, International Committee for the Sociology of Sport*. Vancouver: University of British Columbia.

Cantelon, H., and R.S. Gruneau (1988). "The production of sport for television," in J. Harvey and H. Cantelon, eds., *Not just a game*. Ottawa: University of Ottawa Press.

Carroll, M. (1988). "It's not how you play the game, it's whether you win or lose: The need for criminal sanctions to curb violence in professional sports," *Hamline Law Review*, 12, pp. 71-90.

Cavallo, D. (1981). *Muscles and morals: Organized playgrounds and urban reform, 1880-1920*. Philadelphia: University of Pennsylvania Press.

Chamberlain, N.C. (1983). "Soccer, multiculturalism and the Canadian state," Master's thesis, University of Alberta.

Chandler, J.M. (1988). *Television and national sport: The United States and Britain*. Urbana: University of Illinois Press.

Chivers, B. (1976). "Friendly games: Edmonton's Olympic alternative," in J. Lorimer and E. Ross, eds., *The city book: The politics and planning of Canada's cities*. Toronto: James Lorimer.

Christie, J. (1989a). "U.S. colleges majoring in hockey," *Globe and Mail*, February 11, p. C8.

Christie, J. (1989b). "MP calls lack of university sport bureaucrats disgraceful," *Globe and Mail*, September 4, p. C3.

Christie, J. (1990). "McMurtry wants Canadian pivots in CFL," *Globe and Mail*, May 2, p. A17.

Clark, S.D. (1942). *The social development of Canada*. Toronto: University of Toronto Press.

Coakley, J. (1986). "Socialization and youth sports," in C.R. Rees and A.W. Miracle, eds., *Sport and social theory*. Champaign, Ill.: Human Kinetics.

Coakley, J. (1990). *Sport in society: Issues and controversies* (4th ed.). St. Louis: Times Mirror/Mosby.

Colquhoun, D. (1989). "Health related fitness and individualism: Continuing the debate," *British Journal of Physical Education*, 20, pp. 118-22.

Connell, R.W. (1983). "Men's bodies," in *Which way is up?: Essays on class, sex and culture*. Sydney: George Allen & Unwin.

Cosentino, F. (1989). "Football," in D. Morrow et al., *A concise history of sport in Canada*. Toronto: Oxford University Press.

Cosentino, F. (1990). "Sport for sport's sake? Not when showbiz takes over," *Globe and Mail*, May 17, p. A7.

Cosentino, F., and M.L. Howell (1971). *A history of physical education in Canada*. Toronto: General Publishing Company.

Coulombe, S., and M. Lavoie (1985). "Les francophones dans la Ligue nationale de hockey: une analyse économique de la discrimination," *L'Actualité Économique*, 61, pp. 73-92.

Coutts, J., and M. Polanyi (1990). "Bidding for the spectacular," *Globe and Mail*, June 9, p. D2.

Crawford, R. (1977). "You are dangerous to your health: The ideology and politics of victim blaming," *International Journal of Health Services*, 7, pp. 663-80.

Crawford, R. (1980). "Healthism and the medicalization of everyday life," *International Journal of Health Services*, 10, pp. 365-88.

Crawford, R. (1984). "A cultural account of health: Control, release and the social body," in J.B. McKinlay, ed., *Issues in the political economy of health care*. New York: Tavistock.

Csikszentmihalyi, M. (1975). *Beyond boredom and anxiety*. San Francisco: Jossey-Bass.

Csikszentmihalyi, M. (1990). *Flow: The psychology of optimal experience*. New York: Harper and Row.

Curtis, J.E., and B.G. Milton (1976). "Social status and the active society: National data on correlates of leisure-time physical and sport activities," in R.S. Gruneau and J.G. Albinson, eds., *Canadian sport: Sociological perspectives*. Don Mills, Ont.: Addison-Wesley (Canada).

Curtis, J.E., and P.G. White (1984). "Age and sport participation: Decline in participation or increased specialization with age," in N. Theberge and P. Donnelly, eds., *Sport and the sociological imagination*. Fort Worth: Texas Christian University Press.

Curtis, J.E., and B.D. McPherson (1987). "Regional differences in the leisure physical activity of Canadians: Testing some alternative interpretations," *Sociology of Sport Journal*, 4, pp. 363-75.

Czerny, M., and J. Swift (1988). *Getting started on social analysis in Canada* (2nd edition). Toronto: Between the Lines.

Darroch, G. (1986). "Class and stratification," in L. Tepperman and R.J. Richardson, eds., *The social world: An introduction to sociology*. Toronto: McGraw-Hill Ryerson.

Davidson, J. (1985). "Girls just want to play hockey," *Globe and Mail*, November 2, pp. D1, D3.

Davidson, J. (1987). "Runners take dollar stride," *Globe and Mail*, May 4, p. A16.

Davidson, J. (1989). "Canadians passionate for sport – U.S. style," *Globe and Mail*, October 14, pp. D1, D8.

Davies, P. (1990). "Hot shoes," *The Globe and Mail Report on Business Magazine*, May, pp. 91-95.

Davis, L.E. (1974). "Self regulation in baseball," in R.G. Noll, ed., *Government and the sports business*. Washington: The Brookings Institute.

Day, R.D. (1981). "Ethnic soccer clubs in London, Canada: A study of assimilation," *International Review of Sport Sociology*, 16, 1, pp. 37-50.

Devereux, E.C. (1976). "Backyard versus Little League Baseball: The impoverishment of children's games," in D.M. Landers, ed., *Social problems in athletics: Essays in the sociology of sport*. Urbana: University of Illinois Press.

Dominion Law Reports (1983). 13, 4th series, pp. 485-525.

Donnelly, P., and K. Young (1988). "The construction and confirmation of identity in sport subcultures," *Sociology of Sport Journal*, 5, pp. 223-40.

Downey, D. (1986). "NFL still big favorite of betting crowd," *Globe and Mail*, March 13, p. A8.

Drahozal, C. (1986). "The impact of free agency on the distribution of talent in major league baseball," *Journal of Economics and Business*, 38, pp. 113-21.

Dryden, K. (1983). *The game*. Toronto: Totem Books.

Dryden, K., and R. MacGregor (1989). *Home game: Hockey and life in Canada*. Toronto: McClelland & Stewart.

Dubin, C.L. (1990). *Commission of inquiry into the use of drugs and banned practices intended to increase athletic performance*. Ottawa: Minister of Supply and Services.

Duncan, M.C., and C.A. Hasbrook (1988). "Denial of power in televised women's sports," *Sociology of Sport Journal*, 5, pp. 1-21.

Dunning, E. (1986). "Sport as a male preserve: Notes on the social sources of masculine identity and its transformation," *Theory, Culture & Society*, 3, 1, pp. 79-90.

Dunning, E., and K. Sheard (1979). *Barbarians, gentlemen, and players: A sociological study of the development of rugby football*. Oxford: Robertson.

Duquin, M.E. (1989). "Fashion and fitness: Images of women's magazine advertisements," *Arena Review*, 13, 2, pp. 97-109.

Dyer, K. (1982). *Challenging the men: Women in sport*. St. Lucia: University of Queensland Press.

Eitzen, D.S. (1985). "Violence in professional sports and public policy," in A.T. Johnson and J.H. Frey, eds., *Government and sport: The public policy issues*. Totowa, N.J.: Rowman & Allanheld.

Eitzen, D.S., and G.H. Sage (1989). *Sociology of North American Sport* (4th ed.). Dubuque, Iowa: Wm. C. Brown.

Elias, N., and E. Dunning (1986). *The quest for excitement: Sport and leisure in the civilizing process*. New York: Blackwell.

Enchin, H. (1989). "Canadien fans take religion seriously," *Globe and Mail*, February 27, p. C4.

Epp, J. (1986). *Achieving health for all: A framework for health promotion*. Ottawa: Government of Canada.

Eynon, R.B., P.D. Kitchen, and D.M. Semotiuk (1980). "The economics of age-group swimming in Ontario," *Canadian Journal of Applied Sport Sciences*, 5, pp. 132-36.

Fabiano, D. (1984). "Minority managers in professional baseball," *Sociology of Sport Journal*, 1, pp. 163-71.

Fennell, T., and D. Jenish (1990). "The riches of sport," *Maclean's*, April 9, pp. 42-45.

Finch, P. (1989). "The golf club with a handicap all its own," *Business Week*, May, pp. 126, 130.

Fine, G.A. (1987). *With the boys: Little League baseball and preadolescent culture*. Chicago: University of Chicago Press.

Fisher, M. (1984). "Podborski won't spell it out, but he's probably a millionaire," *Globe and Mail*, April 6, p. M5.

Fisher, M. (1985). "Jelinek out to tap corporate purse," *Globe and Mail*, May 6, p. S2.

Fisher, M. (1989a). "The failure of Canadian sports journalism in relation to Olympic sports," in R. Jackson and T. McPhail, eds., *The Olympic movement and the mass media*. Calgary: Hurford.

Fisher, M. (1989b). "Broncos bust out after bucking disaster," *Globe and Mail*, March 27, p. A16.

Fishwick, L., and S. Greendorfer (1987). "Socialization revisited: A critique of the sport-related research," *Quest*, 39, pp. 1-8.

Fitness and Amateur Sport (1986). *Sport Canada policy on women in sport*. Ottawa: Government of Canada.

Fitness and Amateur Sport (1987). *Sport Canada marketing support program for national sport organizations: Funding guidelines 1987-1988*. Ottawa: Government of Canada.

Fitness and Amateur Sport (1988). *Toward 2000: Building Canada's sport system* (The Report of the Task Force on National Sport Policy). Ottawa: Government of Canada.

Fitness and Amateur Sport (1990). *Doping related matters*. Discussion paper prepared for consultation on the Dubin Report. Ottawa: Government of Canada.

Fletcher, S. (1984). *Women first: The female tradition in English physical education 1880-1980*. London: Athlone Press.

Foley, D. (1990). "The great American football ritual: Reproducing race, class, and gender inequality," *Sociology of Sport Journal*, 7, pp. 111-35.

Franks, C.E.S., M. Hawes, and D. Macintosh (1988). "Sport and Canadian diplomacy," *International Journal*, 43, pp. 665-82.

Gantz, W. (1981). "An exploration of viewing motives and behaviors associated with televised sports," *Journal of Broadcasting*, 25, pp. 263-75.

Garrison, B. (1989). "The evolution of professionalism in sports reporting," in R. Jackson and T. McPhail, eds., *The Olympic movement and the mass media*. Calgary: Hurford.

Gaskell, J. (1981). "Equal educational opportunity for women," in J.D. Wilson, ed., *Canadian*

Education in the 1980s. Calgary: Detselig Enterprises.

Geddert, R.L., and R.K. Semple (1987). "A National Hockey League franchise: The modified threshold concept in central place theory," *Leisure Sciences*, 9, pp. 1-13.

Gelinas, M., and N. Theberge (1986). "A content analysis of the coverage of physical activity in two Canadian newspapers," *International Review for the Sociology of Sport*, 21, pp. 141-51.

Gerth, H.H., and C.W. Mills (1953). *Character and social structure: The psychology of social institutions.* New York: Harcourt, Brace.

Giddens, A. (1982). *Sociology: A brief but critical introduction.* New York: Harcourt Brace Jovanovich.

Glassford, R.G. (1976). *Application of a theory of games to the transitional Eskimo culture.* New York: Arno Press.

Goldlust, J. (1987). *Playing for keeps: Sport, the media and society.* Melbourne: Longman Cheshire.

Gray, M. (1989). "Play ball!" *Maclean's*, June 12, pp. 40-47.

Greendorfer, S.H. (1981). "Sport and the mass media," in G.R.F. Lüschen and G.H. Sage, eds., *Handbook of social science of sport.* Champaign, Ill.: Stipes.

Greer, D.L., and M.L. Stewart (1989). "Children's attitudes toward play: An investigation of their context specificity and relationship to organized sport," *Journal of Sport and Exercise Psychology*, 11, pp. 336-42.

Grenier, G., and M. Lavoie (1988). *Francophones in the National Hockey League: Test of entry and salary discrimination*, Department of Economics Research Paper 8805. Ottawa: University of Ottawa.

Griffin, P. (1989). "Assessment of equitable instructional practices in the gym," *CAHPER Journal*, 55, 2, pp. 19-26.

Grignon, G. (1989). "The packaging of sport," *Champion*, 13, pp. 53-55.

Gruneau, R.S. (1975). "Sport, social differentiation and social inequality," in D.W. Ball and J.W. Loy, eds., *Sport and social order: Contributions to the sociology of sport.* Reading, Mass.: Addison-Wesley.

Gruneau, R.S. (1976). "Class or mass: Notes on the democratization of Canadian amateur sport," in R.S. Gruneau and J.G. Albinson, eds., *Canadian sport: Sociological perspectives.* Don Mills, Ont.: Addison-Wesley (Canada).

Gruneau, R.S. (1978). "Elites, class and corporate power in Canadian sport: Some preliminary findings," in F. Landry and W. Orban, eds., *Sociology of sport.* Miami: Symposia Specialists.

Gruneau, R.S. (1981). "Considerations on the politics of play and youth sport," in A. Ingham and E. Broom, eds., *Career patterns and career contingencies in sport. Proceedings of the 1st Regional Symposium, International Committee for the Sociology of Sport.* Vancouver: University of British Columbia.

Gruneau, R.S. (1983). *Class, sports and social development.* Amherst: University of Massachusetts Press.

Gruneau, R.S. (1984). "Capitalism, commercialism and the Olympics," in A. Tomlinson and G. Whannel, eds., *Five ring circus: Money, power and politics at the Olympic games*. London: Pluto Press.

Gruneau, R.S. (1988). "Modernization or hegemony: Two views of sport and social development," in J. Harvey and H. Cantelon, eds., *Not just a game*. Ottawa: University of Ottawa Press.

Gruneau, R.S. (1989a). "Television, the Olympics, and the question of ideology," in R. Jackson and T. McPhail, eds., *The Olympic movement and the mass media*. Calgary: Hurford.

Gruneau, R.S. (1989b). "Making spectacle: A case study in television sports production," in L.A. Wenner, ed., *Media, sports & society*. Newbury Park, Calif.: Sage.

Gruneau, R.S., D. Whitson, and H. Cantelon (1988). "Method and media: Studying the sports television discourse," *Society and Leisure*, 11, pp. 265-81.

Guay, D. (1973). "Problems de l'integration du sport dans la sociale Canadienne 1830-1865: Le case des courses de chevaux," *Canadian Journal of the History of Sport and Physical Education*, 4, 2, pp. 70-92.

Gurney, H. (n.d.). *A century of progress: Girls' sports in Ontario high schools*. Don Mills, Ont.: Ontario Federation of Schools Athletic Associations.

Guttmann, A. (1978). *From ritual to record: The nature of modern sports*. New York: Columbia University Press.

Guttmann, A. (1984). *The games must go on: Avery Brundage and the Olympic movement*. New York: Columbia University Press.

Guttmann, A. (1988). *A whole new ball game: An interpretation of American sports*. Chapel Hill: University of North Carolina Press.

Gzowski, P. (1981). *The game of our lives*. Toronto: McClelland and Stewart.

Hall, M.A. (1987). "Women Olympians in the Canadian sport bureaucracy," in T. Slack and C.R. Hinings, eds., *The organization and administration of sport*. London, Ont.: Sport Dynamics.

Hall, M.A. (1988). "The discourse of gender and sport: From femininity to feminism," *Sociology of Sport Journal*, 5, pp. 330-40.

Hall, M.A. (1990). "How should we theorize gender in the context of sport?" in M.A. Messner and D.F. Sabo, eds., *Sport, men, and the gender order: Critical feminist perspectives*. Champaign, Ill.: Human Kinetics.

Hall, M.A., D. Cullen, and T. Slack (1989). "Organizational elites recreating themselves: The gender structure of national sport organizations," *Quest*, 41, pp. 28-45.

Hall, M.A., D. Cullen, and T. Slack (1990). *The gender structure of national sport organizations*. Sport Canada Occasional Papers, No. 2, December.

Hall, M.A., and D.A. Richardson (1982). *Fair Ball: Toward sex equality in Canadian sport*. Ottawa: Canadian Advisory Council on the Status of Women.

Hall, S. (1981). "Notes on deconstructing 'the popular'," in R. Samuel, ed., *People's history and socialist theory.* London: Routledge & Kegan Paul.

Hall-Dennis Report (1968). Ontario: Provincial Committee on the Aims and Objectives of Education in the Schools of Ontario.

Hardy, S. (1982). *How Boston played: Sport, recreation, and community, 1865-1915.* Boston: Northeastern University Press.

Hardy, S. (1986). "Entrepreneurs, organizations, and the sport marketplace: Subjects in search of historians," *Journal of Sport History*, 13, pp. 14-33.

Hargreaves, Jennifer (1984). "Women and the Olympic phenomenon," in A. Tomlinson and G. Whannel, eds., *Five ring circus: Money, power and politics at the Olympic games.* London: Pluto Press.

Hargreaves, Jennifer (1986). "Where's the virtue? Where's the grace? A discussion of the social production of gender relations in and through sport," *Theory, Culture & Society*, 3, 1, pp. 109-21.

Hargreaves, John (1986). *Sport, power and culture.* Oxford: Polity Press.

Harney, R.F. (1985). "Homo ludens and ethnicity," *Polyphony: The Bulletin of the Multicultural History Society of Ontario*, 7, 1, pp. 1-12.

Harris, S. (1988). "Why Judge Harris put Ciccarelli in jail," *Toronto Star*, August 26, p. D3.

Harvey, J. (1983). *Le corps programmé ou la rhétorique de Kino-Québec.* Montréal: Albert Saint-Martin.

Harvey, J. (1988). "Sport policy and the welfare state: An outline of the Canadian case," *Sociology of Sport Journal*, 5, pp. 315-29.

Harvey, J., and R. Proulx (1988). "Sport and the state in Canada," in J. Harvey and H. Cantelon, eds., *Not just a game.* Ottawa: University of Ottawa Press.

Heinz, R. (1988). *Many are called – few are signed: Hard realities of professional hockey.* Toronto: Heinz Publishing.

Hellison, D.R. (1973). *Humanistic physical education.* Englewood Cliffs, N.J.: Prentice-Hall.

Helmes, R. (1978). *Ideology and social control in Canadian sport: A theoretical review.* Working Papers in the Sociological Study of Sport and Leisure, Vol. 1, No. 4. Kingston: Queen's University.

Hershfield, L. (1980). *The Jewish athlete: A nostalgic view.* Winnipeg: Lieble Hershfield.

Hilliard, D.C. (1984). "Media images of male and female professional athletes: An interpretive analysis of magazine articles," *Sociology of Sport Journal*, 1, pp. 251-62.

Hirsch, F. (1976). *Social limits to growth.* Cambridge, Mass.: Harvard University Press.

Hollands, R.G., and R.S. Gruneau (1979). *Social class and voluntary action in the administration of Canadian amateur sport,* Working Papers in the Sociological Study of Sport and Leisure, Vol. 2, No. 3. Kingston: Queen's University.

Homel, G.H. (1981). "Sliders and backsliders: Toronto's Sunday tobogganing controversy of 1912," *Urban History Review*, 10, 2, pp. 25-34.

Houston, W. (1990). "Time may be right to sell TSN," *Globe and Mail*, June 15, p. A15.

Howell, D., and P. Lindsay (1986). "Social gospel and the young boy problem, 1895-1925," *Canadian Journal of History of Sport*, 17, 1, pp. 75-87.

Huizinga, J. (1955). *Homo ludens: A study of the play element in culture*. Boston: Beacon Press. (Original work published in 1950.)

Humber, W. (1983). *Cheering for the home team: The story of baseball in Canada*. Erin, Ont.: The Boston Mills Press.

Hunter, J. (1984). "Pickings prove slim for most medalists," *Globe and Mail*, October 20, p. S1.

Hyndman, L. (1989). *The rainbow report: Our vision for health*. Final report of the Premier's Commission on Future Health Care for Albertans, Vol.1. Edmonton: Government of Alberta.

Ingham, A.G. (1985). "From public issue to personal trouble: Well-being and the fiscal crisis of the state," *Sociology of Sport Journal*, 2, pp. 43-55.

Ingham, A.G., and S. Hardy (1984). "Sport: Structuration, subjugation and hegemony," *Theory, Culture & Society*, 2, 2, pp. 85-103.

Ingham, A.G., and J.W. Loy (1974). "The structure of ludic action," *International Review of Sport Sociology*, 9, 1, pp. 23-36.

Ingham, A.G., J. Howell, and T. Schilperoort (1988). "Professional sports and community: A review and exegesis," in K. Pandolf, ed., *Exercise and Sport Science Reviews*, Vol. 16. New York: Macmillan.

Inglis, F. (1977). *The name of the game: Sport and society*. London: Heinemann Educational.

Inglis, S.E. (1988). "The representation of women in university athletic programs," *Journal of Sport Management*, 2, 14-25.

Jackson, R., and T. McPhail, eds. (1989). *The Olympic movement and the mass media: Past, present and future issues*. Calgary: Hurford.

Jameson, A. (1965). *Winter studies and summer rambles in Canada*. Toronto: McClelland and Stewart. (Original work published in 1838.)

Johns, D.P., K.J. Linder, and K. Wolko (1990). "Understanding attrition in female competitive gymnastics: Applying social exchange theory," *Sociology of Sport Journal*, 7, pp. 154-71.

Johnson, T. (1972). *Professions and power*. Basingstoke, Hants: Macmillan Education.

Jones, J., and W. Walsh (1987). "The World Hockey Association and player exploitation in the National Hockey League," *Quarterly Review of Economics and Business*, 27, pp. 87-101.

Kereliuk, S. (1982). "The Canadian boycott of the 1980 Olympics," Master's thesis, University of Alberta.

Kerwin, K. (1989). "L.A. Gear is going where the boys are," *Business Week*, June, p. 54.

Kidd, B. (1978). *The political economy of sport*. Ottawa: CAHPER Sociology of Sport Monograph Series.

Kidd, B. (1980). *Tom Longboat*. Toronto: Fitzhenry and Whiteside.

Kidd, B. (1981). "The Canadian state and

sport: The dilemma of intervention," in *Annual conference proceedings of the National Association for Physical Education in Higher Education*. Brainerd, Minn.: Human Kinetics.

Kidd, B. (1982). "Sport, dependency and the Canadian state," in H. Cantelon and R.S. Gruneau, eds., *Sport, culture and the modern state*. Toronto: University of Toronto Press.

Kidd, B. (1983). "In defence of Tom Longboat," *Canadian Journal of History of Sport*, 14, 1, pp. 34-63.

Kidd, B. (1987). "Sports and masculinity," in M. Kaufman, ed., *Beyond patriarchy: Essays by men*. Toronto: Oxford University Press.

Kidd, B. (1988a). "The philosophy of excellence: Olympic performances, class power, and the Canadian state," in P.J. Galasso, ed., *Philosophy of sport and physical activity: Issues and concepts*. Toronto: Canadian Scholars' Press.

Kidd, B. (1988b). "The elite athlete," in J. Harvey and H. Cantelon, eds., *Not just a game*. Ottawa: University of Ottawa Press.

Kidd, B. (1988c). "The campaign against sport in South Africa," *International Journal*, 43, pp. 643-64.

Kidd, B. (1989). "We must maintain a balance between propaganda and serious athletics – the workers' sport movement in Canada, 1924-1936," in M. Mott, ed., *Sports in Canada: Historical readings*. Toronto: Copp Clark Pitman.

Kidd, B. (1990). "For the Toronto Olympics and the Toronto Olympic commitment. A brief to the City of Toronto," January 15.

Kidd, B., and M. Eberts (1982). *Athletes' rights in Canada*. Toronto: Ministry of Tourism and Recreation.

Kidd, B., and J. Macfarlane (1972). *The death of hockey*. Toronto: New Press.

Killanin, L., and J. Rodda (1983). *The Olympic Games 1984*. London: Collins.

Kirsh, C., B. Dixon, and M. Bond (1973). *A leisure study – Canada 1972*. Ottawa: Government of Canada.

Kjeldson, E.K. (1984). "Integration of minorities into Olympic sport in Canada and the USA," *Journal of Sport and Social Issues*, 8, 2, pp. 29-44.

Knoppers, A. (1985). "Professionalization of attitudes: A review and critique," *Quest*, 37, pp. 92-102.

Knoppers, A., M. Zuidema, and B. Meyer (1989). "Play to win or playing to play?" *Sociology of Sport Journal*, 6, pp. 70-76.

Koppett, L. (1981). *Sports illusion, sports reality: A reporter's view of sports, journalism and society*. Boston: Houghton Mifflin.

Laberge, S., and D. Sankoff (1988). "Physical activities, body *habitus*, and lifestyles," in J. Harvey and H. Cantelon, eds., *Not just a game*. Ottawa: University of Ottawa Press.

Labonté, R. (1983). "Good health: Individual or social," *Canadian Forum*, April, pp. 10-13.

Larson, M.S. (1977). *The rise of professionalism: A sociological analysis*. Berkeley: University of California Press.

Lasch, C. (1979). *The culture of narcissism*. New York: Warner Books.

Lavoie, M. (1989). "Stacking, performance differentials, and salary discrimination in professional ice hockey: A survey of evidence," *Sociology of Sport Journal*, 6, pp. 17-35.

Lenskyj, H. (1985). *Female participation in sport: The issue of integration versus separate-but-equal*. A discussion paper prepared for the Canadian Association for the Advancement of Women and Sport, February.

Lenskyj, H. (1986). *Out of bounds: Women, sport and sexuality*. Toronto: The Women's Press.

Lenskyj, H. (1988). *Women, sport and physical activity: Research and Bibliography*. Ottawa: Fitness and Amateur Sport.

Lenskyj, H. (1989). "Femininity first: Sport and physical education for Ontario girls, 1890-1930," in M. Mott, ed., *Sports in Canada: Historical readings*. Toronto: Copp Clark Pitman.

Lesieur, H.R. (1989). "Pathological gambling in Canada," in C.S. Campbell and J. Lowman, eds., *Gambling in Canada: Golden goose or Trojan horse?* Burnaby, B.C.: Simon Fraser School of Criminology.

Lever, J. (1983). *Soccer madness*. Chicago: The University of Chicago Press.

Lorimer, R., and J. McNulty (1987). *Mass communication in Canada*. Toronto: McClelland and Stewart.

Lower, A.R.M. (1958). *Canadians in the making*. Toronto: Longmans.

MacAloon, J.J. (1989). "Steroids and the state: Dubin, melodrama, and the accomplishment of innocence," paper presented at the North American Society of Sport Sociology annual meetings. Washington, D.C., November.

Macintosh, D. (1982). "Socio-economic, educational and status characteristics of Ontario interschool athletes," *Canadian Journal of Applied Sport Sciences*, 7, pp. 272-83.

Macintosh, D. (1986). "Intercollegiate athletics in Canadian universities: An historical perspective," in A.W. Taylor, ed., *The role of interuniversity athletics: A Canadian perspective*. London, Ont.: Sports Dynamics.

Macintosh, D. (1989a). "Interschool sport programs in Canada," unpublished paper, Queen's University, School of Physical and Health Education.

Macintosh, D. (1989b). "Female participation in Ontario inter-university sport programs," *CAHPER Journal*, 55, 2, pp. 7-8.

Macintosh, D., T. Bedecki, and C.E.S. Franks (1987). *Sport and politics in Canada: Federal government involvement since 1961*. Kingston, Ont.: McGill-Queen's University Press.

Macintosh, D., and R. Beamish (1987). "Class or credentials?: Recruitment to administrative positions in Canada's high performance delivery system," in T. Slack and C.R. Hinings, eds., *The organization and administration of sport*. London, Ont.: Sports Dynamics.

Macintosh, D., and D. Whitson (1990). *The game planners: Transforming Canada's sport system*. Kingston, Ont.: McGill-Queen's University Press.

MacNeill, M. (1988). "Active women, media representations, and ideology," in J. Harvey and H. Cantelon, eds., *Not just a game*. Ottawa: University of Ottawa Press.

Maguire, J. (1990). "More than a sporting touchdown: The making of American football in England 1982-1990," *Sociology of Sport Journal*, 7, pp. 213-37.

Mangan, J.A. (1981). *Athleticism in the Victorian and Edwardian public schools: The emergence and consolidation of an educational ideology*. Cambridge: Cambridge University Press.

Mantel, R.C., and L. Vander Velden (1974). "The relationship between the professionalization of attitude toward play of adolescent boys and participation in organized sport," in G.H. Sage, ed., *Sport and American society*. Reading, Mass.: Addison-Wesley.

Marchak, M.P. (1988). *Ideological perspectives on Canada* (3rd ed.). Toronto: McGraw-Hill Ryerson.

Marcuse, H. (1964). *One dimensional man*. London: Routledge & Kegan Paul.

Mark, M., F.B. Bryant, and D.R. Lehman (1983). "Perceived injustice and sports violence," in J.H. Goldstein, ed., *Sports violence*. New York: Springer-Verlag.

Martens, R., ed. (1978). *Joy and sadness in children's sports*. Champaign, Ill.: Human Kinetics.

Maynard, R. (1987). "Win some, lose some," *The Globe and Mail Report on Business Magazine*, March, pp. 50-56.

McCormack, J.B., and L. Chalip (1988). "Sport as socialization: A critique of methodological premises," *Social Science Journal*, 25, pp. 83-92.

McCrone, K. (1988). *Playing the game: Sport and the physical emancipation of English women, 1870-1914*. Lexington: University of Kentucky Press.

McGregor, C. (1983). *Pop goes the culture*. London: Pluto Press.

McIntosh, P. (1979). *Fair play: Ethics in sport and education*. London: Heinemann.

McKay, J. (1975). "Sport and ethnicity: Acculturation, structural assimilation, and voluntary association involvement among Italian immigrants in metropolitan Toronto," Master's thesis, University of Waterloo.

McKenzie, R.T. (1892). "Rugby football in Canada," *The Dominion Illustrated Monthly*, 1, 1, pp. 11-19.

McKie, C., and K. Thompson (1990). *Canadian social trends*. Toronto: Thompson Educational Publishing.

McMillen, J. (1989). "The future: Golden goose or Trojan horse? – symposium summation," in C.S. Campbell and J. Lowman, eds., *Gambling in Canada: Golden goose or Trojan horse?* Burnaby, B.C.: Simon Fraser School of Criminology.

McMurtry, W.R. (1974). *Investigation and inquiry into violence in amateur hockey*. Toronto: Ontario Government Bookstore.

McPherson, B.D. (1981). "Socialization into and through sport," in G. Lüschen and G. Sage, eds., *Handbook of social science of sport*. Champaign, Ill.: Stipes.

McPherson, B.D. (1984). "Sport participation across the life cycle: A review of the literature and suggestions for future research," *Sociology of Sport Journal*, 1, pp. 213-30.

McPherson, B.D. (1986). "Socialization theory and research: Toward a 'new wave' of scholarly inquiry in a sport context," in C.R. Rees and A.W. Miracle, eds., *Sport and social theory*. Champaign, Ill.: Human Kinetics.

McPherson, B.D., and B.A. Brown (1988). "The structure, processes, and consequences of sport for children," in F.L. Smoll, R.A. Magill, and M.J. Ash, eds., *Children in Sport*. Champaign, Ill.: Human Kinetics.

McPherson, B.D., and L. Davidson (1980). *Minor hockey in Ontario*. Toronto: Ministry of Culture and Recreation.

McQuail, D. (1983). *Mass communication theory: An introduction*. Beverly Hills, Calif.: Sage.

McTeer, W., and J.E. Curtis (1984). "Sociological profiles of marathoners," in N. Theberge and P. Donnelly, eds., *Sport and the sociological imagination*. Fort Worth: Texas Christian University Press.

Medoff, M. (1976). "On monopsonistic exploitation in professional baseball," *Quarterly Review of Economics and Business*, 16, pp. 113-21.

Messner, M. (1988). "Sports and male domination: The female athlete as contested ideological terrain," *Sociology of Sport Journal*, 5, pp. 197-211.

Messner, M. (1990). "When bodies are weapons: Masculinity and violence in sport," *International Review for the Sociology of Sport*, 25, pp. 203-19.

Messner, M, and D. Sabo, eds. (1990). *Sport, men, and the gender order: Critical feminist perspectives*. Champaign, Ill.: Human Kinetics.

Metcalfe, A. (1978). *Working class physical recreation in Montreal, 1860-1895*, Working Papers in the Sociological Study of Sport and Leisure, Vol. 1, No. 2. Kingston: Queen's University.

Metcalfe, A. (1987). *Canada learns to play: The emergence of organized sport, 1807-1914*. Toronto: McClelland and Stewart.

Mills, C.W. (1959). *The sociological imagination*. New York: Oxford University Press.

Mills, D. (1990). "The battle of Alberta: Entrepreneurs and the business of hockey in Edmonton and Calgary," *Alberta: Studies in the Arts and Sciences*, 2, 2, pp. 1-25.

Mills, D. (1991). "The blue line and the bottom line: Entrepreneurs and the business of hockey in Canada, 1927-1988," in J.A. Mangan and P. Staudohar, eds., *American professional sports: Social, historical, economic and legal perspectives*. Urbana: University of Illinois Press.

Milton, B.G. (1975). *Social status and leisure time activities: National survey findings for adult Canadians*. Montreal: Canadian Sociology and Anthropology Association Monograph Series.

Mitchell, R.G. (1983). *Mountain experience: The psychology and sociology of adventure*. Chicago: University of Chicago Press.

Moodie, S. (1962). *Roughing it in the bush*.

Toronto: McClelland and Stewart. (Original work published in 1853.)

Morley, D. (1986). *Family television: Cultural power and domestic leisure.* London: Comedia.

Morrow, D. (1981). "The powerhouse of Canadian sport: The Montreal Amateur Athletic Association, inception to 1909," *Journal of Sport History,* 8, 3, pp. 20-39.

Morrow, D. (1986). "A case-study in amateur conflict: The athletic war in Canada, 1906-1908," *British Journal of Sports History,* 3, pp. 173-90.

Morrow, D. (1988). "The knights of the snowshoe: A study of the evolution of sport in nineteenth century Montreal," *Journal of Sport History,* 15, pp. 5-40.

Morrow, D. (1989). "Baseball," in D. Morrow *et al., A concise history of sport in Canada.* Toronto: Oxford University Press.

Morrow, D., M. Keyes, W. Simpson, F. Cosentino, and R. Lappage (1989). *A concise history of sport in Canada.* Toronto: Oxford University Press.

Mott, M. (1980). "The British protestant pioneers and the establishment of manly sports in Manitoba, 1870-1886," *Journal of Sport History,* 7, pp. 25-36.

Mott, M. (1983). "One solution to the urban crisis: Manly sports and Winnipeggers, 1900-1914," *Urban History Review,* 12, 2, pp. 57-70.

Mott, M. (1989a). "Games and contests of the first 'Manitobans'," in M. Mott, ed., *Sports in Canada: Historical readings.* Toronto: Copp Clark Pitman.

Mott, M. (1989b). *Sports in Canada: Historical readings.* Toronto: Copp Clark Pitman.

Mottram, D.R. (1988). "Introduction – Drugs and their use in sport," in D.R. Mottram, ed., *Drugs in sport.* Champaign, Ill.: Human Kinetics.

Mrozek, D.J. (1987). "Games and sport in the Arctic," *Journal of the West,* 26, 1, pp. 34-46.

Munro, J. (1970). *A proposed sport policy for Canadians.* Ottawa: Department of Health and Welfare.

Nattrass, S. (1988). "Sport and television in Canada: 1952 to 1982," Ph.D. thesis, University of Alberta.

Neff, C. (1987). "Portrait of a sportswriter as a young man," *Gannett Center Journal,* 1, 2, pp. 47-55.

Nelson, B. (1988). "Olympics, Inc.," *Financial Times of Canada,* January 25, pp. 16, 18.

Néron, G. (1977). *Violence in hockey.* Quebec City: Government of Quebec, High Commission for Youth, Leisure and Sport.

Nicholson, G. (1978). *The great bike race.* London: Methuen.

Noll, R.G. (1974a). "The U.S. team sports industry: An introduction," in R.G. Noll, ed., *Government and the sports business.* Washington, D.C.: The Brookings Institute.

Noll, R.G. (1974b). "Alternatives in sports policy," in R.G. Noll, ed., *Government and the sports business*. Washington: The Brookings Institute.

Novak, M. (1976). *The joy of sports*. New York: Basic Books.

Offe, C. (1984). *Contradictions of the welfare state*. London: Hutchinson.

Olafson, G. (1986). "Canadian international sport policy and the Gleneagles agreement," in J.A. Mangan and R.B. Small, eds., *Sport, culture and society*. London: E. & F.N. Spon.

Olafson, G., and C.L. Brown-John (1986). "Canadian international sport policy: A public policy analysis," in G. Redmond, ed., *Sport and politics*. Champaign, Ill.: Human Kinetics.

Olympic Charter (1990). Lausanne: The International Olympic Committee.

Orlick, T. (1977). "Traditional Inuit games, looking back to looking forward," *CAHPER Journal*, 43, 5, pp. 6-10.

Orlick, T. (1978). *The cooperative sports and games book*. London: Writers and Readers Publishing Cooperative.

Orlick, T., and C. Botterill (1975). *Every kid can win*. Chicago: Nelson-Hall.

Palmer, B. (1979). *A culture in conflict: Skilled workers and industrial capitalism in Hamilton, Ontario, 1860-1914*. Montreal: McGill-Queen's University Press.

Panitch, L. (1977). "The role and nature of the Canadian state," in L. Panitch, ed., *The Canadian state: Political economy and political power*. Toronto: University of Toronto Press.

Paraschak, V. (1982). "The heterotransplantation of organized sport: A Northwest Territories case study," in B. Kidd, ed., *Proceedings of the Fifth Canadian Symposium on the History of Sport and Physical Education*. Toronto: School of Physical and Health Education, University of Toronto.

Paraschak, V. (1989). "Native sports history: Pitfalls and promise," *Canadian Journal of History of Sport*, 20, 1, pp. 57-68.

Petrie, B. (1975). "Sport and politics," in D.W. Ball and J.W. Loy, eds., *Sport and social order*. Reading, Mass.: Addison-Wesley.

Picard, A. (1990). "Quebeckers are still paying for '76 Olympics," *Globe and Mail*, June 9, p. D2.

Polanyi, Margaret (1990). " 'Bid book' for Olympics cost backers $800,000," *Globe and Mail*, January 20, p. A12.

Polanyi, Michael. (1958). *Personal knowledge: Towards a post-critical philosophy*. Chicago: University of Chicago Press.

Pooley, J.C. (1987). "The sociology of university athletic awards," *Arena Review*, 11, 2, pp. 101-07.

Porter, J. (1967). *The vertical mosaic: An analysis of class and power in Canada*. Toronto: University of Toronto Press.

Rader, B.G. (1984). *In its own image: How television has transformed sports*. New York: Free Press.

Randall, M. (1988). "Feminism and the state: Questions for theory and practice," *Resources for*

Feminist Research, 17, 3, pp. 10-16.

Reasons, C. (1984). "It's just a game?: The 1988 Winter Olympics," in C. Reasons, ed., *Stampede City: Power and Politics in the West*. Toronto: Between the Lines.

Rigauer, B. (1981). *Sport and work*, A. Guttmann, trans. New York: Columbia University Press. (Original work published in 1969.)

Rintala, J., and S. Birrell (1984). "Fair treatment of the active female: A content analysis of *Young Athlete* Magazine," *Sociology of Sport Journal*, 1, pp. 231-50.

Robinson, R.G. (1983). "The history of the law of gaming in Canada," a paper prepared for the R.C.M.P. Gaming Specialist Field Understudy Program.

Rodriguez, C. (1990). "Steeped in scandal," *Globe and Mail*, July 5, p. A15.

Ronberg, G. (1975). *The violent game*. Englewood Cliffs, N.J.: Prentice-Hall.

Rosengren, K.F., L.A. Wenner, and P. Palmgren, eds. (1985). *Media gratifications research: Current perspectives*. Beverly Hills, Calif.: Sage.

Russell, G., S. DiLullo, and D. DiLullo (1989). "Effects of observing competitive and violent versions of a sport," *Current Psychology: Research and Reviews*, 7, pp. 312-21.

Sage, G.H. (1987). "Pursuit of knowledge in sociology of sport: Issues and prospects," *Quest*, 39, pp. 255-81.

Salter, M. (1972). "The effect of acculturation on the game of lacrosse and on its role as an agent of Indian survival," *Canadian Journal of History of Sport and Physical Education*, 3, 2, pp. 28-43.

Sax, J. (1980). *Mountains without handrails*. Ann Arbor: University of Michigan Press.

Schrodt, B., G. Redmond, and R. Baka (1980). *Sport canadiana*. Edmonton: Executive Sport Publications.

Schultz, D. (1981). *The Hammer: Confessions of a hockey enforcer*. Toronto: Collins.

Scraton, S. (1986). "Images of femininity and the teaching of girls' physical education," in J. Evans, ed., *Physical education, sport and schooling*. London: The Falmer Press.

Scraton, S. (1987). " 'Boys muscle in where angels fear to tread' – girls' sub-cultures and physical activities," in J. Horne, D. Jary, and A. Tomlinson, eds., *Sport, leisure and social relations*. London: Routledge & Kegan Paul.

Scully, G. (1974). "Pay and performance in major league baseball," *American Economic Review*, 64, pp. 915-30.

Sennett, R., and J. Cobb (1972). *The hidden injuries of class*. New York: Vintage Books.

Sewart, J.J. (1987). "The commodification of sport," *International Review for the Sociology of Sport*, 22, pp. 171-91.

Shephard, R.J. (1988). "Fitness boom or bust – A Canadian perspective," *Research Quarterly for Exercise and Sport*, 59, pp. 265-69.

Shephard, R.J. (1990). "Costs and benefits of an exercising versus a nonexercising society," in

C. Bouchard *et al.*, *Exercise, Fitness and Health: A Consensus of Current Knowledge.* Champaign, Ill.: Human Kinetics.

Shotter, J. (1974). "The development of personal powers," in M. Richards, ed., *The integration of a child into a social world.* London: Cambridge University Press.

Shotter, J. (1984). *Social accountability and selfhood.* Oxford: Basil Blackwell.

Simpson, R.W. (1987). "The elite and sport club membership in Toronto 1827-1881," Ph.D. thesis, University of Alberta.

Simpson, R.W. (1989). "Hockey," in D. Morrow *et al.*, *A concise history of sport in Canada.* Toronto: Oxford University Press.

Singer, C. (1989). "The ethics of gambling," in C.S. Campbell and J. Lowman, eds., *Gambling in Canada: Golden goose or Trojan horse?* Burnaby, B.C.: Simon Fraser School of Criminology.

Skolnick, J. (1978). *House of cards.* Boston: Little, Brown.

Slack, T. (1985). "The bureaucratization of a voluntary sport organization," *International Review for the Sociology of Sport.* 20, pp. 145-65.

Slack, T., and C.R. Hinings (1987). "Planning and organizational change: A conceptual framework for the analysis of amateur sport organizations," *Canadian Journal of Sport Science,* 12, pp. 185-93.

Smith, C. (1987). "The mixing of a new generation," *Athletics,* February/March, pp. 8-9.

Smith, G.J. (1976). "A study of a sports journalist," *International Review of Sport Sociology,* 11, 3, pp. 5-25.

Smith, G.J. (1987). "Gambling and sport: The Canadian experience," *Arena Review,* 11, 1, pp. 25-36.

Smith, G.J. (1988). "The noble sports fan," *Journal of Sport and Social Issues,* 12, 1, pp. 54-65.

Smith, G.J. (1990). "Pools, parlays and point spreads: A sociological consideration of the legalization of sports gambling," *Sociology of Sport Journal,* 7, pp. 271-86.

Smith, G.J., and C. Blackman (1978). *Sport in the mass media.* Ottawa: CAHPER Sociology of Sport Monograph Series.

Smith, G.J., and C.F. Grindstaff (1972). "Race and sport in Canada," in A.W. Taylor and M.L. Howell, eds., *Training: Scientific basis and application.* Springfield, Ill.: Charles C. Thomas.

Smith, G.J., and T.A. Valeriote (1983). "Ethics in sports journalism," *Arena Review,* 7, 2, pp. 7-14.

Smith, G.J., B. Williams, and R. Pitter (1989). "How Alberta amateur sport groups prosper through legalized gambling," in C.S. Campbell and J. Lowman, eds., *Gambling in Canada: Golden goose or Trojan horse?* Burnaby, B.C.: Simon Fraser School of Criminology.

Smith, M.D. (1983). *Violence and sport.* Toronto: Butterworths.

Sparkes, A. (1989). "Health related fitness: An example of innovation without change," *British*

Journal of Physical Education, 20, pp. 60-63.

Sparks, R. (1990). "Social practice, the bodily professions and the state," *Sociology of Sport Journal*, 7, pp. 72-82.

Statistics Canada (1978). *Culture statistics: Recreational activities 1976*. Ottawa: Statistics Canada.

Statistics Canada (1988). *Television viewing in Canada*. Ottawa: Statistics Canada.

Staudohar, P.D. (1989). *The sports industry and collective bargaining* (2nd ed.). Ithaca, N.Y.: IRL Press, Cornell University.

Stebbins, R.A. (1987). *Canadian football: The view from the helmet*. London: Centre for Social and Humanities Studies, University of Western Ontario.

Stephens, T., and C.L. Craig (1990). *The well-being of Canadians: Highlights of the 1988 Campbell's survey*. Ottawa: Canadian Fitness and Lifestyle Research Institute.

Stevenson, C.L. (1975). "Socialization effects of participation in sport: A critical review of the research," *Research Quarterly*, 46, pp. 287-301.

Steward, H. (1977). "Fitness: The great Canadian shape-up," *Maclean's*, January 24, pp. 41-44.

Stock, C. (1990). "Horse racing catering to bettors," *Edmonton Journal*, June 9, p. H3.

Stoddart, B. (1986). *Saturday afternoon fever: Sport in Australian culture*. North Ryde, New South Wales: Angus & Robertson.

Strachan, A. (1989). "Brier ranks as ultimate Canadian sports event," *Globe and Mail*, March 13, p. A12.

Strachan, A. (1990). "Everything's coming up roses in this spring's playoffs," *Globe and Mail*, May 21, p. A11.

Struna, N.L. (1988). "Sport and society in early America," *International Journal of the History of Sport*, 5, pp. 292-311.

Suransky, V.P. (1982). *The erosion of childhood*. Chicago: University of Chicago Press.

Sweeney, D. (1986). "Pedaling new wares," *High Technology*, February, pp. 54-56.

Talbot, M. (1989). "Professionals working together toward equality of opportunity," *CAHPER Journal*, 55, 2, pp. 12-18.

Taylor, T. (1986). "Politics and the Olympic spirit," in L. Allison, ed., *The politics of sport*. Manchester: Manchester University Press.

Task Force Report (1969). *Report of the Task Force on Sport for Canadians*. Ottawa: Department of National Health and Welfare.

Telander, R. (1984). "The written word: Player-press relationships in American sports" *Sociology of Sport Journal*, 1, pp. 3-14.

Telander, R. (1990). "Your sneakers or your life," *Sports Illustrated*, May 14, pp. 36-49.

Theberge, N. (1984a). "Some evidence on the existence of a sexual double standard in mobility to leadership positions in sport," *International Review for the Sociology of Sport*, 19, pp. 186-95.

Theberge, N. (1984b). "On the need for a more adequate theory of sport participation," *Sociology of Sport Journal*, 1, pp. 26-33.

Theberge, N. (1985). "Toward a feminist alternative to sport as a male preserve," *Quest*, 37, pp. 193-202.

Theberge, N. (1985b). "Sport and feminism in North America," *West Georgia College Studies in the Social Sciences*, 24, pp. 41-53.

Theberge, N. (1987). "Sport and women's empowerment," *Women's Studies International Forum*, 10, pp. 387-93.

Theberge, N. (1989a). "A feminist analysis of responses to sports violence: Media coverage of the 1987 World Junior Hockey Championship," *Sociology of Sport Journal*, 6, pp. 247-56.

Theberge, N. (1989b). "Women's athletics and the myth of female frailty," in J. Freeman, ed., *Women: A feminist perspective*. Mountain View, Calif.: Mayfield.

Theberge, N., and A. Cronk (1986). "Work routines in newspaper sports departments and the coverage of women's sports," *Sociology of Sport Journal*, 3, pp. 195-203.

Thérien, R. (1989) *Rapport Thérien: Rapport final du groupe de travail sur le hockey mineur au Québec*. Québec: Government du Québec.

Todd, T. (1987). "Anabolic steroids: The gremlins of sport," *Journal of Sport History*, 14, pp. 87-107.

Tomlinson, A. (1989). "Representation, ideology and the Olympic games: A reading of the opening and closing ceremonies of the 1984 Los Angeles Olympic games," in R. Jackson and T. McPhail, eds., *The Olympic movement and the mass media*. Calgary: Hurford.

Tomlinson, A., and G. Whannel (1986). *Off the ball: The football world cup*. London: Pluto Press.

Valeriote, T.A., and L. Hansen (1986). "Youth sport in Canada," in M.R. Weiss and D. Gould, eds., *Sport for children and youths*. Champaign, Ill.: Human Kinetics.

Varpalotai, A. (1987). "The hidden curriculum in leisure: An analysis of a girls' sport subculture," *Women's Studies International Forum*, 10, pp. 411-22.

Vaz, E. (1982). *The professionalization of young hockey players*. Lincoln: University of Nebraska Press.

Veblen, T. (1934). *The theory of the leisure class: An economic study of institutions*. New York: The Modern Library. (Original work published in 1899.)

Vincent, I. (1990). "Lottery changes spark controversy," *Globe and Mail*, June 16, p. C4.

Voisey, P. (1981). "Boosting the small prairie town, 1904-1931: An example from southern Alberta," in A.F.J. Artibise, ed., *Town and city: Aspects of western Canadian urban development*. Regina: University of Regina, Canadian Plains Research Centre.

Watson, G.G., and R. Collis (1982). "Adolescent values in sport: A case of conflicting interest," *International Review of Sport Sociology*, 3, pp. 73-89.

Wayne, J. (1988). "Johnson fiasco rocks sport funding," *The Financial Post*, October 1-3, pp. 1, 6.

Webb, H. (1969). "Professionalization of attitudes toward play among adolescents," in G.S. Kenyon, ed., *Aspects of contemporary sport sociology*. Chicago: The Athletic Institute

Wenner, L.A., ed. (1989). *Media, sports, & society*. Newbury Park, Calif.: Sage.

Westell, D. (1990). "Financing the Skydome," *Globe and Mail*, March 10, pp. D1, D8.

Whannel, G. (1984). "Fields in vision: Sport and representation," *Screen*, 25, 3, pp. 99-107.

Whannel, G. (1989). "History is being made: Television sport and the selective tradition," in R. Jackson and T. McPhail, eds., *The Olympic movement and the mass media*. Calgary: Hurford.

Wheeler, R.F. (1978). "Organized sport and organized labour: The workers' sports movement," *Journal of Contempory History*, 13, pp. 191-210.

White, P.G., and J.E. Curtis (1990a). "Participation in competitive sport among anglophones and francophones in Canada: Testing competing hypotheses," *International Review for the Sociology of Sport*, 25, pp. 125-39.

White, P.G., and J.E. Curtis (1990b). "English/French Canadian differences in types of sport participation: Testing the school socialization explanation," *Sociology of Sport Journal*, 7, pp. 347-68.

Whitson, D. (1984). "Sport and hegemony: On the construction of the dominant culture," *Sociology of Sport Journal*, 1, pp. 64-78.

Whitson, D. (1990). "Sport in the social construction of masculinity," in M.A. Messner and D.F. Sabo, eds., *Sport, men, and the gender order: Critical feminist perspectives*. Champaign, Ill.: Human Kinetics.

Whitson, D., and D. Macintosh (1988). "The professionalization of Canadian amateur sport: Questions of power and purpose," *Arena Review*, 12, pp. 81-96.

Whitson, D., and D. Macintosh (1989). "Gender and power: Explanations of gender inequalities in Canadian national sport organizations," *International Review for the Sociology of Sport*, 24, pp. 137-50.

Whitson, D., and D. Macintosh (1990). "The scientization of physical education: Discourses of performance," *Quest*, 42, pp. 40-51.

Williams, C.L., G. Laurence, and D. Rowe (1985). "Women and sport: A lost ideal," *Women's Studies International Forum*, 8, pp. 639-45.

Williams, R. (1980). *Problems in materialism and culture: Selected essays*. London: Verso.

Willis, P. (1982). "Women in sport in ideology," in J. Hargreaves, ed., *Sport, culture and ideology*. London: Routledge & Kegan Paul.

Wilson, J. (1988). *Politics and leisure*. London: Unwin Hyman.

Wilson, S. (1986). "Mass media and influence," in L. Tepperman and R.J. Richardson, *The social world: An introduction to sociology*. Toronto: McGraw-Hill Ryerson.

Wilson, W. (1990). "Social discontent and the

growth of wilderness sport," in G. Sage, ed., *Sport and American society* (3rd. ed.). Reading, Mass.: Addison-Wesley.

Wise, S.F. (1974). "Sport and class values in old Ontario and Quebec," in W.H. Heick and R. Graham, eds., *His own man: Essays in honour of A.R.M. Lower.* Montreal: McGill-Queen's University Press.

Worsley, P., ed. (1987). *The new introducing sociology.* London: Penguin.

Young, I.M. (1979). "The exclusion of women from sport: Conceptual and existential dimensions," *Philosophy in Context*, 9, pp. 44-53.

Young, I.M. (1980). "Throwing like a girl: A phenomenology of feminine body comportment, motility and space," *Human Studies*, 3, pp. 137-56.

Young, K., and M.D. Smith (1989). "Mass media treatment of violence in sports and its effects," *Current Psychology: Research and Reviews*, 1, pp. 298-312.

Zeigler, E.F. (1989). "Let's preserve educational sport in Canadian higher education," *CAHPER Journal*, 55, 3, pp. 2-4.

Zeman, B. (1988). *To run with Longboat: Twelve stories of Indian athletes in Canada.* Edmonton: GMS2 Ventures.

AUTHOR INDEX

SUBJECT INDEX

Printed in Canada